FROMMER'S
DOLLARWISE GUIDE TO PORTUGAL, MADEIRA & THE AZORES

by Darwin Porter

1982-1983 Edition

Copyright © 1970, 1972, 1974, 1976, 1978, 1980, 1982

All rights reserved
including the right of reproduction
in whole or in part in any form

Published by Frommer/Pasmantier Publishers
A Simon & Schuster Division of
Gulf & Western Corporation
1230 Avenue of the Americas
New York, New York 10020

ISBN 0-671-43624-4

Manufactured in the United States of America

*Although every effort was made to ensure the accuracy
of price information appearing in this book,
it should be kept in mind that prices
can and do fluctuate in the course of time.*

CONTENTS

Introduction	**A DOLLARWISE GUIDE TO PORTUGAL**	1
	The Reason Why	1
Chapter I	**GETTING THERE**	10
	1. Plane Economics	10
	2. Traveling Within Portugal	11
Chapter II	**THE SCENE IN PORTUGAL**	14
	1. A Capsule History	16
	2. Dining and Wining	20
	3. The Hotel Outlook	24
Chapter III	**SETTLING INTO LISBON**	26
	1. Navigating Your Way	29
	2. Public Transportation	31
	3. The ABC'S of Life	32
Chapter IV	**THE HOTELS OF LISBON**	37
	1. The Deluxe Choices	38
	2. Leading First-Class Hotels	40
	3. Middle-Bracket Hotels	43
	4. Full-Board Bargains	46
	5. The Budget Range	47
Chapter V	**THE RESTAURANTS OF LISBON**	49
	1. The Deluxe Quartet	49
	2. The Medium-Priced Range	51
	3. Less Expensive Restaurants	53
	4. The Budget Range	55
	5. Seafood on the Left Bank	57
	6. The Foreign Colony	57
	7. The Special Spots	59
Chapter VI	**ESTORIL, CASCAIS, AND SINTRA**	63
	1. Estoril	65
	2. Cascais	71
	3. Oltavos	79

	4. Guincho	79
	5. Queluz	81
	6. Sintra	82
	7. Mafra Palace	90
	8. Ericeira	91
	9. Vale do Lobos	92
Chapter VII	**SHOPPING IN PORTUGAL**	93
	1. The Best Buys in Lisbon	93
	2. Porto	96
	3. Barcelos	96
	4. Madeira	97
Chapter VIII	**THE SIGHTS OF LISBON**	98
	1. The Alfama	99
	2. Belém	102
	3. Museums and Galleries	107
	4. The Churches of Lisbon	110
	5. A Bullfight Spectacle	112
	6. Other Sights	112
Chapter IX	**NIGHTLIFE IN AND AROUND LISBON**	115
	1. The Fado Clubs	116
	2. The Capital After Dark	117
	3. Estoril by Night	120
	4. The Clubs of Cascais	122
Chapter X	**SOUTH OF THE TAGUS**	124
	1. Azeitão	125
	2. Sesimbra	126
	3. Portinho da Arrábida	128
	4. Setúbal	128
	5. Palmela	131
Chapter XI	**ESTREMADURA**	133
	1. Óbidos	134
	2. Caldas da Rainha	136
	3. Berlenga Islands	137
	4. Alcobaça	137
	5. Aljubarrota	138
	6. São Martinho do Pôrto	138
	7. Nazaré	139
	8. Batalha	142
	9. Fátima	143

Chapter XII	**THE ALGARVE**		**146**
	1. Sagres		149
	2. Lagos		151
	3. Portimão		156
	4. Praia da Rocha		159
	5. Silves		163
	6. Armação de Pêra		164
	7. Albufeira		166
	8. Praia de Quarteira		173
	9. Vilamoura		175
	10. Vale do Lobo		177
	11. Faro		178
	12. São Brás de Alportel		180
	13. Olhão		181
	14. Monte Gordo		182
Chapter XIII	**ALENTEJO AND RIBATEJO**		**185**
	1. Évora		186
	2. Beja		189
	3. Vila Viçosa		191
	4. Elvas		193
	5. Marvão		194
	6. Castelo de Vide		194
	7. Estremoz		195
	8. Vila Franca de Xira		196
	9. Santarém		197
	10. Tomar		198
Chapter XIV	**COIMBRA AND THE BEIRAS**		**201**
	1. Leiria		202
	2. Figueira da Foz		203
	3. Coimbra		205
	4. Conimbriga		210
	5. Buçaco		211
	6. Curía and Luso		212
	7. Aveiro		213
	8. Caramulo		215
	9. Viseu		217
	10. Sêrra da Estrêla		218
	11. Castelo Branco		219
	12. Abrantes		219
	13. Guarda		220

Chapter XV	**PORTO AND ITS ENVIRONS**	221
	1. The Hotels	222
	2. Where to Dine	225
	3. What to See and Do	227
	4. Exploring the Coast	231
	5. Deep in the Environs	234
Chapter XVI	**THE MINHO DISTRICT**	237
	1. Guimarães	238
	2. Braga	240
	3. Barcelos	242
	4. Esposende	243
	5. Viana do Castelo	243
	6. Valença	246
	7. Pousada-Hopping in Minho	247
Chapter XVII	**MADEIRA AND THE AZORES**	249
	1. Settling into Funchal	250
	2. Excursions in Madeira	261
	3. Discovering the Azores	264
	4. Ponta Delgada	267
	5. Exploring São Miguel	269
	6. Terceira	270
	7. Faial	272
Chapter XVIII	**A GRAB BAG OF CHARTS**	274
	1. Menu Translations	274
	2. A Capsule Vocabulary	277
	3. Currency Exchange	278

MAPS

Portugal	17
Lisbon: The Major Boulevards	28

For Stanley Haggart

Inflation Alert!!!

The author of this book has spent laborious hours of research trying to ensure the accuracy of prices appearing in this guide. As we go to press, we believe he has obtained the most reliable data possible—but we cannot predict, during this latest wave of inflation battering the countries of the world, how long these prices will hold.

Portugal has witnessed some of the worst inflation in Europe. Once one of the cheapest countries of Europe, and still cheaper than many, it is now moving closer to the continent, at least in the tariffs it charges. Although the dollarwise bargain hunter will still find good values galore, know that some overeager hoteliers, in their leap forward, have actually increased their prices from 100% to 150% within a one- to two-year period. Of course, that is the exception rather than the rule. Most hotels and restaurants in this guide will probably raise their tariffs during the lifetime of this edition, but perhaps by no more than 20% to 30%, which is painful enough. If you use this guide in planning a budget for your trip, you would be wise to take into account the probable increases.

When a $ is not a $

Portugal is one of the most inexpensive countries in which to travel in Europe. But first-time American visitors often panic at price quotations, because Portugal uses the same $ sign to designate its currency. The **escudo** is written as 1$00. The dollar sign is written between the escudo and the **centavo,** of which there are 100 to the escudo.

There is no fixed rate of exchange between the escudo and the dollar. At press time, one escudo was worth approximately 1.53¢ in U.S. coinage. meaning you could buy 65.50 escudos with one dollar. There is no way to predict what the escudo will be worth when you arrive—so check with a banker, at home or in Portugal, for the latest information.

Introduction

A DOLLARWISE GUIDE TO PORTUGAL

The Reason Why

AT THE DAWN of the Renaissance Age of Exploration, mariners believed that two-headed, fork-tongued monsters big as houses lurked across the Sea of Darkness, waiting to gulp a caravel down their fire-lined throats. It was even feared that white men turned black if they ventured near the equator.

In spite of these formidable problems, Portugal—in what has been called its "épopée of yesteryears"—launched legendary caravels on missions that became historic: Vasco da Gama to India, Ferdinand Magellan to circumnavigate the globe, Dias to round the Cape of Good Hope. In time, Portuguese navigators explored two-thirds of the earth.

Although the Iberian country was in the vanguard of worldwide exploration, it has never been as successful in attracting visitors to its own shores. Outside of Greater Lisbon, the Algarve, and Madeira, it was in the past unknown and undiscovered by the main-line tourist. That fact is particularly lamentable because Portugal offers so much in the way of sandy beaches, art treasures, a respectable cuisine, unique Manueline architecture, cut-rate handicraft shopping buys, a mild climate, moderate hotel tariffs, and friendly people.

The country may be small—roughly about the size of Maine—but, like Mighty Mouse, it packs a powerful punch. Connecting you with its life forces is one of the aims of this book.

I have set for myself the formidable task of seeking out the finest in Portugal, its best way of life, and condensing that between the covers of this book. The finest includes not only descriptions of cities, towns, villages, and attractions, but recommendations of hotels, restaurants, bars, coffeehouses, and nightspots as well.

Part of the philosophy of this book is based on the premise that the best need not be the most expensive. Hence, my ultimate aim, beyond that of familiarizing you with the offerings of Portugal, is to stretch your dollar power, to reveal to you that you need not always pay scalper's prices for charm, top-grade comfort, and first-rate food.

In this guide, I'll devote a great deal of attention to those old meccas—Lisbon, Estoril, Cascais, Sintra—focusing on both their obvious and hidden treasures. But they are not the full reason for this book. Important as they are, they do not reflect fully the widely diverse and complicated country that Portugal is. To discover that, you must venture deep into the provinces.

Unlike many nations in Europe, Portugal defies a clear, logical, coherent plan of sightseeing. It is a patchwork of treasures, with many of the choicest items tucked away in remote corners. To sample the best of Portugal, especially some of its most intriguing living conditions, you'll have to seek out a faraway country estate deep in the heartland, or perhaps a 14th-century monastery now converted into a pousada (tourist inn) in the old Roman city of Evora in Alentejo, even an 18th-century palace in Seteais, where Lord Byron worked on *Childe Harold* in the front garden. Living outside of Lisbon whenever possible will, of course, give you a chance to get acquainted with the Portuguese, a more difficult task in most capital-city hotels.

THE PEOPLE OF PORTUGAL: Meeting the Portuguese, after all, is perhaps the major reason for making the jaunt. They have developed a decidedly different character from the people of Spain, their sister nation on the Iberian peninsula. Those who travel among and mingle with the Portuguese usually return home filled with a special warm response for the people. They are easily approachable, helpful, and you may find after you've left that you have cultivated several lifetime friends and correspondents.

Physically (generally speaking, of course) the Portuguese are rather short in stature with swarthy complexions. The women are quite attractive, although their bodies are often hidden behind a regional garb if they live in the country. The men play their roles well, with bravura flair at times, especially when they fancy themselves as *conquistadores*.

In Lisbon, the people generally dress well, at least in the business district. However, in the country, you'll meet the people of the heartland with their all-purpose, all-weather clothing. Women with black shawls draped around their shoulders carry baskets of produce balanced on their heads. These same women work in the fields with their men, sowing seed, guiding oxen, carrying milk jugs, harvesting. Forming a colorful sight, they wear folded clothing, their hands bandaged, wide caps covering their heads from the powerful summer sun. Children are often attired in sweaters and labor in the fields alongside their parents.

The north of Portugal is more industrial, especially in and around Porto; while in the south, the Algarve, the approach to life seems more casual, the attitude more relaxed and friendly.

In Portugal, the family as an institution remains firmly entrenched. Many of its people have no close friends outside the family unit. The Catholic church still enjoys strong power and prestige over many segments of society. It is rare to meet a Portuguese Protestant or members of other faiths.

Although ladies of the *sociedade* have become increasingly sophisticated in the past few years, their counterparts down the economic and social scale are still of a more traditional character. Unlike Finland, where women have achieved equal status with men in all professional fields, the Portuguese woman remains in her time-honored position. But she usually has more than a housewife's share of work. If her husband's a fisherman, she may help repair the nets, then sell the catch in the streets. If she's married to a farmer, she'll spend part of her day in the fields with her husband, retiring to their cottage in the evening to do all the housework, cooking, and the mending. It's a hard life.

In all, the Portuguese are a proud people worthy of knowing.

It may be presumptuous to give you reasons why to go to Portugal. Dozens may have already occurred to you, ranging from trying to find where you hid that microfilm when you were spying for the Allies in World War II, to putting a tracer on your ancestors to determine if you are descended from royalty or hangmen. We'll merely add a few that you may not have thought about.

To Learn the Meaning of Saudade

The word is hard to translate, evoking a mood of melancholy, a sense of sadness expressed most dramatically in Portuguese music. One scholar called it ". . . the nostalgic memory of past greatness, the myth of a golden century, the deep sense of loss which has been called Atlantic melancholy." You'll want to listen to saudade's most heart-throbbing and poignant expression, the fado—Portugal's most authentic and absorbing art form. Classically beautiful singers, such as Celeste Rodrigues, sister of the world-famed Amália, will entertain you in Lisbon. Clutching a traditional black shawl around herself, she raises her sensitive voice in the dimly lit tavern near the Alfama and the docks, singing the plaintive and poetic songs of her people. It doesn't matter whether you understand the words. The power of dynamic quality of the lament transcends language, forming its own vocabulary, finding its own reality.

To Do Something Majestic

Atop the highest turret of the seemingly impregnable fortress of St. George in Lisbon, the sounds of the quays and streets merely hum far below. A great eagle encaged within the fortress bewails its captivity. And whenever all sounds seem to have faded, the unnerving screams of one of the castle's white peacocks knifes the tranquility. Then you understand why the ancients trembled at the harsh, discordant shrieks of this bird—supposedly ill omens, harbingers of war, blood, and death.

Below, great ocean-going vessels trudge out of the custard-brown harbor toward the blue Atlantic. Cast before you are ancient facades and chipped slate backsides; teeming narrow city streets and rolling hills; awesome religious monuments; and steel-and-glass testimonies to technology. You can sit straddled upon a giant cannon which once protected the wealthiest of maritime empires and which trembled through many an earth tremor. In a glance you can view Roman occupation, Visigothic walls, Moorish remains, conflict with Spain, the cradle of the Portuguese empire, the modern world—a continuum of time unbroken.

To Wander Back into the Middle Ages

Involve yourself in the rural life, the very soul of Portugal. To sample a way of life fast disappearing, go to, say, Entrocamento, in the bull-breeding province of Ribatejo. This village, like so many others in Portugal, exudes the simple rusticity and warmth of a people still connected spiritually to the grapes and the land on which they grow.

From any street you can see the outskirts of the vineyards, in which cork trees are abundantly interspersed. Streams flow swiftly through the vineyards on their way to the nearby Tagus. You can follow one up into the foothills; and if you possess or can borrow a string and hook, chances are that you'll be having fish for supper.

The men come in from the fields at dusk, heading directly for the taverns for many carafes of deep purple wine topped with an inch of froth. An entire family—including the mother, the father, the children, even the friends—works behind the serving tables, drawing glasses from the damp, cool casks. Once inside one of these bustling taverns, an olive-skinned habitué will motion you toward a serving table, give a quick jerk on his earlobe, a wink of the eye from under a dark beret, and a repeated flip of his thumb toward his lips—the lever on the cask creaks.

To Build Bridges to Other People

As crusty as cork bark, as hard as an olive pit, yet as warm as life really ought to be, the people of Portugal are the greatest experience in this still provincial country. Their bridges of giving are strong and sturdy. Those travelers accustomed to a smile or friendly gesture used to cover an ulterior motive may find themselves clumsy in dealing with the Portuguese. But once you let yourself go, venturing into the countryside and exposing yourself to the Portuguese way of life, you'll feel the organic kindness of a remarkable people.

For example, you might stop a white-bearded farmer in Alentejo, innocently inquiring about directions. Don't be surprised if he invites you inside his family compound, where all the activity really takes place. It is here where he grows the produce that feeds his large family, barters with his neighbors, and generally carries on the business of living. He'll ask you to warm yourself at a corner hearthside fire, while he takes out a large loaf of bread, slicing it and spreading it with home-churned butter, then coating it with farm-grown honey kept in a large crock. Wine made from his own grapes will be offered in ceramic mugs.

When you leave, again don't be surprised if he tells you with conviction that the next time you pass through, you're to bed down as a guest of his family.

To Feel the Impact of the Sea

While the Portuguese fishermen are the challengers of the sea, the women are the guardians and sentinels. At Nazaré, Portugal's most colorful fishing village (north of Lisbon), the ritual of launching and bringing in those brightly painted Phoenician-inspired boats is as regular as the tidal rhythm of the sea. The bearded fishermen, in their long, tasseled stocking caps and plaid shirts, push out to the sea, paddling furiously, riding through the fury of the first breaker. When at sea, they search for the best fish-producing waters, letting down their nets and depositing their catch at the bottom of the boat. Hopefully, they will return to shore early with smiles of victory; but too often their return is delayed. Tragically, an occasional storm may rise suddenly to strike them down.

As the sun sinks, the women of Nazaré, frozen like classical women in stone, wait on the beach for the return of their men. They have spent the first portion of the day gossiping and repairing nets; but when it's time for the homecoming of the fleet, they gather quietly at the water's edge. Standing there in lonely vigil, they say not a word, as there is a silent understanding among them. While the custom of the young girls is to wear seven bright petticoats, the older women are nearly always draped in black. There is no one who has not lost a father, a brother, or a son. Tightening their woolen black shawls around themselves, they gaze out to the now-darkening sea, squinting their eyes, searching for the first signs of the high-bowed seeing-eye boats.

When the fleet appears, the women cross themselves many times in gratefulness to their protector saint, then rush out to do their part in unloading the boat. Teams of oxen are hitched up, ready to bring the boats in safely on the beach, so as not to lose the precious cargo.

The sea gives life and it takes it away.

We'll turn now to a closer examination of our pleasant task.

INTRODUCTION

DOLLARWISE—WHAT IT MEANS: In brief, this is a guidebook giving specific details (including prices) about Portuguese hotels, restaurants, bars, sightseeing attractions, nightlife, and tours. Establishments in *all* price ranges have been documented and described.

About 10% of the recommendations include the luxury hotels such as the Palácio at Estoril, while another 35% suggest inexpensive accommodations: budget hotels, guest houses, or country inns such as the Estalagem da Santa Iria in the heart of the scenic Templars town of Tomar, offering provincial-style bedrooms with private baths overlooking a gently flowing river, and costing only $22 a night for two persons.

On the other hand, the greater number, 55%, falls in that large in-between price category of the middle bracket. For example, in Lisbon you can ensconce yourself at the ultracontemporary Tivoli Jardim in the center of the city, where your colorful bedroom with its tiled bath goes for around $60 nightly for a double.

In all cases, establishments have been judged by a strict yardstick of value. If they measured up, they were included, regardless of price classification. The uniqueness of the book, I think, lies in the fact that it could be used either by a society matron with lorgnette ("We always stay at the Albatroz in Cascais") or by an escudo-lean collegian ("There's this little restaurant in Lisbon that serves you a big spread for two dollars").

But the major focus of the book is centered neither on the impecunious nor on the affluent whose gold rests in numbered accounts in Zurich. Rather, my chief concern is the average, middle-income-bracket voyager who'd like to patronize the almost wholly undocumented establishments in Portugal—that is, the first-class hotels or some of the better, but less heralded, restaurants, where you can often get a superb dinner.

In Portugal, of course, a first-time visitor is often bewildered as to what to see. The country suffers from lack of publicity. People know of Lisbon, and that's about it.

However, I've penetrated deep into remote villages, such as baroque Lamego in that province over the mountains, Tras-os-Montes. Naturally, all the big-time attractions are explored as well, ranging from Byron's glorious Eden at Sintra, to the sunny beaches of the Algarve, to the coastal villages of the north.

To show you what I have in mind in the way of where you'll be sleeping and dining, here is . . .

A CALDEIRADA OF BARGAINS: Borrowing the title of this heading from the classic fish stew of Portugal, we'll preview some of the delectable establishments awaiting you. In my journeys through every province of the country, I have discovered charm and comfort offered for little cost, or else establishments where the homemade or creative touch of their proprietors lifts them far above the ordinary. For an understanding of what Dollarwise means, I'll recall only a few as examples, although you'll meet dozens more in the pages ahead, perhaps discover some all on your own when you actually go to Portugal.

—A converted hillside monastery providing living in Lisbon, overlooking the Tagus River. The 16th-century convent, called York House, offers today's comforts blended with the mellowed atmosphere of yesterday: antique-filled bedrooms, corridors, and living rooms; ecclesiastical sculpture; bronze torchères; time-aged paintings. Oddly shaped bedrooms open onto a cloistered garden. For all of this, including three top-quality meals provided by a spirited Gallic owner, you'll pay $45.90 daily for two persons.

6 □ DOLLARWISE GUIDE TO PORTUGAL

—Or perhaps a crow's nest, stone-built modern inn, perched near the crest of a mountain of Caramulo. This estalagem retreat is favored by artists who appreciate a genuine Dufy on the wall, a blazing fire before an open hearth for after-dinner coffee, a panoramic view from the dining room, and immaculately kept and cozy bedrooms with private balconies and tiled baths. All this, plus three country-style meals (lots of second helpings), costs only $19 per person daily.

—Or perhaps you'll be drawn to the splendid life in the historic Roman city of Évora, staying at a luxury pousada (a government-run tourist inn). In this converted 14th-century convent you'll pay only about $34 per day for a bedroom filled with antique reproductions, and a tiled private bath, with breakfast. You can wander through a Manueline-style cloister, pause beside a gurgling marble fountain, and drink the local wine in the former dining hall.

—Finally, you may want to become a guest in an ancient stately home (quinta) on the faraway island of Madeira, at a converted private estate, with its own sun-pocket swimming pool. Two persons can stay here in individualized bedrooms with antiques for $40 daily. That figure includes a breakfast served on a silver tray on the flagstone terrace overlooking the harbor.

What about restaurants?

—In the kitchen of the former royal palace at Queluz, outside of Lisbon on the road to Sintra, you can enjoy a first-class meal in a regal setting. You dine seated on high ladder-backed chairs under a towering vaulted ceiling, with stone arches, a fireplace, and a 15-foot marble-topped chef's table laden with appetizing food. For $15, you can order a dinner, such as a regional soup, seafood bubbly with cheese, plus assorted cheeses from the neighboring countryside, as well as fresh fruit.

—Back on the island of Madeira, you can savor a hearty meal in a provincial hillside tavern, a setting of sun terraces overlooking the bay at Funchal. For only $3.67, an order of skewers of garlic-studded charcoal-broiled hunks of tender beef will be hung on a hook over your table. The rich juices are mopped up with crusty homemade bread fresh from the oven.

SOME DISCLAIMERS: No restaurant, inn, hotel, pensão, or nightclub paid to be mentioned in this book. What you read are entirely personal recommendations—in many cases, the proprietors never knew their establishments were being visited or investigated for inclusion in a travel guide.

A word of warning: Unfortunately, costs change, and they rarely go downward. The government virtually imposes rent control on its hotels, and many establishments have gone two or three years before changing their tariffs. Owing to sudden improvements or upgrading, other places have skyrocketed their tabs.

Always, when checking into a hotel, inquire about the tariff. This policy can save much embarrassment and disappointment when the time comes to settle your bill. Unfortunately, you cannot ever insist on being charged the precise prices quoted in this book, although every effort has been made to secure the accurate tariffs as much as they were foreseeable.

THE ORGANIZATION OF THIS BOOK: Here's how *Dollarwise Guide to Portugal* (*plus Madeira and the Azores*) sets forth the information it provides:

Chapter I, directly ahead, deals with ways of flying to Portugal, and then with various modes of transportation within the country. Naturally, the focus is on the least expensive means of transport, on such items as excursion fares and off-season discounts.

Chapter II turns the spotlight on "The Scene in Portugal"; it's meant to fortify you for your plunge into the country by outlining its history, providing tips on food specialties and wine, and previewing the hotel outlook.

Chapters III through IX take on a huge task—that of exploring the hotels, restaurants, shopping, attractions, and nightlife not only of **Lisbon,** but of the leading resorts along the Costa do Sol (**Estoril** and **Cascais**), and of **Sintra.** Documented first are the deluxe and first-class hotels, followed by those in the middle bracket and budget range. Beginning with the most expensive and elegant restaurants, such as Tavares and Aviz, the list continues downward to the lowly beer tavern serving an icy-cold stein and a juicy steak. Nightlife, especially fado, can be found in a wide variety of places, ranging from a rowdy sailors' bar in Lisbon to a posh disco in Cascais.

Chapters X and XI move outside of Lisbon for a trip south of the Tagus to the fishing port of **Setúbal** and the three-castle district, to the resort village of **Sesimbra,** and to the cove of **Portinho da Arrabida** at the foot of the Arrabida hills. Heading north, although still based in Lisbon, you can explore the fortress town of **Óbidos;** the 12th-century Cistercian monastery of **Alcobaça;** the 14th-century battle abbey at **Batalha;** the fishing village of **Nazaré;** the world-famed pilgrimage shrine at **Fátima;** and the historic Templars city of **Tomar.**

Chapter XII heads to the **Algarve,** the African-looking, southernmost province of Portugal. Stretching along the coast from Sagres to Vila Real de Santo António, it spans a distance of about 94 miles. For those who like beaches and sunshine, it sends out a call, and the tariffs are moderate.

Chapter XIII also bites off a big hunk, **Alentejo** and **Ribatejo.** Ribatejo is a land of pastures known for its bull breeding. The chief target is Tomar. The Alentejo is a district of olive trees and cork, its major goal the old Roman city of **Évora.**

Chapter XIV explores **Coimbra,** famous for its university dating from 1290, and the environs, especially the former royal palace and forest of **Buçaco** and the remains of a Roman settlement at **Conimbriga.**

Chapters XV and XVI do the same for Portugal's second city, **Porto** (where port wine is shipped out to the world), and for the **Minho** district in the northwestern corner of the country. Hotels, pousadas, sights, whatever, are detailed.

Chapter XVII heads out into the Atlantic for the mountainous, vegetation-rich island of **Madeira,** centering at **Funchal.** Finally, our trip concludes in the remote **Azores,** referred to as the "daughters of the ocean" and discovered in the 15th century.

Chapter XVIII caps the book with vital minutiae: menu translations, capsule vocabularies, and a currency conversion.

AN INVITATION TO READERS: Like all the Dollarwise books, *Dollarwise Guide to Portugal (plus Madeira and the Azores)* hopes to maintain a continuing dialogue between its writer and its readers. All of us share a common aim—to travel as widely and as well as possible, at the best value for our money—and in achieving that aim, your comments and suggestions can be of aid to others. Therefore, if you come across an appealing hotel, restaurant, nightclub, even sightseeing attraction, please don't keep it to yourself. I'll send free copies of the next edition of this book to readers whose suggestions are printed in it. And the letters need not only apply to new establishments, but

8 □ DOLLARWISE GUIDE TO PORTUGAL

to hotels and restaurants already recommended in this guide. The fact that a listing appears in this edition doesn't give it squatter's rights in future publications. If its services have deteriorated, its chef grown stale, its prices risen unfairly, whatever, these failings need to be known. Even if you enjoyed every place and found every description accurate, a letter letting me know that, too, can cheer a gray day. Send your comments to Darwin Porter, c/o Frommer/Pasmantier Publishers, 1230 Avenue of the Americas, New York, NY 10020.

THE $15-A-DAY TRAVEL CLUB: In this book we'll be looking at how to get your money's worth in Portugal, Madeira, and the Azores, but there is a "device" for saving money and determining value on *all* your trips. It's the popular, international $15-a-Day Travel Club, now in its 19th successful year of operation. The Club was formed at the urging of numerous readers of the $$$-Day and Dollarwise Guides, who felt that such an organization could provide continuing travel information and a sense of community to value-minded travelers in all parts of the world. And so it does!

In keeping with the budget concept, the membership fee is low and is immediately exceeded by the value of your benefits. Upon receipt of $12 (U.S., Canadian, and Mexican residents), or $15 (other foreign residents) in U.S. currency to cover one year's membership, we will send all new members, by return mail (book rate), the following items:

(1) The latest edition of *any two* of the following books (please designate in your letter which two you wish to receive):

Europe on $20 a Day
Australia on $20 a Day
England and Scotland on $25 a Day
Greece on $20 a Day
Hawaii on $25 a Day
Ireland on $25 a Day
Israel on $25 & $30 a Day
Mexico and Guatemala on $15 & $20 a Day
New Zealand on $20 & $25 a Day
Scandinavia on $25 a Day
South America on $25 a Day
Spain and Morocco (plus the Canary Is.) on $20 a Day
Washington, D.C. on $25 a Day

Dollarwise Guide to Canada
Dollarwise Guide to the Caribbean (including Bermuda and the Bahamas)
Dollarwise Guide to Egypt
Dollarwise Guide to England and Scotland
Dollarwise Guide to France
Dollarwise Guide to Germany
Dollarwise Guide to Italy
Dollarwise Guide to Portugal (plus Madeira and the Azores)
Dollarwise Guide to California and Las Vegas
Dollarwise Guide to Florida
Dollarwise Guide to New England
Dollarwise Guide to the Southeast and New Orleans
(Dollarwise Guides discuss accommodations and facilities in all price ranges, with emphasis on the medium-priced.)

INTRODUCTION 9

How to Beat the High Cost of Travel
(This practical guide details how to save money on absolutely all travel items—accommodations, transportation, dining, sightseeing, shopping, taxes, and more. Includes special budget information for seniors, students, singles, and families.)

How to Live in Florida on $10,000 a Year
(For the resident or anyone contemplating the move, this book provides all the information needed to live economically but well in the Sunshine State.)

Where to Stay USA (By the Council on International Educational Exchange, this extraordinary guide is the first to list accommodations in all 50 states that cost anywhere from $3 to $25 per night.)

(2) A copy of **Arthur Frommer's Guide to New York,** a newly revised pocket-size guide to hotels, and restaurants, night spots, and sightseeing attractions in all price ranges throughout the New York area.

(3) A one-year subscription to the quarterly Club newsletter—**The Wonderful World of Budget Travel** (about which more below)—which keeps members up-to-date on fast-breaking developments in low-cost travel to all areas of the world.

(4) Your personal membership card, which, once received, entitles you to purchase through the Club all Arthur Frommer Publications for a third to a half off their regular retail prices during the term of your membership.

Those are the immediate and definite benefits which we can assure to members of the Club at this time. Further benefits, which it has been our continuing aim to achieve for members, are announced to members in *The Wonderful World of Budget Travel (WWBT).* An eight-page, full-size newspaper, *WWBT* carries such continuing features as "The Traveler's Directory" (a list of members all over the world who are willing to provide hospitality to other members as they pass through their home cities) and "Share-a-Trip" (offers and requests from members for travel companions who can share costs); worldwide travel news and feature stories by our expert travel writers; plus tips and articles on specific plans and methods for travel savings.

If you would like to join this hardy band of international budgeteers and participate in its exchange of travel information and hospitality, simply send your name and address, together with your membership fee of $12 (U.S., Canadian, and Mexican residents), or $15 (other foreign residents) in U.S. currency to: $15-a-Day Travel Club, Inc., 1230 Avenue of the Americas, New York, NY 10020. All foreign residents please pay by international postage money order in U.S. funds, or by a check drawn on a U.S. bank. Remember to specify which *two* of the books in section (1) above you wish to receive in your initial package of members' benefits. Or, if you prefer, use the last page of this book, simply checking off the two books you want and enclosing $12 or $15 in U.S. currency.

Chapter I

GETTING THERE

1. Plane Economics
2. Traveling Within Portugal

ALTHOUGH LISBON is a major gateway city to Europe, in bygone days travelers went to France or England first and then began their Grand Tour, perhaps (but most likely not) stopping over in Portugal.

Air transportation has changed this habit, and more and more sun-seeking travelers are beginning their European adventure in Lisbon. Portugal is, in fact, one of the closest of all European countries to North America, and it costs less to fly from New York to Lisbon than from New York to Paris, Amsterdam, Frankfurt, Geneva, Munich, or Copenhagen.

In the paragraphs that follow we'll describe the basic structure of airfares, exploring various methods of cutting your air transportation costs, and then we'll deal with methods of traveling within Portugal once you arrive.

1. Plane Economics

Since deregulation under the Carter administration, the airlines have competed fiercely with one another for traffic. To many destinations, an airline now proposes a fare structure; another airline then files a competing and perhaps different fare structure. A process of jockeying occurs which may or may not result in a uniform price structure for all airlines flying to that particular country.

It all adds up to chaos—but often *beneficial* chaos for the alert traveler willing to study and consider all the fares available. The key to bargain airfares is to shop around.

In what follows we'll point out the current options available for flying directly to Portugal—only two airlines do so and they are TAP (the Portuguese international airline) and TWA. If you don't want to fly directly to Portugal, then remember to check all the airlines to find the most inexpensive transatlantic fare that coincides with your itinerary and travel plans.

Please note that the fares below are TAP's and are current as of autumn 1981; they are subject to change and meant to serve only as a guide.

LEAST EXPENSIVE FARES: Currently your cheapest direct flight options fall into two categories.

APEX Fare

This means Advance Purchase Excursion and is probably the most popular fare used to cross the Atlantic. It's valid for a stay abroad of from 7 to 60 days and must be purchased at least 21 days in advance of your outbound flight to Lisbon. There is a cancellation charge of $50 for nonuse of a ticket.

The peak-season fare (round trip between New York and Lisbon) is, as of this writing, $564, but is subject to change by the summer of 1982, an anticipated rise of 6%. Peak season begins June 15, ending August 15.

Shoulder season is from April 1 to June 15 and from August 15 to October 31. The round-trip fare between New York and Lisbon is $543, dropping to $532 for a round-trip between New York and the Azores (Santa Maria or Terceira).

The cheapest fare is in the winter, known as the basic season. The round-trip New York-Lisbon fare is $499, dropping to $489 for a round-trip excursion between New York and the Azores.

Excursion Fare

Finally, one more discount fare—the 14- to 90-day excursion fare, which features a 14-day minimum stay and a 90-day maximum stay. The current excursion fare charged by TAP between New York and Lisbon (round trip) is $850 in peak season, $770 in basic (which begins after September 14). TAP also flies on Monday and Friday to the Azores. A typical round-trip fare between New York and, say, Terceira, goes for $840 in peak season, $759 in basic.

THE REGULAR FARES: If you can't take advantage of any of the above fares, which should be unlikely, here are the regular round-trip fares offered by TAP: $1092 basic, $1382 peak. On TAP, this fare is known as "executive class," and is the equivalent of a first-class fare. Departures are only on 747s on Thursday, Saturday, and Sunday from New York's Kennedy Airport.

2. Traveling Within Portugal

TRAINS IN PORTUGAL: The railway system is underdeveloped when stacked against the more industrialized nations of Western Europe. Still, the connections between the capital and more than 20 major towns are mainly electric and diesel. Express trains run between Lisbon and Coimbra (the university city), as well as Porto. Leaving from Lisbon's waterfront, electric trains travel along the Costa do Sol (Estorial and Cascais) and on to Queluz and Sintra.

At any rate, nobody complains about the prices charged: 0$72 (1¢) per kilometer in first class, a little more than 0$40 (½¢) per kilometer in second class. Discounts up to 20% are granted on Weekend Tickets, valid only from 5 p.m. on Friday till noon on Sunday. Parties of ten or more can apply at any Portuguese railway station for substantial reductions if the total combined rail miles exceeds 31.

In Lisbon at the **Statium Apolônia**, connections can be made for international services and the Northern and Eastern Lines. **Rossio** serves Sintra and the Western Lines; and at the **Cais do Sodré** connections are made for the Costa do Sol resorts of Estoril and Cascais. Finally, trains leave from the **Sul e Sueste** for the Alentejo and the Algarve. In addition, express trains connect

Lisbon to all the major capitals of Western Europe, and there is a direct link with Seville.

Railway information and tickets on the **Portuguese National Railroad** may be obtained in North America from its representative, the **French National Railways,** 610 Fifth Ave., New York, NY 10017 (tel. 212/582-2110); 360 Post St., San Francisco, CA 94108 (tel. 415/982-1993); 946 Wilshire Blvd., Beverly Hills, CA 90212 (tel. 213/274-6934); 11 East Adams St., Chicago, IL 60603 (tel. 312/427-8691); 1500 Stanley St., Montréal, Québec (tel. 514/288-8255).

Eurailpass

This pass is obtainable for periods of 15 days, 21 days, and one, two, or three months at the price of $200, $250, $300, $400, and $500, respectively. The holder is entitled to unlimited **first-class** rail transportation and many bonuses —either free or with substantial reductions. Travel on this pass must begin within six months of the day of issue, and the first day of validity has to be stamped in at the railroad station where travel is commenced.

Travel agents in all towns, and railway agents in major cities in the United States, sell Eurailpasses. Readers who live elsewhere can write to: Eurailpass, Box Q, Staten Island, NY 10305.

The pass is sold worldwide except in Europe and North Africa, and it is good throughout Western Europe, except in the British Isles and Finland.

Youth Pass

This is available in North America to young people under 26 years of age. It's valid for two months of unlimited **second-class** travel in some 15 countries. However, supplements and seat reservation fees aren't included in the $260 price. The bonuses are the same as for Eurailpass.

Before leaving for Portugal, you can get complete details from travel agents in all towns and railway agents in such major cities as New York, Montréal, Los Angeles, San Francisco, Miami, Vancouver, Toronto, Houston, or Chicago. You can also write to Eurailpass, Box Q, Staten Island, NY 10305.

CAR RENTAL: For most travelers, it's best to have a rented car at your command. That way, you're your own free agent, capable of savoring the hidden charms of Portugal that are often inaccessible by public transportation. While there are no superhighways, the roads are quite good, providing access to hard-to-reach gems, undiscovered villages, mountain passes with panoramic views and waterfalls, rustic country inns, and off-the-beaten-track sandy beaches and coves.

You'll have to decide if it's more economical for you to rent a car with a straight daily or weekly charge, plus either a per-kilometer rate, or an unlimited-mileage arrangement. Many agencies do not offer you a choice, but a firm that does is **Avis.** The office is at the airport. However, Avis also has as many as 14 convenient offices in Lisbon and Estoril. The main office is at Avenida Praia de Victoria in Lisbon (tel. 56-11-77). Tariffs range from 750$ ($11.48) daily, plus 7$50 (12¢) per kilometer for a car in Class A (Morris Mini or Fiat 127), up to 3830$ ($58.60) daily for a Mercedes Diesel, plus 30$20 (46¢) per extra kilometer.

Unlimited mileage is only available by the week at a rate of 12,810$ ($195.99) for cars in Class A to 58,500$ ($895.05) for vehicles in Class I.

Write to or speak with the friendly and most helpful manager Victor Manique. He'll send you a detailed brochure and will reserve a car for your arrival. If you want to tour in the grand manner, Mr. Manique will arrange it at a lower cost than any competitive car-rental firm in Portugal.

By now you've bought your plane tickets and are on your way. Coming up next—some handy reading matter during your flight about the food, history, and hotels of Portugal.

Chapter II

THE SCENE IN PORTUGAL

1. A Capsule History
2. Dining and Wining
3. The Hotel Outlook

IN AN INCREASINGLY mechanized age, there is still Portugal.

It is a land of gardens and natural produce, of abundant flowers, a place that still values the artful homemade touch. The wine you drink may be from your host's own casks, the tablecloth before you made by his wife, the bread fresh from the oven and baked by a daughter-in-law.

A long line of expatriates, including exiled royalty, knows what has long been called "the last foreign country of Europe." The society has been termed feudal, and that forms part of its medieval charm for many. But change is in the air. Even so, visitors are still rare in the more remote parts of Portugal. One Canadian couple were themselves the subject of sightseeing interest as they made their way through a village en route to a church built in the 14th century.

A small country at the southwestern edge of Europe, Portugal measures only 136 miles at its widest point, 350 miles at its longest span.

You can divide your Portuguese holiday into four parts, spending the first part of your trip in **Lisbon** and at the Costa do Sol resorts of **Estoril** and **Cascais**. Perhaps you'll allow time for a series of day trips from the capital, going to **Sintra, Nazaré, Tomar, Fátima, Óbidos**, as well as the scenic spots south of the **Tagus**.

Maybe you'll devote the second phase to one of the hotels on the **Algarve** in the south, studded with sandy beaches. En route to the Algarve, you can detour through the Alentejo district, stopping at the old Roman city of **Évora**.

Before leaving continental Portugal, you should experience the relatively unknown north. Go there to see towns and monuments—**Coimbra, Porto** (home of port wine), **Viana do Castelo**—and some of the country's finest scenery. Before beginning your homeward trek, you can wind down in the islands, either **Madeira** or in the more remote **Azores**.

Hopefully, on your Portuguese holiday you'll allow for recuperative days in the sun and at the sea, all of which will fortify you to drink from Lisbon's chalice: hearing fado songs, seeing its museums, attending a bullfight, an opera, dining in a palace, browsing through numerous handicraft shops.

When traveling through the countryside, it's best to plot your trips so that you'll stop over at the government-owned pousadas (tourist inns), ranging from restored castles on the Atlantic coast to mountain chalets.

Essentially, Portugal is a land of . . .

SOUNDS, SMELLS, AND SIGHTS: Windmills clacking in the Atlantic wind . . . farmers burning dried eucalyptus leaves . . . the plaintive sound of fado echoing through the narrow streets of Lisbon's Alfama . . . lonely *varinas* draped in black, waiting at the surf, their melancholy faces wrinkled by the harsh sea wind . . . purple wisteria cascading over the walls of mosaic courtyards . . . starfish-scattered sands . . . plodding oxen pulling carts along ribbon roads . . . sun-baked, grape-yielding slopes . . . the stark ruggedness of the seascape . . . sun-scorched, bull-breeding plains . . . houses bathed in birthday-cake colors with contrasting azulejos in ivory white, mustard gold, indigo blue, and emerald green . . .

Wicker baskets of eels steeped in the scent of the sea . . . terraced rice fields evoking the Orient . . . the pine groves of Leiria . . . bullock carts trundling across arched bridges . . . a ringing of a church bell in a mountain village . . . fields of cork . . . coasts of cliffs . . . the singsong litany of a fish auction . . . lemons, snowy almonds, and cactus . . . richly embroidered regional costumes . . . black-shawled women mending nets . . . horseback-riding *campinos* . . . the violent grandeur of the Mouth of Hell . . . pagan festivals . . . medieval monasteries . . . and women filling their jugs at fountains, as in biblical times.

THE SEASONS: "We didn't know we had an April," one Lisbon resident said, "until *that* song came out." "April in Portugal" is famous, both the song and the season. Then there are those who prefer May, or a day in late September, and especially October. Summer may be the most popular season, vacations being timed as they are; but for the traveler who can chart his or her own course, spring and autumn are the delectable seasons.

For North Americans, the climate of Portugal most closely parallels that of California. The Portuguese, of course, consider their climate one of the most ideal in Europe, and it is. As in California, there are only slight fluctuations in temperature between summer and winter, the overall mean ranging from 77 degrees Fahrenheit in summer to about 58 degrees Fahrenheit in winter. However, the rainy season begins in November, usually lasting through January.

The proximity of the Gulf Stream allows Portugal's northernmost province, the **Minho**, to enjoy mild, albeit very rainy, winters, even though it's at approximately the same latitude as New York.

Snow brings many skiing enthusiasts to the **Sêrra de Estrêla** mountains in north-central Portugal; but, for the most part, winter entails only some rain and lower temperatures in the other provinces.

The **Algarve** and especially **Madeira** are the exceptions to the rule: they enjoy warm and temperate winters. Madeira, in fact, basks in its high season in winter. The Algarve, too, is somewhat of a winter Riviera, attracting sunworshipers from both North America and Europe. Summers in both the Algarve and Madeira tend to be long and hot, crystal clear and dry.

Lisbon and **Estoril** enjoy 46- to 65-degree Fahrenheit temperatures in winter, those figures rising to between 60 and 82 degrees Fahrenheit in summer.

Travelers have dubbed the country whose terrain ranges from wooded fertile valleys, to mountains, to sun-baked slopes, to flat coastal expanses, to rolling pasturelands, to windswept plains, to sandy beaches—a "country for all seasons."

1. A Capsule History

Early in their history, the 12th century to be exact, the ancestors of today's Portuguese decided they didn't want to be associated with their Spanish neighbors in León and Castile. The split that was to occur followed a typical medieval pattern of indiscretion, ambition, jealousy, open conflict, and the emergence of a popular hero around whom the people could rally in a cause of independence.

First, the indiscretion. The 11th-century ruler of the Spanish kingdoms of León and Castile, Ferdinand the Great (otherwise the First), handed over the county of Portugal to his illegitimate daughter Teresa. The land south of the Tagus was at that time held by the Moors. Unknowingly, the king had launched a course of events that was to lead eventually to the birth of another nation.

Ambition. Teresa, although born out of wedlock herself, was firmly and securely bound in marriage to Henry, a count of Burgundy. Count Henry seemed to accept his father-in-law's gift of Portugal as his wife's dowry. Upon the king's death, Henry perhaps coveted the territories in Spain as well, but his own demise cut short further aggrandizement of territory.

Jealousy. Teresa now ruled in Portugal, casting a disdainful eye and an interfering nose into her legitimate sister's kingdom in Spain. Teresa lost no time mourning poor Henry, but took as a lover a Galician count, Fernao Peres. Teresa's constant refusal to guard her own affair with Peres and stay out of everyone else's affairs led to open strife with León.

Her son, Afonso Henriques, was terribly displeased with his mother's actions. Life being so short in those days, he probably wanted to hurry the day when he could rule in her place. Their armies met at São Mamade in 1128. Teresa lost and was banished along with her lover.

Ungrateful son or not, Afonso Henriques was to become the George Washington of Portugal. In 1143 he was proclaimed king, and official recognition eventually came from the Vatican in 1178. His enemies in Spain temporarily quieted, Afonso turned his roving eye toward the Moorish conquerors in the south of Portugal. Beefed up by the armed might of the Crusaders from the north, the Portuguese conquered Santarém and Lisbon in 1147. Upon his death in 1185, Afonso was succeeded by his son Sancho I, who continued his father's work of consolidation of the newly emerged nation, which was threatened with recurring attacks by the Moors. His heir Afonso II ruled for 12 years, beginning in 1211. Like his father and grandfather, he carried on the war against the Moors.

Sancho II was an adolescent when he ascended the throne. Extremely devout, he returned much to the clergy that had been confiscated during his father's reign. He scored numerous victories over the Moors. However, he couldn't pacify the clergy and was eventually excommunicated. His brother Afonso III was named king, ruling from 1248 to 1279. During the latter's reign, the Algarve, the southern district of Portugal, was finally taken from the Moors, and the capital was moved from Coimbra to Lisbon.

The new king Dinis, the son of a bigamous marriage, ruled Portugal from 1279 to 1325. He is sometimes known as the poet king or the farmer king. He founded the country's first university, in Lisbon, in 1290. Dinis married an Aragonese princess, Isabella, who was later canonized, although evidence indicates that the vigorous young king would have preferred a less saintly wife. Isabella was especially interested in poor people, and they spread a legend about

HISTORY OF PORTUGAL 17

her. It seems that she was sneaking bread out of the palace to feed them when her husband spotted her and inquired as to what she was concealing. When she revealed the contents to Dinis, the bread miraculously turned into roses, so the story goes.

The son of these two famous monarchs, Afonso IV, could hardly wait until his father stepped down from the throne. He, too, was involved in wars with Castile and the Moors, chiefly the 1340 battle of Salado; but he is remembered today for having had assassins murder his son's mistress, the legendary Inês de Castro.

Early in life Afonso's son, who would later rule as Pedro I, was betrothed to marry a Spanish princess. However, he fell in love with her beautiful lady-in-waiting. Inês was deeply attracted to him, and their affair blossomed. Eventually, Inês was banished from the country, although she returned upon the death of the Spanish princess to live openly with Pedro. Jealous sycophants in court persuaded Afonso IV to sanction her murder, which was especially blood-curdling. Although he was to know other women, Pedro never recovered from the shock of seeing his dead mistress. Patiently he waited until his father died. Upon his becoming king, he set out to seek revenge. Tracking the assassins to Spain, he had them returned by force to Portugal, where he had their hearts torn out. (One of the assassins managed to escape to France.) But the king did not stop there. He ordered that the body of Inês be exhumed. The members of the court were summoned and forced to pay homage by kissing the hand of Inês, who had been interred for at least four or five years. She was then royally attired and regally placed on the throne beside her husband. Inês, and later Pedro, were buried at Alcobaça, where their tombs are visited frequently today.

During Pedro's reign (1357–1367), the influential representative body, the Cortes (an assembly of clergy, nobility, and commoners), began to gain ascendancy, while the majority of the clergy, pretentious and greedy for power, fought the sovereign's reform measures, thus allying the people more strongly with the crown. Pedro's son, Ferdinand I (1367–1373), saw Portugal invaded by Castilian forces, Lisbon besieged, and the final demise of his dynasty.

In 1383, rather than submit to Spanish rule, the Portuguese people chose the illegitimate son of Pedro as regent. The house of Avís was thereby established. João de Avís (1383-1433) secured Portuguese independence by defeating Castilian forces at Aljubarrota in 1385. His union with Philippa, the granddaughter of Edward III of England, produced the seed which was to mark the emergence of Portugal as an empire, Prince Henry the Navigator.

Henry's demand for geographical accuracy and exploration, his desire to attain the legendary wealth in gold and ivory, slaves, and spices of the East and "Terra Incognita," and his patriotic and spiritual desires to promote Christianity by joining with the fabled Christian kingdom of Prester John and driving the Moslems out of North Africa—all drove Henry to explore. Facing him was a Sea of Darkness, where ships supposedly melted in the equatorial regions, sea serpents flourished, and strange beasts sought to destroy any interloper.

Henry established a community of scholars at Sagres on the south coast of Portugal to develop navigational and cartographical techniques. He infused the court with his zeal and brought his nation to face a destiny imminent from the time of their earliest contacts with Phoenician and Greek mariners. Henry was responsible for the discovery of Madeira, the Azores, Cape Verde, Senegal, and Sierra Leone, and he established the blueprint for continued exploration during the reigns of Duarte I (1433–1438), Afonso V (1438–1481), and João II (1481–1495).

In 1482 Portuguese ships explored the mouth of the Congo; in 1488 Dias rounded the Cape of Good Hope; and in 1497 Vasco da Gama reached Calicut

(Kozhikode) on India's west coast, clearing the way for trade in spices, porcelain, silks, ivory, and slaves. The original appellation of the Cape of Good Hope, the Cape of Storms, might have been a more prophetic one.

The Treaty of Tordesillas, negotiated by João II in 1494 for as yet undiscovered lands in the Western Hemisphere, ensured Portugal's possession of Brazil, not discovered until 1500. Utilizing the inflowing wealth of the whole empire, Manuel I (the Fortunate, 1495-1521) imprinted his imagination and name upon great monuments of art and architecture. His reign inspired Portugal's Golden Age. By 1521 the country had begun to tap the natural resources of Brazil and had broken the spice-trade monopoly formerly held by the Venetians. She was mistress of nearly all accesses to the Indian Ocean. At her noontide, she stood as the first of the great maritime world empires.

João III (1527–1557) ushered the Inquisition and the Jesuits into his unwieldy empire. With his son Sebastian's disappearance in action in Morocco in 1578, leaving Portugal without an heir, the way was opened for Spanish control. Philip II of Spain claimed the throne and began 60 years of Spanish domination. In the East, Portugal's strength had been undermined by Dutch and English traders.

A nationalist revolution in 1640 brought a descendant of an illegitimate son of João I to the throne, João IV. This began the house of Braganza, which was to rule until the 20th century, as well as a long series of revolutions and intrigues in Portugal's history. João IV arranged an English alliance, wedding his daughter to Charles II. For her dowry he "threw in" Bombay and Tangier.

The Treaty of Lisbon with Spain in 1668 gave Portugal recognized independence. In that same year the Cortes ousted King Afonso VI, replacing him with Pedro II.

All Saints Day, 1755. The great earthquake destroyed virtually all of Lisbon. In six minutes 15,000 people were killed, many thousands while attending morning masses. The Marquês de Pombal, adviser to King José (1750–1777), became a dictator, completing the process he had begun years before, transforming the inert absolutism into an active depotism. Much that he did, such as limiting the power of the Inquisition and rebuilding Lisbon after the earthquake, was good. He beefed up such industries as silk, fishing, even diamonds. But his expulsion of the Jesuits in 1759 earned him powerful enemies throughout Europe.

In 1793, under the threat of Napoleon, Portugal joined a coalition with England and Spain. An insane queen, Maria I (1777–1816), plus an exiled royal family, made military overthrow an easy job. The Cortes was summoned by the military junta, a constitution was drawn up, and Maria's son, João VI, accepted the position of constitutional monarch in 1821. João's son Pedro declared independence for Brazil in 1822; and in 1853, after a series of intrigues and battles within the royal family, he returned to Portugal and restored the constitution.

The years 1853–1908 felt the rumble of republican movements that assaulted the very existence of the monarchists, as exemplified by the dictatorial government of Carlos I, "the painter king." In 1908 Carlos and the crown prince were assassinated at Black Horse Square in Lisbon. Manuel II ruled for two years before being overthrown in an outright revolution on October 5, 1910. (He died in England in 1932, the last of the Portuguese monarchs.)

Portugal was a republic.

Instability was the watchword of the newly proclaimed republic, with revolutions occurring two or three times a year. Portugal failed in her attempts to remain neutral in World War I. Influenced by her old ally, England, she commandeered German ships in the Lisbon harbor, which promptly brought a declaration of war from Germany.

The precarious foundations of the republic collapsed in 1926 when a military revolt established a dictatorship, with Fragoso da Carmona at its head. He remained president until 1951, but only as a figurehead. António Salazar became his finance minister in 1928, rescuing the country from a morass of financial difficulties. He went on to become the head of state. In World War II, he asserted his country's neutrality, although he allowed British and American troops to occupy the Azores in 1943.

In 1955, Portugal joined the United Nations. Salazar suffered a stroke in 1968 (he died in 1970), and Premier Marcelo Caetano succeeded him.

The old dictatorship was overthrown on April 25, 1974, in a coup dubbed "the flower revolution" because the soldiers wore red carnations instead of carrying guns. Change swept across the land, as Portugal drifted into near anarchy.

But, happily, things have returned to order now, with a freely elected president. The revolutionary slogans and hammers and sickles are gradually being removed from national monuments. Tourists are reappearing by the thousands, and Portugal is now considered one of the safest countries in all of Europe in which to travel.

2. Dining and Wining

Portuguese food was summed up well by Mary Jean Kempner in her *Invitation to Portugal:* "The best Portuguese food is provincial, indigenous, eccentric, and proud—a reflection of the chauvinism of this complex people. It takes no sides, assumes no airs, makes no concessions or bows to Brillat-Savarin—and usually tastes wonderful."

WHAT TO EXPECT: The first main dish you're likely to encounter on any menu is bacalhau (salted codfish), the *o fiel amigo* (faithful friend) to the Portuguese. As you drive through fishing villages in the north, you'll see racks and racks on which the fish is drying in the sun. It has literally saved the lives of thousands from starvation, and the Portuguese not only are grateful to it, they like it as well.

Foreigners may not wax as rhapsodical about bacalhau, although it's prepared in imaginative ways, reportedly one for every day of the year. Common ways of serving it include bacalhau cozido (boiled with vegetables such as carrots, cabbage, and spinach, then baked in a mixture); bacalhau à Bras (fried in olive oil with onions and potatoes and flavored with garlic); bacalhau à Gomes de Sá (codfish that has been stewed with black olives, potatoes, onions, then baked and topped with a sliced boiled egg); and, finally, bacalhau no churrasco (barbecued).

A Kettle of Fruits of the Sea

Aside from codfish, the classic national dish is *caldeirada,* once described as the Portuguese version of a savory Mediterranean bouillabaisse. Prepared by the lady of the house, it is a simple kettle of fish, with bits and pieces of the latest catch. From the kitchen of a competent chef, it's a pungent stew with choice bits and pieces of fruits of the sea.

Next on the platter is the Portuguese sardine, which many gastronomes have called elegant. This unassuming fish goes by the pompous name of *Clupea Pilchardus,* and is found off the Atlantic coasts of Iberia as well as France.

Many of the sardines come from Setúbal, a city south of the Tagus which is most often visited on a day trip from Lisbon. As you stroll through the alleys of the Alfama, or pass along the main streets of small villages throughout Portugal, you'll see women kneeling in front of braziers on their front doorsteps, grilling these large sardines left behind for domestic consumption. To have them grilled, order *sardinhas assadas.*

Shellfish is one of the great delicacies of the Portuguese table. Its scarcity and the demand of foreign markets have led to astronomical price tags.

However, tourists devour them, many lamenting later when the bill is presented to settle damages. The price of lobster or crabs literally changes every day, depending on market quotations. Therefore, the tariff doesn't appear on the menu. Rather, you'll see the abbreviation, "Preço V.," meaning variable price. When the waiter brings one of these crustaceans to your table, inquire as to the price. That way you'll avoid shock when your sin is tallied up.

If you do decide to splurge, make sure you get fresh shellfish. Many of these creatures from the deep, such as king-size crabs, are cooked, then displayed in restaurant windows. If they don't sell that day, we suspect the chef places them there tomorrow.

When fresh, *santola* (crab) is a delicacy. It's often served stuffed (*santola recheada*), although this specialty may be too pungent for unaccustomed Western palates, *Amêijoas,* the baby clams, are a reliable item of the Portuguese kitchen. *Lagosta* is translated as lobster; in fact, it's really a crayfish, best when served without adornment. If you see the words "piri-piri" on the menu following lobster, rush for the nearest exit. This is a sauce made of hot pepper from Angola. Jennings Parrott once wrote: "After tasting it you will understand why Angola wanted to get it out of the country."

In Pursuit of an Incomparable Morsel

Many Portuguese begin their meals with *percêbes,* roughly translated as goose barnacles. These little devils are the subject of much controversy. One local newspaper in Lisbon suggested to tourists that if they "can bear their repulsive appearance," they'll find "an incomparable morsel of delicious seafood" within. Others claim that all they taste from barnacles is brackish sea water.

There will be no controversy among those who are partial to *camarãoes* (shrimps). Most restaurants serve a heaping, delectable platter full, but be forewarned: after devouring the meal, you will most asuredly need a bath.

A wide variety of good-tasting and inexpensive fish dishes are also available: *salmonete* (Red mullet) from Setúbal; *robalo* (bass); *lenguado* (sole); and the sweet-tasting *pescada* (hake). Perhaps less appealing to to the average diner, but preferred by many discriminating palates, are *eirós* (eels), *polvo* (octopus), and *lampreías* (lampreys), the latter a seasonal feature in the northern Minho district.

Of course, another way of beginning your repast is to select from the offerings of trays of *acepipes variados,* Portuguese hors d'oeuvres, which might include everything from a sea creature known as "knife" to the inevitable olives and tuna fish.

Meat, especially beef and veal, is less satisfying. Porto residents are known as "tripe eaters." The specialty is *dobrada,* tripe with beans, a favorite of the workers. The *cozido à Portuguesa* is another dish much in demand: a stew often employing both beef and pork, along with fresh vegetables and sausages. The chief offering of the beer tavern is *bife na frigideira,* beef in a mustard sauce, usually served with a fried egg on top, all piping hot in a brown ceramic dish. Thinly sliced *iscas* (calves' livers) are usually well prepared and sauteed with onion.

The best meat in Portugal is *porco* (pork), which is usually tender and juicy. In particular, order porco Alentejano, fried pork in a succulent sauce with baby clams, often cooked with herb-flavored onions and tomatoes. In the same province, *cabrito* (roast kid) is another treat, flavored with herbs and garlic. Chicken tends to be hit and miss, and is perhaps best when spit roasted a golden brown (*frango no espeto*).

In season, game is good, especially *perdiz* (partridge) and *codorniz estufada* (pan-roasted quail).

The Question of Olive Oil and Garlic

From the soup kitchen, the most popular broth is *caldo verde*, literally green broth. Made from cabbage, sausage, potatoes, and olive oil, it is commonly encountered in the north. Another ubiquitous soup is *sopa alentejana*, simmered with garlic and bread among other ingredients. The Portuguese housewife is canny, knowing how to gain every last morsel of nutrition from her fish, meat, and vegetables. The fishwives make a *sopa de mariscos* by boiling the shells from fish, then richly flavoring the stock and lacing it with white wine.

The basis of much Portuguese cooking is olive oil. However, the oil seems blander than that used extensively in Spain. Furthermore, chefs in most Portuguese hotels, certainly first-class ones, offer more of a routine international fare than they do the regional cuisine. If you don't like olive oil, ask that your fish or meat be prepared *sem azeite* (without olive oil) but *com manteiga* (with butter). Garlic is also used extensively and forms the basis of many dishes. However, if you select anything prepared to order you can request that it be *sem alho* (without garlic).

Time and time again in Portuguese restaurants you'll be asked: "Do you want a second helping?" It's customary in most establishments to order soup (invariably a big bowl filled to the brim), then a fish and a meat course. Potatoes and/or rice are likely to accompany both the meat and fish platters. This banquet is simply too much for many, particularly those second helpings.

Menus are not usually posted in the windows of Portuguese restaurants, making shopping around impossible. In many restaurants, the chef features a *prato do dia*—that is, a plate of the day which is actually several listings. These dishes are prepared fresh that day, and often are cheaper than the regular offerings. In regional dining rooms (not in first-class restaurants and hotels), you'll sometimes see two price listings after an entree. The first price is the tariff if one person orders the dish, the second tab is if two persons select the same main course. This system is known as the famous "double portions" of Portugal. Having two persons order the same main dish amounts to only a small saving, but the custom is highly favored in escudowise Portugal.

The Sugaring of the Egg

Locked away in isolated and remote convents and monasteries, nuns and monks created such original sweet-tooth concoctions that they surely had to confess their sins. Many of these same delectable dessert specialties have been handed down over the years and are nowadays sold in little pastry shops throughout Portugal. In Lisbon or Porto, and a few other Portuguese cities, you can visit a salão de chá (tea salon) at four o'clock in the afternoon where you can sample these delicacies. Regrettably, too few restaurants feature regional desserts, many relying on caramel custard or fresh fruit.

Portugal doesn't offer many egg dishes, except for the omelet, which countries enjoy. However, the egg is used extensively in many of the sweets. Although egg yolks cooked in sugar may not appeal to you, you may want to try some of the more original offerings. Perhaps the best known are *ovos moles* (soft eggs sold in colorful barrels) that originate in Aveiro. From the same district capital comes *ovos de fio* (string eggs).

The most typical dessert is *arroz doce,* rice pudding flavored with cinnamon. As mentioned, flan, or caramel custard, appears on all menus. If you're in Portugal in summer, ask for a peach from Alcobaça. One of these juicy, succulent yellow fruits will spoil all other peaches for you forever. In first-class restaurants, the waiters go through an elaborate ritual of skinning it in front of you. Sintra is known for its strawberries, Setúbal for its orange groves, the Algarve for its almonds and figs, Elvas for its plums, the Azores for their pineapple, and Madeira for its passion fruit. Some people believe that if you eat too much of the latter, you'll be driven insane.

Cheese (*queijo*) is usually eaten separately and not with the fruit, as in France. The most common varieties of Portuguese cheese are made from sheep or goat's milk. Popular entrees include *queijo da sêrra* (literally, cheese from the hills). Another much-in-demand cheese is queijo do Alentejo, plus queijo de Azeitão. Many prefer queijo Flamengo (similar to the Dutch Gouda cheese).

Dining hours in Portugal are much earlier than they are in Spain. The best time for lunch is between 1 and 2:30 p.m., from 7:30 to 9 p.m. for dinner.

The Pleasures of Port

One of the joys of dining in Portugal is to discover its regional wines. With the exception of port and Madeira, they remain little known in Europe.

Port wine is produced in a specially designated region on the arid slopes of the **Douro.** Only vineyards within this area are recognized as yielding genuine port wine. The wine is shipped from Portugal's second-largest city, Porto, which the English have dubbed Oporto.

Port, drunk in tulip-shaped glasses, comes in many different colors and flavors. The pale dry port makes an ideal apéritif, and you can request it at the same time you might normally order dry sherry. The ruby or tawny port is sweet or medium dry, usually drunk as a liqueur after dessert. The most valuable port is either vintage or crusted wine. Crusted port does not mean vintage—rather, it takes its name from the decanting of its crust. Vintage port is the very best wine. In a period of a decade, only three years may be declared vintage.

Port is blended to assure a consistency of taste. Cyril Ray called it "one of the heartiest and handsomest of wines." Matured in wooden casks, the wood ports are either white, tawny, or ruby red. At first, the wine is a deep ruby color, turning more the color of straw as it ages.

Port wine had "perpetuated and glorified the fame of Porto," as one citizen put it. The first foreigners to be won over by it were the English, a drinking tradition dating back to the 17th century. In more recent times, however, the French import more of the wine than the British. The grapes are still crushed by barefoot men; but this shouldn't alarm you as the wine is purified before it's bottled.

Falstaff's Soul for a Glass of Madeira

Although its greatest chic was in times gone by, Madeira wine remains popular. It was highly favored by the early American colonies. Made with grapes grown in volcanic soil, it is fortified with brandy before it's shipped out.

The major types of Madeira are Sercial (a dry wine, drunk as an apéritif, once a favorite with characters in Galsworthy novels); Malmsey (the dessert wine that the Duke of Clarence allegedly asked to drown in to escape torture at the hands of his brother); and Boal (a heady wine used on many different occasions, everyplace from a banquet following a hunt to an off-the-record tête-à-tête).

Perhaps one of the finest statements ever made for Madeira wines is the following: "It gives vivacity to a social gathering, profundity to a solitary meditation, helps a man to think well of his friends and to forgive his enemies. . . ."

Feminine, but Virile

Among the table wines, my personal favorites are from the mountainous wine district known as Dão. Its red wines are ruby-colored, their taste often described as velvety, whereas the white wines are light and delicate enough to make a fit accompaniment to Portuguese shellfish. From the sandy dunes of the Colares wine district, near Sintra, emerges a full-bodied wine made from Ramisco grapes (this wine is served at the Palácio de Seteais hotel). Of Colares wine, a Portuguese writer once noted that it has "a feminine complexion, but a virile energy."

The vinhos verdes (green wines) have many adherents. These light wines, low in alcoholic content, come from the northwestern corner of Portugal, the Minho district. The wine is gaseous, as it's made from grapes not fully matured. Near Estoril, the Carcavelos district produces an esoteric wine, commonly served as an apéritif or else with dessert. As it mellows, its bouquet is more powerful. Finally, the Busselas district, near Lisbon, makes a wine from the Arinto grape, among others. Its best known wine is white, with a bit of an acid taste.

Water and Beer

Drinking water is safe in Lisbon, along the Costa do Sol (Estoril and Cascais), and in Porto. In less visited towns and villages, you may want to be extra cautious and order bottled water. You can ask for it to be with or without "gas."

Beer (cerveja) is gaining new followers yearly. One of the best of the home brews is sold under the name of Sagres, honoring the town in the Algarve which enjoyed associations with Henry the Navigator.

3. The Hotel Outlook

The government-sponsored **pousadas**, similar to Spain's paradores, were originally created for Portuguese holiday seekers in remote sections of the country. Now they are crowded during the peak months. The pousadas, usually in a setting of physical beauty, perhaps on the ledge of a mountain, are strategically located. Often they are in accommodation-lean sections: everywhere from a cliffside inn at Henry the Navigator's Sagres to a feudal castle in the walled town of Óbidos. The tariffs are moderate, and a guest can't stay more than five days, as there is usually a waiting line of other pilgrims. Special terms are granted to honeymoon couples.

Not only the capital, but the Costa do Sol resorts are riddled with attractive, serviceable, small, contemporary, and inexpensive accommodations, with a tiled private bath going with every room. Accommodations are available to fit all pocketbooks, ranging from the Lisbon Ritz to the Palácio at Estoril down to the lowliest pensão (boarding house).

In the 1960s, many enterprising and cost-concerned Germans and Scandinavians discovered the **Algarve** coast, that southernmost strip of Portugal, with its miles of some of the finest beaches in Europe. The sun-seekers from the Teutonic lands poured in like the invading Visigoths of old. They were subsequently followed by Americans and Canadians, all wanting in on the suntanning and surf-riding bonanza. The Algarve at present boasts some deluxe hotels, as well as dozens of first- and second-class establishments, plus lots of low-cost boarding houses.

In the north, **Porto** has also wakened from its hotel slumber, its newest hotels finding immediate acceptance. Many provincial towns, such as **Viseu, Tomar,** and **Leiria,** have well-run, first-class hotels. However, other out-of-the-way towns and villages have not yet aroused themselves to meet the needs of projected tourism. Although some of the most interesting centers don't offer enough varied quality accommodations as of yet, there are ways to work around this handicap. For example, one can often bed down in the vicinity of a tourist zone, visiting important shrines or sights on day trips from a more pleasing base elsewhere.

Funchal, the capital of **Madeira,** is well stocked with top-grade hotels, notably the famed Reid's. For budgeteers, many cost-saving accommodations are available, especially the quintas (old stately homes converted into inns, usually surrounded by gardens and furnished with family antiques). Even the **Azores** offer pleasant lodgings, but they're very limited.

For a more detailed breakdown of the hotel classifications and price guidelines, refer to the introduction to "The Hotels of Lisbon," Chapter IV.

There's just so much to learn about a country before plunging into it. Now it's time for the actual experience. Our plane is about to land in Lisbon, where our voyage of discovery will begin.

Chapter III

SETTLING INTO LISBON

1. Navigating Your Way
2. Public Transportation
3. The ABC'S of Life

IN ITS GOLDEN AGE, it was called the eighth wonder of the world. Travelers returning from a trip to Lisbon reported that its riches rivaled those of Venice.

As one of the greatest maritime centers in history, the Portuguese capital has enjoyed exotic riches from the far-flung corners of its empire. Aside from the wealth of cultural influences, Lisbon stockpiled goods, beginning with its earliest contacts with the Calicut and Malabar coasts.

Treasures from the Orient brought in on Chinese junks to Indian seaports eventually found their way back to Lisbon: porcelain, luxurious silks, rubies, pearls, and other rare gems: The abundance and variety of spices from the East—tea, indigo, turmeric, ginger, pepper, coconut, cumin, betel—were to rival even Keats's vision of "silken Samarkand."

From the wilds of the Americas came red dye-wood (Brazil-wood), coffee, gold (discovered in 1698), diamonds (unearthed in 1729), and gem stones. All this extensive contact signaled a new era in world trade, with Lisbon sitting as the grande dame of maritime empires, the hub of commerce between Europe, Africa, and Asia. And then came . . .

THE GREAT EARTHQUAKE: "From Scotland to Asia Minor, people ran out of doors and looked at the sky, and fearfully waited. It was, of course, an earthquake," as once chronicled a *Holiday* article. Tidal waves, 50 feet high, swept over Algeciras, Spain. The capitals of Europe shook.

It was 9:40 on the morning of All Saints Day, November 1, 1755. The churches were packed to overflowing; smoky tapers and incense burned upon the altars. After the initial shock, 22 spasms followed. Roofs caved in; hospitals (with more than 1000 patients), prisons, public buildings, royal palaces, aristocratic town houses, fishermen's cottages, churches, and houses of prostitution —all were toppled. Overturned candles helped ignite a fire that would consume the once-proud capital in six days, leaving her a gutted, charred shambles.

Voltaire captured much of the spiritual and fatalistic tenor of the feelings of the people in *Candide*. In one part, he wrote: "The sea boiled up in the harbor and smashed the vessels lying at anchor. Whirlwinds of flame and ashes covered the streets and squares, houses collapsed, roofs were thrown onto foundations and the foundations crumbled." All told, 30,000 inhabitants were crushed beneath the tumbling debris.

When the survivors of the initial shocks ran from their burning homes toward the mighty Tagus, they were met with walls of water 40 feet high. Estimates vary, but the final tally of all who died in drownings and the six-day holocaust that followed is put at around 60,000.

Voltaire was cynical in commenting on the aftermath of the disaster, particularly the *auto-da-fé* that followed: "It was decided by the University of Coimbra that the sight of several people being slowly burned with great ceremony was an infallible means of preventing the earth from quaking."

PLAYING THE COQUETTE GAME: Today, the "new" Lisbon is distinctly feminine. In fact, she was once called a coquette. Under a stark blue sky, her medley of pastel-washed houses dazzles, like a city in North Africa. The Tagus has been called her eternal lover.

Sea gulls take flight from her harbor, where trawlers from Africa unload their freight. Pigeons sweep down on Black Horse Square. From the Bairro Alto (upper city), cable cars carry Lisbon's denizens down to the waterfront. On narrow lanes and dark cobbled alleyways, barefoot *varinas* rush by with wicker baskets of fresh fish on their heads. The sidewalks are more characteristic, the black and white mosaics forming arabesques.

At times, a country town atmosphere prevails. From many Lisbon hotel rooms, you are wakened in the morning by the crowing of roosters. Streets bear colorful names of designations, such as the Rua do Açúcar (Street of Sugar). Fountains abound: one, the Samaritan, dates from the 16th century. Wide, symmetrical boulevards split through the city to new high-rise apartment houses, while in other quarters laundry hanging from 18th-century houses laps the wind.

It is a city that gives nicknames to everything from its districts (the Chiado, named after a poet) to its kings. Fernando, who built one of the most characteristic walls around Lisbon, was honored with the appellation "The Beautiful."

THE LEGEND OF ULYSSES: Lisboans have always known they were special. Regardless of how fanciful the legend, it has its adherents. In the Alfama, many of the residents claim unabashedly that Ulysses founded their city. Others more scholarly maintain that the Phoenicians or the Carthaginians were the original settlers. The body of the country's patron saint, Vincent, is said to have arrived in Portugal on an abandoned boat, with only two ravens to guide it. It is further alleged that the birds lived in the cathedral tower until as late as the 19th century.

The Romans settled in Lisbon in the first century B.C., building a fortification on what is now St. George's Castle. The city was captured by the Visigoths in the fifth century A.D., this conquest later followed by long centuries of Moorish domination beginning in A.D. 714. The first king of Portugal, Afonso Henriques, captured Lisbon in 1147. But it wasn't until 1256 that King Afonso III moved the capital there, deserting Coimbra, the major university city of Portugal.

Now in its seventh century as the headquarters of the Portuguese nation, Lisbon is the westernmost capital of continental Europe. Part of its legend is that it spreads across seven hills, like Rome. If that statement were ever true, it has long since become historical, as Lisbon now sprawls across more hills than that. Most of it lies on the right bank of the Tagus.

1. Navigating Your Way

No one ever claimed that getting around Lisbon was easy. Streets rise and fall across the legendary seven hills, at times dwindling into mere alleyways. But exploring it and ultimate discovery make the effort worthwhile.

Lisbon is best approached by way of its gateway, the **Praça do Comércio**, bordering the Tagus. Like a formal parlor, it is one of the most perfectly planned squares in Europe, rivaled perhaps only by the Piazza dell'-Unitá d'Italia in Trieste, Italy.

Before the earthquake of 1755, Commerce Square was known as **Terreiro do Paço**, the palace grounds, as the king and his court lived in now-destroyed buildings on that site. To further confuse matters, English-speaking residents refer to it as **Black Horse Square**, so named because of a statue (actually a bronze green) of José I, a Portuguese king. The monument from the 18th century was created by Machado de Castro, who dominated Portuguese sculpture in his era.

Today, the square houses the Stock Exchange and various ministries of government. Its center is used as a parking lot, which destroys some of the harmonious effect of its praça. In 1908, its most monumental event occurred, the reverberations of which were heard around the world. King Carlos I and his older son, Luís Filipe, were fatally shot by an assassin. Although it would hold on for another two years under the rule of a younger prince, the House of Braganza collapsed that day on Black Horse Square.

Directly to the west of the square stands the City Hall fronting the **Praça do Município.** The building was erected in the latter 19th century by the architect Domingos Parente.

Heading north from Black Horse or Commerce Square, you enter the hustle-bustle of the Praça Dom Pedro IV, popularly known as **The Rossio.** The "drunken" undulation of the sidewalks, with their arabesques of black and white, have led to the appellation, used mainly by tourists, of "the dizzy praça." Here you can sit, sipping strong unblended coffee from the former Portuguese provinces in Africa, while a boy gives you one of the cheapest and slickest shoeshines in Europe. The statue on the square is that of the emperor of Brazil, Pedro IV, himself a Portuguese.

Opening onto the Rossio is the **Teatro Nacional Dona Maria II,** a free-standing building whose facade has been preserved. In 1967-1970, workmen gutted the interior to rebuild it completely. If you arrive by train, you'll enter the **Estação do Rossio,** whose Manueline exuberance offends those sensitive to architecture. The Tourist Bureau on this square is in the Palácio Foz.

Separating the Rossio from the Avenida da Liberdade is the **Praça dos Restauradores,** named in honor of the restoration—that is, when the Portuguese chose their own king and freed themselves from 60 years of rule by Spain. That event is marked by an obelisk.

The main avenue of Lisbon is the **Avenida da Liberdade,** a handsomely laid out street dating from 1880, and once called the antechamber of Lisbon. The Avenue of Liberty is like a mile-long park, with shade trees, gardens, and center walks for the promenading crowds. Flanking it are some of the finest shops, headquarters for many major airlines, travel agents, coffeehouses with sidewalk tables, and such important hotels as the Tivoli. The comparable street in Paris would be the Champs-Élysées; in Rome, the Via Veneto.

At the top of the avenue is the **Praça Marquês de Pombal,** with a statue erected in honor of Pombal, the 18th-century prime minister credited with the reconstruction of Lisbon in the aftermath of the earthquake. He is depicted with a lion.

Proceeding north, you'll enter the splendid **Parque Eduardo VII,** named to honor the son of Queen Victoria, who paid a state visit to Lisbon. In the park is the **Estufa Fria,** a greenhouse that is well worth a visit.

The business district of Lisbon is called **Baixa,** its architecture characterized as Pombaline, referring to the 18th-century prime minister again. Many of the major Portuguese banks have their headquarters here. Running south, the main street of Baixa separates Black Horse Square from the Rossio. In fact, a triumphal arch leads from Black Horse Square to the **Rua Augusta,** itself sheltering many clothing stores. The two most important streets of Baixa are the Street of Silver (Rua da Prata) and the Street of Gold (Rua da Ouro). Of course, they were never paved with gold or silver, but take their names from the silver- and goldsmiths whose shops were (and still are) found there. The best known one is Sarmento.

If you head west from Baixa, you'll enter an even more fashionable shopping district known as the **Chiado.** From its perch on a hill, it is traversed by the **Rua Garrett,** honoring the Portuguese poet and dandy of the 19th century. Many of the finest shops in the city, such as the Vista Alegre, a china and porcelain house, are here. One coffeehouse, in particular, A Brasileira, has been a traditional gathering spot for the Portuguese literati.

Continuing our ascent, we arrive at the **Bairro Alto** (the upper city). This sector, reached by trolley car, occupies one of the legendary seven hills of Lisbon. Many of its buildings were left fairly intact from the 1755 earthquake. Containing much of the charm and color of the Alfama, it is of interest mainly because it is the center of some of the finest fado cafés in Lisbon, including A Severa, Lisboa a Noite, and Adega Machado. In addition, some of the best restaurants in the city are found here, as well as unpretentious taverns featuring hearty Portuguese cuisine.

To the east of Black Horse Square lies the oldest district of Lisbon, the **Alfama**. For a more detailed description of this section, refer to Chapter VIII, "The Sights of Lisbon." Saved only in part from the devastation of the earthquake, the Alfama was the Moorish sector of the capital. Centuries later, before the earthquake struck, it was the residential district of aristocrats. Nowadays, it is occupied mainly by stevedores, plus fishermen and their barefoot varinas.

Overlooking the Alfama is **St. George's Castle,** once a Visigothic fortification, although it was used by the Romans before that. Destroyed and rebuilt so many times that its history is a jumble, the present castle dates from the 12th century.

On the way to the Alfama, on the Rua dos Bacalheiros, stands the **Casa dos Bicos** (the House of the Pointed Stones). Although this early 16th-century town house is not open to the public, the mansion is graced with a facade studded with diamond-shaped stones. And while it was partially demolished by the earthquake, it remains an impressive sight.

In the west, on the coastal road to Estoril, is the suburb of **Belém** (Bethlehem). It contains some of the finest monuments in Portugal, a few of which were built during the Age of Discovery, near the point where the caravels set out to conquer new worlds (at Belém, the Tagus reaches the sea). At one time, before the earthquake, Belém was an aristocratic sector filled with elegant town houses.

Two of the principal attractions in all of Portugal stand here: the **Jerónimos Monastery,** erected in the 16th century in the Manueline style, and the **National Coach Museum,** the finest of its kind in the world. Actually, Belém is Lisbon's museumland, containing as it does the **Museum of Popular Art,** the **Ethnological Museum,** and the galley-stuffed **Naval Museum.**

On the south side of the Tagus, where a puce-colored smoke billows out from the factories, is the left-bank settlement of **Cacilhas**. It is inhabited mainly by the working class, although visited by right-bank denizens for its seafood restaurants, such as the Floresta (see my dining recommendations). You can reach the settlement by way of a bridge or by taking a ferryboat across, leaving from Black Horse Square.

Of course, the most dramatic way to cross the Tagus is on the **Ponte 25 de Abril,** the longest and most expensive suspension bridge ever erected in Europe, the total outlay exceeding $75 million. The bridge opened up that sector of Portugal lying south of the Tagus. Its towers peaking at 625 feet, the bridge is 7473 feet long. Standing guard on the left bank is a monumental statue of Christ, depicted with his arms outstretched.

If you don't have a private car, you'll need to know something about:

2. Public Transportation

Public transport is inexpensive but inadequate at times. Yet considering the hilly terrain of the city and the fact that many of the streets were designed for donkey carts, the Portuguese manage very well. However, even the most skilled chauffeurs have been known to scrape the fenders of their clients' rented limousines while maneuvering through the narrow alleyways.

A lot of the city can be walked around, especially by those adept at hill climbing. However, to get from one point to the other—say from the Alfama to the suburb of Belém—you'll need public transport or your own car.

THE TAXIS: Taxis in Lisbon tend to be cheap and are a popular means of transport for all but the most economy minded of tourists. The taxis usually are diesel-engined Mercedes, charging a basic fare of 15$ (23¢) for the first 500 yards. After that, you'll be assessed another pittance for each additional 250 yards. The driver is allowed by law to tack on another 50% to your bill if your total luggage weighs in at more than 66 pounds.

Many visitors anchor in at one of the Costa do Sol resort hotels, such as the Palácio in Estoril and the Cidadela in Cascais. If that is your situation, then you'll probably find taxi connections from Lisbon prohibitively expensive. The fare must be negotiated. The driver has a choice of turning the meter down and letting it tick up a fat tab, or else of setting a straight fare for the journey. Whichever he elects, it's not cheap. Far preferable for Costa do Sol visitors is the electric train system (see below).

TRAMS AND BUSES: These are among the cheapest in Europe. You'll pay only 6$ (9¢) to 15$ (23¢) for a ride. The trolley cars, such as those that make the steep run up to the Bairro Alto, are usually painted a rich Roman gold. The green double-decker buses, on the other hand, come from London and look as if they need Big Ben in the background to complete the picture. If you're trying to stand on the platform at the back of a jammed bus, by the way, you'll need both hands free to hold on.

At the foot of the Santa Justa elevator, that Eiffel-designed structure lying on the Rua do Ouro, or Street of Gold, a stand will give you a schedule pinpointing the zigzagging route of these trams and buses. Your hotel concierge also should be of help to you.

SUBWAYS: Lisbon's Metro stations are designated by large M signs, but some readers have reported difficulty in locating them, as several are missing. A single fare is only 15$ (23¢). One of the most popular trips, and likely to be jam-packed on corrida days, is from the Avenida da Liberdade to the Campo Pequeno, that brick bullring away from the center of the city.

FERRYBOATS: Long before the advent of the Ponte 25 de Abril, the reliable ferryboats chugged across the Tagus, connecting the left bank with the right. They still do, and are as popular as ever, as many Portuguese find the bridge too expensive to traverse with their automobiles. Therefore, they leave their cars at home and take the ferryboat to work.

Most of the boats leave from Praça do Comércio, heading for Barreiro and Cacilhas. The one-way fare on the ferryboat is about 10$ (15¢) per passenger. You can take your car over on the ferry as well for around 50$ (77¢). Or else you can drive on the:

PONTE 25 DE ABRIL: As mentioned, this suspension bridge, the largest ever built in Europe, connects Lisbon with its left bank and the district south of the Tagus. For a small car, the toll charge is 20$ (31¢), increasing to 50$ (77¢), for a larger automobile. Not only can you take the bridge to reach Cacilhas, but you can use it for such cities as Setúbal in the south, and Évora, the old Roman city in the east.

Finally, there is that most important means of transport, the:

ELECTRIC TRAINS: Lisbon is connected with all the towns and villages along the Portuguese Riviera by a smooth-running electric train system. You can board the train at the waterfront **Cais do Sodré** station in Lisbon, heading up the coast all the way to Cascais, the end of the run where you'll be delivered practically to the doorstep of the Fim do Mundo (End of the World) restaurant.

Both first- and second-class seats are offered, and the rides are cheap. For example, if you go all the way—that is, Lisbon to Cascais—in a first-class seat, the one-way fare is 25$ (38¢). From Lisbon to Estoril, the one-way fare in a first-class seat is also 25$. Sintra, that third major destination in the environs, is not reached by the electric train. You must go to the Estação do Rossio station, opening onto the Praça Dom Pedro IV or the Rossio, where frequent connections can be made.

3. The ABC'S of Life

It's maddening to have your trip marred by an incident which could have been avoided if you'd been tipped off previously. Hocking your watch, renting a fur, seeking medical care, getting your hair cut, and ferreting out the nearest toilet can at times become paramount problems. Although we don't promise to answer all these needs, there are a variety of services in Lisbon that can ease your adjustment into the capital.

The concierge in your hotel is a usually reliable dispenser of information, bullfight tickets, advice about whether you can "bring somebody back to the room," or assistance in pleading with your wife to speak to you again after your too-friendly attention to a fadista. However, should your hotel not be staffed with an English-speaking person, or should you desire more immediate or more detailed answers to your questions, the following brief summary of some of Lisbon's facets of life may prove helpful.

LISBON: ABC'S   33

AIRLINES: For ticket sales, flight reservations, information about the city and the country, you can get in touch with the polite and efficient personnel of **Transportes Aéreos Portuguêses (TAP)** at 3 Praça Marquês de Pombal (tel. 53-88-52).

AMERICAN EXPRESS: Will hold or forward mail for you. There, too, you can buy travelers checks, tickets for tours, or exchange currency. **STAR** in Lisbon is the representative of American Express and accommodates your banking and mailing needs from its offices at 4-A Avenida Sidónio Pais (tel. 53-98-71). It is open daily from 9 a.m. until 12:30 p.m. and from 2 to 6 p.m. weekdays; closed on Saturday and Sunday. The offices are near the Pombal and easily reached by bus.

BABYSITTING: Check with the staff at your hotel for arrangements. Most first-class hotels can provide competent women or young girls for babysitting from lists which the concierge keeps. At smaller establishments, the girl is likely to be the daughter of the proprietor. Rates are low. Remember to request a babysitter in the morning if you're going out that evening.

BANKS: Check with your home bank before your departure, as many banks in Canada and the United States may not have affiliates in Lisbon. The majority of banks open at 9 a.m., close at noon. Afternoon hours are from 2 to 3:30. A trio of major Portuguese banks: the **Banco Português do Atlântico,** 112 Rua Aurea; the **Banco Espírito Santo e Comercial de Lisboa,** 95 Rua do Comércio; at the airport, a branch of **Banco Totta & Açores** is open at all hours day and night including holidays.

CURRENCY: The exchange rate is approximately 65.50 escudos to the U.S. dollar.

CUSTOMS: You may be asked how much tobacco you're bringing in: the limit is 200 cigarettes or 50 cigars. One still camera with five unexposed reels of film is allowed duty free; also a small movie camera with two reels; a portable tape recorder; a portable record player with ten "used" records; a portable typewriter; a portable radio; a portable musical instrument; and a bicycle (not motor bikes).

Campers and sports persons are allowed to bring in one tent and camping accessories (including a kayak not exceeding 18 feet), a pair of skis, two tennis racquets, a tackle set, and a small firearm (for hunting only) with 50 bullets.

Pets brought into the country must have the okay of a local veterinarian and a health certificate from their home country. A normal-size bottle of wine and half a pint of hard alcohol are permitted, as are a "small quantity" of perfume and a half pint of toilet water.

ELECTRIC CURRENT: Many North Americans find that their plugs will not fit into sockets in Portugal, where the voltage is 220 AC, 50 cycles. Adapters and transformers may be purchased once you're in Lisbon.

HOLIDAYS: Watch those holidays and adjust your banking needs, or whatever, accordingly. Aside from the regular holidays, Portugal has a few of its own:

Universal Brotherhood Day on January 1; the anniversary of the Republic, October 5; a Memorial Day to the country's greatest poet, Camões, June 10; Assumption Day, August 15; All Saints Day on November 1 (ironically, this was the date Lisbon was destroyed in the earthquake of 1755); Independence Day on December 1; and the Feast of the Immaculate Conception on December 8. Good Friday and the Feast of Corpus Christi are also holidays, but their dates are different every year.

LANGUAGE: One writer suggested that Portuguese "has the hiss and rush of surf crashing against the bleak rocks at Sagres." French and English are commonly spoken in Lisbon, along the Costa do Sol, and in Porto. In most small villages and towns, hotel staffs and guides usually speak French, although English is making greater inroads. The native tongue is difficult, but the people are helpful and patient. Gestures often suffice.

LAUNDRY: Most hotels in this guide provide laundry services, but if you want your garment returned on the same day, you'll often be charged anywhere from 20% to 40% more. Simply present your maid or valet with your laundry or dry cleaning (usually lists are provided). *Note:* Materials such as synthetics needing special treatment should be called to the attention of the person handling your laundry. Some establishments we've dealt with treated every fabric as if it were cotton.

MEDICAL CARE: The concierge at your hotel can usually put you in touch with the house doctor, or summon him in case of emergencies. You can also call the American Embassy, 39 Avenida Duque Loulé (tel. 55-51-41), and ask the staff there to recommend a physician who speaks English; or the British Hospital (tel. 67-10-07), where the telephone operator, staff, and doctors all speak English, of course.

NEWSPAPERS AND MAGAZINES: The international edition of the *Herald Tribune* is sold at most newsstands in Lisbon, either in major hotels or along the street. The *Trib* is also sold in leading newsstands throughout the country, in Porto, and in the Algarve.

PASSPORTS: If you lose your passport, and if you're an American citizen, you can apply for a new one at the **American Embassy,** 47 Duque de Loulé (tel. 57-01-02). Hours are from 8:30 a.m. to 12:30 p.m. and 1:30 to 4 p.m. If you've lost your passport, a photographer will be recommended who can provide the proper size photos for American passports, a 24-hour service.

PHARMACIES: The Portuguese government requires selected pharmacies *(farmacias)* to stay open at all times of the day and night. This is effected by means of a rotation system. So check with your concierge for locations and hours of the nearby drugstore. The local newspapers list the ones open 24 hours each day.

POST OFFICE: While in Portugal you may have your mail directed to your hotel or hotels, to the American Express representative, or to General Delivery,

LISBON: ABC'S 35

Lisbon. Your passport must later be presented for mail pickups. Open 24 hours a day, the General Post Office is at Praça dos Restauradores.

TIPPING: The following tips on tipping are merely guidelines:
Hotels: The hotels add a service charge (known as a *servico*), which is divided among the entire staff. But individual tipping is also the rule of the day: 30$ (46¢) to the bellhop for errands run; 25$ (38¢) to the doorman who calls you a cab; 25$ to the porter for each piece of luggage carried; 130$ ($1.99) to the wine steward if you've dined often at the hotel (more if your stay has been extended beyond a week); 110$ ($1.68) to the chambermaid on short stays.

In the first-class or deluxe hotels, the concierge will present you with a separate bill, outlining your little or big extras, such as charges for bullfight tickets, etc. A gratuity is expected in addition to the charge, the amount depending entirely upon the number of requests you've put to him.

Hairdressers: For a normal haircut, men should leave 30$ (46¢) behind as a tip to their barbers. But if your hair is cut at the Ritz, don't dare leave less than 50$ (77¢). Beauticians get 75$ ($1.15); a manicurist, around 50$ (77¢).

Taxis: Figure on about 20% of the regular fare for short runs. For longer treks—as, for example, from the airport to Cascais—15% is adequate.

Porters: The porters at the airport or train stations generally charge you 25$ (38¢) per piece of luggage. In addition to that, you should add 15$ (23¢).

Restaurants: Restaurants and nightclubs include service and government taxes. As in hotels, this serviço is distributed among the entire staff, including the waiter's mistress and the proprietor's grandfather—so extra tipping is required. Add about 5% to the bill in moderately priced restaurants, up to 10% in deluxe or first-class establishments.

Services: Hatcheck girls in fado houses, restaurants, and nightclubs expect at least 25$ (38¢) as do the women who stand on sentinel duty in the washrooms. The shoeshine boys of Portugal are the most undertipped creatures in Portuguese society. Here we recommend greater generosity if you feel like it.

Helpful Hints: Learn the value of Portugal's currency and its relation to the people as you dispense your gratuities. Tips in the country are generally low, higher in Lisbon and Estoril. However, service personnel expect more every year. It is well to remember that exorbitant tipping in another country, given its economic structure, can be as unwise as undertipping is cruel.

TOURIST OFFICE: The **Portuguese National Tourist Board** is at 86 Avenida António Augusto de Aguiar in Lisbon (tel. 57-59-81). The public information section is housed in the Palácio Foz at Praça dos Restauradores (tel. 36-33-14) and at the Lisbon Airport (tel. 89-36-89). If you desire travel information or facts about Portugal before heading there, you can make contact with the **Portuguese National Tourist Office**, 548 Fifth Ave., New York, NY 10036 (tel. 212/354-4403), or their regional branches at Palmer House, Suite 500, 17 East Monroe St., Chicago, IL 60603 (tel. 312/236-6603), and 1 Park Place, Suite 1305, 3250 Wilshire Blvd., Los Angeles, CA 90010 (tel. 213/380-6459).

TOURS: Lisbon travel agents will book you on organized tours. One of the most popular such agencies is **STAR**, the Lisbon representative for American Express, at 4-A Avenida Sidónio Pais (main office, tel. 53-98-71), close to Eduardo VII Park-South (Marquês de Pombal Square), starting point of its tours. It also has a downtown branch office at 14 Restauradores Square (tel. 36-25-01).

At the height of the season, from March 1 to October 31, most of the major tours are operated on a daily basis, excluding Monday and holidays. St. George's Castle, Belém's Jerônimos Monastery, the National Art Gallery—all are highlighted by different city tours which stress particularly fascinating cultural, historical, or scenic attractions.

"**Touristic Lisbon**" and "**Old Lisbon**" are popular morning tours, departing at 9:30 a.m. "**Touristic Lisbon**" and "**Artistic Lisbon**" are afternoon trips leaving at 2:30 p.m.

The **Lisbon-Mafra-Sintra-Escoril** special departs daily, except Tuesday at 9:30 a.m., and includes lunch. It's a beautiful excursion out into the environs.

You can journey north on a 12-hour trip to the walled city of **Óbidos** and the fishing village of **Nazaré**. The jaunt departs on Tuesday, Thursday, and Saturday from April 1 to October 31, at 8:30 a.m. Another popular year-round 12-hour tour is to **Nazaré-Fátima**.

In the next chapter, we'll tackle the more specific problem of settling into Lisbon—that is, finding a suitable hotel in the price range you desire.

Chapter IV

THE HOTELS OF LISBON

**1. The Deluxe Choices
2. Leading First-Class Hotels
3. Middle-Bracket Hotels
4. Full-Board Bargains
5. The Budget Range**

WHEN YOU CHECK into a hotel, you'll see the official tariffs posted in the main lobby as well as somewhere in your room, perhaps at the bottom of the closet. These rates are dictated by the Directorate of Tourism and are strictly regulated. It's really a form of rent control. They include the 13.1% service charge and tourist tax which in previous years were added on separately.

Most hotels will allow you to keep your room or deposit your luggage there until noon. From that point on, the manager can add the cost of an additional full day's rent to your bill.

When checking into a hotel, clear up the all-important question of how many meals, if any, you plan to take in the dining room. Full pension means a room and three meals a day; half pension means a room, breakfast, and at least one other meal. It is proper for the hotel clerk to ask which of those main meals, either lunch or dinner, you'll be taking. Those on the half- or full-pension plans must pay for a meal even if they miss it. It saves you money to take full or half board, as you are granted a reduction in the overall rate, as opposed to staying at a hotel and taking your meals there on an à la carte basis. But the manager is not obliged to grant you a discount on a pension plan unless you are staying at his establishment two full days and nights.

Should an infraction such as overcharging occur, you may demand to be given the Official Complaints Book. In this tome you can write your allegations. The hotel manager is then obligated to turn your comments over to the Directorate of Tourism, where they are reviewed by a staff to see if any punitive action should be taken against the establishment.

Hotels in Portugal are rated from five stars to one star. The difference between a five-star hotel and a four-star hotel will not always be apparent to the casual visitor. Often the distinction is based on square footage of bathrooms and other technical differences.

When you go below this level, you enter the realm of the second-class hotel and the third-class, the latter comprising the most raw-boned and least recommended hotels in Portugal, although some can be good.

Tourist inns, not government run, are known as **estalagems**. Often these offer some of the finest accommodations in Portugal, many decorated in the native or *típico* style and representing top-notch bargains.

The **residências** are a form of boarding house, except without board. Only a room and breakfast are offered at these establishments. The **pensão** is a Portuguese boarding house that charges the lowest tariffs in the country. The deluxe pensão is a misnomer. The term simply means that the pensão enjoys the highest rating in its category, although the accommodation is decidedly not luxurious. A luxury pensão is generally the equivalent of a second-class hotel. The boarding houses are finds for the budget hunter. Often many of them prepare a good local cuisine with generous helpings. For bottom-of-the-barrel type of living, there are both first-class and second-class boarding houses.

Coastal hotels, especially those in the Algarve, are required to grant off-season (November to February) visitors a 15% reduction on the regular tariff. To attract more off-season business, a number of establishments extend this, starting the reduced rates in mid-October and granting them until April 1.

1. The Deluxe Choices

THE TOP CHOICE: American ladies in boots, black velvet pants, and chinchilla swagger jackets walk their pet poodles on the grassy center strip fronting the entrance. Where does this scene take place? At **The Ritz**, 88 Rua Rodrigo da Fonseca (tel. 68-41-31). Now a landmark, the hotel was built in the late 1950s.

The Ritz was once given worldwide exposure in a many-page spread in *Life* magazine. There in dazzling color you saw the richness of its lavish suites, furnished with museum-quality antiques or reproductions (many of which were made at the Fundação Ricardo do Espirito Santo Silva). Of course, in *Life* you were shown the romantically contrived suites. If you book into a typically modern room, you'll more likely get unfrilly blonde furnishings. The duality in the decor has its amusing moments, especially when teddy bear wooly armchairs are set in vast bank-style lobbies.

The suites have the finest style and decorative taste of all first-class Portuguese hotels. Slender mahogany canopied beds, with fringed swags, marquetry desks, satinwood dressing tables with tip-mirrors, plush carpeting—no wonder the Ritz was preferred by such famous guests as the late President Eisenhower, Walter Mondale, Germany's Kurt Georg Kiesinger, Faisal of Saudi Arabia, even Jerry Lewis, Audrey Hepburn, and Sammy Davis, Jr. The modern rooms facing the avenue are cheaper, the more expensive ones with terraces open onto Edward VII Park. All are air-conditioned and soundproof, with modern tiled baths with double basins.

For a double room, including a continental breakfast, the tariff ranges from $102 (U.S.) to $140. In a single, the rate goes from $85 to $118. Suites with antiques or reproductions rent for anywhere from $124 to $225. All rates include service, taxes, and a continental breakfast.

The main dining room, Varanda, is dignified and pleasant, and the Grill Room is traditionally decorated (see my restaurant recommendations in the next chapter). Breakfast is usually brought to your room on a tray, but alternatively there is a breakfast room overlooking the avenue, with wooden marquetry panels on its gleaming marble walls. In addition to the bridge and reading rooms, the Ritz Bar is a magnet. Lodged in a corner of the hotel, overlooking the terrace and park, it offers everything from a Pimm's No. 1 Cup to a mint julep.

The Ritz is operated by Intercontinental Hotels, a wholly owned subsidiary of Pan American World Airways. Reservations can be made through travel agents or any Pan Am or Intercontinental sales or reservations office worldwide.

OTHER DELUXE HOTELS: Hotel Diplomático, 74 Rua Castilho (tel. 56-20-41), is a semiluxurious structure in the gilt-edged section of the city, near the Ritz and Edward VII Park. The two-story-high lobby and lounge is dominated by an overscale mural in reds and oranges, the creation of George Brandeiro, who exhibits in modern galleries. Guests receive visitors in the hidden-away mezzanine lounge, with its brightly colored contemporary furnishings. There is an open sundeck terrace, where you can relax and enjoy a panoramic view of most of the hills of Lisbon. On the ground floor is a modernistic dining room—enlivened by wall murals, a Cubist-style ceiling, and a highly polished silver meat trolley. A complete table d'hôte meal costs $12 (U.S.). The Cosy Corner Bar is a favorite gathering place, and there is also a coffeeshop for snacks.

Spread among the 11 floors are the tasteful bedrooms, which have small balconies and excellent city views, plus central heating, air conditioning, and TV if required. The majority of the rooms are clean-cut, with no extra frills, each dominated by a long built-in headboard, with "airplane pilot" buttons to summon room service or the maid. Pristine walls with simple flowing draperies create a restful background for well-selected furnishings, such as built-in chests, armchairs, and desks. The baths, one to each room, are tiled. The manager has set price levels based on the size and location of the room. Singles range from $37 (U.S.) in low season to a peak of $44 in high season, and doubles go from $48 in low season to $56 in high season. Low season is from November 1 through February 28, and high season is from March 1 to October 31. Breakfast and taxes are included in the prices.

Sheraton, 1 Rua Latino Coelho (tel. 57-57-57), a huge 30-story colossus, was opened in 1972 and contains 400 rooms. It can be seen from miles away, and in turn the views from its windows are panoramic, sweeping over the whole of Lisbon. Like most other Sheratons around the world, its emphasis is on slick American-type comfort.

This blockbuster of a hotel, in the modern part of Lisbon, not far from Pombal Square, features a penthouse restaurant called the Panorama, where à la carte dishes go for about 450$ ($6.89) to 900$ ($13.77). Downstairs is the Alfama Grill, serving Portuguese specialties and providing fado music. There's also a Caravella coffeeshop, with a table d'hôte menu for 600$ ($9.18), including beverages. Hamburgers here cost 300$ ($4.59), a ham steak goes for 440$ ($6.73), and a sirloin with salad is 450$ ($6.89). The hotel has many amenities, including a garage, a pool, and a complete health club. The rooms are comfortably furnished, with individually controlled heating and air conditioning, wall-to-wall carpeting, marble sinks in the bathrooms, and direct-dial telephones. The rather steep price of a single is 4000$ ($61.20). Doubles cost 6000$ ($91.80), including breakfast.

Avenida Palace, 123 Rua 1 de Dezembro (tel. 36-01-51), is Lisbon's leading hotel link to the past, a world reflected in crystal and antiques. The second-floor drawing room attracts those partial to the age of silk-brocaded wall paneling, fringed velvet draperies, crystal chandeliers, marquetry tables, consoles, and hand-woven Portuguese carpets. Five tall windows in the dining room overlook the avenue. The location is bull's eye, right at the Rossio, minutes from fado clubs, restaurants, and some of Lisbon's major shops.

Major renovations have prevented the Avenida Palace from slipping to a level of disrepair and deterioration. Most of the rooms have been redone. Frankly, the rooms given a new lease on life are more tasteful and enjoyable than the average sterile ones at the Ritz—and go for less than half the price.

The redecorated bedrooms are furnished in a traditional manner, with 18th-century antiques or else artwork (most often reproductions), and are air-conditioned and centrally heated. The walls are paneled, often with gilt trim. The spacious bathrooms are faced in Portuguese marble. A single room rents for 3500$ ($53.55), with breakfast, rising to 4800$ ($73.44) in a twin-bedded room. If ordered separately, a lunch or a dinner costs 1000$ ($15.30), taxes and service included.

2. Leading First-Class Hotels

Hotel Tivoli, 185 Avenida da Liberdade (tel. 53-01-81), has many enticing features that make it the first choice of many seasoned travelers. First, its location is choice, right on the main boulevard of Lisbon. Second, it's large enough to accommodate more than 600 guests—hence, its public facilities are bountiful. Third, its prices are in line, considering its amenities. The two-story-high reception lobby with an encircling mezzanine lounge is almost arena-size, with comfortable islands of furniture arranged on Oriental rugs.

The wood-paneled O Zodiaco restaurant is decorated with Easter-egg-colored chairs and a wall plaque depicting astrological signs. Meals are all à la carte. Adjoining the restaurant is a homelike salon with a wood-burning fireplace, Oriental rugs, and restrained accoutrements. On the top floor, the O Terraço offers a view of Lisbon. Here, à la carte meals are provided, with the emphasis on steaks and chops, which you select yourself and have cooked on a tiled charcoal grill.

The regular room prices are scaled according to position—the larger and more expensive ones facing the boulevard. Singles with breakfast are $58 (U.S.) to $64; doubles are $66 to $73. The air-conditioned rooms contain a mixture of modern and traditional pieces, with solid fabrics and walls making for a restful background. All have private baths. Taxes and service are included in the tariffs.

Tivoli Jardim, 7-9 Rua Júlio C. Machado (tel. 53-99-71), is the sister to the above-mentioned hotel. Here you'll find more contemporary design in the lounges and bedrooms than at the Tivoli. Set in back of its namesake, avoiding the traffic noises from the Avenida da Liberdade, it features a free parking area for guests. The air-conditioned structure is graced with cliff-hanging balconies, two shafts of elevators, and well-styled bedrooms.

The rooms are consistent, with a restrained decor. The walls are rough white plaster, the carpets scarlet, the furnishings basic built-in, with reading lights, maid-summoning bells, channel music, as well as comfortable armchairs with coffee tables, and a wall glass (curtained off at night) leading to the balcony with its rattan furniture. The baths have overall patterned tile, with a bidet, shower, and tub. For a room and breakfast, a single person is charged $53 (U.S.) in high season, a double costs $60, including breakfast. The rooms overlooking the garden in the rear are a little cheaper.

There are adequate public lounges. Portuguese business people have found the Jardim ideal for meeting clients in the cathedral-high lobby, with its wall of glass through which the Iberian sun pours in. Dominating everything is a ceiling-high tapestry, in sunburst colors. The tiled and marbled floors are peacock blue and emerald green, the staircase leading to the mezzanine a blood red. The dining room is tasteful, with its white brick walls and green tables, its wall niches filled with Portuguese ceramics. Within view of most of the tables is a convoluted bronze sculpture, framed by a picture window.

Hotel Plaza, Avenida da Liberdade, Parque Mayer (tel. 37-03-31), is a charmer, right in the heart of the city. A four-star hotel, the Plaza has many appealing art nouveau touches, including its facade. My favorite rendezvous point is the 1900-style bar, with its soothing olive colors and tufted leather chairs. Through another art nouveau entrance you enter the restaurant with its selection of international dishes. The rooms are well styled and comfortable, with color-coordinated accessories. Singles cost $40 (U.S.); doubles, $50; and some triples are available at $60. It's also possible to stay here on either full- or half-pension terms. For example, one person pays $52 for half board, including all taxes and service. The hotel is air-conditioned and contains private car-parking facilities as well.

Príncipe Real, 53 Rua de Alegria (tel. 36-01-16), is a remarkable little hotel. It has one of the most skillful and efficient staffs of any hotel in Lisbon, but a surprisingly large one considering the size of the establishment. For example, one maid is assigned only six rooms. That way, things are kept more personal and homelike.

The modern hotel, a convenient five-minute walk from the Avenida da Liberdade, is quite disarming. Behind its rather impersonal facade lies a petite world of fine living. No wonder the Ritz uses it for overflow guests. The living room, quite private seeming, is eclectic, revealing the tastes of the owner, Maria C. Rezende. Carved wooden pieces, ecclesiastical figures, Oriental rugs, a wide stone fireplace, an ornate pirate's chest, copper water jugs with flowers—whatever, it's warm and inviting. Guests get acquainted in the adjoining small bar, dramatically styled with fire-engine-red tiled tables, ebony banquettes, and wood-paneled walls.

The same selectivity and care extends to the individualized bedrooms—compact, tasteful little worlds. The beds are reproductions of fine antiques, with excellent mattresses. Each room is color coordinated, a happy blending of plain fabrics with florals. In the bathroom, you're likely to find purple towels, lavender toilet paper, and a lilac stemmed glass for your toothbrush. You'll be charged $31 (U.S.) in a single room, $50 in a double, and $67 in a triple—these tariffs including a continental breakfast, taxes, and service. Breakfast is served in a glassed-in rooftop room. Here early risers are treated to Lisbon's sensational sunrise. The sun first backlights St. George's Castle, topping the mountain on the far side of the city, as if some master electrician had wired the setting for a *son et lumière* show. When the sun pops over the mountain, red rays catch the tops of taller buildings, gradually illuminating their sides with gold. A fantastic shadow play. The breakfast room has a beamed ceiling and 18th-century-style red velvet chairs. What a way to meet the new day in Lisbon! And the waitress, who has one of the prettiest smiles in a city where smiles are prettier than most, usually remembers whether or not you prefer tea or coffee.

A *Los Angeles Times* columnist called the Príncipe Real " . . . one of the finest small hotels in Europe." We concur. We had to go to the cellar one day to get a packing box—there the floors sparkled too, as well-scrubbed as those in the lobby. A beautifully kept hotel, indeed.

Dom Carlos, 121 Avenida Duque de Loulé (tel. 53-90-71), just off the Praça Marquês de Pombal, faces its own triangular park, dedicated to the partially blind Camilo Castelo Branco, a 19th-century "eternity poet." The curvy facade of the hotel is all glass, giving guests an indoor-outdoor feeling, reinforced by green trees and beds of orange and red canna. In summer, there is air conditioning; in winter, central heating.

The hotel offers 73 bedrooms, including 17 suites. The bedrooms, all with private baths and some with television, are paneled in reddish Portuguese wood. The Nordic-inspired furnishings are softened by the occasional use of accessories, such as a hand-carved cherub or collage. The single rate is 1500$ ($22.95) daily, increasing to 2500$ ($38.25) in a double. In a suite, suitable for three guests, the tariff is 3500$ ($53.55) daily, including breakfast.

The lobby-lounge is satisfactory, but even more inviting is the mezzanine salon, where sofas and chairs face the park. The dining room is intriguing with its curving glass, polished Danish chairs, and slat-board ceiling. In addition, there's a miniature drinking bar, with leather chairs, ideal for a tête-à-tête. The hotel also has a sauna.

Around the corner is a fire station, and guests at the Dom Carlos are likely to hear frequent sirens. Upstairs over the fire station, teenagers on weekends play live rock music for many hours at night. Therefore, avoid any of the rooms to the left of the elevator, as you face the hotel.

Flórida Hotel, 32 Rua Duque de Palmela (tel. 57-61-45), is one of the many hotels clustered around the circular Praça Marquês de Pombal, with its statue of the prime minister who rebuilt Lisbon after the earthquake. Against a contemporary background, the public rooms utilize a palette of colors. Facing a glass wall, the main lounge is decorated with pillars of Portuguese marble. Against one wall is a painting by António Alfredo. The grill room provides meals in a setting of Nordic-style armchairs and plaid draperies. A snackbar opens onto a view of the plaza. There's yet another "view" dining room, more conservatively decorated in shades of midnight blue. In the Bar de Inverno guests congregate for drinks.

The bedrooms are well designed, fitting the shape of the curving building and making use of stark, primitive colors. Often you'll get a U-shaped desk and sofa as a room divider, with two armchairs forming a living room area. The rooms contain wall-to-wall windows, blond furniture, minuscule closets, and bathrooms with wide-grain marble. Singles range in price from 2000$ ($30.60), and doubles are in the 3500$ ($53.55) category. Taxes, service, and a continental breakfast are included.

Hotel Lutécia, 52 Avenida Frei Miguel Contreiras (tel. 80-31-21), is in a new shopping center, five minutes by underground from old Lisbon, toward the airport, offering 143 air-conditioned rooms, plus eight suites, that have distilled beauty and space and yet are utter simplicity. The ambience is caused by the slimline leather and wood armchairs, the wall-hung desk and dressing table, a room-wide headboard and walnut and leather paneling complete with push-buttons, reading lights, and telephones. The baths are tiled, with a tub and shower combination, and large wrap-around towels on heated rods. Breakfast is available either on your private balcony or in the roof restaurant. The tariff for one person is $40 (U.S.) per day, increasing to $50 for a double. Two persons in one suite pay $80, taxes and services included.

Its 12 stories are set back from a busy thoroughfare, with a formal driveway entrance. The public lounges consume most of the first two floors, although you must take an elevator to the top for the open-view dining room. Also up in the sky is a bar with red leather love seats and stools, potted palms, prints of schooners, and a picture-window view of Lisbon. The snackbar is open till 2 a.m., where a hearty meal will run around $10, including taxes.

Mundial Hotel, 4 Rua Dom Duarte (tel. 86-31-01), right in the heart of everything, rises eight floors on the curve of a street. The top-floor restaurant offers a view of St. George's Castle and the Alfama. A short walk to the Rossio, theaters, and shops, the Mundial is well managed. The staff generates an efficient, friendly atmosphere. Everything is properly manicured and polished, and the hotel is high on the preference list of European business people.

The rooms, 150 in all with private bath, are comfortable, spacious, and restrained in decor. The baths are tiled, each with a bidet, shower/tub combination, and plenty of mirrors and shelf space for toilet articles. In a single, the rate is 2000$ ($30.60). Doubles rent for 3600$ ($55.08), breakfast included.

The lobby is sedate, with a glass wall of ivy and gift displays. The sky-view dining room provides both indoor and outdoor meals, according to the weather. You can get a better-than-average four-course table d'hôte meal here. Tucked away is the tiny Oriental-style bar on the roof, ideal for that special tête-à-tête. The birds in the cages sing love songs.

3. Middle-Bracket Hotels

Hotel Albergaria da Senhora do Monte, 39 Calçada do Monte (tel. 86-28-46), is a special little hilltop hotel with a unique character. It's perched near a belvedere, the Miradouro Senhorado Monte, in the Graça district, a spot where a knowing Lisboan takes his favorite person for a memorable nighttime view of the city, the Castle of St. George, and the Tagus.

Built originally as an apartment house, the hotel has been converted into a clublike establishment, with lots of semilavish touches for those seeking an unusual atmosphere. The living room is intimate, with large tufted sofas and overscale tables and lamps. The drinking lounge is yet another favored gathering spot.

Many-leveled corridors lead to the excellent bedrooms, all 27 of which contain private baths and verandas. The rooms reveal the touch of the decorator, especially the gilt-edged door panels, the grass-cloth walls, and the tiled baths with bronze fixtures. No room is a rubberstamp duplicate. A single with bath rents for 1300$ ($19.89), a double with bath for 1700$ ($26.01). The tariffs include a continental breakfast and taxes. In a suite for two, the rate is 2500$ ($38.25).

Hotel Fenix, 8 Praça Marquês de Pombal (tel. 53-51-21), enjoys a frontrow position on the circular plaza dedicated to the 18th-century prime minister of Portugal. From most of its bedrooms, you can view the trees on the avenue and in Edward VII Park. A semimodern hotel, the Fenis is run by the Torralta chain.

The hotel is favored by many clients who have time-tested their stays here, enjoying its cleanliness and comfort, the tiled baths, the Nordic-type furnishings. Each of the compact 125 bedrooms is uncluttered, containing upholstered armchairs and many amenities. In a double or twin-bedded room the daily rate is 3500$ ($53.55), 2000$ ($30.60) in a single, including breakfast.

The brightly furnished and air-conditioned two-floor reception lounge, with a cozy bar-lounge on the mezzanine, is much favored. Another plus is the grill room in the hotel, the Bodegón, worthy of a separate recommendation as a restaurant.

Dom Manuel, 187 Avenida Duque d'Avila (tel. 57-61-60), may be a small hotel, but its style level is high, and for such an atmosphere the rates are low. It's a little out of the very heart of Lisbon, on a tree-lined avenue. Its guest lounge is like a private home in an estate, with an open fireplace to make it cozy. Flanking white sofas are set on an Oriental area rug. On one wall is an Aubusson tapestry, and a picture window looks out onto an interior planter with subtropical greenery. On a mezzanine there is an intimate little cocktail lounge with brass light fixtures. You dine on the lower level which is very

Portuguese, with formal leather armchairs and elegant floor torchères. Letting in filtered light is a stained-glass rose window. Each of the bedrooms is in a restrained modern style, with muted color coordination, built-in headboards, a desk and armchair, bed lights, and all-tiled baths. Singles are 1750$ ($26.78) daily; doubles, 2250$ ($34.43) daily—including a continental breakfast.

Infante Santo, 14 Rua Tenente Valadim (tel. 60-01-44), is on a secluded tree-shaded street near the docks where the great liners tie in, lying 1.4 miles from the Cais do Sodré, the electric train departure point for the Costa do Sol resorts. Built on the side of a high-rising hill, it has two tiny elevators to take you to the top of its eight floors. Almost all of its 27 bedrooms contain good-size balconies where you can order your morning breakfast, while enjoying the Tagus.

The emphasis is on modern bedrooms with space for sitting, adequate closets, and amenities such as radios, televisions, and reading lamps. The bedspreads and draperies are in simple yet vibrant tones, contrasting with warm grained wood and pastel walls. Tiled baths with a shower/tub combination come with each room. For a double, tariffs range from 1400$ ($21.42) to 1800$ ($27.54) daily; in a single room, from 1100$ ($16.83) to 1400$ ($21.42). Service and taxes are included.

Breakfast, included in the price, is the only meal served. Mostly, guests like to utilize the drinking lounge, decorated with oak walls, leather armchairs, and tiled abstract fish scenes on the walls. The corridors have pleasant touches, using decorative framed tiles of regional scenes.

Jorge V Hotel, 3 Rua Mouzinho da Silveira (tel. 56-25-25), is a neat little hotel of today's design, with good amenities, moderate prices, and a choice location a block off the Avenida da Liberdade. Its facade contains rows of cellular balconies, roomy enough for guests to have breakfast or afternoon "coolers." A wee-size elevator takes you to a variety of rooms at different price levels. The rooms aren't generous in size, but adequate—not glamorous, but comfortable in a compact way. All have small tiled bathrooms, telephones, and radios.

Tariffs vary according to position, with the cheaper rooms facing the rear. Singles cost 1500$ ($22.95) including breakfast, with doubles renting for 2500$ ($38.25).

The reception lounge shares space with a bar in bright, stark colors played against white. For 500$ ($7.65) you can order a table d'hôte meal in the dining room, pleasantly decorated and dominated by a central table with baskets of fresh fruit and cheese. But the room most favored by guests is a regional-style combination drinking bar and breakfast room of nicely melded aggregate stone and wood paneling. Napery is a crisp white, and a center table tempts with fruits piled high in baskets and a big condiment tray.

Flamingo Hotel, 41 Rua Castilho (tel. 53-21-91), has an informal, friendly atmosphere. The hotel lies in the "Park Avenue" section of Lisbon, near the Ritz, close to the best shops and restaurants. On its seven floors, the hotel offers 35 compact bedrooms, decorated and maintained in a homey fashion, with a liberal use of modestly contemporary furnishings. Including breakfast, service, and taxes, the rate for a double or twin-bedded room ranges from 1600$ ($24.48) to 2000$ ($30.60). In a single, the tariff is 1500$ ($22.95) to 1900$ ($29.07) nightly. Every room has a private bath with a shower/tub combination, plus a bidet.

In winter, everything is kept snug by central heating; in summer, a few rooms are air-conditioned. The dining room is decorated in white and puce, with overhead indirect lighting. Off the lounge is a little bar, where the bartender quickly learns to mix your favorite drink. The most important community area is the rear garden terrace, where summer furniture is set up and surrounded by vines and semitropical greenery.

Presidente Hotel, 13 Rua Alexandre Herculano (tel. 53-95-01), is a small-scale establishment near the Avenida da Liberdade on a busy street corner. It's recommended to families, as children under 9 are granted a 50% reduction; babysitting can be arranged, there's a laundry on the premises, and a permanent medical service.

The general atmosphere, including the furnishings, is of good taste. Although the 59 bedrooms are small, they are nicely laid out, with chestnut built-in headboards, including radios, bed lights, and telephones. There are double-view windows, a small entry with two closets, bathrooms tiled in happy colors, papered walls, and even a valet stand. The high-season rate, with breakfast, for a double is 2500$ ($38.25); in a single, 1500$ ($22.95). In the wood-paneled mezzanine lounge, only breakfast is served.

The public rooms, all the suites, and the bedrooms are air-conditioned. The modest-size reception lounges are on three levels, connected by wide marble steps.

Rex Hotel, 169 Rua Castilho (tel. 68-21-61), is another family favorite, a modern hotel only minutes from the Ritz, the Avenida da Liberdade, and Edward VII Park. Every one of the 77 bedrooms at the Rex is complete with a tiled private bath and is furnished in a homelike manner, with matching fabrics, sitting area, carpeting, radio, telephone, TV, refrigerator, air conditioning, and (in some rooms) balconies. The bedrooms are priced according to placement and size. The cost of a double room is 2500$ ($38.25); in a single, 1500$ ($22.95).

Guests seek out the cozy bar, Club 37, or the solarium terrace and breakfast room on the top floor, where the view of Lisbon is memorable. There's a restaurant on the top floor with a panoramic view.

The **Hotel do Reno,** 195–197 Avenida Duque d'Avila (tel. 54-81-81), and the **Hotel Príncipe,** 201 Avenida Duque d'Avila (tel. 53-61-51), lie only about a ten-minute taxi ride from the heart of Lisbon. Although run as competitors by different owners, they are two almost identical small modern hotels, heretofore enjoying heavy patronage by Germans and Scandinavians. But they attract English and American visitors as well. Both of them provide good, substantial, and clean rooms with private baths (and, in most cases, private balconies). Each puts an emphasis on the bedrooms rather than the public lounges, although providing a small lobby and bar, along with separate dining room for breakfast.

The first of the economy twins, the Do Reno has been upgraded to three stars. It has a nice bar at the main entrance, and its sitting room has been enlarged. The bedrooms are tailored and contemporary, each provided with a small sitting area that includes a desk and an armchair. Single cost 1600$ ($24.48), with breakfast; doubles, 2000$ ($30.60), including a continental breakfast.

The Príncipe (not to be confused with the first-class Príncipe Real recommended previously) is the second of these compact, quite commercial, but comfortable little hotels. Also a successful three-star choice, it enjoys lounges and a very good dining room. For a room with breakfast, the rate for a single is 1600$ ($24.48), that tariff increasing to 2000$ ($30.60) for a double or twin-bedded room with breakfast. Spread among the hotel's eight floors are enough beds to accommodate 100 travelers, who use two elevators for their ascent. At both establishments, children up to 8 years are granted a 50% reduction.

Miraparque 12 Avenida Sidónio Pais (tel. 57-80-70), is a first-class modern hotel on a secluded quiet street, opposite Edward VII Park. While not modish, it still is very presentable, designed in a conservative manner. The lounges are furnished in simulated brown leather with wood-paneled walls. Likewise, the tiny bar, with stools and lounge chairs, has a neat and comfortable ambience. The dining room, also wood-paneled with contemporary chairs, has a wall-wide mural as a decorative feature. Bedrooms have the same modified contemporary styling, with pastel colors. All units have private baths. For bed and breakfast, the rate is $30 (U.S.) in a single, rising to $40 in a double, $50 in a triple. Dinner is another $8.

4. Full-Board Bargains

York House, 32 Rua das Janelas Verdes (tel. 66-25-44), provides the drama of the past with the conveniences of the 20th century. York House was once a 16th-century convent and is outside the center of traffic-filled Lisbon, attracting those who want peace and tranquility. Long known to the English and embassy personnel, it is almost opposite the National Art Gallery, sitting high on a hillside street overlooking the Tagus.

You go past an old iron gate and ascend a flight of stone steps past trailing ivy and rugged walls. You enter York House through a garden cloister, where guests congregate under gnarled trees. Owned and run by a Frenchwoman, Madame Andrée Goldstein, York House is knowingly furnished with flair by her son, who is one of the most distinguished designers for theater, opera, and villas in Lisbon. Each bedroom is tastefully furnished with antique beds, soft mattresses, and a liberal use of 18th- and 19th-century pieces. Almost all of the bedrooms contain private baths.

All year the charge is 1500$ ($22.95) per person per day based on double occupancy, including all meals. Single rooms with bath and full board go for 2000$ ($30.60) daily. Preference is given to those requesting full board.

The guest book reveals that York House is favored by the embassies, artists, writers, poets, professors, and ministers of the present government. Writers often stay here when on sabbatical leave, doing research on sociological studies of Portugal.

Everything is homelike. In the public rooms antiques are used: inlaid chests, coats of armor, carved ecclesiastical paintings and figures, ornate ceramics, gilt and bronze chandeliers. The former monks' dining hall has deep-set windows, large niches for antiques, and best of all, a combined French and Portuguese cuisine. Guests gather in the two-level lounge for before- or after-dinner drinks under a beamed ceiling, in a setting of ecclesiastical sculpture, 17th-century paintings, decorative torchères, and church candlesticks made into table lamps.

Madame has acquired a former town house at no. 47, down the street, adjacent to the museum. Here you can book larger, more luxurious rooms, with abundant closet space and tiled private bathrooms. Only breakfast is served here, although main meals are provided back at the convent. Singles are 1200$ ($18.36) with breakfast; doubles, 1700$ ($26.01).

The lounge is Victorian, predominantly red, turn-of-the-century Lisbon. Over the fireplace is a grotesque portrait of Alfonso, the former king of Spain, as a child. The bedrooms have a unified color theme, antiques, and large, tiled baths. Breakfast is brought on a tray to your room, to the lounge, or to the rear walled-in terrace with its garden furniture and antique iron spiral staircase with its steps filled with potted flowering plants.

Estalagem do Cavalo Branco (The White Horse Inn), 146 Avenida do Almirante Gago Coutinho (tel. 88-61-21). To stay here requires a sense of adventure, humor, and a love of the fantastic. This former villa on a residential boulevard leading to the airport was taken over by Frederico de Eca Leal, a collector of Iberian antiques, a gourmet, and an interior decorator. He offers not only inexpensive rooms, but excellent meals in an unusual setting.

The bedrooms are individually decorated in a theatrical way, using bright colors and occasional antiques. A group of rooms on the lower level is for use in an emergency only, but generally the better rooms, up and down short flights of steps, are quite comfortable and never boring. A personal favorite is the amusing attic room, with red walls and black furniture. The price for two persons, with breakfast included, is 1850$ ($28.31), dropping to 1200$ ($18.36) for one. All the rooms have individual bathrooms (either a tub or shower), plus radio or TV. Taxes and service are included.

Dining at the inn is festive in one of its series of midget rooms, crowded with antiques. One dining room has oak furniture against a background of opera-red walls and gilded cherubs. If you're dropping in just for dinner, the à la carte menu includes both fish and meat dishes. Every surface downstairs is covered with bric-a-brac, gilded torchères, painted wooden chests, and window swags. On the stairway rests a clock collection, and in the open-beamed bar is a fireplace and an assemblage of more than 100 decorative oddments.

5. The Budget Range

Capitol Hotel, 24 Rua Eça de Queirós (tel. 53-68-11), is a fine little bargain, just minutes from the top of the Avenida da Liberdade and the Praça Marquês de Pombal. It nestles on a quiet street, away from busy boulevards, and opens onto a wedge-shaped park with weeping willows and oaks.

Attracting budgeteers, the Capitol places the emphasis on good, roomy chambers with private baths, all of which are furnished in a restrained, utilitarian fashion. The more expensive rooms open onto private balconies. Singles pay 1400$ ($21.42) nightly; doubles, 1950$ ($29.84); triples, 2200$ ($33.76)—including breakfast. On the premises are a bar, snackbar, and restaurant.

Hotel Excelsior, 172 Rua Rodrigues Sampaio (tel. 53-71-51), enjoys a setting one block from Marquês de Pombal Square, at the entrance to Edward VII Park. Right off the upper regions of Lisbon's major boulevard, it contains 90 good-size bedrooms, each with its own private bath.

Most of the rooms have a small sitting area, with a combination desk and dressing table. For a single, the maximum rate is $29 (U.S.), increasing to $38 for the most expensive double. Breakfast and taxes are included in the tariffs. In a room with shower, but no tub, the tariffs are reduced. In addition to the air-conditioned, wood-paneled bar, with bamboo planters for semitropical foliage, there's a spacious breakfast room which has large-view windows.

Residência Imperador, 55 Avenida 5 de Outubro (tel. 57-48-84), not far from the center, provides rooms with private baths for 850$ ($13.01) in a single, 1500$ ($22.95) in a double. The front entranceway, designed in Portuguese pine wood, is barely large enough to set down one's suitcase. However, the bedrooms and upper lounge are adequate in size. Opening onto balconies, the front bedrooms face a tiny private garden. The rooms are contemporary in concept, neatly planned with built-in beds and simple lines. Muted colors are used on the walls and in the fabrics.

The residência has only one owner, A. T. Carvalho, who provides personalized service. On the top floor is an airy public room and terrace with a glass front, where breakfast is served. Tram 1 or 21 and the Metro (Saldanha station) can whisk you into the city center.

Borges Hotel, 108 Rua Garrett (tel. 36-19-51), has undergone a facelifting. The beehive reception area is as crowded as the 19th-century coffeehouse next door, A Brasileira, the traditional gathering spot for the Portuguese literati. On the second floor of the Borges, the dining room partially escaped the contemporary treatment, its paneled walls and crystal chandeliers intact.

The 93 bedrooms and 12 suites have been refurnished in a semicontemporary manner, with traditional draperies and counterpanes. All the rooms have private baths or showers, the doubles ranging from 1500$ ($22.75) to 1800$ ($27.54), the singles going for anywhere from 1200$ ($18.36) to 1500$ ($22.95). Breakfast, taxes, and service are included. The location is persuasive, in the Chiado district, minutes from some of Lisbon's best known restaurants and fado clubs, as well as the shops of Baixa.

Hotel da Torre, 8 Rua dos Jerónimos (tel. 63-62-62), is in Belém, a suburb of Lisbon, near an estuary of the Tagus. As such, it is suitable primarily for those who want to be in the belt of Lisbon's museumland. The renovated inn rises three stories, and is furnished in a regional style. Doubles with breakfast peak at 2500$ ($38.25), and singles are charged 1500$ ($22.95). The air conditioning is confined to the public rooms and the wood-paneled bar, with its plastic lounge chairs. Regional food is served in the provincial restaurant.

READERS' HOTEL SELECTIONS: "We found a very comfortable and reasonable room at the **Pensão-Santana,** 30 Rua Luciano Cordeiro (tel. 57-61-41). It was one of the cleanest we came across in our travels, and the owner and one of his sons speak understandable English as well as being most obliging. We would not hesitate to recommend this accommodation or return there ourselves. For 750$ ($11.48) per night, we had a large room for two with private toilet, shower, and bidet" (P. F. Deary, Grand Bend, Ontario, Canada).... "A great pensão borders St. George's Castle and has a magnificent view. It's **Pensão Ninho de Aguias,** 74 Costa do Castelo (tel. 86-21-51). It is also extremely reasonable, charging 1200$ ($18.36) for a very large room which opens up onto the patio and includes a bathroom and a small entrance hall with a couch where our two children slept. The staff is friendly" (Nelson and Dotty Gonsalves, Hayward, Calif.).

"I have investigated many hotels in the Lisbon area, but the best value for location and service seems to be the **Hotel Lis,** 180 Avenida da Liberdade (tel. 56-34-34). It is impossible to quote definite prices as they depend on the type of room, but we obtained a very large double room facing the street, with bath and toilet, for 1800$ ($27.54). There are cheaper rooms. English is spoken, the breakfast is adequate, and the elevator works. The desk staff is helpful, and, above all, taxis are plentiful past the door. It is only a short walk to Thomas Cook's, the post office, and the restaurant area. All major bus operators call there to pick up for tours" (Dr. Gerald Noble, North Balwyn, Victoria, Australia). ... "An excellent pensione in Lisbon is the **Residêncial Aleleuia,** 32 Rua Luciano Cordeiro (tel. 57-37-02). It is completely modern, and a room containing a private bathroom and shower costs 1000$ ($15.30) for two. The rooms are immaculate with a beautiful decor. The owner, Tony, and his wife are especially helpful and furnish transportation to and from the railway station. Tony speaks good English. His pensione is in the modern section of the city, two blocks from the Praça Marquês de Pombal and Avenida da Liberdade. You can have an excellent breakfast for about $1 (U.S.), consisting of fresh fruits, coffee, tea, or chocolate, rolls and butter, and fresh Portuguese cheese. Residêncial Aleluia is two subway stops from the Alfama, or you can walk there in 15 minutes" (Thomas and Glenda Bagnato, Richmond Hill, N.Y.).

Chapter V

THE RESTAURANTS OF LISBON

1. The Deluxe Quartet
2. The Medium-Priced Range
3. Less Expensive Restaurants
4. The Budget Range
5. Seafood on the Left Bank
6. The Foreign Colony
7. The Special Spots

LISBON OFFERS A WIDE RANGE of dining places, headed by such restaurants as Aviz and Tavares. The cuisine in these establishments is of a high standard, ranking justifiably with leading places in other European capitals. Here, you'll encounter the best of Portuguese dishes, intermixed with the classics from the continental repertoire. In such establishments, a knowledgeable maître d'hôtel and a wine steward are at your elbow to guide you toward culinary decisions.

But you needn't pay high prices for top-quality food in Lisbon and its environs. There are many noteworthy regional restaurants, offering Portuguese cooking, even foreign viands, at various price levels, ranging from a simple beer and steak tavern, to a formal town-house-style dining chamber, to a cliffside restaurant with a panoramic view.

Aside from the recommendations contained within this chapter, you may also want to consider having your evening meal at one of the fado cafés (see our suggestions in Chapter IX).

Portuguese friends often confide that it takes two hours for people of their country to dine—"one hour to talk, another to eat."

1. The Deluxe Quartet

Restaurante Aviz, 12-B Rua Serpa Pinto (tel. 32-83-91), is Portugal's poshest restaurant, a visual reminder of the city's past. Known for its top-notch gourmet cuisine to prime ministers, exiled kings, and Mr. and Mrs. John Doe of Kansas City, the Aviz is a treasure. What is now the Aviz was saved from the demolition of the famed hotel of the same name, once (in the pre-Ritz days) the only deluxe hotel in Lisbon. Salvaged from the ruins was the nucleus of the hotel staff, including the maître d'hôtel Anibal Espírito Santo Silva, and the chef João da Cruz Ribeiro. The bartender Tony Fadda is also part owner.

You ascend a staircase into an elegant setting. While drinks are served in the foyer lounge, menu selections are made. The ambience is that of a private club with mahogany paneling, tufted black leather chairs, green marble columns, and crystal. The hotel staff brought not only parts of the torn-down establishment with them, including all the silver, a meat trolley, and the wall torchères, but the secrets of the kitchen as well.

Aviz turns out many specialties, so making decisions is difficult. For an unusual beginning, try espadon fumé (smoked swordfish), for 400$ ($6.12). This is served with quartered lemons wrapped in tulle tutus. An alternative choice might be a creamy vichyssoise at 250$ ($3.82). For a main course, the following dishes are recommended as exciting treats: entrecôte au poivre (pepper steak), 550$ ($8.42); fettuccine (ribbon-thin egg noodles) alla Bolognese, 245$ ($3.75); and suprême de volaille Holstein (an elegant chicken suprême), 420$ ($6.43). For dessert, fine offerings include gâteau Aviz, 250$ ($3.82), and bananas flambé with kirsch for the same price. To the charge quoted will be added the local tax, service charge, and cover charge.

Your table must be reserved in one of the trio of intimate dining rooms, preferably the larger green and gold chamber, with its ornate bronze and frosted glass, globed chandelier, and circular display of specialty foods (foie gras de Strasbourg, chilled cooked pears, cheese, and decorative flowers). The Aviz (closed Sunday) offers two evening settings, at 8 and 10 p.m. The last orders are taken at 2 p.m. for lunch, 10:30 p.m. for dinner. Your bill will be presented in an enclosed gold-embossed leather folder on a silver tray.

Clement Freud went looking for the "best restaurant in Europe," and when he arrived at the Aviz, discovered he'd found it.

Restaurante Tavares, 37 Rua da Misericórdia (tel. 32-11-12), is a gilt and crystal world under a glass bell. This slice of the past offers a palace-style setting and a superb cuisine. White and gold paneled walls, three chandeliers, freshly arranged table roses, Louis XV armchairs—all keep intact the spirit of the 19th century.

Actually, Tavares was originally a café, dating from 1784 when a man known as O Talao founded it. When the two Tavares brothers died in the 19th century, half a dozen waiters formed a partnership and took over the restaurant. It is still owned by a combine of waiters, who continue its high standards. It is the oldest restaurant in Lisbon, attracting many diplomatic and government heads, as well as the literati.

Drinks are served in the petite front salon, where you can plan your meal. Fernando Lopes, the wine steward, aids you in your selection (he tries to provide a pleasant wine and does not push the most expensive bottles). Perhaps Carvalho Ribeiro Ferreirniepoort, one of the owners, will take your order.

A beginning might be crêpes de marisco, at 550$ ($3.82), or a vichyssoise, costing 250$ ($3.82). A main-course selection might be the sole in champagne, 800$ ($12.24), a real delicacy, or tournedos Grand Duc, also 800$. Many continental dishes are scattered throughout the menu, including the classic scallops of veal Viennoise, 500$ ($7.65). However, the restaurant nearly always serves sardines and salted codfish, so secure is it in its reputation.

For a wine, perhaps you'll try Colares Reserva Tavares, costing 550$ ($8.42) and hailing from the wine caves of Tavares. To complete your meal, why not try the chef's dessert specialty, a high-rise soufflé for 300$ ($4.59), followed by a café filtro?

Tagide, 18 Largo da Biblioteca Publica (tel. 32-07-20) has had a prestigious past, and now it is a distinguished place to dine in the Chiado. Its situation is colorful—up from the docks, on a steep hill on a ledge overlooking the old part of Lisbon and the Tagus. Once the town house of a diplomat, then a leading nightclub, it now is one of Lisbon's leading restaurants.

It's very old, with a museum look to it. You go up marble steps with shiny brass balustrades. The dining room has view windows, overlooking moored ships and the port. Set into the white plaster walls are overscale figures made of blue and white tiles, each depicting a famous queen. The chairs are provincial, the tablecloths have hand-crocheted edges. Glittering above are crystal chandeliers.

Both Portuguese dishes of quality as well as selections from the international repertoire are featured and are beautifully served. For an opener, we'd suggest the salmon pâté at 380$ ($5.81), or else the cream of shrimp soup at 220$ ($3.37), and perhaps the soufflé Tagide. Other well-recommended dishes include rabbit, Minho style, 480$ ($7.34), duck liver with fresh mushrooms, or sauteed quail at the same price; and filet of sole, 560$ ($8.57). I'm also fond of the pork coriander, 550$ ($8.42). The restaurant is closed on Sunday. Always call for a reservation.

The **Ritz Grill Room,** 88 Rua Rodrigo da Fonseca (tel. 68-41-31), is in the Ritz Hotel, overlooking the terrace and the Edward VII Park, but fortunately set apart from the main hotel lobby.

This restaurant features a completely new gastronomic concept in Lisbon, *Cuisine Moderne,* with each dish specially prepared with the freshest ingredients. The cream of lobster soup goes for $8.50 (U.S.) and the dried smoked Chaves ham for $6.50. Among meat specialties, you can have filet of beef in red wine and green peppercorn sauce at $13, or mignons of beef with morels and truffle juice at $15. A sophisticated touch is found in fish entrees, such as ragoût of sole and langoustines ($18) or braised sea bass with Ricard for two persons ($23). A pastry trolley will be brought to your table, with a choice of cake costing $3.70 per portion. For a finish, try filtered coffee ($2). Service and taxes are included in the prices.

The Ritz Grill can become a habit hard to break, even on short stays in Lisbon. It opens at 7:30 p.m.

2. The Medium-Priced Range

Gambrinus, 25 Rua das Portas de Santo Antão (tel. 32-14-66), is an establishment whose stature among Lisbon's leading restaurants is justified. Intimate dining rooms are clustered around an open blue-tiled kitchen, where expert chefs in starched white hats prepare fine meals, using large copper pots and a charcoal grill. The location is a breeze for those who want to dine in the heart of the city, off the Rossio, near the railway station, and on a little square in back of the National Theater.

You can have your meal while sitting on leather chairs in the rear under a cathedral-beamed ceiling, or else select a little table beside a fireplace upon the raised end of the room. All is dominated by an impressionistic tapestry along one wall. There is also an alcove with a stained-glass enclosure, all primitively modern. The walls of the back room are sedate with paneling, not unlike a country lodge. For before-dinner drinks, a front bar beckons.

Although there is a diversified à la carte menu, don't fail to check the *especialidades do dia.* The soups are good, everything from bisque of shellfish to onion soup for 150$ ($2.30). Fish dishes range from conha com mariscos à thermidor (conch with shellfish) for 450$ ($6.89) to tobalo (bass) minhote at 580$ ($8.87). A Germanic meat dish, salsichas de Frankforte com choucroûte (frankfurters with sauerkraut), costs 480$ ($7.34), and the specialty is rumpsteak Gambrinus, 620$ ($9.49). The restaurant offers elaborate desserts, such as a soufflé de baunilha (vanilla) at 270$ ($4.13) and crêpes suzette at 480$ ($7.34). Coffee with a 30-year-old brandy complements the meal perfectly.

Chester, 87 Rua Rodrigo da Fonseca (tel. 657-347), near the Ritz Hotel, is an attractive restaurant and bar, with a good cellar. Its specialty is grilled steaks. The pepper steak is tempting at 340$ ($5.20), as is the rib steak for two, 750$ ($11.48). Entrecôte with whiskey sauce goes for 350$ ($5.36), and the fondue bourguignonne costs 900$ ($13.77) for two persons. You might begin with a crab cocktail at 275$ ($4.21), finishing with flambéed pineapple, 450$ ($6.89) for two persons. The restaurant is upstairs, and the cozy little bar lies below. Service is friendly, and reservations are suggested.

Bodegón, Hotel Fenix, 8 Praça Marquês de Pombal (tel. 53-51-21), is a first-rate grill room attached to a hotel. You dine in a tavern setting, with beamed ceiling, tiled floors, wood-paneled pillars, warm Iberian colors of yellows and browns. Spanish engravings have been placed around the walls, and adjoining is a separate drinking bar.

Some of the house specialties include quail, partridge, and fresh salmon from the north of Portugal. The chef is known for smoking food—try his smoked eel, smoked duck, or smoked swordfish. All year you can order cultivated oysters, although they are at their best after October.

Among the à la carte selections are salmão grelhado (grilled salmon), which is priced depending on size, but do not expect less than 550$ ($8.42); spaghetti Venezia, 300$ ($4.59); sopa de cebola (onion soup), 150$ ($2.30); smoked colin, 400$ ($6.12); and paella à la Valenciana, 500$ ($7.65). For dessert, try crêpes suzette, 175$ ($2.68).

Comodoro, 20-23 Praça D. João de Câmara (tel. 32-74-18), resembles a business people's club at lunch, a supper club in the evening. Between 11 p.m. and 3:30 a.m., upstairs, it changes character completely and is enlivened by music for dancing. By then, its conservative mien has disappeared entirely. The dining room is decorated with wood paneling, old prints of clipper ships, an enlarged photostat of the seaport of Lisbon's past, ships' lanterns, and a display of silver football trophies won by the waiters and kitchen staff.

The cuisine of the house is highly respected, as is the attentive service. A starter might be crème de mariscos (shellfish soup) for 50$ (77¢), or you might prefer a choice of about 21 hors d'oeuvres, priced according to what you select. Main dishes include ameijoas (clams) en cataplana, 400$ ($6.12); and filetes linguados (sole) suchet, 420$ ($6.43). My special favorite is a cutlet of grilled veal with fresh vegetables, 450$ ($6.89).

Pabe, 27A Rua Duque de Palmela (tel. 53-56-75), is the Portuguese name for pub, and that's what this cozy English-style place is. Convenient to the Praça do Pombal, the pub has done its best to emulate English establishments. There's a soft red carpet on the floor, mugs hanging over the long bar, a beamed ceiling, coats-of-arms, and engravings of hunting scenes around the walls. Two saloon-type doors lead into a wood-paneled dining room, where you can sup on meat specially imported from the U.S. A chateaubriand for two has a 1000$ ($15.30) tab. If you prefer local fare, start off with a shrimp cocktail for 480$ ($7.34), then Portuguese veal liver for 450$ ($6.89), or a supremo de galinha (white chicken with mushrooms), 380$ ($5.81). Finish with sherbert for 160$ ($2.45).

The crowd tends to be a well-groomed Portuguese set as well as resident Yanks and Britons. The Pabe is closed on Sunday.

Sancho, 6A Travessa dos Gloria (tel. 36-97-80), is a cozy, rustic-style place just off the Avenida da Liberdade, close to the Praça dos Restauradores. After passing a pleasant bar, you enter a dining room with red plush draperies over the windows, a beamed ceiling, a fireplace, and leather and wood chairs. A second adjoining room is equally pleasant. The walls are stuccoed, flowers are placed all around, and paintings hang on the walls. In summer the Sancho is air-conditioned. A fish gratinée soup costs 85$ ($1.30); a cream of tomato, 60$ (92¢); robalo (bass) al forno, 255$ ($3.90); slices of turbot, also 255$; veal scallopine, 300$ ($4.59); fried chicken, 175$ ($2.68); bife na frigideira, 270$ ($4.13); crêpes suzette, 180$ ($2.75); house tart, 70$ ($1.07); a mousse, 60$ (92¢). Also good is a chicken dish, churrasco de frango au piri-piri, for those who like hot seasonings, 175$ ($2.68). For milder tastes, there is always sole meunière, 300$ ($4.59).

Telheiro, 10A Rua Latíno Coelho (tel. 53-40-07), means "The Roof" in Portuguese, and it's a bistro-like place not far from the Sheraton Hotel. The ceilings are beamed, and you sit on wooden chairs with heart shapes carved out of their backs. The friendly waiters are clad in scarlet waistcoats. Peppers hang from the chandeliers. Pâté, butter, and rolls are placed on your table before you even order. Specialties are the gazpacho, a French bean and tomato soup at 35$ (54¢); mussels, 320$ ($4.90); turkey, 270$ ($4.13); leitão (suckling pig), also 270$; and the fried fresh sea bass, 450$ ($6.89). For dessert, try the rum omelet, 110$ ($1.68), or a honey ball, 60$ (92¢).

Escorial, 47 Rua Portas de Santo Antão (tel. 3-37-58). You can dine here with Spanish flair. Although right in the heart of Lisbon's restaurant district, this Spanish-owned establishment combines classic Spanish dishes with an inviting ambience. The dining room walls are paneled in rosewood, with frosted globe lighting. Around the scarlet-clothed tables, armchairs have been placed, stemmed glasses lined up, and napkins rolled like Roman scrolls. Before dinner you can have a drink in a cocktail lounge, the Art Room, called that because it has exhibits of contemporary Portuguese artists.

The menu is English (always look for the course of the day). An order of onion soup with cheese goes for 210$ ($3.21); a bisque of shellfish for 270$ ($4.13). Excellently prepared fish dishes include baked whiting with clams or a mixed fry, both 600$ ($9.18). A meat specialty is marinated pork cutlets served in a clay dish, and the chef does a good beef Stroganoff, both again 600$ ($9.18). Desserts include a choice of tarts at 140$ ($2.14). Taxes are included.

One touch indicates why Escorial is a fine dining room. Your brandy glass is flamed to just the right temperature before a drop of liqueur is poured. Senhor José Costa has assembled an admirable staff. Such things pay off, as Escorial attracts an interesting crowd from Lisbon, Estoril, and Cascais.

3. Less Expensive Restaurants

António Restaurante, 63 Rua Tomás Ribeiro (tel. 53-87-80), was created especially for Portuguese business people who want a relaxing ambience and good food. A corner establishment, just a bit away from the din of central traffic, it is a refreshing oasis with blue and white glazed earthenware tiles. In fact, the color scheme of blue and white prevails, with a blue free-form ceiling, blue linen tops over white cloths, even crisp blue jackets on waiters. Pewter service plates and fresh flowers set the taste level.

The menu is in English. You can start with a cream of tomato soup for 25$ (38¢) or shellfish soup for 60$ (92¢). Orders of fish, garnished with vegetables, include filets with tomato sauce, 210$ ($3.21), or baked sole, 420$ ($6.43). Among the meat dishes, try an order of breaded chicken with spaghetti, 190$ ($2.91), or pork with clams, in the Alentejana style, 260$ ($3.98). Chicken de churrasco (barbecued) is another favorite at 190$ ($2.91). The dessert list is extensive, with even a banana split, 100$ ($1.53).

The owner-manager of the restaurant, António Oliveira, came to Lisbon in search of work from Viseu (in the north of Portugal), when he was 17 years old. He recommends his acorda de marisco, a stew-like, breaded dish of shellfish and eggs, which is a treat at 350$ ($5.36).

Restaurante Leão d'Ouro, 105 Rua I de Dezembro (tel. 36-94-95), stands beside the Estação do Rossio, the railway station best described as Victorian Gothic. The atmosphere of a large, old tavern prevails—high brick arches, a beamed ceiling, and a pictorial tile, depicting Portugal's liberation from Spain in 1640.

Food prices are keyed to the sparse Portuguese purse. You can start your meal with a rich-tasting soup, such as crème de camarão (cream of shrimp) for 35$ (54¢) or sopa à alentejana (made with bread and garlic, among other ingredients) for 45$ (69¢). Among the meat dishes, try pork chops prepared in the Alentejana way, 200$ ($3.06), or filet mignon, 300$ ($4.59).

A fowl specialty, if featured, is frango de churrasco, barbecued chicken. If one person orders it, the price is 160$ ($24.48). For dessert try the pêssegos (peaches), the skins like walls of a reservoir holding in all those juices. The price? 35$ (54¢).

Bonjardim, 10 Traverssa de Santo Antão (tel. 32-43-89), quite rightly deserves the enthusiastic approval of a Boston traveler: "I was given the names of eight inexpensive restaurants, including Bonjardim, to try out in Lisbon during my five-day stay. I ended up trying only two of them, as I took the rest of my meals at Bonjardim, sampling a different dish for lunch and dinner every day."

Manuel Castanheira, who owns and manages the restaurant, along with his handsome son, caters mostly to families, providing wholesome meals that fit most budgets. So successful has been their operation that they've taken over a building across the street, where the same menu is offered.

In the main restaurant, the second-floor air-conditioned dining room is in the rustic Portuguese style, with a beamed ceiling and a tile mural depicting farm creatures. The noonday sun pours in through seven windows. The street-floor dining room, with an adjoining bar for premeal drinks, has walls of decorative tiles accented by bunches of garlic and peppers along with a wooden oxen yoke.

During your dinner the aroma of fat chickens roasting to a golden brown on the charcoal spit can only persuade you to try a hen yourself. An order of this house specialty, frango no espeto, costs 175$ ($2.68), adequate for two persons, with a side dish of french fries for 25$ (38¢). The cook also knows how to bake hake in the Portuguese style, for 220$ ($3.37). An alternate dish is pork fried with clams, 200$ ($3.06). For dessert, you can order a cassate at 38$ (58¢). The Bonjardim is open seven days a week from noon to 11:30 p.m.

Restaurante Agricola da Quinta da S. Vicente, 144 Telheiras de Cima (tel. 79-02-11), is an overgrown, once-isolated farm on the edge of the Lumiar district of Lisbon, away from the river. It's snowballed into a Portuguese family tradition to congregate here, and the weekends find many an informal wedding party gaily celebrating with continuous toasts from steins of beer or wine.

There's a huge dining room with a mosaic-decorated bar at one side, a walk-through garden, and a copper-hooded fireplace. Prices are inexpensive. Typical is the frango na pucara, chicken in an earthenware pot, and the frango (chicken) à S. Vicente is the specialty of the house. Both are 260$ ($3.98) per person. Among the game selections, coelho (rabbit) à cacadora stands out at 300$ ($4.59). Many diners begin their meal with a selection of mariscos (shellfish)—especially the ameijoas à espanhola (Spanish-style clams) at 280$

($4.28). For dessert, why not try one of the native Portuguese cheeses, such as queijo sêrra, for 80$ ($1.22)? A fresh fruit salad goes also for only 80$.

The restaurant is run by the sons of Francisco Rodrigues de Alemaida, who bring in an orchestra for dancing on Saturday and Sunday evenings from 9 p.m. to 1 a.m. Closed Tuesday. Ask for the wine of the house, as the sons make their own. The Quinta is best reached by taxi or private car. You head up what at first appears to be a narrow village street, passing tree-shaded picnickers along the way.

Well-meaning Lisbon friends advise that "Americans won't like this place —it's too Portuguese." I think they're wrong!

O Funil (The Funnel), 82-A Avenida Elias Garcia (tel. 76-60-07). You have to be Portuguese to know about this place. It specializes in *cozinha Portuguesa,* and does the cooking so well and so inexpensively that a line forms at the door, and it's hard to get a table. You enter into a street-floor tavern with crowded tables. But chances are you'll be directed to the lower level, where you can wait at the tiny bar while a table is made ready. The Funnel is owned by three men who offer their *vinho da casa* in three different sizes of pitcher. If you'd prefer a bottle, then we'd recommend the red Valpacos at 105$ ($1.61). Featured dishes include clams (ameijoas) at 270$ ($4.13) and roast pork at 280$ ($4.28). Also recommendable is the swordfish at 300$ ($4.59). The almond tart at 80$ ($1.22) is a tasty dessert.

Toni dos Bifes, 50-E Avenida Praia da Vitória (tel. 53-60-80), is an old Lisbon standby where hungry Portuguese and foreigners have been going for years to get a good, inexpensive, and copious meal. Near the Monumental cinema, the restaurant has a plain but pleasant decor, with a counter on one side of the dining room and small tables on the other. Some tables and chairs are placed outdoors as well, in French café style, with a glass enclosure. You begin with small portions of pâté and butter and toast, bread and roll, and then you can launch into the homemade tomato soup, 30$ (46¢), or maybe a seafood omelet for 140$ ($2.14), followed by an entrecôte steak, 255$ ($3.91). Other specialties include the bacalhau (cod), 220$ ($3.37); pork Alentejana style, 210$ ($3.21); bife de atum grelhado (grilled tuna fish), 198$ ($3.03); and breaded veal, 280$ ($4.28). Finish with a melon with ham, 90$ ($1.38), or a peach melba, 75$ ($1.15). Bananas and cream cost 65$ (99¢).

4. The Budget Range

Dona Maria, 7 Largo do Regedo (tel. 36-49-82), is a rapid step away from the Teatro Nacional Dona Maria II at the Rossio. Go here for completely unpretentious Portuguese cuisine. The restaurant, popular with bullfight aficionados, is on the second floor of the building flanked by the fire department on one side, one of Lisbon's top restaurants, the Gambrinus, on the other. Inside, the dining room is informal, with a Spanish-style decor. A bas-relief of an Iberian village adorns the wall under a ceiling frieze of painted flowers. The manager, Benigno Casal Amoedo, is proud of his good food.

Considering the quality of the cooking, the low prices may astonish you. For only 35$ (54¢), you can order a healthy-size bowl of black bean soup, a Brazilian specialty. The fish courses are a meal in themselves: a specialty is bacalhau à Braz, dried codfish fried with potatoes, eggs, and onions, for 320$ ($4.90).

Meat courses start at 330$ ($5.05), the price for pork chops. Favorite main dishes include ribs of beef in the style of the province of Trás-os-Montes, 325$ ($4.97). Desserts are numerous, with a rice pudding costing only 60$ (92¢). A typical Portuguese dessert is orange pudding, also 60$. Dona Maria will offer a second person a reduction if two order the same dish. Closed Sunday.

Novo Dia, 4D Rua Dom Antão de Almada, off the Largo de São Domingos, is most centrally located in the economy restaurant belt of Lisbon. It's owned by Alberto Sena da Silva, a doctor of economics, who offers Portuguese dishes at moderate prices in an atmosphere evoking Lisbon's past as a seaport. Behind its ornate tiled facade is a compact air-conditioned dining room with four groups of stone arches, blue and white decorative azulejos walls, and wrought-iron chandeliers casting soft lights over the starched linen tablecloths.

First courses include such soups as crème de mariscos (cream of shellfish) or caldo verde (cabbage and potato), a big bowl of either one going for 25$ (38¢). The best buys are the servings for two, listed under the pratos do dia (plates of the day): Ameijoas à espanhola (Spanish-style clams in a savory sauce), 220$ ($3.37); linguado grelhado (grilled sole), 330$ ($5.05); carne de porco Alentejana (pork in the Alentejana style), 240$ ($3.67). Desserts such as flan (caramel custard) cost 25$ (38¢); a chocolate mousse, 30$ (46¢).

For further local color, visit the fruit market and grocery directly across the street. Note the displays of cheese, wine, coffee, and tea, all casting an aromatic spell.

Choupal, 9 Rua do Salitre (tel. 4-29-63), is a stylized taverna, one minute from the Avenida da Liberdade, where regional dishes are often served family style. Its walls have aqua and olive tiles, combined with wood paneling, and the ceiling is in a warm brown cork. Chairs are natural wood, the tables have bright cloths, and there is an English menu. The waiter usually suggests that food portions be shared as they are that large. He brings a loaf of crusty bread and a little ceramic jar of mildly seasoned pâté with sweet butter to begin your meal. You might begin with a shellfish soup at 40$ (61¢) or else savory, Spanish-style clams, 240$ ($3.67). Two main-dish specialties are roast chicken at 180$ ($2.75) and lampreys, those tiny eel-like creatures from the north of Portugal, 375$ ($5.74). The chef also does a special beef dish for 180$ ($2.75). The restaurant is open every day from 9 a.m. to midnight.

Pessoa Restaurante, 14 Rua de Santa Justa, is a super-economical place for Portuguese cooking on a street of low-budget restaurants. It's also owned by Alberto Sena da Silva, who seems to be a master of creating fine food for economical prices. Much to our good fortune, he likes to share his enthusiasm for regional cuisine with others.

The atmosphere of Pessoa is tavern-style on two floors, with thick arches, walls of black and white tiles, simple tables lit by crudely ornate wrought-iron lanterns, plus an open brick fireplace where steaks and fish are broiled.

If you dine in the air-conditioned upstairs, the food is sent up on a trusty old dumbwaiter. For only 30$ (46¢), you can get a good-size bowl of soup, such as a crème à Carolino. For a second course, a house specialty is fried swordfish, 300$ ($4.59). Another is filetes de linguado (filets of sole meunière), 320$ ($4.90). The menu is extensive: on my most recent visit I counted about 75 main dishes offered. Desserts are simple, however, with flan (caramel custard) going for 35$ (54¢).

Policia, 125A Avenida Donde de Valdom (tel. 76-35-05), has been remodeled and air-conditioned, and can now seat 250 diners comfortably. There's bar service from noon to midnight, and the restaurant operates from noon to 10 p.m., except on Saturday when it opens at noon, closing at 3 p.m. It remains shut all day on Sunday. The owner, Teotónio Lazaro Miranda, has some exceptionally good wines, both white and red, in stock, and sells bottles at reasonable prices.

The menu is good and typically Portuguese, including the chef's specialty, a regional stew "cozido." The choice of fish dishes is limited, but compensatingly fresh. A mixed fish stew, caldeirada mista à Policia, is preferred, and the inevitable codfish is on the menu, given the appendage of "à José do Pipo" here. The chef also does a good roast goat and, when available, rabbit. Veal is sweet and tender, and if you're dining light, expect to find a selection of omelets. For a complete meal, the charge is likely to be 750$ ($11.48) or more.

Bonjardim, run by the previously mentioned restaurant of the same name, has a nearby self-service cafeteria at 41 Rua do Jardim do Regedor. Sample dishes: seafood soup, 25$ (38¢); half a roast chicken with trimmings, 125$ ($1.91); garoupa fish à Bretone, 380$ ($5.81); and mousse, 22$ (34¢). The decor is simple, plastic, and efficient. The cafeteria is near the Rossio.

5. Seafood on the Left Bank

Floresta do Ginjal, 7 Ginjal (tel. 27-00-87), overlooks the waterfront on the left bank of the Tagus in Cacilhas. You dine on some of the best cooked fish dinners in the area, while overlooking the river life and the hills of Lisbon. Floresta is reached by ferryboat, from Praça do Comércio or from Cais do Sodré. You can buy tickets right on the boat—someone comes around to collect the money.

The approach to the two-level dining room is by way of a long staircase, the walls covered with varieties of decoratively placed seashells. Owned by José Alves de Melo and his sons for more than 42 years, the restaurant draws a thriving family trade from right-bank Lisbon families, especially on Sunday afternoons.

While there is a complete menu of meat and fowl dishes, the fish sets the pace. The fishermen's stew, or caldeirada, at 250$ ($3.82) is a meal in itself. Another main course might be fried eels at 300$ ($4.59) or turbot meunière at 320$ ($4.90). A dessert favorite is manjor de príncipe, made of eggs and almonds, 55$ (84¢), although you can also order strawberries with sugar at 110$ ($1.68).

A few steps farther down the quay in Gijan are two restaurants for those on a tighter budget. Both are simple family places, with no frills.

At the **O Grande Elias,** next to the Floresta Restaurant, you can have a complete meal for only 320$ ($4.90) to 500$ ($7.65), including bread, wine, soup, a dish of eggs, fish, or meat, followed by cheese, fruit, or a dessert. Farther down the street, you come to **Gonçalves,** featuring a good oceanside view from the upstairs part, with a tourist menu for 310$ ($4.74), a gastronomic menu for 450$ ($6.89). Downstairs is a large dining room which seats eight at each table. À la carte entrees go for 200$ ($3.06) to 350$ ($5.36).

6. The Foreign Colony

Michel, 5 Largo de Santa Cruz do Castelo (tel. 86-43-38), is a good bistro-style French restaurant, with plenty of atmosphere and a hard-to-beat location right on the corner of a pocket-size plaza near St. George's Castle. The restaurant's a remake of three buildings: a barbershop, blacksmith's shop, and a wine tavern, all renovated and decorated in a tastefully rustic manner. Antique wood chests are used for coffee tables in the tavern portion, and a refectory table holding desserts stands in the walk-in fireplace. The skylight is canopy covered, and the walls contain everything from violins to zithers to stirrups and ceramics.

Star performer is the chef-owner, Michel, a youthful, energetic host with a keen eye for food preparation and service. Morocco born, Michel was trained in cooking in southern France. Now he has his own Julia Child–style cooking show on Lisbon television. At his restaurant he not only provides gourmet food, but seductive background music from a balladeer. The menu includes such items as French onion soup at 90$ ($1.38)—crusty with freshly baked cheese on top. Specialties include blinis with smoked swordfish at 380$ ($5.81); sole Don Fernando, 630$ ($9.64); and duck with green peppercorns, 510$ ($7.80). Closed Sunday.

Portas do Sol, 86 Rua de S. Tomé (tel. 86-16-33), is a leading French bistro restaurant, above the Alfama on a belvedere plaza. It's almost next to the Fundação Ricardo do Espírito Santa Silva and the Museum of Decorative Art.

Two arched windows open onto a bar-lounge, where most guests gather for an apéritif. The dining room invites with its rough white plaster walls, hand-carved tables, and high-back leather chairs. Even the cloths are handmade, a good background for deep blue floral dishes and ruby-red glasses. The kitchen is ruled over by a Frenchwoman, who, with the help of her family, turns out excellent dishes.

The main course might include a steak au poivre at 325$ ($4.97), or veal kidneys in a smooth, light-tasting cream sauce, 190$ ($2.91). To finish your meal, you may choose fresh banana flambé, 140$ ($2.14). After coffee, you can visit the boutique, then stroll over to the belvedere for a view.

Xangai (Shanghai), 20B Avenida Duque de Loulé (tel. 55-73-78), is a good Chinese restaurant near the American Embassy. An authentic cuisine is served here on green and pink plates imported from Macão. The setting is an impersonal one, with Oriental touches provided by the black and scarlet tasseled lanterns, the blue carpet, and lacquered screens.

As in most Chinese restaurants, dishes are best shared. Outstanding among the soups are bird's nest at 130$ ($1.99). Among the main dishes are hot-and-sweet shrimps at 180$ ($2.75), chicken and almonds at 210$ ($3.21), pork with green peppers and bamboo shoots at 200$ ($3.06), duck and pineapple at 225$ ($3.44), and shrimps with soy sauce at 310$ ($4.74). Especially tasty is a beef dish in an oyster sauce, 240$ ($3.67).

Desserts feature an apple dipped in an egg batter and fried, then served with a sprinkling of sugar, 70$ ($1.07). Be sure to order a pot of delicate jasmine tea, with blossoms floating on top.

Restaurante Macão, 37A Rua Barata Salgueiro (tel. 55-88-88), is centered in the swankier section of Lisbon, and is the oldest Chinese restaurant in the city. The dining room is highlighted by red pagoda pillars and bright tasseled lanterns that lend a certain authenticity. Fernando O, the bright multilingual son of the owner, was born in Macão. He manages the restaurant.

The menu is big, each dish numbered and translated into English. Both Peking and Cantonese cuisine are featured. Soup specialties include corn at 77¢ ($1.18). Egg roll is 70$ ($1.07). Dishes personally sampled and preferred include sweet-and-sour fish, 225$ ($3.44); lobster in a sauce (prices vary daily); a king-size prawn with lobster sauce, 395$ ($6.04). Nearly ten choices of dessert are offered, including a fried apple at 102$50 ($1.57) or fried bananas for the same price. The Macão is open from noon to 3:30 p.m. and 7 to 11 p.m. Closed on Sunday and for Monday lunch.

Dionysos, 124 Rua de Belém (tel. 64-35-35), is a Greek restaurant, and a good one, lying out in the suburb of Belém, the ideal place for lunch if you're visiting the nearby coach museum. The atmosphere is cozy, and because the tables, particularly at lunch, are always full, you may have to wait. However, once seated, you'll find the service friendly and efficient. A Greek salad for two costs 100$ ($1.53), or else you can order a mixed salad for just 90$ ($1.38). Souvlaki costs 210$ ($3.21), and homemade desserts average 95$ ($1.45).

Velha-Goa, 41-B Rua Tomás de Anunciação (tel. 60-04-46), evokes memories of the Portuguese empire. The Portuguese colony of Goa was forcibly annexed by India in 1961, but the aura still lingers on in this restaurant. The background is Oriental, but the cuisine is Goanese, and all dishes are prepared according to the taste of the diners—that is mild, pungent, and *very* pungent. House specialties include curries—prawns, chicken, Madrasta—but the chef also serves beef and pork chops in case you're dining with someone who doesn't like Indian food. Expect to pay about 350$ ($5.36) for a meal in the dining hall. The snackbar has been converted into a pub where you can enjoy a drink and listen to Indian or jazz music (live) on weekends. The meal begins with the appetizer, samuchas. The restaurant is open from noon to midnight, although you must arrive before 10:30 p.m.

7. The Special Spots

SHELLFISH, STEAKS, AND BEEF: Cervejaria Ribadouro, 155 Avenida da Liberdade (tel. 54-94-11), is one of the typical shellfish and beer emporiums in central Lisbon, midway along the city's major boulevard at the corner of the Rua do Salitre. There's a minimum of decor in this tavern-style restaurant, as the management thus far has steered clear of gimmicks.

Instead, the emphasis is on the varieties of fish offered. You select from more than 50 fish and meat dishes, highlighted by the crustaceans and "sea fruit" recommendations. Try the bacalhau (codfish) à Braz, 160$ ($2.45). You can dine lightly as well, particularly at lunch, ordering such plates as shrimp omelet for only 180$ ($2.75).

Many diners often follow fish with a meat dish. If so, a good choice is sauteed veal cutlets with mushrooms, 200$ ($3.06). However, only those who've been trained for at least 25 years on the most mouth-wilting of Indian curry should try the sauteed pork cutlets with piri-piri, the latter made with red hot peppers from Angola, 200$ ($3.06). A wedge of Portuguese cheese "from the hills" goes for 65$ (99¢) and finishes off the meal nicely.

Cervejaria da Trindade, 20-B Rua Nova de Trindade (tel. 32-35-06), is a combination of a German beer hall and a Portuguese tavern—the oldest of them all, owned by the brewers of Sagres beer. Here you can order tasty little steaks and heaps of crisp french-fried potatoes for 125$ ($1.91) per person. The meat is garnished with a dollop of country butter and a slice of aromatic lemon. Many of the Portuguese prefer bife na frigideira—that is, steak with a mustard sauce and a fried egg accompaniment, all in a clay frying pan. The tavern also features shellfish, which come from private fish ponds, and the house specialties are ameijoas (clams) à Trindade, 250$ ($3.82), and the giant prawns. To go with your main course, a small stein of beer costs 21$ (32¢). For dessert, a good selection is a slice of queijo da sêrra (cheese from the mountains) and coffee. This restaurant was formerly a convent and later on a brewery. Its walls, which resisted the 1755 earthquake, are tiled with Portuguese scenes, such as one depicting a sunburst, a cornucopia of fruit, tropical birds, and a gentleman holding a 17th-century stein. Meals are served in the inner courtyard on sunny days.

Cervejaria a Brilhante, 103 Rua Portas de Santo Antão, is where to go if you enjoy seafood with beer. Lisboans from every walk of life stop off for a stein of beer and mariscos. Opposite the Coliseu, the tavern is decorated with stone arches, wood-paneled walls, and pictorial tiles depicting sea life. You can dine either at the bar or at marble tables.

The front window is packed with an appetizing array of king crab, oysters, lobster, baby clams, shrimps, even barnacles. And they aren't cheap. The price changes every day, depending on market quotations, and you pay by the kilo. Among the fixed-price items, a steaming bowl of shellfish soup is 50$ (77¢); an order of baked codfish, 250$ ($3.82); a filet of sole, 340$ ($5.20); a fresh fruit salad, 60$ (92¢).

VEGETARIAN AND MACROBIOTIC: Restaurante A Colmeia, 110 Rua da Emenda (tel. 37-05-00), is a center of healthy eating and living. On the top floor of this corner building are two entirely separate kitchens and cuisines, both vegetarian and macrobiotic. In addition, you'll find a miniature shop where you can purchase such natural ingredients as nuts, raisins, herbs, even pastries and black breads.

You enter on the street floor through an old hall with a stone floor, then ascend scrubbed wooden steps, with old Portuguese tiled dado. The top floor has a narrow hallway lined with shelves of books dealing with metaphysics as well as healthful living.

Along one wall is a large menu board, with the offerings of the two cuisines, the dishes of the day, and, of course, the prices. Special plates range from 60$ (92¢) to 130$ ($1.99). A salad of the house costs 35$ (54¢); tea, 7$50 (12¢).

Through the open doors of the two kitchens you'll see the delicious and aromatic pastries. Three dining rooms, each with large windows, are decorated differently. One is in aqua with mystical paintings, another in the Moorish style with low cushions.

The restaurant is open from noon to 3 p.m. and from 7 to 8:30 p.m. On Saturday it closes after the 3 p.m. lunch and remains so on Sunday.

THE COFFEEHOUSES OF LISBON: How can one to go Lisbon without visiting one of the traditional coffeehouses? It's like a trip to England without four o'clock tea, or to Munich without a stein in a beer hall. To the Portuguese, the coffeehouse is an institution, a democratic parlor where they can drop in for their favorite beverage, abandon their worries, relax, smoke a cigarette, read the paper, write a letter, or chat with friends about tomorrow's football match or last night's lover.

The coffeehouse in Portugal is revered, although the older and more colorful ones with their turn-of-the-century charm are rapidly being replaced by the 20th-century world of chrome and plastic. According to the Portuguese, coffee from such places as Timor and Angola is the best in the world. They may be right, although its powerful flavor may not please the palate of percolator or freeze-dried devotees.

One of the oldest coffeehouses in Lisbon is **A Brasileira**, 102-A Rua Garrett (tel. 36-87-92), in the Chiado district. It's a 19th-century emporium, a favorite gathering place (today and yesterday) for the literati, who sit on its leather chairs and banquettes, sipping coffee from demitasse on tiny marble-topped round tables against a background of framed mirrors. A newspaper vendor wends his way through the crowd.

Outside, the street speaks of its past associations with men of letters. Garrett, a romantic dandy of the 19th century, was one of Portugal's leading poets (the street is named after him). The district itself, the Chiado, was named for another poet. On the square near the café a statue honors António Ribeiro, a 16th-century poet. Yet another poet, Bocage of Setúbal, used to frequent this coffeehouse. When once accosted by a bandit, he is said to have replied, "I am going to the Brasileira, but if you shoot me I am going to another world."

A demitasse of coffee, a bica, costs 35$ (54¢), including a tip, a small amount to pay for the privilege of savoring another era.

SNACKBARS, RITZ-STYLE: **Ritz Snack Bars,** 77-C Rua Castilho, is a three-level dining establishment within the Ritz Hotel compound, although it has a separate entrance facing the Edward VII Park. It wasn't long ago when it was an innovation for Lisboans to be served meals at a counter, but they are taking to it enthusiastically—enough so that they stand behind stools waiting for a vacant spot.

The same basic menu is used on each floor, featuring some Indian, Portuguese, and Italian specialties, including lasagne, 200$ ($3.06), and pizza, 200$ also.

On the separate and lengthy dessert menu, you'll find ten varieties of fruit salad, five kinds of cheese, seven different cakes, tarts, and puddings, and ten kinds of ice-cream delicacies, everything from Niagara at 110$ ($1.68) to Himalaya at 110$ also. And don't worry if the waiter doesn't speak English—the menu has photos of the dishes, so just point. The snackbar opens at noon and closes at 1:30 a.m.

Progresso, 2 Rua Barata Salgueiro (tel. 417-12), run by José Ricardo da Costa, who speaks some English, serves good food at inexpensive prices. You might choose his excellent febras de porcos (pork) Aljibarrota for 185$ ($2.83), or a portion of grilled espadon (swordfish) for 170$ ($2.60). Soups run for as low as 25$ (38¢), and there is a choice of desserts from 30$ (46¢).

THE ENJOYMENT OF PORT: **Solar do Vinho do Porto,** 45 Rua de S. Pedro de Alcântara (tel. 36-64-44), is a bar devoted exclusively to the drinking and enjoyment of port in all its known types. The choice is staggering, with nearly 100 wines from which to choose. The Solar is near the Bairro Alto, with its fado houses. In the rear of a large building, it offers a quiet and relaxing atmosphere, the feeling enhanced by an open stone fireplace.

Owned and sponsored by the Port Wine Institute, it displays many artifacts related to the industry. But the real reason for dropping in here during the day is for its *lista de vinhos*—you can have a glass (cálice) of extra-seco (dry) for anywhere from 20$ (31¢) to 195$ ($2.98).

READERS' RESTAURANT SELECTIONS: "A good restaurant is **Restaurante 111,** 111 Rua dos Remédios in the Alfama (tel. 87-53-53). The interior is decorated with horse pictures and rustic wood, and candles flicker at your table. Bacalhau com natas (cod) is superb at $6 (U.S.). Rosé and fresh fruit wines cost about $3. It was one of the best meals we had in all of Lisbon" (W. Michael Sharpe, Windsor, Ontario, Canada).... "We found a wonderful restaurant, **Tasca da Mafalda,** 14 Travessa do Guarda Mor (tel. 36-53-50). It has all the requirements of a good restaurant: tasty food, pleasing decor, friendly service. It also has what we appreciate, reasonable prices and an English-speaking waiter. One day we had shrimp croquettes for 170$ ($2.60); a large steak of espada, a delicious, unfishy-tasting swordfish, 190$ ($2.91); and sole for 240$ ($3.67). We liked this restaurant best of all the ones we went to in Lisbon. It's in the Bairro Alto section, just around the corner from the Misericórdia Church. The restaurant is owned by a Portuguese family which makes everyone feel welcome and very much at home" (Nelson and Dotty Gonsalves, Hayward, Calif.).

"Our highest praise goes to **Celta Restaurante,** 148 Rua Gomes Freire (tel. 57-30-69). We received attentive and personalized service. Our waiter offered to select our meal for us, and his choices were wonderful. After apéritifs, we dined on fish with rice and vegetable, followed by chicken (a specialty) with potato and vegetable, rosé wine, a sumptuous dessert (ice-cream soufflé cake), and coffee—all really excellent and all for only a well-spent 1500$ ($22.95). Budget-minded travelers should note that it is possible to dine here for less money very well. After dinner, we were served a complimentary Portuguese cherry liqueur" (Sandra A. Ciullo and Gary R. Donner, Brookline, Mass.). . . . **"Restaurante Isaura,** 4-B Avenida de Paris (tel. 88-08-38), has several tables on the ground floor, but the main dining room is in the basement. The atmosphere here is more subdued than in the typical budget-priced restaurant, which might make it more agreeable to North American visitors. The room is attractively decorated, with brick and colorful wine bottles and decanters. We had a well-prepared grilled codfish and the puffy, baked apples for dessert. Dinner for four, including four entrees, two soups, bread, a bottle of Dão wine, one beer, and four desserts, came to 1200$ ($18.36). Service is personal and excellent" (Kathleen M. James, Phoenix, Md.). . . . "We bumped into a restaurant called **Cervejaria Inglesa,** 42 Rua das Portas de St. Antão, very near the center (tel. 32-41-88). There we had a good seafood meal. Dishes cost from 200$ ($3.06) each" (Jerry Rosen, New York, N.Y.).

"Restaurante Clara lies in Campos Martires da Patria. It is in an old residence elegantly furnished in Louis XVI style. The entry, public dining area, and private areas are exquisite. A tiny bar as you enter invites you to explore further. The prices are fairly reasonable, the service is excellent, and the food is gourmet. Lunch costs about $10 (U.S.). . . . A restaurant near the Sheraton Hotel, **Restaurante Forno da Brites,** 75 Rua Tomás Ribeiro (tel. 54-27-24), has been in business for some 20 years. It is small but attractive with red and white tablecloths, excellent service, and reasonably priced food. Dishes are prepared at your table and served elegantly. The baby clams with pork are superb. Dinner prices range from $8 (U.S.) to $12 for a complete meal, including fish and meat dishes. The servings are more than ample and can be shared between two persons" (Marie Lindsay, Redondo Beach, Calif.). . . . "We would like to recommend a good Chinese restaurant which is near the Presidente Hotel, **Restaurante Hong Kong,** Rua Camilo Castelo (tel. 53-86-65). For about 600$ ($9.18) we had three different dishes with rice, mineral water, and coffee. Wines, of course, are also served although we didn't have any. Every dish we tried was fantastic and comparable to some of the good restaurants in Hong Kong and Singapore. The service was also good and prompt, with waiters who are willing to suggest especially good dishes if their advice is asked. For the price, we could not ask for a more satisfactory meal" (Bernadette Lim, Singapore).

"The most pleasant economy meal I had was at the **Manila,** 47 Rua 10 de Dezembro. This is a cluster of dining facilities, including an excellent cafeteria in the basement open for lunch, counter service on the street floor for lunch and dinner, and two more elaborate restaurants, plus ice cream and pastry counters. Three-course meals here come to less than $3 (U.S.) each" (Joan E. Edelstein, New York, N.Y.). . . . "You know how difficult it is to find a restaurant where you can get a real lunch, not a full dinner, in Portugal. **Via Marquês Restaurante/Bar,** 6-E Avenida Fontes Pereira de Melo (tel. 57-85-78), is a delightful place which we found on a rainy day in Lisbon when we didn't want to sit outdoors under a dripping awning. They offer the best salads, with an assortment of meats or fish, vegetables, and greens, all arranged in a most pleasing manner. It's definitely Portuguese food but with an unusual, light luncheon approach. It's open from 8 a.m. to midnight" (Mrs. Gordon R. Blakeney, Concord, N.H.). . . . "Almost diagonally across from the Flamingo Hotel at 41 Rua Castilho, there's a cafeteria called **Self Service,** 9 Rua Braamcamp, open from 8 a.m. to 10 p.m., which is good and reasonable. You can't miss it as it's right on the corner. Walk up one flight of stairs, then take the escalator to the next floor. The cashier speaks English and is helpful to visitors. There is a good selection of cold and hot dishes. I had a fresh tuna-fish salad with mayonnaise, lettuce, tomatoes, and other fresh greens for about $ 1.50 (U.S.), and the portion was so large it could be shared" (Ruth Gross, North Hollywood, Calif.).

Not all the best restaurants or hotels are in Lisbon, as you'll soon see in the chapter coming up.

Chapter VI

ESTORIL, CASCAIS, AND SINTRA

1. Estoril
2. Cascais
3. Oitavos
4. Guincho
5. Queluz
6. Sintra
7. Mafra Palace
8. Ericeira
9. Vale do Lobos

THE ENVIRONS OF LISBON are so intriguing that many fail to see the capital itself, so lured are they by the siren call of **Guincho** (near the westernmost point in continental Europe), the roar from the **Mouth of Hell**, the soft muted song from Lord Byron's "glorious Eden" at **Sintra**. Another day could be spent drinking in the wonders of the library at the monastery-palace of **Mafra** (Portugal's El Escorial), dining in and touring the pretty pink rococo palace at **Queluz**, or enjoying a shore dinner at the Atlantic beach resort of **Ericeira**.

However, the chief magnet remains the **Costa do Sol**, that string of beach resorts, such as **Estoril** and **Cascais**, that form the Portuguese Riviera on the northern banks of the mouth of the Tagus. In fact, if you arrive in Lisbon when the sun is shining, the air balmy, you should consider seeking lodgings along this cabana-studded shoreline. So near to Lisbon is Estoril that it's easy to dart in and out of the capital on sightseeing jaunts or fado sprees, while ensconced at a base in a hotel by the sea. An inexpensive electric train leaving from the Cais do Sodré in Lisbon makes the trip frequently throughout the day and evening, ending its run in Cascais.

The sun coast is sometimes known as A Costa dos Reis, the coast of kings, because of all the deposed royalty who have settled there—everybody from exiled kings, to pretenders, marquises from Italy, princesses from Russia, and baronesses from Germany.

These aristocrats may live simply, perhaps as a virtual recluse in an unpretentious villa, in the manner of the late Princess Elena of Rumania (Magda Lupescu); or they may insist on rigid court ambience, as does Umberto, the one-month king of Italy in 1946. Forced into exile when a plebiscite went against the monarchy, Umberto is well settled in Portugal. "He spends his days cataloging family medallions, art works and books, and playing with grandchildren," or so wrote Charlotte Curtis.

Tending his cows in "baggy trousers and muddy boots" in Sintra is the Count of Paris, the pretender to the throne of France. A descendant of Louis Philippe, he was the son of the Duke of Guise. In 1969, another pretender, Don Juan, the Count of Barcelona, was short-changed the Spanish throne in favor of his son, Don Juan Carlos, named by the late Generalísimo Franco as his successor. The older Don Juan is the son of Alfonso XIII, the former king of Spain who was forced into exile in 1931. At one time, the Count of Barcelona was an officer in the British navy and is today a noted yachtsman. Other nobility includes Joanna, the former queen of Bulgaria, and the Infanta Dona Maria Adelaide de Braganza, sister of the Portuguese pretender.

The Riviera is a microcosm of Portugal. Take the ride out on the train, even if you don't plan to lodge there. Along the way, you'll pass pastel-washed houses, with red-tiled roofs and facades of antique blue and white tiles; luxuriant vegetation such as rows of canna, pines, mimosa, and eucalyptus; swimming pools; and in the background green hills studded with villas and chalets.

ON THE WAY TO ESTORIL: Leaving Lisbon by electric train, our first stop along the Sun Coast is . . .

Oeiras

In the 18th century, this ancient town was considered one of the most beautiful spots outside of Lisbon. On the coastal road, about eight miles from the capital, it was selected by the Marquês de Pombal as the site of his petunia-pink country estate. The prime minister, of course, was the one who rebuilt Lisbon after the 1755 earthquake.

For many years, Pombal's palace housed artworks belonging to the Calouste Gulbenkian Foundation. Now that the foundation has its own sparkling museum in Lisbon, the estate is closed to the public and guarded by the military.

Most visitors head for Oeiras for surf and sandy beaches, anchoring in at the following medium-priced motel: **Continental Holiday Motel,** Estrada Marginal (tel. 243-11-86). It is the kind of seaside-resort-style motel that most North Americans will readily appreciate and understand. Unequaled is its prime position, sandwiched between the road to Estoril and long strands of beach along the rugged coastline. It's such a complete recreational zone that one may never go farther afield, preferring to swim in its free-form pools built into the rocks, with flagstoned terraces for sun-soaking.

Each of its cottages has its own front terrace, opening either onto the garden of flowers and pines or else onto an ocean view. The Continental is a self-contained colony, with a large-scale self-service restaurant, the Leopard Bar, a post office, a laundromat, and a host of recreational facilities, including boating, waterskiing, mini-golf, and a children's playground under the pines.

In a typical unit the space includes a sitting area, an adjoining sleeping section with single beds, a separate shower and bath, a kitchen with a refrigerator, and a car port. Some of the rooms contain balconies with two beds. Maid service is provided, as are linens and kitchen utensils. In high season, the rate in a double is 2200$ ($33.66). A single is 1800$ ($27.54) plus a 10% surcharge.

An additional person sharing the room pays 500$ ($7.65). From October 15 to March, 30% reductions are granted.

A short drive farther up the coast delivers us to . . .

Carcavelos

On the road between Lisbon and Estoril, this seaside town boasts the longest stretch of beach along the Costa do Sol. Often considered its gateway, it commands a view of the white Manueline-style Tower of Belém farther back.

Carcavelos was noted for its fortress, São Julião, which once held prisoner so-called left-wing radicals during the Miguelite wars. The fortress, with its pale yellow walls and curious turrets, is of a unique design that is attributed to the theories of Sebastien Le Prestre de Vauban, a French engineer.

The resort lies about 13½ miles outside of Lisbon and is easily reached on the electric train from the Cais do Sodré. Even if you don't go to Carcavelos, you may want to sample some of its full-bodied wine, praised by the Duke of Wellington.

The finest medium-priced accommodation there is provided by the following recommendation:

Hotel Praia-Mar, Quinta do Junqueiro, 16 (tel. 247-31-30). Everywhere you look there is a commendable blend of the best of contemporary architectural and furnishing design with Portuguese provincial. The all-glass walls, the wood paneling, the stark plaster are perfect foils for the assemblage of antiques and reproductions. The more expensive bedrooms facing the sea have terraces with garden furniture, ideal for suntanning or breakfast.

In the private rooms, old-style carved Portuguese beds, high wooden chests with black marble tops, intricate high-back chairs, black oak end tables, and handmade rag rugs tastefully adorn the units. The baths, one with every bedroom, offer plenty of soft towels and fixtures such as bidets. In high season, from March 1 to October 31, rates depend on the view and whether you have a terrace. In a single, the tariff ranges between $31 (U.S.) and $46.50 daily; for a double, anywhere between $39 and $54.50.

In the main lounge, islands of streamlined modern groupings of furniture, such as black leather and teak, abound. An adjoining bar containing antiqued mirrors and art nouveau sculpture opens onto a small patio with a fountain. There's even a boîte, as intimate as a pillbox, for disco dancing. A top-floor bar, paneled in walnut, invites lounging on its sleek brown and black armchairs. The vast, but personalized, dining room crowns the Praia-Mar, offering a panoramic view of the sea from almost every table.

The hotel is set back from the ocean and coastal road. Although many clients like to trek down to the public beach, others relax around the free-form swimming pool with its sun terrace. The electric train stop to Lisbon or Estoril lies about a two-minute walk from the entrance to the hotel.

Coming up, the King of the Costa do Sol.

1. Estoril

This chic resort along the Portuguese Riviera has long basked in its reputation as a playground of kings. Fading countesses arrive at the railway station, monarchs in exile drop in at the Palácio Hotel for dinner, the sons of assassinated dictators sunbathe by the pool—and an international joie de vivre pervades the air.

Once Estoril was a figment of somebody's imagination, a vision of Fausto Figueiredo, the founding father of the deluxe Palácio and the Casino. Before the First World War, Fausto Figueiredo envisioned hundreds of people strolling through the marble corridors and down mosaic sidewalks to the ocean as he gazed out over scrub pines and sandy hills.

Before the Second World War, Estoril was firmly entrenched in the resort sweepstakes. As Nazi troops advanced across Europe, many collapsed courts fled to Estoril to wait out the war in a neutral country. Word arrived daily from resistance movements, and hopes rose of regaining now-lost thrones.

The **Parque Estoril,** in the center, represents magnificent landscaping, a subtropical setting with the plants swaying in the breeze. At night when it's floodlit, fashionable guests go for a stroll. The palm trees studding the grounds have prompted many to call it "a corner of Africa." At the top of the park sits the **Casino,** offering not only gambling, but international floor shows, dancing, and movies.

Across the railroad tracks is the beach, where some of the most beautiful women in Europe sun themselves on the peppermint-striped canvas chairs along the Tamariz Esplanade. The atmosphere is cosmopolitan, and the beach is sandy, unlike the pebbly strand at Nice. If you don't want to swim in the ocean, you can check in at an oceanfront swimming pool for a plunge instead.

To the east is **São João do Estoril,** which also boasts a beach and many handsome private villas. Most visitors go here to dine and dance at **A Choupana** (refer to our nightlife recommendations).

FOR GOLFERS: In the foothills of Sintra, a three-minute drive from the Casino, lies the **Clube de Golf do Estoril.** An attraction for international sports figures, it offers a fairway set against a vista of pine and mimosa. The quality of the course is so acclaimed as one of the finest in Europe that it is selected for international championship matches. Both a 9-hole and an 18-hole course are offered. Guests play from around 7:30 a.m. till sunset daily. On weekdays, you'll pay a 800$ ($12.24) greens fee, 950$ ($14.54) on weekends and holidays. For 18 holes, a first-rate caddie charges 250$ ($3.82). You can also rent clubs and a locker. Guests of the Estoril Palácio Hotel are entitled to a 50% reduction on the above greens fees.

Estoril lies 15 miles west of Lisbon and is reached by an electric train from the waterfront Cais do Sodré. By private car, Estoril is approached either by the coastal road or an island route.

WHERE TO STAY IN ESTORIL: Estoril has several recommended accommodations from which to choose.

A Deluxe Hotel

Palácio Hotel, Parque Estoril (tel. 26-04-00), is legendary as a retreat for exiled royalty and as a center of World War II espionage. It scarcely seems possible that so much old-world elegance could have accumulated since 1930; but fast-breaking events, tumultuous happenings, and thronging international society telescoped its development and its prestige until it now has acquired a lustrous patina.

Its founding father was Fausto Figueiredo, and his descendants still own and run the hotel. At its debut, the Palácio received the honeymooning Japanese crown prince and his new bride. In time, other royalty would follow: Umberto of Italy; Don Juan, the Count of Barcelona. In World War II, when people escaped with a case of jewels and the clothes on their back, diamonds and rubies and gold were accepted instead of money.

The reception rooms are Pompeian, with sienna-colored marble pillars, bold bands of orange, and handmade carpets. Ideal for a tête-à-tête are the series of intimate communicating salons, with Wedgwood blue-and-white friezes on pilasters and walls, draped crystal chandeliers, and high arched windows with silk draperies. In the classic central drawing room, with black and white marble checkerboard floors, groups of antique furnishings are arranged for guests to have after-dinner coffee.

Dining is an event in one of the stateliest rooms along the Riviera. That jeweled choker or string of pearls, even the princess, is for real. The wine steward has a real working knowledge of his country's wines, quickly learning your tastes.

The bedrooms are traditional with fine furnishings, such as an occasional brass bed, always a desk, a marble-topped chest, and twin wardrobes. Bedside buttons summon a maid or valet, but somehow the staff has a radar understanding of when you need fresh towels. The baths are large and marble-faced, with bidets and heated racks. In high season, the single rate is 3500$ ($53.55); the double tariffs, from 6000$ ($91.80). Service, breakfast, and taxes are included. Full board is 4800$ ($73.44) daily in a single, 4300$ ($65.79) per person in a double.

Starting early in the morning, guests gather at the poolside terrace, overlooking the pool which is encircled by a reflection pool. A buffet luncheon is served on your chaise lounge or at a table beside a garland hedge of bougainvillea. The hotel opens onto the side of Estoril Park, capped by the Casino; the beach is only a short walk away. Golfers are given a free temporary membership in the local professional course at Estoril. Seven clay surface championship tennis courts are right next door to the hotel. Three courts are floodlit for nighttime play.

The Medium-Priced Range

Hotel Alvorada, 3 Rua de Lisboa (tel. 268-00-70), opened its doors late in 1969 to provide Iberian parador living on a small scale, opposite the Casino and the formally styled Estoril Parque. Just a three-minute trek from the sands, it is recommended to those desiring well-styled bedrooms and a walk-in private kitchenette, complete with refrigerator and cooking utensils.

Each room is furnished like a studio, with an open iron grille screen between the sleeping and dining sections. The highest tabs are for the rooms with views of the sea and park. In high season, the rate in a double is 2100$ ($32.13). Some of the above rooms are virtual suites and include a twin-bedded room, a sitting area, bath, kitchenette, and balcony. Four persons can book a super-suite with two bedrooms for 2800$ ($42.84).

The public rooms are personalized and well conceived. Off the reception area, the drinking lounge is decorated with modern Portuguese paintings and provincial-style furnishings. Breakfast, at 150$ ($2.30), is provided in the top-floor panoramic beamed-ceilinged room with its roof terrace, a setting enhanced by Portuguese artistry.

Hotel Cibra, Estrada Marginal (tel. 268-18-11), was built next door to its glamorous neighbor, the Palácio. Its nine floors with walls of glass soar high, about half the rooms boasting good-size balconies overlooking a view of the water and the Casino with its formal gardens. Only a minute or so from the seafront and the electric train station, it is in the center of Estoril's boutique district.

The upper-floor dining room provides unobstructed vistas of the sea and the nearby hills studded with villas. On many evenings a white-capped chef stands proudly in front of his specialty display table. In the marble-floored lounge and drinking bar, a good sense of contemporary design prevails, with plenty of museum-like space. Soft tufted leather chairs are gathered around marble-topped tables.

The bedrooms are not only trim, utilitarian, and uncluttered, but many have sitting areas, with wood-grained pieces. French doors open onto balconies in most of the rooms. All have shiny tiled private baths with a shower. Half board in high season, June through September, is 3900$ ($59.67) in a single, 3000$ ($45.90) per person in a double.

Lennox Country Club, 5 Rua Eng. Alvaro Pedro de Sousa (tel. 268-04-24), is a private hillside villa now converted into a small hotel. It has a special appeal for those interested in golf, with a great course almost next door, as well as for those interested in lounging. A circular garden swimming pool completes the perfect setting. Guests from Britain, America, and the rest of the world relax here, taking their meals, reveling in dips in the heated water, sunbathing, and enjoying the rock garden with its beds of red and gold cannas, banks of geraniums, and orange and purple bougainvillea.

The Lennox has a staff of 29 to look after just 32 guests, an example of the way in which the hotel gives first-class service.

The bedrooms are individually furnished, no two the same. All have private bathroom facilities and all but two have balconies. The living rooms are tastefully furnished, giving guests a "home away from home" atmosphere.

The hotel presents occasional film shows in the main lounge or throws a barbecue party with dancing afterward, all included in the daily rate, along with free unlimited wine, coffee, and tea. Prices start at 2450$ ($37.49) per person daily for half board.

Estalagem Claridada, 14 Rua Mouzinho de Albuquerque (tel. 268-34-34), is a hillside villa near that of the Count of Barcelona. Liverpool-born Dorothy Habbick and her Scottish husband George welcome you in one of their ten bedrooms, many of them decorated with antiques or traditionally styled reproductions. All accommodations have private baths. The half-board tariff for two persons is 3400$ ($52.02) in high season. One person pays 2250$ ($34.43) for half board. Some of the rooms contain terraces as well. Guests gather in the top-floor dining room to enjoy good meals, a view of the ocean, and later, the sunbathing terrace. In addition, at the small bamboo bar, you help yourself to drinks—it's the honor system here. From the center of Estoril, a taxi delivers you to the door.

READERS' PENSION SELECTIONS: "We stayed at the **Pansão São Mamede,** Estrada Marginal (tel. 268-15-41), across from the post office, for seven days. For half board, the rate is 1200$ ($18.36) for one person, increasing to 1800$ ($27.54) for two. There's a bar, plus a lounge with magazines. It's run by an Irishman who sees that it's kept very clean. It's a two-minute walk to the sandy beach" (Shelley Mills, Thetis Island, B.C., Canada). ... "Nowhere is there a more remarkable lodgings find than **Casa Smart** (tel. 268-21-64), a ten-minute walk from the beach. It's run by a delightful and inimitable young English woman, Tess Smart. With some of the rooms in this old, huge mansion permanently occupied by retired English persons, the atmosphere is very British. To savor it at its best, stay in for at least one evening and have a tasty and inexpensive dinner with Tess and her guests for only 300$ ($4.59). The eight or ten bedrooms are enormous, some with a view of the ocean, others looking out on the grounds, all quiet and with high ceilings. Ours had a sink and was next door to the bathroom. There are porches and terraces, a piano, and a relaxed, homey atmosphere. And all this costs 750$ ($11.48) a night for two, including a continental breakfast in bed. Tess, who is not shy about sharing her opinions, will also drive you to the airport for a charge less than the going taxi rate. Exact address is available at the tourist bureau" (David Mermelstein, Brooklyn, N.Y.).

ESTORIL/MONTE ESTORIL 69

STAYING IN MONTE ESTORIL: A satellite of Estoril, Monte Estoril lies directly to the west on the road to Cascais, half a mile away. Built across the slope of a hill and containing many moderately priced hotels, it opens onto a vista of Cascais Bay and the Atlantic beyond. In accommodations, the following are recommended:

The Medium-Priced Range

Grande Hotel, Avenida Sabóia (tel. 268-46-09), is a modern compound, just a few minutes up from the beach, next to the Hotel Monte Estoril. It offers seven floors of spacious rooms with private baths, about half of which have balconies large enough for breakfast and sunbathing. Guests relax and swim in its L-shaped pool opening off a cocktail terrace, with a view of eucalyptus and palm trees.

The air-conditioned main dining room is undistinguished, although adequate meals are provided. The large sitting room is popular, with a fireplace, built-in TV, and groupings of comfortable furniture. An international collection of visitors wanders into the open wood-paneled lobby and into the chestnut-fronted drinking lounge.

The bedrooms are furnished in blond moderno (bedside tables, chest-desk combinations), the severity lightened by simple color schemes of avocado or sunflower yellow and white. The hotel charges its highest tariffs from March 1 to October 31: 2600$ ($39.78) in a single, 3600$ ($55.08) in a double, taxes, breakfast, and service included. A continental breakfast is extra. Children under 8 are given a 50% reduction if they share a room with their parents. A few rooms have sitting areas, for which you'll pay more, of course. For a room and full board, the high-season tariff is 5200$ ($79.56) for two persons, including service and tax. The better rooms open onto sea views.

Zenith, 1 Rua Belmonte (tel. 268-02-02), is a six-story structure, with functionally designed rooms and lounge areas. The dining room is a little cramped, and there's a cocktail lounge on the top floor with a good view. With breakfast, a single rents for 1500$ ($22.95), going up to 2500$ ($38.25) in a double. On the full-board plan, two persons can stay here at a daily rate of 4200$ ($64.26).

Lido, Rua do Alentejo Estoril (tel. 268-40-98). The dominant decorative note is out-and-out modern and slightly aseptic, but comfort prevails throughout. This hotel charges 1400$ ($21.42) for a single room and breakfast, 2000$ ($30.60) for a double. A large swimming pool is its most attractive feature.

Hotel Atlântico, 7 Estrada Marginal (tel. 268-02-70), is a self-contained playground, almost directly on the sandy beach, that charges low tariffs. Travelwise visitors, who know how to reserve the best rooms in advance, get a lot for their escudos here. The hotel's separated from the beach by the electric train tracks from Lisbon. Its disadvantages are the whizzing coastal-road traffic in front, the clatter of the train in the rear. However, if you get a room high enough up facing the sea, you can be assured of quiet.

Between the lower floor of the hotel and the tracks is a wide sun terrace, with a seawater swimming pool. The dining room, built cave-like under the width of the hotel, has a view through an all-glass wall overlooking the pool and the sea. The lobby and lounges are dominated by hand-painted murals with a sealife motif.

The bedrooms are medium size and moderately well furnished, with built-in headboards, reading lights, telephones, Swedish-style desks and armchairs, and tiled baths and showers. The decor may not soar with individuality or high style, but it's restful, nevertheless, with many comforts installed. Accommodations are priced according to the view. High season lasts from March 1 to October 31, at which time the single rate is 2000$ ($30.60), including breakfast, with doubles going for 2200$ ($33.66) with breakfast. Two persons can take half board here for 3000$ ($45.90). Service and taxes are included.

The Budget Range

Miramar Hotel, 1 Avenida Sabóia (tel. 268-40-50), offers a well-preserved ambience. Surrounded by semitropical gardens, it is white framed, evoking a rambling turn-of-the century resort hotel. Set back peacefully from the ocean and the coastal road, it has installed a swimming pool with five tree-studded islets in the center of its little park. The Miramar is a pleasant change of pace along the Riviera. To quote an American woman: "I came here for a few days and stayed a month. I love it—and I've traveled everywhere. This is the best bargain I know."

The tabs of the rooms depend on the view and the plumbing, the more expensive ones opening onto the sea and containing private baths. Singles with bath go for 1100$ ($16.83), doubles with bath for 1750$ ($26.78). The price of three meals is 850$ ($13.01) per person extra. The rooms vary greatly in size, exposure, and furnishings. In all cases, however, they are well scrubbed, the decor homelike and comfortable. The best chambers on the front contain an adjoining room in a tower.

Access to the rooms is via an Iron Age elevator. Opening onto the front terrace, the main sitting room is decorated with overstuffed chairs covered in chintz and a few crystal chandeliers. Homemade meals are served in a room painted a churned-butter yellow, with a crisp white molding. You dine seated on old Portuguese handtooled chairs, studded with brass buttons. Open all year, the Miramar is centrally heated in winter.

Vale do Sol, in the Rua do Viveiro (tel. 268-33-85), is a modern apartment-house complex with accommodations for two or four persons. All are fully equipped with kitchenette, bathroom, terrace, TV, radio, and air conditioning. Cleaning service is available, and there are a supermarket, hairdresser, and restaurant on the premises. An apartment for two costs from 1400$ ($21.42) to 2200$ ($33.66), with single occupancy priced from 1100$ ($16.83) to 1600$ ($24.48). An apartment for four persons costs from 2300$ ($35.19) to 3200$ ($48.96). The prices depend on the time of year. The Vale do Sol is near the Hotel Londres.

WHERE TO DINE IN ESTORIL: **English Bar,** Estrada Marginal (tel. 26-12-54). Many couples come here just to watch the sunsets over the Bay of Cascais. Although its mock Elizabethan facade may lead you to think of steak-and-kidney pie and tankards of ale, the food is essentially Portuguese, and it's superb.

Try for a window seat in the handsome dining room, with its wide-plank floors, comfortable wood and leather-backed chairs. There are numerous English-style decorations: heraldic symbols, horsey prints, and bric-a-brac. From the à la carte menu, you can sample such pretested and highly recommended dishes as a savory créme de mariscos (cream of shellfish soup), 80$ ($1.22), or onion soup, 120$ ($1.84).

The chef's specialty is cherne na canoa, a turbot dish served with baby clams and a succulent sauce, 480$ ($7.34). In season you can order perdiz Sêrra Morena (roast partridge). An excellent dessert is a mousse made with nuts, 110$ ($1.68).

ESTORIL/CASCAIS 71

Tamariz, on Estoril Beach, is the most popular gathering spot on the beach. Bathing attire is not only permitted but encouraged. Some of the most attractive visitors on the Costa do Sol fill some of the most imaginative bathing suits from the boutiques of Europe. They sit for hours at canopied tables on a terrace projecting out toward the beach. Light fare and snacks are the order of the day. A hamburger costs 180$ ($2.75); combination plates, 220$ ($3.37); coffee, 40$ (61¢); and a milkshake, from 65$ (99¢) to 105$ ($1.61). Shower facilities and lockers adjoin, and the swimming pool is open all year. Service may be a bit slow, but who's in a hurry?

BETWEEN SINTRA AND ESTORIL: Sintra Estoril Hotel, No. 9 ão km. 6 (Junto ão Autodromo) (tel. 269-07-20), is a crescent-shaped hotel at a triangle of Sintra, Cascais, and Estoril. It looks on the outside like a stadium, with encircling balconies. It's not unlike a modern museum inside, with its bedroom balconies opening onto a large playground area and Olympic-size swimming pool, tennis and volleyball courts. Its lounges are varied, lofty, and warmly colored, with overscale furniture and a generous use of greenery. A few public rooms have drama, with shimmering mirrored walls, circular white sofas, or a wall of abstract sculpture.

Even the bedrooms have their own contemporary character, with built-in headboards, telephones, radios, and piped-in music. All have two double beds, air conditioning, a terrace, and tiled bath. In high season, a single rents for 1200$ ($18.36), rising to 2100$ ($32.13) in a double or twin. From mid-September until the end of March, major reductions are granted—from 1000$ ($15.30) in a single, from 1800$ ($27.54) in a double. For half-board, add another 500$ ($7.65) per person daily.

READER'S RESTAURANT SELECTION: "In Estoril São João we ate dinner several times at the **Mini Cafe** in the one shopping area in the town, near the railway station. It was quite inexpensive, and the food was always good. The young waiter knew some English, and the owner and chef worked for many years as head chef at one of the larger hotels in Estoril and certainly knows his profession. They offered to choose the kind of fish we wanted for dinner the next night on the beach at Cascais during the afternoon. It really could not be much fresher than that. One of their soups which I remember with longing for the recipe was soupa feijão, made of potato, cabbage, and beans, among other ingredients" (Mrs. Gordon R. Blakeney, Concord, N.H.).

2. Cascais

Back in the 1930s Cascais was a tiny fishing village, attracting artists and writers to its little cottages. But its history as a resort is old. In fact, it was once known as a royal village, because it enjoyed the patronage of Portugal's first family. Even when the monarchy died, the big brass moved in. Gen. António de Fragoso Carmona, president of Portugal until 1951, the man responsible for naming Dr. Salazar as minister of finance, once occupied the 17th-century fort guarding the Portuguese Riviera.

That Cascais is growing is an understatement. It's leapfrogging! At one entrance to the resort, someone penciled in the word "City" after Cascais. Although not officially recognized as such, it is well on its way. Apartment houses, new hotels, and the finest restaurants along the Costa do Sol draw a never-ending stream every year.

However, the life of the simple fisherman still goes on. Auctions, called *lotas,* at which the latest catch is sold, still take place on the main square, except a modern hotel has sprouted up in the background. In the small harbor, rainbow-colored fishing boats must share space with pleasure craft owned by an international set which flocks to Cascais from early spring until autumn.

The tie that Cascais has with the sea is old. If you speak Portuguese, any of the local fishermen, with their weather-beaten faces, could tell you that one of their own, Afonso Sanches, discovered America in 1482, that Columbus learned of his accidental find, stole the secret, and enjoyed the subsequent acclaim.

Cascais lies only 4 miles west of Estoril, 18 miles from Lisbon proper. It's reached by the electric train which begins its run at the Cais do Sodré waterfront station, ending it in the center of town, across from the Fim do Mundo (End of the World) restaurant. Trains leave every 15 minutes.

Many visitors, both foreign and domestic, drive out to Cascais on a road-clogged summer Sunday to attend the bullfights at the **Monumental de Cascais,** a ring outside the "city" center. A restaurant, **O Guizo,** has been installed underneath the spectator seats, so you can make plans to dine there before or after watching a *corrida.*

The most popular excursion outside of Cascais is to the **Boca de Inferno** (Mouth of Hell). Reached by heading out the highway to Guincho, then turning left toward the sea, the Boca deserves its ferocious reputation. However, if you should arrive when the sea is calm, you'll wonder why it's called a caldron. At their peak, thundering waves sweep in with such power and fury that they have long ago carved a wide hole, or boca, in the cliffs. The Mouth of Hell can be a windswept roar if you don't stumble over too many souvenir hawkers. Take a bus from Cascais station for 15$ (23¢).

WHERE TO STAY: Cascais has a number of accommodations in all price ranges.

The Top Hotels

Estoril Sol, Parque Palmela (tel. 28-28-31), is a luxury high-rise holiday world, perched on a ledge, with the coastal highway and electric train tracks separating it from the beach. It represents a dream come true for its late owner José Teodoro dos Santos, a self-made personality, who originally arrived in Lisbon with less than a dollar in his pocket. He also built a new casino at Estoril, and his work is now being continued by his children, headed by his son-in-law, Dr. Manuel Telles.

A modern land of resort living has been created: a gymnasium, an Olympic-size pool for adults, a smaller one for children, tennis courts, a complete sauna, a health club with squash courts and bowling alley, facilities for horseback riding, waterskiing, a shopping arcade, a garage and service station, and public rooms large enough for a great invasion of sun-seeking visitors.

The result was that the air-conditioned Estoril Sol ended up as the largest hotel in Portugal, with 400 bedrooms and suites overlooking the sea or the hills beyond. It boasts the largest dining room on the Costa do Sol, the most spacious main lounge (a traffic cop would be helpful here), the greatest number of bars (five in all), the most expansive veranda on the peninsula, and a beach reached by an underground passageway. More recently, a Grill Room has opened.

Already the roster shows such check-in names as Gloria Swanson, Omar Sharif, Melina Mercouri, Juliette Greco, and Prince Rainier and Princess Grace. Even Zsa Zsa Gabor has made one of her famous exits here. The designers have furnished the public rooms and bedrooms in a modified Miami

Beach style. The more expensive rooms have sea views and balconies. Naturally, every room has a complete tiled bath with gadgets.

Single rooms range in price from $60 (U.S.) to $75, doubles from $75 to $105. Lunch or dinner costs $20.

Estalagem Albatroz, 100 Rua Frederico Arouca (tel. 28-28-21). The wandering albatross, of course, is a bird noted as a master of gliding flight, capable of staying airborne on motionless wings for hours on end. What an appropriate symbol for what is perhaps the most delectable treasure on the Costa do Sol. Whether you're seeking food, lodgings, or both, the inn is your good luck choice.

Positioned out on a ledge of rocks, it is screened from the road by a garden. A neoclassic villa, it was built as a luxurious holiday retreat by the Duke of Loulé, then acquired in the 19th century by the Count and Countess of Foz. Sometime in this century it was converted into an inn, and in time received such guests as Anthony Eden, Cary Grant, Chief Justice Warren Burger, the Duke and Duchess of Bedford, Claudette Colbert, William Holden, Amy Vanderbilt, and the former queen of Bulgaria.

Your bedroom will either overlook the sea (you can hear the surf pounding on the rocks at night) or a quiet garden. The bedrooms are enjoyably furnished, with many comfortable pieces (all 16 rooms have private baths). There's a liberal sprinkling of good antiques throughout the chambers, plus paintings, bric-a-brac, and other decorative accessories collected from the corners of the earth. The prices of rooms fall into three categories, based on location, size, and view. Two persons can stay here and have full board (the food is one of the reasons for booking at the inn) for 5000$ ($76.50), including service and taxes. A room and breakfast for two costs 3500$ ($53.55). In a single, the cost of full board is 3200$ ($48.96).

In a small waterside garden, you'll find some white busts on pilasters, set in the midst of greenery, much admired by two former guests, Prince Rainier and Princess Grace. For a preview of the food, refer to our dining section in Cascais.

Hotel Cidadela, Avenida 25 de Abril (tel. 28-29-21). Architecturally and decoratively, this hotel is a citadel of high taste. Elegantly furnished in a restrained way, spacious in concept both in its private and public rooms, and gracious in its reception and amenities, it is emerging as the sleeper of the Sun Coast. Many Riviera-bound guests have deserted their old favorites for this holiday rendezvous.

Although you can reserve a first-class room, built into the central block with balconies, the Cidadela will also place you in womb-like comfort in one of its twin-bedded, terraced suites, or else in one of its apartment-like duplexes, the latter usually sheltering a ménage of anywhere from three to six persons. Priced at from 2000$ ($30.60) to 3600$ ($55.08) during peak season, a regular double is tastefully furnished, the white walls becoming foils for the vibrant plaids. The range in tariffs depends largely on the view. The rear rooms, sheltered from the noise of traffic are preferable.

Two wings of rooms and duplexes face a garden with a large open swimming pool, partially edged by a wading pond. The duplexes are as complete as an apartment: a living room, dining room, and a fully equipped kitchenette on the lower floor, with a staircase leading to the upstairs bedrooms, two or three each, with private baths. Each floor opens onto verandas with garden furniture. For four persons, these suites rent for 4500$ ($68.85), dropping to 3500$ ($53.55) if occupied by two. Service and taxes are included.

The three major public rooms are pleasantly decorated, the main living room with low modern groups of furniture in various primary colors. In the good-size dining room, the sturdy armchairs, upholstered with Portuguese fabric, seat many diners desiring top-quality cooking. You can take all meals here for 1000$ ($15.30) extra per person. However, nearby is a supermarket for those wanting to whip up their own concoctions.

The intimate bar is done in lipstick red with gray-blue armchairs and "medievalesque" helmets and breast plates. On the premises are a garage, a boutique, a hairdresser, plus a concierge skilled at arranging boating and fishing trips, tennis games, a day at the golf course, horseback riding, or a ticket for the bullfight. The hotel divorces itself from the hustle-bustle of summering Cascais, and is reached by heading out on a tree-shaded avenue, past restaurants, boutiques, and nightclubs.

The Medium-Priced Range

Hotel Baía, Estrada Marginal (tel. 28-10-33), sits on what many consider the best spot in Cascais. Its harborfront balconies (a premium at regatta time) and terraces are almost on the Praia da Ribeira, where fishing boats and yachts tie in. Built in 1962 at the hub of the resort, the hotel was constructed of rugged terracotta brick, rising four stories high and offering private sun balconies with 66 of its 85 bedrooms. The lower level, especially the sidewalk cafés, have blossomed into the social center of Cascais.

Informality reigns inside the Baía (bay). The roof-top terrace is large, good for sunbathing, and commands a view over the bay of Cascais.

The bedrooms are comfortably furnished in a modern style, all with private bath, telephone, radio, and glass doors opening onto balconies. In a single, the tariff is 1500$ ($22.95), including breakfast; for a double, 2500$ ($38.25) with breakfast. For full board, two persons pay 4200$ ($64.26), taxes and service included.

In a renovation program, all public rooms are improved: the lounge is now larger and more comfortable and the restaurant air-conditioned.

Estalagem do Farol, 7 Estrada da Boca de Inferno (tel. 28-01-73), is what is happening to the great old waterfront estates. They become waterfront restaurants or small hotels of character. This white building with three sun-catching bay windows and a surrounding garden with a swimming pool at the water's edge is now an inn. Dining is as important as the sea view here. Double rooms go for 1900$ ($29.07) daily with a mountain view, increasing to 2500$ ($38.25) with a sea view and balcony. In low season, these tariffs drop to 1500$ ($22.95) and 1900$ ($29.07) daily. Bedrooms have retained their original architectural character—paneled walls, plenty of space, and attractive furnishings. The atmosphere is congenial, especially in the wood-paneled and fishnet drinking lounge on the waterfront, where guests from Scandinavia, Germany, and England congregate for drinks.

The Budget Range

Albergaria Valbom, 14 Avenida Valbom (tel. 286-58-01), is right in the center of Cascais, providing 45 modern, comfortable rooms. There is little decor to speak of, but the prices are most attractive: single rooms cost 1300$ ($19.89), dropping to 900$ ($13.77) in off-season. Doubles go for 1800$ ($27.54) in season, 1000$ ($15.30) in winter. Breakfast is included, although no other meals are served.

WHERE TO DINE: Outside of Lisbon, this sprawling resort offers the heaviest concentration of high-quality restaurants in all of Portugal. Even if you're based in the capital, you should trek out to Cascais to sample the viands—both Portuguese and international dishes. Once you've tasted cognac-simmered lobster, mint-flavored shellfish soup, stuffed cuttlefish, shrimp pâté, even baked Virginia ham and southern fried chicken, you may become a total refugee from your hotel dining room.

Regrettably, from the customer's—not the owner's—point of view, many of the restaurants in Cascais tend to be overcrowded in summer, as they are so popular and quite reasonably priced. However, since many are excellent, press on to the next recommendation if you can't find a seat at your first choice. What follows is a wide-ranging survey of the best of the lot, in all price ranges.

The Top Choices

Estalagem Albatroz, 100 Rua Frederico Arouca (tel. 28-28-21), is considered the finest and most elegant restaurant in Cascais. The dining room is in the oldest part of the villa, built originally as a holiday retreat for the Duke of Loulé. Against a background of antiques, many celebrities have taken rooms here just so they can enjoy the cuisine. Portuguese and international cooking are featured.

On the à la carte menu, house specialties include cherne (turbot) à la marinière, 630$ ($9.64), and canard à l'orange, 600$ ($9.18). Dessert choices such as crêpes suzette, 390$ ($5.97), are offered. The wine cellar is varied and well stocked. Start your meal in the green room, a favorite of guests who enjoy its cozy ambience near the sea.

Restaurante do Pescador, 9 Rua das Flores (tel. 28-20-54). The name, The Fisherman; the lane, the Street of Flowers; and the proximity to the fish market may lead you to expect a simple café. But after you've smacked your lips at its caldeirada de lagosta com frango, you'll know differently. This savory concoction, on which the tab fluctuates daily, is made with fresh lobster and tender chicken, simmered in a base sauce of cognac and rum with the natural juices, then served in a crockery pot.

The decor is tavern-style, with hand-hewn beams, iron lanters, cork and wood paneling, lobster baskets, ships' models, smoked fish and meats, and strings of garlic, red pepper, and onions. Everything sets the mood for fine eating. An appetizing table in the front displays a mouthwatering selection of prepared foods, fruit, wines, and cheeses.

Features, of course, are the fish dishes. Even if you decide to forgo the house specialty, you may not want to pass up sopa marisco (shellfish soup) for 140$ ($2.14), which is prepared with a savory tomato base and flavored with a sprig of mint. Another recommendation is bacalhau (codfish) à pescador, 420$ ($6.43). Finally, another Portuguese dish is espeteda du lulos com gambras (shrimp), 580$ ($8.74).

The owner, Ramiro Lueiano Pinto, has his own nursery at Guincho, near the Cabo Raso Lighthouse, where his collection of lobster, crayfish, and other mariscos are tended to. Attracted to his Fisherman are a host of well-known personalities. The café serves till midnight.

The Medium-Priced Range

Reijos Restaurant, 35 Rua Frederico Arouca (tel. 28-03-11). First, you should be warned that it's likely to be crowded, and that you'll either have to wait for a table or abandon all hope in high season. This intimate, informal bistro is that good. The fine foods of two countries, the United States and Portugal, are combined on the menu, and the result is altogether pleasing. An

American citizen, Ray Ettinger, who is a purser for a transatlantic airline, has teamed up with a Portuguese, Tony Brito, pooling their talents in the running of this successful enterprise. Often, Mr. Ettinger brings in hard-to-get items by airplane.

At times, to the homesick Mr. Ettinger, nothing is more delectable than roast beef à l'inglese, 280$ ($4.28), or baked Virginia ham, 250$ ($3.82), with cole slaw, 70$ ($1.07) extra. Other popular items include lobster thermidor at 650$ ($9.95); beef Stroganoff, 280$ ($4.28); pepper steak, 395$ ($6.04); and shrimp curry, 360$ ($5.51). From Macão, two Chinese dishes are prepared at your table: beef with garden peppers at 270$ ($4.13) and shrimp and cucumbers at 380$ ($5.81). Unlike many European restaurants, Reijos serves fresh vegetables at no extra cost with its main dishes. In addition, it has an outstanding selection of desserts made on the premises from fresh seasonal ingredients. Lunch is served from 12:30 to 3:30 p.m.; dinner, 7 to 11 p.m. (telephone first). The service from the young staff is excellent.

Restaurante "O Batel," 4 Travessa das Flores (tel. 28-02-15), fronts the fish market. It's giving the better restaurants of Cascais quite a scare, as it is real competition. Styled as a country inn, it doesn't overdo with touristy gimmicks. The atmosphere is semirustic, with rough white walls and old beamed ceilings. The light filters in through bottle glass onto a collection of fishing-boat models. A display indicates the ingenuity of the chef, his wares enhanced by a basket of figs, plums, peaches, and fresh flowers.

The prices are reasonable, and that, balanced with the superb viands, explains why the tiny tables are usually filled at every meal. Lobster thermidor and lobster stewed in cognac are the house specialties, but the price on these items changes daily. For something less expensive, I recommend Cascais sole with banana, 350$ ($5.36); a savory dish, clams with cream, 330$ ($5.05); and mixed shellfish with rice, 900$ ($13.77). For an appetizer, you can try prawn cocktail, 400$ ($6.12). To complete your meal, if you're still hungry, such desserts as pineapple with Madeira wine, 150$ ($2.30), and crêpes suzette, 450$ ($6.89), are offered. *Wine tip:* Order a Casal Mendes rosé, a cool choice.

Restaurante Gil Vicente, 22–30 Rua dos Navegantes (tel. 28-20-32). This is the kind of bistro you usually find on a back street in a town along the Côte d'Azur. Set on the rise of a hill above the harbor, it was converted from a fisherman's cottage. Both the cuisine and the ambience reflect the mood of its owner, who sees to it that excellent dinners are served at candlelit tables. Lunch isn't offered, but dinner is likely to extend until the early hours of the morning.

The name of the tavern, Gil Vicente, honors a 16th-century writer who is sometimes considered the father of Portuguese drama, a virtual Iberian Shakespeare if you will. In spite of his lyricism, the decor of the restaurant is simple—a setting of plaster walls, an old stone fireplace, windows recessed with pots of greenery. To spice up matters, an ornate iron washstand has been adapted for condiments, and the walls contain heads of old iron bedsteads, now gaily painted.

You're likely to be won over by the cooking (pâté, crêpes, shellfish, or grilled chicken and steaks)—and the reasonable tariffs. To whet your appetite, try the assortment of hors d'oeuvres; the pâté maison, 125$ ($1.91); or the bisque of shellfish, 55$ (84¢). At least three main dishes hit the mark every night: sole Colbert, priced according to weight; coloin grillé, 300$ ($4.59); and grilled steak with mushrooms, 350$ ($5.36). Among the desserts, you can settle for a fruit salad or a chocolate mousse at 45$ (69¢), or a banana flambé at 100$ ($1.52).

The John Bull (Brittania Restaurant), 4-A Largo Luís de Camões (tel. 28-01-54). With its black and white timbered Elizabethan facade and an owner nicknamed Kim, you'd expect a wedge of Merrie Old England. But it's merely a mock-up, and the owner Mr. Couto is Portuguese. However, he's imported many of the trappings from England to create, or rather to recreate, the atmosphere. The restaurant is open from noon to 4 p.m. and from 7 p.m. to midnight.

In the street-floor pub, the John Bull, you can order an iced pint of lager. The setting is appropriate—wood paneling, oak beams, a fireplace, crude tavern stools and tables, pewter pots, and ceramic jugs.

The meals at the second-floor Britannia Restaurant feature a medley of English and Portuguese, even American, dishes. A rarity on any Portuguese menu is American southern fried chicken, 275$ ($4.21), and T-bone steak at 440$ ($6.73) is another familiar Yankee favorite. For English tastes, specialties include calves' liver, bacon, and french fries, 320$ ($48.96). A winning dessert is a homemade cake, 90$ ($1.38), or vanilla ice cream for the same price.

O Guizo, Praça de Toiros (tel. 28-34-34), is built right into the lower tier of the Cascais bullring. Not by accident, it is a favorite choice with both Portuguese and Spanish matadors, who often meet their friends here, celebrating victories or cheering themselves up after defeats. The restaurant is colorfully styled with bullfight memorabilia, cart wheels, blue plates, brightly hued oxen tassels, and copper pieces. The atmosphere is enlivened with tablecloths in red, turquoise, and yellow, around which red cowhide-covered chairs are placed.

The chef proclaims that he prepares "the real Portuguese food," as opposed to the standard restaurant fare. The menu changes daily, but examples of what he means are provided by such dishes as soup du jour at 40$ (61¢) or a rich-tasting chicken and rice soup for 75$ ($1.15). Leading off the grandes especialidades of the house is bacalhau (salted codfish) que nunca chega, 190$ ($2.91), and a roast veal, 220$ ($3.37). For dessert, select the cake of the house at 55$ (84¢), or a pudding made of eggs and coconut for the same price. Joaquim Caetano, who owns the restaurant, especially recommends the sauteed pork with rice to his American friends. In the evenings, there's often dancing to records, sometimes as late as 3 a.m., although the restaurant usually closes at midnight. Lunches are served only on Saturday and Sunday.

Salinha Saloia, 14C Rua da Palmeira (tel. 28-61-17), is a cozy, bistro-like place with candles and flowers on all tables, and a rustic Portuguese decor. The charming surroundings are completed by top-notch meals. Best here is the açorda de marisco (grated peasant bread, baked with a raw egg, spices, and seafood) for 260$ ($39.78), or a charcoil-broiled chicken, 220$ ($3.37). Another good selection is the ham and mutton, 205$ ($3.14), a fine beginner.

Farta Pão, Estrada da Malveira (tel. 28-05-68), was originally a barn that has been converted into a restaurant, an ideal setting for country dining. The name of the restaurant means "more you cannot eat." The large barn-like dining room has two huge open fireplaces, tiled floors, and rustic ornaments such as pitchforks, strings of garlic, hoes, and pots. Outside is a terrace with more tables for al fresco dining.

You can start off your repast with a seafood soup for 100$ ($1.53). Grilled sea bass goes for 250$ ($3.82), but the specialty is sargo da roca (white sea bass) which costs 300$ ($4.59) for two persons. You can finish off with an orange pudding at 42$ (64¢). The house wine goes for 100$ ($1.53) a bottle. To find the Farta Pão, take the road to Malveira da Sêrra for about 2½ miles, then turn left down a short dirt road when you see the sign on the right reading Cacos Velhos.

Snobissimo, 12 Rua Xavier Palmerim (tel. 28-21-25), is an art nouveau dream come true. It's a fun place for drinks and meals. The restaurant is so packed full of curious items and decorations that it takes half the evening just to look at everything. One room is a complete library; another has its walls covered with photographs of habitués. Within its rooms, on two floors, is a wealth of old mahogany, marble, and overscale art nouveau sculpture. An aged bronze cash register clanks out your payment. Upstairs is a fabulous fin-de-siècle cocktail lounge and bar, with bronze statues, cartoons, and photos of celebrities. One table is actually made out of an old roulette wheel. The owner, Paulo Guilherme, is an interior decorator.

As for meals, onion soup goes for 115$ ($1.76); a special salad, 125$ ($1.91); fish of the day, 180$ ($27.54); and tournedos, 420$ ($64.26). For dessert, have the crêpe satanic, 110$ ($1.68). At night if you want to enjoy the dancing, expect to pay from 200$ ($3.06) for a whiskey, 100$ ($1.53) for a beer, or 90$ ($1.38) for soft drinks. A minimum of 100$ ($1.53) is required.

The Budget Range

Estribinho, Largo das Grutas (tel. 28-19-01), is a success story. This rustic tavern, offering some of the best yet least expensive food in Cascais, is the fulfillment of the dream of one of two partners, Cezar Pereira and Fernando Jorge da Cruz Antunes. Originally, Senhor Pereira had gone to America to seek his fortune, becoming a marine captain in World War II, seeing action in Japan. Later, he returned to his home country to create this little restaurant, which surrounds his guests with Portuguese symbols of good country eating.

Hanging from the ceiling are garlands of onions, strings of peppers, pigtails of garlic, smoked sausages, pineapples, and glass steins. There's a rough wooden dado, with many nooks for intimate dining,. Offering two levels, it's just off a little square to the right of the leading movie house of Cascais.

The menu is extensive. A soup of the day is always featured at 50$ (77¢), and you can try the chef's delicacy, shellfish soup, also for 50$. A good main dish is the tournedos, 280$ ($4.28). The meat and poultry dishes are served with vegetables. The shellfish, especially the freshly gathered clams at 380$ ($5.81), are also well recommended. Each day a special dessert is offered. For a change of pace, why not try the house sangría? The Estribinho is open most of the time: from 8 a.m. till 4 a.m., a fine choice for off-hours snacks. Closed Thursday.

Costa Azul, 3 Rua Sebastião José de Carvalho e Melo (tel. 28-11-40). The Blue Coast is likely to attract the natives of Casais, not just visitors. A blackboard standing out front announces the special regional fare of the day. The restaurant is usually crowded with hungry diners, and it may be difficult to get a table. All the typically Portuguese trappings are here, including pineapples, pigtails of garlic, and sprigs of bay leaf hanging from the ceiling. Often featured are clam soup at 50$ (77¢); pork Alentejano, 200$ ($3.06); bacalhau (cod) à Costa Azul, also 200$; lombinhos (pork steak with a special sauce), 240$ ($3.67); and shrimp with piri-piri, 280$ ($4.28). Closed Tuesday.

READERS' RESTAURANT SELECTIONS: "Os Doze Restaurante, 71 R. Frederico Arouca (tel. 28-53-34), offers some of the best food in Portugal. We especially liked the appetizer, avocado stuffed with shrimp sauce for 200$ ($3.06), and the oxtail soup at 48$ (73¢) was also tasty. My husband and I feel whatever your selection you'll find it well prepared. The service is good also, as is the selection of wines. If you have trouble making up your mind, the proprietor Mr. Baptista will make it up for you. He's a gem and makes everybody comfortable. The cavern-like restaurant is small, with a lounge in front. Port-oysters cost 125$ ($1.91) for six; turtle soup, 70$ ($1.07); chicken curry, 135$ ($2.07); pork chops, 165$ ($2. 53); and a good house wine, only 50$ (77¢) for a half bottle. It's closed Wednesday" (Mr. and Mrs. James Borsil, Chicago, Ill.).... "Alaúde is a good place to eat economically in a town where many restaurants have become overpriced. It has only 12 tables, most of which were filled by local Portuguese people. We had soup, fish with rice and vegetable, mineral water, coffee, and dessert for 850$ ($13.01). Everything was very good. Alaúde is centrally located on a small street behind the Hotel Baía" (Sandra A. Ciullo and Gary R. Donner, Brookline, Mass.). . . . "Just opposite the railway station in Cascais there is a large **supermarket.** You can't miss it, as it has a large parking lot with carts, American style. The prices are surprisingly reasonable, and you can buy food items for picnicking as well as accessories for the beach. I might add that it is a nice walk along the beach from Estoril to Cascais, scenic and with no traffic at all" (Ruth Gross, North Hollywood, Calif.).

3. Oitavos

Restaurante de Oitavas, Estrada do Guincho (tel. 28-92-77), is reached by a winding road. You arrive at a restaurant and teahouse on a plateau with a view of the coast. In the background loom the hills of Sintra. The restaurant is in the modern style, designed with glass walls to show off the view. The cuisine features regional fare. You might begin with a shrimp cocktail at 400$ ($6.12) or perhaps grilled sardines at 180$ ($2.75). For a main dish, it's best to stick to the fish dishes. Sole is prepared in an interesting number of ways, costing 400$ ($6.12). Frango (chicken) à piri-piri at 200$ ($3.06) is the "hottest" item on the menu. Among the desserts, the most lavish is a banana flambé at 80$ ($1.22).

4. Guincho

Guincho means caterwaul, screech, shriek, yell, the cry that swallows make while darting among the air currents over the wild sea. These swallows at Guincho are to be seen all year, unlike their fickle fair-weather counterparts at San Juan Capistrano, California. Sometimes at night the sea, driven into a frenzy, howls like a wailing banshee, and that, too, is guincho. The settlement is near the westernmost point on the European continent, known to the Portuguese as **Cabo da Roca.** The beaches are spacious and sandy; the sunshine incandescent; the nearby promontories, jutting out amid white-tipped Atlantic waves, spectacular. The windswept dunes are backed by wooded hills, and to the east the Sêrra de Sintra is silhouetted upon the distant horizon.

The **Praia do Guincho** draws large beach crowds each season. However, it's wise to keep in mind the advice of Jennings Parrott, writing in the *International Herald Tribune:* "If you are caught up by the current, don't fight it. Don't panic. The wind forces it to circle, so you will be brought back to shore." A local fisherman, however, advises that you take a box lunch along. "Sometimes it takes several days to make this circle." The undertow is treacherous— be forewarned.

Guincho lies about four miles from Cascais, about six from Estoril. To reach it, you have to either drive or take a bus from Cascais. One of the primary reasons for coming to Guincho is, of course, to sample its seafood restaurants, described below. You can try, for example, the crayfish-size, box-jaw lobsters known as *bruxas,* which in Portuguese means sorcerer, wizard, witch doctor, even a nocturnal moth. To be totally Portuguese, you must also sample the barnacles, called *percêbes,* meaning to perceive, to understand, to comprehend. After devouring these creatures, many foreign visitors fail to comprehend or perceive their popularity with the Portuguese. The fresh lobsters and crabs are cultivated in nearby shellfish beds, a fascinating sight.

If you're staying over at one of the recommendations described below, the night calls of the "sirens" may enrapture you.

THE UPPER BRACKET: Hotel do Guincho (tel. 285-04-91) is a remake of a 16th-century fortress, standing on a rocky coast, not far from Cabo da Roca. Orson Welles once stayed here, fascinated by the mist and the surging roar of waves as they dashed against the stone cliffs.

You enter through a cloister-like arcaded courtyard, with a four-sided balcony and four stone water wells. The one-time arsenal that once quartered troops now has deluxe bedrooms, all with private baths. The individualized bedrooms echo the castle's various architectural features: arched, deeply set windows, stone or plaster walls, plus a combination of antiques or reproductions. The charge is from 2900$ ($44.37) to 3500$ ($53.55) in a single, from 4000$ ($61.20) to 5250$ ($80.33) in a double, depending on the season.

There are several lounges, each richly decorated. To dine, you enter a spacious ocean-view room, with hand-embroidered draperies, high-backed chairs, and an overscale antique armoire. The food and service are excellent. Lunch costs 875$ ($13.39); dinner, 1000$ ($15.30).

THE MEDIUM-PRICED RANGE: Estalagem Muchaxo, Praia do Guincho (tel. 285-02-21), was begun more than 30 years ago as a simple straw hut set up on rugged wave-dashed rocks, with the father of the present owner selling brandy and coffee to the fishermen. Gradually, the senior Muchaxo started to cook for them. In time, beach-loving Germans discovered the place, and eventually even royalty, such as ex-king Umberto of Italy, arrived wanting to be fed.

Nowadays, the new has absorbed the old, although the straw shack remains to please traditionalists. António Muchaxo and his sons operate this overblown hacienda, placing emphasis on the rustic blended with a mild dose of the contemporary. The Estalagem is rectangular-shape, with windows of bedrooms overlooking either the courtyard or the nearby coast and hills. At one side, thrust out onto rock walls, is a swimming pool with terraces and diving boards.

After a day of swimming, guests gather in the chalet-style living room to warm themselves at the huge raised stone fireplace. They use a natural stone milling wheel as a coffee table and relax in rattan chairs brought in from Madeira.

There's a choice of two dining rooms, one modern, the other with bamboo ceiling, staccato black and white covered tables, and hand-painted provincial furniture. People drive from miles around just to sample the Muchaxo culinary wares, highly praised by such discriminating Iberian travelers as author James A. Michener.

The adventurous will begin their meals with barnacles, described previously. The house specialty is lobster, Barraca style, but the price is likely to change daily. An order of grilled sea bass is decidedly less expensive at 500$ ($7.65). A dish worth recommending is the chateaubriand at 450$ ($6.89). However, unless your throat is lined with asbestos, avoid ordering the chicken with piri-piri sauce made with hot pepper from Angola. One diner is said to have fainted after tasting this concoction. An excellent finish to a meal here would be banana fritters, 80$ ($1.22).

Those who want to anchor in will find a choice of 24 rooms in three price ranges—the most expensive directly overlooking the sea, the middle price group with side views of the ocean, and the cheapest facing the blue-green hills on the horizon. A single goes for 1970$ ($30.14) nightly. Two persons can stay here and take all their meals for 4170$ ($63.80) daily. All rooms have private baths, telephones, and central heating.

Each bedroom is unique, although most of them have basic stark white walls with beamed ceilings. Original use is made of provincial hand-painted furniture and accessories. Carved ox yokes serve as headboards for the beds, and the floors are spotted with black and white calfskin rugs.

Mar do Guincho Estalagem, Praia do Guincho (tel. 285-02-51). While this modern inn contains relatively inexpensive bedrooms, its success stems from its superb kitchen. The owners can look with pride at a plaque from *Holiday* magazine honoring their establishment as one of the most outstanding in Portugal.

The stone inn is simple, uncluttered—rather starkly modern—set on a low cliff, with its bedrooms and dining room facing the pounding surf. From the à la carte menu, you can order freshly made shrimp soup for only 70$ ($1.07). Oysters are sometimes difficult to obtain, but when they appear on the menu, they go for 30$ (46¢) apiece.

Shellfish is the house specialty, although the prices are beyond the means of many diners. However, you can order shrimp, barnacles, stuffed crab, grilled lobster, and panada, a very good local shellfish. The sweet-tasting, freshly caught clams—served in their natural state—will cost 300$ ($4.59). Meat eaters will find an excellent pork Alentejano (with clams), also for 300$. A wide range of fruits from the Portuguese heartland is offered for dessert, along with such desserts as almond cake, 80$ ($1.22).

Sea-view double bedrooms cost 2350$ ($35.96), with breakfast included. Slightly cheaper rooms are available sans sea view. The bedrooms contain private baths and balconies. If you're tempted to stay here, you'll dine well, living informally in casual attire, sunbathing, playing in the surf, and falling asleep listening to the constant rhythm of the waves breaking on the rocks below your balcony.

READER'S RESTAURANT SELECTION OUTSIDE CASCAIS: "The **Adega Crossas Restaurant** lies outside Cascais in Areia, Guincho (tel. 28-99-60). It serves tasty food at reasonable prices. They always offer what one person called 'white lightning,' a very strong licorice-flavored brandy, following dinner. It's a perfect ending to a good meal" (Mrs. Gordon R. Blakeney, Concord, N.H.).

Back in Lisbon, we strike out this time on quite a different excursion:

5. Queluz

On the highway to Sintra, 9½ miles from the capital, Queluz shimmers in the sunlight, a brilliant example of the rococo in Portugal. An evocation of the 18th century is effected by the faded cotton-candy decoration, inspired in part by Versailles.

Pedro III ordered its construction in 1747, and the work dragged on until 1787. The architect Mateus Vicente de Oliveira was later joined by French decorator and designer Jean-Baptiste Robillon. The latter was largely responsible for the planning of the garden and lakeland setting, through which the promiscuous queen Carlotta Joaquina, with her beet-colored nose jutting forth, raced to her next indiscretion.

A fire in 1934 destroyed a great deal of Queluz, but tasteful and sensitive reconstruction has restored the light-hearted aura of the 18th century.

The topiary effects, with closely trimmed vines and sculptured box hedges, are highlighted by blossoming mauve petunias and red geraniums. Lavender, purplish-red porphyry, and pink are the colors on the palette. Fountain pools on which lilies float are lined with blue azulejos (earthenware tiles), reflecting the muted facade, the statuary, and the finely cut balustrades.

Inside, you can wander through the dressing room of the queen, lined with painted panels depicting a children's romp; stroll through the Don Quixote Chamber (Dom Pedro was born here and returned from Brazil to die in the same bed); pause in the Music Room, complete with a French grande pianoforte, an 18th-century English harpsichord, and a gilded sacrificial patera; and stand in the mirrored throne room adorned with crystal chandeliers. In the way that the Spanish use La Granja, the Portuguese still hold state banquets here.

Festooning the palace are all the eclectic props of the romantic era—the inevitable chinoiserie panels (these from the Portuguese overseas province of Macão); Florentine marbles from quarries once worked by Michelangelo; Iberian and Flemish tapestries; Empire antiques; indigo blue ceramics from Delft; 18th-century Hepplewhite armchairs; porcelains from Austria; carpets from Rabat; Portuguese Chippendale furnishings; and wood pieces (jacaranda) from Brazil—all of which are of exquisite quality. When he visited Portugal, the late President Eisenhower was housed in the 30-chambered Pavilion of D. Maria I, as was Queen Elizabeth II on another occasion. These storybook chambers, refurbished by the Portuguese government, are said to have reverberated with the rantings of the grief-stricken mad monarch Maria I, who, it is alleged, had to be strapped to her bed at times.

The admission to the palace is a well-spent 10$ (15¢); the hours are from 10 a.m. to 5 p.m., except on Tuesday when it is closed. From Lisbon, you can visit Queluz by a train departing from the central station at the Rossio.

DINING IN AN 18TH-CENTURY KITCHEN: Cozinha Velha (Old Kitchen), Palácio Nacional de Queluz (tel. 95-02-32). If you have only two or three meals in all of Portugal, take one of them here. Once it was the kitchen of the palace, built in the grand style; now it has been converted into a colorful dining room that finds favor with gourmets, royalty, and the average visitor seeking a romantic setting for a fine dinner.

The entrance is through a garden patio. The dining room is like a small chapel, with high stone arches, a walk-in free-standing fireplace, marble columns, and the original spits. Along one side is a 20-foot marble chef's table that's a virtual still life of the culinary skill of the chef, augmented by baskets of fruit and vases of flowers. You sit on ladderback chairs in a setting of shiny copper, oil paintings, and torchères. And the trained waitresses are costumed in regional dress.

Fortunately, meals are served seven days a week (luncheon, noon to 3 p.m.; dinner, 7:30 to 10 p.m.). We'd suggest the hors d'oeuvres for two persons at 470$ ($7.19), followed by such recommendable main courses as filet steak, 475$ ($7.28); poached sea bass, 400$ ($6.12); grilled pork on a spit, 325$ ($4.97); or whiting with capers, 360$ ($5.51). To finish, you might try the Serpa cheese, at 130$ ($1.99), or else a vanilla soufflé for two persons, 370$ ($5.66).

6. Sintra

"It is indeed a fairytale setting and gives one the feeling that this is where Sleeping Beauty must have rested all those years." These were the words of a publicist singing the praises of Sintra. Writers have been doing that ever since Portugal's greatest poet Luís Vas de Camõës proclaimed its glory in *Os Lusíadas* (The Portuguese).

Lord Byron called it "glorious Eden" when he and his companion John Cam Hobhouse included Sintra in their grand tour of 1809. Subsequently,

English romantics thrilled to the description in the poet's autobiographical *Childe Harold*.

Picture a town on a hillside, decaying birthday cake villas covered with azulejos coming loose in the damp mist hovering like a veil over Sleeping Beauty. What would Sintra be without its luxuriant vegetation? It's all here: camellias for melancholic romantics, ferns behind which lizards dart, pink and purple bougainvillea crawling over garden trelliswork, red geraniums sitting out on wrought-iron balconies, eucalyptus branches fluttering in the wind, lemon trees studding the groves, succulent strawberries weighing down plants in the surrounding countryside, and honey-sweet mimosa scenting the air.

Be duly warned: there are those who visit Sintra, fall under its spell, and stay forever!

Sintra is one of the oldest towns in the country. When the Christian Crusaders captured it in 1147, they fought bitterly against the Moors firmly entrenched in their hilltop castle, the ruins of which remain today.

The town, 18 miles from Lisbon, is on the northern slope of the granite Sintra Range. A 45-minute train ride from the neo-Manueline-style railway station at the Rossio in Lisbon will deposit you here. Visitors staying in the Costa do Sol hotels can make bus connections at both Cascais and Estoril. Sintra is also visited on many organized tours departing from Lisbon, although this latter method allows no time for personal discovery, which is essentially what Sintra is all about.

THE SIGHTS: The specific sights of Sintra are set forth below, but the task of selection is difficult. Byron put it well: "Ah me! What hand can pencil guide, or pen, to follow half on which the eye dilates."

Opening onto the central square of the resort town is the:

National Palace of Sintra

Until 1910 this was a royal palace. Its last royal inhabitant was Queen Maria Pía, the Italian grandmother of Manuel II, the last king of Portugal. Much of the palace was constructed in the days of the first Manuel the Fortunate.

Outside, two conically shaped chimneys tower into the sky, forming the most distinctive landmark on the Sintra skyline. Long before the arrival of the conquering Christian Crusaders under Afonso Henriques, this was a summer palace of Moorish sultans, filled with dancing harem girls who performed in front of bubbling fountains. Although the original was torn down, the Moorish style of architecture was incorporated in latter-day versions of the palace. The entire effect is rather a conglomeration of styles, with Gothic and the original Manueline predominant.

The glazed earthenware tiles or azulejos lining many of the chambers are among the best you'll find in Portugal. João I, one of the founding kings, was fond of the Swan Room, João was the father of Henry the Navigator and the husband of Philippa of Lancaster.

It is said that one day the English queen came upon her king embracing one of the ladies of the court. Apparently, she did not hold a grudge against him for this one indiscretion, but it grew into a court scandal of which the king became painfully aware. Hoping to end speculation and save his wife further embarrassment, he called in his decorators and gave them a secret mission. The room was locked. When the doors were finally opened to the ladies of the court, they marched in, only to discover that the ceiling was covered with magpies.

The symbol of the chattering birds scored a point, and a new subject of gossip was discovered. Guides now call the salon the Chamber of the Magpies.

The Room of the Sirens or Mermaids is one of the most elegant in the palace. In the Heraldic or Stag Room, coats-of-arms of aristocratic Portuguese families and hunting scenes are depicted. From most of these rooms, wide windows look out onto attractive vistas of the Sintra mountain range. Tile-fronted stoves are found in the Old Kitchen, where the feasts of yore were held, especially game banquets in the reign of Carlos I, the king assassinated in 1908.

The palace is rich in paintings and Iberian and Flemish tapestries. But it is at its best when you wander into a tree- and plant-shaded patio and listen to the water of a fountain. Perhaps the young king Sebastião sat here lost in the dreams of glory that would one day take him and his country on an ill-fated mission to North Africa, a mission that would cost him his life.

As you approach the palace, you can buy a ticket a the kiosk on your left. The cost is 25$ (38¢), one of the best investments you'll make in all of Portugal. Visiting hours are daily from 10 a.m. to 5 p.m., except on Tuesday when it is closed.

The Pena Palace

Towering over Sintra, this palace appeals to special tastes. From its perch on a plateau about 1500 feet above sea level, it stands like a medieval fortress on one peak, looking at the ruins of the old Moorish castle on the opposite hill. Part of the fun of visiting it is the ride up the verdant winding road, through the Parque das Merendas.

At the top you come upon a form of Wagnerian fantasy, perhaps something the mad Bavarian, Ludwig, would have constructed. This castle in the sky was called a "soaring agglomeration of towers, cupolas, and battlemented walls" by *National Geographic*. The inspiration behind it was Ferdinand of Saxe-Coburg-Gotha, the husband of Maria II.

Of course, Ferdinand needed a German to help him build this fantasy. While dreams of the Middle Ages danced in his head, Baron Eschwedge arrived. You can still see a sculptured likeness of the baron by looking out from the Pena at a huge rock across the way. Romantically, the architect fancied himself a soldier, armed with a halberd.

In the early 16th century, Manuel the Fortunate had ordered a monastery built on these lofty grounds for the Jerónimos monks. Even today you can visit a cloister and a small ogival chapel that the latter-day builders decided to preserve.

Crossing over a drawbridge, you'll enter the palace proper, whose last royal occupant was Queen Amélia. On a long-ago morning in 1910, she clearly saw that monarchy in Portugal was drawing to an end. Having already lost her husband and her soldier son two years before, she was determined not to lose her second offspring, King Manuel II. Gathering her most precious items and only the small family heirlooms that could be packed quickly, she fled to Mafra where her son waited.

Behind she left Pena Palace and was not to see it again until 1945, when she returned to Portugal under much more favorable conditions. Pena has remained much as Amélia left it, and that is part of its fascination; it emerges as a rare record of European royal life in the halcyon days preceding World War I.

For an entrance fee of 20$ (31¢), you can visit the palace daily from 10 a.m. until 5 p.m., except on Tuesday when it is closed.

SINTRA 85

Pena Park was designed and planted in a four-year span beginning in 1846. Again, Ferdinand was the controlling factor behind the landscaping. What he achieved was one of the most spectacular parks in Portugal, known for the scope of its plant and tree life. For an eye-opening vista of the park and the palace, you can make the ascent to **Cruz Alta**.

The entrance fee to the park, with a car, is 15$ (23¢).

Forming the third member of the palace-castle triumvirate is . . .

The Moorish Castle

The fortification, the Castelo dos Mouros, had been around for a long time when Scandinavian Crusaders in 1147 besieged and successfully captured it from its Moorish occupants. It was built sometime between the eighth and ninth centuries at a position 1350 feet above sea level. The consort of Maria II, Ferdinand, the German responsible for Pena Palace, attempted restoration in the 19th century, but was relatively unsuccessful.

To reach its decaying ramparts, you take a path that's a ten-minute walk. The path branches off from the road Parque das Merendas (a small sign points the way). There's a parking area for your car, and a guide will send you off in the right direction. From the royal tower, the view of Sintra, its palace and its castle, and of the Atlantic coast is spectacular. Go between 8 a.m. and sunset.

The following and final sight within Sintra is missed by too many visitors —and what a pity. It's one of the gems.

Monserrate

One Englishman, Francis Cook, between 1846 and 1850 set out to make Lord Byron's dream of a glorious Eden even more of a reality. Bringing in landscape artists and flora from everywhere from Africa to Norway, he planned a botanical garden, the rival of which is not to be found either in Spain or Portugal.

The garden scales the slope of a hill—paths cut through to hidden oases— and you need to give it the better part of the afternoon. Walking back is rough on all but seasoned hill scalers. However, it's worth the descent.

At the bottom, Cook built his **Palácio de Monserrate**. It seemed that in his Eden, only a Moorish temple would do. But when Cook died, Monserrate faced a troubled future. An English manufacturer purchased the property and set out virtually to destroy Cook's dreams. He began by selling the antiques in the Palácio, and it's said that he made so much money on the sale that he was paid back for all the cash he sank into Monserrate. He wasn't satisfied. When news leaked out to Lisbon that he was going to subdivide the park and turn it into a housing development of villas, the government belatedly intervened, and well that it did. When you see Monserrate, you'll surely agree that it belongs to all the people, preserved and well maintained.

Lilies float on cool fountains, flowers scent the air, ferns scale the hillside, northern spruce grows tall, and flora from Africa thrives as if it were in its native habitat. The entrance fee is 10$ (15¢). The park is open from 10 a.m. to 6 p.m.

One final stopover, lying outside of Sintra, merits exploration:

Convento de Santa Cruz dos Capuchos

Dom Alvaro de Castro ordered that this curiously structured convent be built for the Capuchins in 1560. Cork was used so extensively in its construction that it is sometimes known as the cork monastery.

You walk up a moss-covered path, like a wayfarer of old approaching for his dole. Ring the bell, and a guide (not a monk) will appear to show you in and out of the miniature cells. The convent is in a secluded area, 4½ miles from Sintra.

It appears forlorn, forgotten. At its finest hour, it probably wasn't too lively. The Capuchins who lived here, perhaps eight in all, had a penchant for the most painstaking of detailed work. For example, they lined the walls of their monastery with cork bark tiles and seashells. They also carved a chapel out of rock, using cork for insulation.

When making toilets or "refrigerators," they displayed ingenuity. A hospital was even installed into the most cramped of quarters. Their monastery is perhaps the coziest in the world. Outside, one of them found time to fresco an altar in honor of St. Francis of Assisi.

In 1834, they left suddenly; but fortunately the curiosity they left behind wasn't destroyed by vandals. The convent can be visited today for a 10$ (15¢) entrance fee.

DINING 18TH-CENTURY STYLE: Hotel Palácio de Seteais, Seteais, Sintra (tel. 293-32-00), is Portugal's most romantic dream palace converted into a hotel. Lord Byron worked on *Childe Harold* in the front garden. The palace is approached via a long private encircling driveway, past shade trees, a wide expanse of lawn, yew hedges, and the silhouette of the building itself. The stone-built architecture is formal, dominated by an arched entryway.

Seteais looks older than it is, having been built in the late 18th century by a Dutch gildemeister. It was subsequently taken over and restored by the fifth Marquis le Marialva, who sponsored many receptions and galas for the aristocrats of his day.

The palácio is on the crest of a hill, with most of its drawing rooms, galleries, and chambers overlooking the lower formal terraces, flower garden, and a vista toward the sea. Upon entering there is a long galleried hall, a dramatic staircase, with white and gilt balustrades and columns, leading to the lower-level dining room, drinking lounge, and garden terraces.

Along the corridor are museum-caliber tapestries, groupings of formal French, Italian, and Portuguese furniture, and a hand-woven decorative carpet. On the left is a library and an adjoining music room, furnished tastefully with period pieces.

The main drawing room is an achievement, with its blend of antiques dominated by a fine mural extending around the cove and onto the ceiling. Large bronze chandeliers with crystal add to the luster. The guest book reads like a Who's Who: glowing comments from Richard Nixon, Gloria Swanson, Claudette Colbert.

However, don't just drive up to the entrance and expect to be given shelter. There are only 18 rooms (almost all with private bath), so advance reservations may be needed. Housed in beautiful rooms furnished with antiques or reproductions, you'll pay from 1800$ ($27.54) for one person to 2800$ ($42.84) for two; breakfast, service, and taxes are included. The full-board rate goes from 3200$ ($48.96) for one person to 5500$ ($84.15) for two.

Lunch or dinner is special, and it's possible to come here just for your meal. In summer, the tables are graced with low clusters of pink or blue hydrangea from the garden and each is set with stemware and silver.

The set meal for 850$ ($13.01) consists of four courses, with dishes such as turbot in a cream sauce browned in the oven with spinach. The hors d'oeuvres are among the best, especially the crayfish and fish mousse. The dessert trolley is intriguing—pastries with light rich cream blended with a flaky crust and fruits. After-dinner coffee is taken on the adjoining terrace and loggia or else in the dining room.

    Galeria Real, Rua Tude de Sousa, in São Pedro de Sintra (tel. 293-16-61), is a unique mixture of antique galleries and an 18th-century-style restaurant. The Galeria Real is one of the most impressive-looking places in Portugal. On the ground floor is a cocktail lounge as well as eight shops crammed with antiques, busts, and paintings. Going up a balustraded staircase, you come to further antique shops and a sumptuous restaurant, lorded over by Francisco Correia. The main dining room has a hand-painted beamed ceiling, tiled floors, small wooden frame windows, flowers on each table, carved wooden chairs, and candles. All this is a perfect setting for unhurried dining in a royal fashion. Each day there is a special menu for 600$ ($9.18) at lunch and dinner which might start with a cream of tomato soup or a melon cocktail, followed by a filet of sole or a queijada de bacalhau (a codfish soufflé which is a specialty of the house). The final course might be veal cutlets or a steak, followed by assorted desserts. À la carte entries include sole for 325$ ($4.97) or tournedos Galeria Real, 410$ ($6.27). The chicken shish kebab and the espeteda de frango, at 280$ ($4.28), are good.

Sampling Portuguese Specialties

    For local specialties, **O Chico,** in Sintra, on the hard-to-find Rua do Arco do Teixeira, in the old part of town, is just the place. At the horseshoe-shaped bar, a delectable variety of food items are turned out, including the green broth of the north, caldo verde. Large codfish hang from the ceiling; a lone chicken will sometimes run in and out, and no one seems to notice. A relaxed and cordial atmosphere prevails, and a guitar is ever available for guests. Regular or vintage port wine ranges in price from 70$ ($1.07) to 200$ ($3.06) per glass. For those in pursuit of local color, O Chico is the leading choice.

A FOUR-STAR HOTEL: Hotel Tivoli Sintra, Praça da República (tel. 293-35-05), opened in 1981. It lies only a few doors to the right of the Central Hotel (recommended below) and the already mentioned National Palace. The hotel is newly constructed, with an abundance of modern conveniences, including a garage (most important in Sintra). However, the decorator stuck to the típico Portuguese style in the decor, and the combination of modern with traditional is successful. In the cavernous lobby the floors are of marble, and you'll find the same marble in your own private bathroom. Brass lamps are used, and many earth tones are among the colors chosen. Bedrooms are spacious and comfortably furnished, with large beds and big easy chairs for relaxation. The balconies and the public rooms look out onto a wooden hill, with excellent views of some of Sintra's quintas. The sight, according to readers Peter and Cynthia Hecker, of Berkeley, California, "could have inspired mad Ludwig of Bavaria or at least Walt Disney." In high season two persons can stay here for 3500$ ($53.55), the price including a continental breakfast.

BUDGET HOTELS AND RESTAURANTS: Quinta dos Lobos, Caminho dos Frades (tel. 293-02-10), is one of the few places that has such individual style, such sophisticated charm, you'll want to settle in for a long stay. This was a former stone-built countryside stable, with more than 35 acres of gardens, on the outskirts of Sintra. In the late 1970s it was bought by two talented and enterprising young men, Marc Zurcher from Switzerland and Arturo Perreira from Bermuda, who undertook the task of creating an unusual, tasteful little inn.

It was a major restoration, but they skillfully retained the original architectural features, adapting their design to the inherent features of the buiding. For instance, the long bedroom loft has ceilings that sweep down low, yet has been divided into small accommodations for a total of 12 guests. One has an old Portuguese carved Bilros bed with crochet lace counterpane; another has a wall of mirrors and a room-size bathroom. All decorative accessories are antiques, selected and placed with care and restraint. There's an intimate room for drinks, with white wrought-iron garden benches, a living room that retains the original fireplace, and chic armchairs and sofa.

The dining room also has its own personality, although according to the mood of the owners you might have breakfast on the terrace. Meals are special, utilizing the experience and international tastes of the owners. They sometimes invite their lodgers to eat with them in the kitchen, which guests are welcome to use, whenever they want to make a special dish. In summer, from May 1 to the end of October, Quinta welcomes nonresident guests for dinner, charging 500$ ($7.65).

The cost for two persons in a double with breakfast is 1800$ ($27.54) daily. If you want a larger room with an ornate bed, it's 2800$ ($42.84) for two. Four persons can rent a suite for 3500$ ($53.55) per day.

Quinta da Capella (tel. 293-02-10) is run by the same people as the previously recommended Quinta dos Lobos. This estalagem lies three kilometers from the Quinta dos Lobos, directly next to and overlooking the botanical gardens and the Palace of Monserrate. In fact, the quinta has its own private entrance to the gardens of Monserrate.

Historically, the quinta was built in the early 16th century. Part of the old palace was restored to what exists today as the main house. Between the rose-covered ruins of the old palace and the main house are French-style gardens, a tea pavilion, a chapel with beautiful 16th-century glazed tiles (where mass is said every Sunday at noon), and a swimming pool.

The quinta offers 11 rooms, all of which open onto views of the unspoiled Sêrra of Sintra and the Pena Palace, as well as Monserrate and the surrounding villages below. This view can also be seen on the terrace in the early morning sun, while you're having breakfast. I'd also suggest you return there for a drink at sunset. A double room with bath rents for 1800$ ($27.54), breakfast included. Some more expensive doubles are tabbed at 2800$ ($42.84).

A three-course dinner, plus coffee, goes for 500$ ($7.65) per person. Dinner is served in a unique church-shaped room with a checkered marble floor. The menu includes not only Portuguese specialties, but main dishes from the kitchens of France and England.

The quinta's added features include horseback riding and large water reserves transformed into swimming pools. The site is just 30 minutes from the center of Lisbon, 10 minutes from the beaches.

Central Hotel, 35 Largo da Rainha D. Amélia (tel. 293-00-63), should be given a heavy check with your pencil if you prefer a charming family-owned-and-operated village inn offering personalized accommodations and good food. The hotel opens onto the main square of Sintra, facing the National Palace.

The owner Laura de Jesus Raio, along with her son and daughter-in-law, have created a homelike inn. The facade is inviting, with decorative blue and white tiles and an awning-covered front veranda with dining tables.

The interior, especially the bedrooms, reflects the English background of the owners (they lived in Surrey, near London, for seven years and have accumulated some antiques). Each room is furnished individually, with a reliance on fine old pieces—polished woods, inlaid desks, and lots more. The baths, one to nearly every room, are well designed, with tiles and happy colors.

The cost for one person in a room with bath is 1505$ ($23.03) nightly, increasing to 1590$ ($24.33) for two. Breakfast is included. You'll be charged 500$ ($7.65) for a complete lunch or dinner. The most economical way is to order all of your meals. Complete pension for two costs 3270$ ($50.03).

The restaurant of the Central offers a choice of dining on the veranda overlooking the village, or in one of the large interior rooms. The cooking is primarily Portuguese, with such main courses featured as escalopes of veal in a Madeira sauce, 300$ ($4.59); veal cutlet Milanese, 280$ ($4.28); beef Portuguese, also 280$; and chateaubriand for two, 800$ ($12.24). A traditional dessert, homemade caramel pudding, goes for 50$ (77¢).

To quote the senhora, with her snowy white hair and sweet face, "My son says I'm everyone's mother—and wants me to refrain. But I say, I am this way."

Estalagem da Raposa, 3 Rua Alfredo Costa (tel. 293-04-65), formerly was a private home which belonged to an old Sintra family. It's been run as an inn for the last quarter of a century, and is centrally located, within walking distance of the railroad station. The house is set back from the street in a fenced and flowered yard.

The inn is owned by a Lisbon family and is under the able attention of Mrs. Margarita Araújo, who speaks French and English. A charming woman, Mrs. Araújo makes you feel at home immediately. She keeps a careful eye on the housekeeping and upkeep of the ten high-ceilinged rental units. Rooms all have tile baths, and they're furnished with old-fashioned pieces that are homey and comfortable.

A double room with breakfast rents for about 2500$ ($38.25). The maid who keeps the rooms in spotless condition is polite, and she runs right up with a ring of keys to open your door the moment she hears you on the carpeted stairs.

Solar dos Mouros, 2 Rua Consigieri Pedroso (tel. 293-17-06), is an old-world tavern, just a two-minute walk from the village center. You descend stairs to a pair of dining rooms, with rugged stone walls, old beamed ceilings, deep white stucco arches, and there you can order either lunch or have afternoon tea. It's open every day from noon to 3 p.m., then for tea at 4 p.m. Dinner is not served. On the luncheon list are soups for 28$ (43¢), and I urge you to taste the caldo verde, the "green broth" famous in the Minho district. Grilled fish ranges between 200$ ($3.06) and 300$ ($4.59), and meats such as veal escalope go for 250$ ($3.82). A bottle of the house wine begins at 60$ (92¢), although the eternal favorite is Mateus, for 225$ ($3.44). Flan or chocolate mousse costs 42$ ($6.23), tea 20$ (31¢), and cake of the day is either 42$ (64¢) or 60$ (92¢).

Restaurante Solar S. Pedro, 12 Praça Don Fernando II, off the Largo da Feira in São Pedro de Sintra (tel. 293-18-60), is run by the helpful and hospitable Francisco Freitas, who speaks English. His place is a popular rendezvous, as diners are drawn not only to his personality but his good selection of continental specialties. The lobster crêpes are a favorite at 320$ ($4.90), and another specialty is a flavorsome filet of sole at 345$ ($5.28). Trout with cream and toasted almonds at 225$ ($3.44) is perfectly balanced. Also excellent is the steak Café Paris at 300$ ($4.59). Many of the beef specialties are distinguished as well, including the pepper steak at 420$ ($6.43) and the entrecôte with mushrooms at 330$ ($5.05).

90 □ DOLLARWISE GUIDE TO PORTUGAL

READERS' RESTAURANT SUGGESTIONS: "**Restaurante Regional de Sintra**, 2 Traversa do Municipio, is a little restaurant around the second corner from the Estalagem da Raposa. It lies opposite the Municipal Building. The service is good and the meals generous. Three courses with wine cost 480$ ($7.34). . . . **Restaurante Santo António**, Quinta de Santo António, 2 Rua Camara Pestana, is new and decorated to look like an ancient castle dining hall. It is frequented mainly by Portuguese, the menu seems designed to suit them. We found the food and service excellent. The place is pleasant and congenial. We highly recommend it. Soup, two quail, salad, wine, and coffee cost us 700$ ($10.71) each. . . . **Restaurante Alcobaça**, 7 Rua dos Padarias (tel. 293-16-51), is off the central plaza. If you want an 'experience,' lunch here. The restaurant is a small shop size, small by our standards, with a similar small room upstairs. It was half full when we arrived, and we got a tiny table (coffee-table size) in the corner, for two. Thirty-one locals on a bus trip then arrived and filled the place to the seams. It was virtually seething with people. The restaurant is run by a man and his wife and a couple of teenagers. They all scuttled around to find enough chairs and even went across the street to borrow from some of the neighbors. They treated the whole thing as a joke, and everyone was happy and good humored. Food was produced and served in an unlimited supply on white, spotless tablecloths. I am sure that if anyone else had tried to get in they would have been welcomed and a place found for them to dine. Appropriately, we had fresh grilled sardines, and they have never tasted so good. Soups cost only 15$ (23¢), and roast sardines are only 80$ ($1.22). Other good dishes include grilled swordfish at 125$ ($1.91) and pork chops at 140$ ($2.14). Fresh cheese is 7$50 (12¢) per serving" (Dr. C. H. Chaffey, Dapto, Australia).

Another fine restaurant is **A Tiborna**, 6 Largo Raínha da Amélia (tel. 293-27-72), just off the main square of Sintra; not far from the Central Hotel. At this clean and charming restaurant, which features a well-stocked bar and balcony dining room, we had two different pork dishes, both excellent, with fried potatoes, fabulous desserts, mineral water, and coffee. Portions were very large, and the service friendly and attentive. Complete meals are served for 700$ ($10.71) per head by Daniel Brito and Jeremias Silva, managers" (Sandra A. Ciullo and Gary R. Donner, Brookline, Mass.).

"A real discovery is **O Retiro do Augusto**, 11 Rua da Pendoa (tel. 293-01-65). Despite our usual policy of choosing a different restaurant every night, we ate three dinners at Augusto's, and it was not in the least crowded. The restaurant is in an inconspicuous spot near the Central Hotel. To get there, you go down the alley to the left of the hotel and make the first right turn; Augusto's is then on the left. It's in the basement of a large residence on a quiet street, and the way is marked by large blue and white signs. We found it on the recommendation of a waiter at the Central Hotel who called it 'a simple place.' The restaurant is spotless, with red tile floors, brilliant white stucco walls inside, and simple wall decorations (e.g., small unglazed clay pots hung like a string of garlic). The menu is varied. We especially liked the sole meunière (linguado à la meuniére) and the beef with mushrooms and cream (bife con cogumelos e natas). The latter is not a Stroganoff but a thin slab of tender, medium-rare flank steak with lots of mushrooms and a light, spare sauce of buttery cream. The strawberries, of course, are scrumptious. The caldo verde is only 15$ (23¢), and entrees are 150$ ($2.30) to 320$ ($4.90)" (Peter and Cynthia Hecker, Berkeley, Calif.).

7. Mafra Palace

This baroque chef d'oeuvre of precision craftsmanship is an ensemble of discipline, grandeur, and majesty. At the peak of its construction, it is said to have employed a working force of 50,000 Portuguese men. A small town was built just to house the corps, the cream of the crop of a small nation's working force.

Its master model was El Escorial, that Daedalian maze constructed by Philip II outside Madrid. Mafra's corridors and complex immurements may not be as impressive, nor as labyrinthine, but the diversity of its contents is amazing. The end product was 880 rooms, housing 300 friars, who could walk through 5000 doorways and stare out 2500 windows.

That devout king of "peace and prosperity," João V, seemingly couldn't sire an heir, and court gossips openly speculated that he was sterile. One day he casually mentioned to a Franciscan that if he were rewarded with an heir, he would erect a monastery to the order. Apparently, the Franciscans, through what the king considered "divine intervention," came through. João produced his heir, and Mafra was born, the work beginning in 1717. Originally, it was to house 13 friars, but that figure rapidly mushroomed into 300, as the Franciscans had a population explosion uniquely their own.

It is said that Mafra, 13 years in the making, was built with gold and diamonds pouring in from the new colony of Brazil. Seeing it now, and considering building methods in those days, one wonders how such a task was ever completed in so short a time.

Its more than 110 chimes, made in Antwerp, can be heard from a distance of 12 to 15 miles when they are played at Sunday recital. Holding the chimes are two towers which flank a basilica, capped by a dome that has been compared to that of St. Paul's in London. The inside of the church is a varied assortment of chapels, 11 in all, expertly crafted with detailed jasper reredos, bas-reliefs, and marble statues from Italy (the musculature of St. Sebastian is awesome).

In the monastery is found the pride of Mafra, a 35,000-volume library with tomes 200 and 300 years old, many gold-leafed. Viewed by some more favorably than the world-famed library at Coimbra, the room is a study in gilded light, decorated in what has been called grisaille rococo. In the Museum of Religious Art, the collection of elaborately decorated vestments is outstanding.

Following the omnipresent red Sintra marble, you enter the monks' pharmacy, hospital, and infirmary, the beds sans mattresses. Later, you can explore the spacious kitchens and the penitents' cells, with the flagellation devices used by the monks.

The summer residence of kings, Mafra was home to such members of Portuguese royalty as the banished Queen Carlotta Joaquina. In addition to his love of painting, Carlos I, the Braganza king assassinated at Praça do Comércio in 1908, was also an avid hunter. In one room, he had chandeliers made out of antlers, upholstery of animal skins. His son, who ruled for two years as Manuel II, spent his last night on Portuguese soil at Mafra, fleeing with his mother Amélia to England.

You can wander through the trompe l'oeil-ceiling audience room; through the sewing room of the mad Maria I; the music room of Carlos. Throughout the apartments hang decaying tapestries, taking their place in a setting of antiques, ceramics, and silverware.

The charge for admission is 10$ (15¢); the hours, from 10 a.m. to 5 p.m. From Sintra, you can make bus connections to Mafra, about 25 miles from Lisbon.

8. Ericeira

Some 32 miles from Lisbon and a quick 13 miles across the countryside from Sintra, this fishing village nestles on the Atlantic shore. Its narrow streets are lined with whitewashed houses, accented by pastel-painted corners and window frames. To the east, the mountains of Sintra appear.

The sea has been giving life to Ericeira for 700 years and continues to do so today. Not only do the fishermen pluck their food from it, but it is the sea, especially the beach, that lures streams of visitors every summer, adding a much-needed shot in the arm to the local economy. Along the coast lobsters are bred in cliffside nurseries, *sêrração.* Anyplace in Ericeira, especially at the Hotel Tourismo da Ericeira, lagosta is la specialité de la maison.

In 1584 Mateus Álvares arrived in Ericeira from the Azores, claiming to be the King Sebastião (The Desired One), who was killed (some say disappeared) on the battlefields of North Africa. Álvares and about two dozen of his chief supporters were finally executed after their defeat by the soldiers of Philip II of Spain; but he is today remembered as the king of Ericeira. It wasn't until an October day in 1910 that the second monumental event occurred at Ericeira. From the harbor, the fleeing Manuel II and his mother Amélia set sail on their yacht to a life of exile in England. The House of Braganza, monarchy itself, had collapsed in Portugal.

For such a small place, there are quite a few sights of religious and historic interest. The **Church of São Pedro** (St. Peter) and the **Misericórdia** (charitable institution) both contain rare 17th- and 18th-century paintings. The **Hermitage of St. Sebastião**, with its Moorish designs, would seem more fitting in North Africa. Rounding out the ecclesiastical ring is one more hermitage honoring **St. Anthony**.

The chloride-rich spring waters (radioactive) of **Santa Maria** attract health-spa enthusiasts. But it is the crescent-shaped sandy **Praia do Sol** that is the favorite of Portuguese and foreign visitors alike. Ericeira maintains bus connections with both Sintra and Lisbon (you can also take the train from Lisbon to Mafra, where connections can be made).

9. Vale do Lobos

This often forlorn-looking Valley of the Wolves is a Sorrento Secreto for lovers, or a place where soccer players like to rest and recuperate between matches at its only hotel. The environs are tranquil, the gentle wooded hills rolling into the distance.

Some 12½ miles north of Lisbon, the Vale is reached via Queluz and Belas, heading in the direction of Sabugo before turning off to the right.

A BUDGET HOTEL: Vale do Lobos Hotel, Vale do Lobos, Sabugo (tel. 30-28-45). This one-time private villa was converted more than 20 years ago into a country inn-hotel, created expressly for those seeking a tranquil retreat. Wedding receptions are held here—there's even a honeymoon suite so couples won't have far to go. Lovers of nature enjoy the garden walks, the open-air swimming pool surrounded by flagstone terraces, and the pathways lined with blue and pink hydrangeas and red geraniums.

The bedrooms, 30 in all with private bath, are small, but quite comfortable and attractive, with old-fashioned provincial-style furniture (high headboards, for example). The tariff for a single room ranges from 1000$ ($15.30) to 1500$ ($22.95). For a double, the price jumps from 1500$ ($22.95) to 2500$ ($38.25), depending on the size of the room and the view. With full board, a single person pays from 1850$ ($28.31) to 2500$ ($38.25); two persons, 3100$ ($47.43) to 4000$ ($61.20).

There are a number of cheerful lounge rooms—homelike, very Portuguese. Dining here is enjoyable. Three walls of windows overlook the garden and its trellis of purple bougainvillea. Many drive all the way out from Lisbon on an excursion to sample the good-tasting home cooking. A table d'hôte is offered, including, say, caldo verde (a potato and cabbage soup), then a fish dish, a mixed salad, perhaps Valencian paella, a dessert, and the fruit of the season, all costing 600$ ($9.18). You don't have to be a guest of the hotel to drop in for dinner.

Now that we've seen, sampled, and eaten our way through the environs, we'll return to Lisbon.

Chapter VII

SHOPPING IN PORTUGAL

                              1. The Best Buys in Lisbon
                                             2. Porto
                                             3. Barcelos
                                             4. Madeira

    PORTUGUESE HANDICRAFTS OFTEN have exotic influences because of the versatility of the Portuguese and their skill of absorbing other styles. The best showing of their work is in Lisbon. The shopkeepers and their buyers hunt out unusual items in the Madeira Islands and the Azores as well as in their own country. But there are also good buys throughout Portugal, especially in Porto, Barcelos, and the Madeira Islands.
    If you want to bargain (although it is not looked on kindly in the more prestigious shops), it is still customary throughout Lisbon. Use both your sixth sense and common sense. A good yardstick is whether or not a store is owner-managed, as smaller ones usually are. In owner-managed stores you might work out a deal.
    Baixia is the major area for browsing, but shops are spread out all over the city. Baixia is the district forming downtown Lisbon. Rua do Ouro (Street of Gold, where the major jewelry shops can be found), Rua da Prata (Street of Silver), and Rua Augusta are Lisbon's three principal streets.
    Especially good handicrafts buys from the Azores and Madeira Islands can be found in Portugal, including handmade embroideries, such as blouses, napkins, tablecloths, and handkerchiefs; products made of cork, from placemats to cigarette boxes; and *azulejos* (decorative glazed tiles). From Vista Alegre there is porcelain and china; there are fishermen's sweaters from Nazaré; filigree jewelry in gold and silver; Arraiolos carpets; local pottery; and, of course, fado records.

1. The Best Buys in Lisbon

    Most stores open at 9 a.m., closing at noon for lunch. They reopen at 2 p.m., closing for the day at 7 p.m. However, many shopkeepers like to take lunch from 1 to 3 p.m., so check before making the trip. On Saturday, most stores in Lisbon, and elsewhere in Portugal for that matter, are open a full day.

EMBROIDERIES FROM THE ISLANDS: Madeira Superbia, with a branch at the Ritz Hotel and a somewhat larger store at 75-A Duque de Loulé (tel. 53-79-68), is an outlet for one of the best embroidery factories on the Madeira Islands. The exquisite craft they showcase, not inexpensive, includes tapestries, linens, and women's apparel, such as petit-point handbags and blouses. Often, high-quality fabrics are imported from Switzerland and Ireland, then embroidered on the islands. The collection of hand-embroidered napkins, tea cloths, pillowcases, and sheets is exceptional. Beautiful placemats often come in organdy with a linen appliqué (some are double-edged with shadow work embroidery). One of the most popular items is monogrammed linen handkerchiefs.

Ann Leacock boutiques, 4 Galeria do Ritz, 77-A Rua Castilho, is another shop where hand-embroidered linens and clothing can be found, as well as items of local craftsmanship.

Casa Regional da Ilha Verde, 4 Rua Paiva de Andrade, specializes in handmade items, especially embroideries from the Azores. That's why it's called the Regional House of the Green Island. Each piece carries a made by hand guarantee. Some of the designs used on the linen placemats with napkins have been in use for centuries. You can get some good buys here.

CHINA AND GLASSWARE: Vista Alegre, 18 Largo do Chiado (tel. 36-14-01), is unparalleled for china and glassware, numbering royalty and diplomats, or whoever demands the very best, among its clientele. The colorful porcelain from Ilhavo, with many of the figurines depicting regional costumes, is of special interest to the casual shopper.

Professional and do-it-yourself decorators are drawn to the porcelain figures and birds. They are amazingly lifelike, but also alarmingly high-priced. If you're bargain hunting, you'd do better buying a fruit bowl or a set of dishes.

THE LEADING GOLDSMITH: W. A. Sarmento, 251 Rua Aurea, celebrated its 100th anniversary, in the hands of the same family-owners, in 1970. The shop, at the foot of the Santa Justa elevator, has been the favorite place for Lisboans to buy treasured confirmation and graduation gifts, and it has customers among the Costa do Sol aristocracy as well as movie stars and diplomats. They are the most distinguished silver- and goldsmiths in Portugal, specializing in lacy filigree jewelry, in gold and silver. Considered a good buy in Portugal, gold is strictly regulated by the government, which requires jewelers to put a minimum of 19¼ karats in jewelry made of this expensive metal. Small gold filigree caravels come in many prices. Their less expensive filigree jewelry is made of silver and plated with gold. These are primarily cufflinks and earrings. For additions to your charm bracelet, Sarmento is the place to go. There are literally dozens of choices.

GLAZED PORTUGAL TILES: Sant'Anna, 95–97 Rua do Alecrim, is Portugal's leading ceramic center and was founded in 1741. Famous for its azulejos (glazed tiles), Sant'Anna is in the Chiado section. The showroom is at the Rua do Alecrim location, but you can also visit the factory at 96 Calcada da Boa Hora; however, you must telephone ahead to make an appointment. Some of the designs that decorate the tiles are created by artisans who are among the finest in Europe, and many of them employ designs in use since the Middle Ages. Bargains I bought recently include a group of framed scenic azulejos; a two-holder candelabrum; an hors d'oeuvres tray (tiled); and a ceramic umbrella stand that is three feet high.

LISBON: SHOPPING 95

A HOUSE OF SUEDE: Caprice, 67-B Rua Joaquim António de Aguiar (tel. 53-85-27), sells a fine line of washable suede items, such as pants suits and jackets. Situated diagonally across from the Ritz Hotel, it is owned by Philippe L. Gaulier, whose mother was a Lanvin stylist. He apparently inherited her good taste. Both he and his wife are English-speaking and will offer you an assortment of aqua-suede in both dresses and coats as well as men's safari shirts. The suede comes in a wide assortment of interesting colors, including pink, dark chocolate, navy, aqua, and caramel. In addition, the Gauliers present a selection of hand-crocheted suits and dresses, but unfortunately, these items are so expensive to produce that they don't fall within the average person's price range.

THE THIEVES MARKET: Here is a place where you can haggle and enjoy the fun of getting a bargain. Called the **Feira da Ladra,** this open-air street market is like the flea markets of Madrid and Paris. Nearly every possible item that can be purchased is seen here in the street stalls. For the best pickings it's best to go in the morning. The vendors here peddle their wares on Tuesday and Saturday.

About a five-minute walk from the waterfront, in the Alfama district, the market sits in back of the Military Museum adjoining the Pantheon of São Vicente. Start your browsing at the Campo de Santa Clara. Portable stalls and individual displays are lined up on this hilly street with its tree-lined center.

You can often pick up a bargain here, but you must search diligently through masses of cheap clothing and lots of junk to find it. Everything from brass scales, oil lamps, portable bidets, cow bells, and old coins, to Macão china, antique watches, and Angola woodcarvings is on display.

ROSSIO RAILWAY STATION SHOPPING MALL: There are some 150 boutiques, shops, and snackbars installed in four of the five floors of the Rossio Railway Station, in the heart of downtown Lisbon. The fifth floor is where the trains arrive and depart. Banks of escalators whisk you from floor to floor, and shopping in the maze of petite shops is easier than walking on the congested streets. Conveniently, the shops are open every day of the year from 9 in the morning to midnight. The street floor is deceivingly shabby—ignore it and take the escalator to the boutiques. You'll find apparel for men, women, and children, shops specializing in jewelry, fado records, whatever. There's a pharmacy for "naturalists," beauty parlors, hair dressers, bookstores, leather goods, sweaters, and Portuguese handicrafts.

ANTIQUE ALLEY: Along both sides of the narrow street Rua de S. José are treasure troves—shops packed with antiques from all over the world. Antique dealers from America come here to pick up bargains. You'll find ornate spool and carved beds, high-back chairs, tables, wardrobes with ornate carving or time-seasoned woods, brass, plaques, copper pans, silver candelabra, crystal sconces, and chandeliers, plus a wide selection of old wooden figures, silver boxes, porcelain plates, and bowls.

A MODERN SHOPPING COMPLEX: Apolo 70, 10 Avenida Julio Dinis (tel. 77-15-94), near the bull ring, is a self-contained unit that includes everything from an interior sidewalk café to a cinema and a leather shop. Wander for an hour or two among the 38 shops, making purchases at a teenage boutique, getting your photograph blown up to poster size, or having your hair styled by experts, after which you can stop in their cozy bar for a cooling drink, on the lower level. Also on the lower level is a restaurant that vaguely evokes a merry-go-round. Main courses include a hamburger at 180$ ($27.54); a typical Portuguese fish stew at 200$ ($3.06); a shrimp or minestrone soup for 45$ (69¢); and a dessert for 60$ (92¢). The restaurant is open till 12:30 a.m.

2. Porto

The capital of the north boasts some of the finest gold- and silversmiths in Portugal. You'll find dozens of shops, especially along the **Rua das Flores,** offering a glittering display in their window cases. The most outstanding one is:

Pedro A. Baptista, 235 Rua das Flores (tel. 25142), which offers an unusual collection of antique as well as new jewelry (often based on traditional designs, however), plus several upper floors of decorator items. In the ground-floor jewelry section, you'll find intricate and delicate lace-like filigree pins, brooches, pillboxes, and bracelets, in both solid gold (19½ karats) or else gold-plated silver, plus an exquisite silver collection, including elaborately decorated tea services.

Antique watches are sold, antique pearl brooches, tie pins, or gold rings, even jeweled opera glasses and a gold-headed cane. The owner buys rare and beautiful antique jewelry which he "offers first to my wife." The decorative bric-a-brac collection upstairs features many ornate gilt pieces, such as a three-foot-high wood-carved church candelabra or a trestle dining table.

The **Fabrica de Loica de Sacavem,** 40 Rua das Carmelitas (tel. 22033), across from the Clerigos Church, is Porto's leading outlet for ceramics and china. Long established, it is important enough to have wares made especially for it. Generally the china selections are sophisticated, although regional motifs are offered as well. Worth considering are some of its decorative vases, based on old designs, four-legged white ceramic cigarette boxes, along with a wide assortment of mugs, tureens, platters, cups, saucers, and glasses. Of course, pastel-colored china comes in many different arrangements at widely varying price levels.

3. Barcelos

Centro do Artesanato de Barcelos, Torre da Porta Nova, is a unique shopping center tucked away in a provincial town. But it displays some of the best regional handicrafts at the most compelling prices of any shop we've encountered in the north. It's in an age-old stone tower, opposite the Church of S. da Cruz. On its street level and upper floor is found a wide display.

Outstanding (and worth the trip to Barcelos) is the collection of witty and sophisticated ceramics from the heirs of Rosa Ramalho, who was known as the Grandma Moses of Portuguese ceramics. Some of these figures were influenced by Picasso. Ms. Ramalho created figures depicting eerie people, some looking as if they stepped out of a painting by Hieronymus Bosch. She put the heads of wolves on nuns, gave goats six legs, and so forth, all in her muted forest green or butterscotch brown.

In addition, there is a good selection of the ceramic, red-combed Barcelos cockerels, with many variations on the traditional motif in red and black. Local wares include black ceramic candlesticks, earthenware bowls traditionally used for caldo verde, hand-knitted pillows, handmade rugs in bold stripes, and hand-loomed bedspreads. As a novelty, the rugs and pillows made from flamboyantly dyed chicken feathers may attract you.

4. Madeira

Casa do Turista, 2 Rua do Conselheiro José Silvestre Ribeiro, near the waterfront, Funchal, is one of the best places on the island at which to purchase handicrafts of Madeira. Privately managed, it has a policy of clearly labeled and "firm" prices unlike many of the bazaars which pick up added business by paying to have cruise-ship passengers directed to their establishments, or else having employees chase you down the street quoting lower tariffs after you've nixed their higher tabs. The setting of the Tourist House is beguiling, in an old quinta, once inhabited by a distinguished local family. Its elegant rooms are a natural setting to show off the beautiful handmade items. You're treated as a guest in a private home.

In the patio, with a fountain and semitropical greenery, is a miniature village, with small-scale typical rooms furnished in the local style. Among the merchandise offered are handmade embroideries in linen or cotton (the fabric is often imported from Switzerland and Ireland), tapestries, wickerwork, Portuguese pottery and ceramics, Madeira wines, fruit, and flowers. You'll find all types of embroidery and appliqué, as well as "shadow work," the tariffs determined by the number of stitches.

Specific merchandise includes embroidered Irish linen handkerchiefs for men (some with monograms); handbags made of banana skins (a new industry), in different sizes; the characteristic goatskin boots; 12-string guitars; 15-piece embroidered placemat and napkin sets; appliquéd tray cloths in shadow work; old Madeira-style tablecloths, and embroidered bridge cloths with four napkins.

In one of the rooms is a display of old wines, with ceramic jugs. Old wines (velho) are sold in their original bottles, some costing very little. In addition, a half pint of sugarcane brandy is for sale in souvenir packages of five miniature varieties.

Other shops include the following:

Casa Oliveira, 1-B Rua da Alfandega, which has an embroidery factory right on the premises.

Likewise, **Jabara**, 59 Rua Dr. Fernão de Ornelas, has its own embroidery factory, and specializes in regional articles.

Marghab, 165 Rua dos Ferreiros, is also known for fine embroidery.

Madeira Gobelins, 194 Rua da Carreira (tel. 22073), is a specialist in art needlework, and you can visit its showroom and factory. In addition to needlework, it specializes in the production of Portuguese rugs, hand-stitched, as well as monogrammed, linens and other items. It also has a second outlet in Funchal, the Savoy Boutique No. 2 on the Avenida do Infante. Although there is no factory in Lisbon, the Madeira house displays its goods there at 40 Rua Castilho (corner of Rua Braamcamp).

Madeira Superbia, 30 Rua do Conselho, is known for its fine embroidery (of excellent quality) and is a specialist in tapestries.

Chapter VIII

THE SIGHTS OF LISBON

1. **The Alfama**
2. **Belém**
3. **Museums and Galleries**
4. **The Churches of Lisbon**
5. **A Bullfight Spectacle**
6. **Other Sights**

IN LISBON IT'S STILL a case of the frame competing with the picture. Although the Portuguese capital offers many worthwhile attractions, its Lorelei environs echo a siren call that few can resist. Many guests end up using Lisbon only as a base, while venturing forth during the day to Lord Byron's "variegated maze of mount and glen" at Sintra, to the sandy beaches along the Portuguese Riviera (Estoril and Cascais), to the monastery and royal palace at Mafra, even as far north as the fishing villages of Nazaré or Fátima, where three shepherd children claimed to have seen a vision of the Virgin Mary on May 13, 1917.

One reason Lisbon gets overlooked is that enough time isn't budgeted for it. One or two days simply isn't adequate for Lisbon and the environs. A minimum of five days is needed. Another reason is that the attractions of Lisbon remain relatively unknown. Seemingly, every stone in Rome has been documented or recorded by someone. But in talks with literally dozens of visitors, the question most often asked is: "What does one do in Lisbon?"

This chapter hopes to answer that question, specifically with regard to sightseeing. If your time is limited, and you can cope only with the most important, then you should explore: (1) the **Coach Museum,** (2) **Jerónimos Monastery,** (3) the **Alfama** and the **Castle of St. George** (for the view if nothing else). At least two art museums, although not of the caliber of Madrid's Prado, merit attention: (1) the **National Art Gallery,** and (2) the **Gulbenkian Center for Arts and Culture.**

These sights are rated for those in a hurry. Readers who enjoy more leisure time can visit the **Fundação Richardo do Espírito Santa Silva** and watch reproductions of antiques being turned out, or books being gold-leafed; or you can see the gilded royal galleys at the **Naval Museum;** or wander through the **fish market;** or explore the arts and crafts of a **Belém folk museum,** and lots more.

More important, the Lisbon voyager will discover just by walking its streets, a city unique in the world, a capital that extended its power across continents.

1. The Alfama

Lisbon of old lives on in the most typical quarter of the city. The wall built by the Visigoths and incorporated into some of the old houses is mute testimony to its ancient past. In East Lisbon, the Alfama was the Saracen sector of the city centuries before its conquest by the Christians.

Some of the buildings were thankfully spared from the earthquake of 1755, and the Alfama has retained much of its original charm, characterized by narrow cobblestone streets; cages of canaries chirping in the afternoon sun; fish in baskets balanced on the heads of *varinas;* strings of garlic and pepper inviting you inside a *típico* tavern; old street markets; and charming balconies.

The 19th-century Lisbon historian Norberto de Araújo wrote of ". . . its perpetual resigned human tragedy from the habit of living it." In a colorful description he pointed up some of its elements: ". . . labyrinth, confused, heaped up, multicolored; twisted and retwisted, lots of embracing narrow streets and kissing eaves; archways, backyards, blind alleys, stairways and terraces; commons and courtyards. . . ."

But perhaps the most exciting sight is to see a little boy racing down a stone stairway in his droopy underwear (or wearing nothing at all) to hug his sailor father. The boy's mother will go to a fountain and return, balancing a jug of fresh water on her head, to prepare a steaming pot of caldeirada, the traditional fishermen's stew, for her family.

When that same boy isn't racing to greet his father or isn't on an errand for his mother, he'll likely join one of Norberto de Araújo's "waves of little truants" who like to attach themselves to visitors. These children appear in ripples, always with an alert eye for a lost tourist. With hands outstretched and eyes soulfully pleading, they beg you to let them lead you to an open street market. Once there, you can wander in a maze of stacks of brightly colored vegetables from the country, bananas from Madeira, pineapple from the Azores, and fish from the sea.

Much of the charm of the Alfama lies in its armies of cats roaming the streets at will, asserting their unique rights. It is said that without these cats the sector would be rat infested. Occasionally, a black-shawled old woman, stooping over a brazier grilling sardines in front of her house, will toss one of these felines a fish head.

The houses are so close together that in many places it's impossible to stretch your arms to their fullest length. That proximity was dramatically expressed by the poet Frederico de Brito: "Your house is so close to mine! In the starry night's bliss, to exchange a tender kiss, our lips easily meet, high across the narrow street."

Once aristocrats lived in the Alfama, their memory perpetuated by the coats-of-arms of noble families slowly decaying on the fronts of some of the 16th-century houses. Some still do live there. One of the surviving members of an old family refuses to move, despite the pleadings of her relatives. "I will always live here," she said. "When I die, then you can remove my body."

The best known of the aristocratic mansions is the one once occupied by the Count of Arcos, the last viceroy of Brazil. Constructed in the 16th century and spared, in part, from the earthquake, it lies on the Largo da Salvador.

Stevedores, fishmongers, and sailors occupy the Alfama. From the smallest houses that virtually hold hands, streamers of laundry protrude. The fishwives make early-morning appearances on their iron balconies, where they water their pots of geraniums.

On your exploration, you'll suddenly come upon a belvedere and be rewarded with an overall perspective of the contrasting styles of the Alfama, from a simple tile-roofed fishmonger's abode to a gaily decorated baroque church.

One of the best views is from the belvedere of the **Largo das Portas do Sol**, near the Museum of Decorative Art. It's a balcony opening onto the sea, overlooking the typical houses as they sweep down to the Tagus.

One of the oldest churches is that of **St. Estevão** (St. Stephen), at the Largo de Santo Estevão. It was originally constructed in the 13th century, although the present marble structure dates from the 18th century.

Also of medieval origin is the **Church of São Miguel** (St. Michael), at the Largo São Miguel, deep in the Alfama on a palm-tree-shaded square. The guardian angel of the church is an elderly and devout Alfama woman, who spends her time lighting the main altar for visitors or else working or repairing a decaying curtain while sitting outside soaking up the afternoon sun. The interior is richly decorated, with 18th-century gilt and trompe l'oeil walls. The church was reconstructed after the earthquake.

The **Rua da Judiaria** (The Street of Jews) is yet another reminder of the past. It was settled largely by refugees fleeing Spain to escape the Inquisition.

At night the spirit changes. Although the Bairro Alto is the traditional fado quarter of Lisbon, the Alfama also reverberates to the plaintive sound of the fadista. The packs of little boys will be only too glad to guide you to the **Nau Catrineta** or the **Parreirinha d'Alfama**, even to a place where Celeste Rodrigues, sister of Amália, is singing. You'll recall that in the vicinity of the dockland she and her celebrated sister got their start, selling flowers to tourists arriving on boats.

The Alfama was well summed up by another Portuguese writer who called it "... a sort of old curiosity shop, under a veil of humility here and there, ever inclined to be romantic and childish."

ST. GEORGE'S CASTLE: The local people speak of it as the cradle of their city. Yet it hovers over Lisbon more like a protecting mother than a baby. **Castelo São Jorge** may well have been the spot on which the Portuguese capital began in times too distant to be known. Although it is believed to have predated the Romans, the hilltop was used by these warriors as a fortress guarding the Tagus and its settlement below.

From the fifth century A.D., it was a Visigothic fortification, falling in the early eighth century to the Saracens. Much of the walls which still remain were erected during the centuries of Moorish domination. The Moors were in control until 1147, a historic year for the Portuguese, for it was then that Afonso Henriques, the first king of the country, chased them out and extended his kingdom south. Even before Lisbon was made the capital of a newly emerging nation, the site was used as a royal palace.

For what many consider the finest view of the Tagus and the Alfama, walk the esplanades and climb the ramparts of the old castle. The structure takes its name, St. George, in commemoration of an Anglo-Portuguese pact dating from as early as 1371. (Portugal and England have been traditional allies, although their relationship was strained in 1961 when India, a member of the British Commonwealth, seized the Portuguese overseas territory of Goa, Diu, and Damão.)

Huddling close to the protection of the moated castle is a sector that appears almost medieval (many houses still retain their Moorish courtyards, although others have been greatly altered).

At the entrance to the castle, visitors pause at the Castle Belvedere. The Portuguese refer to this spot as their ancient window overlooking the Alfama, the Sêrras of Monsanto and of Sintra, the Ponte 25 de Abril spanning the Tagus, the Praça do Comércio, and the tiled roofs of the Portuguese capital. In the square stands a heroic statue—sword in one hand, shield in the other—of the first king, Afonso Henriques.

Inside the castle grounds, you can stroll through a setting of olive, pine, and cork trees, all graced by the appearance of a flamingo. In bad weather when rain is sweeping the city, you'll focus on a cannon and think of the massacres that must have occurred on this blood-soaked hill. On a fair day, you'll perhaps notice that only the willows weep or the oleander dazzles. Swans with white bodies and black necks glide in a silence shattered by the bloodcurdling scream of the rare white peacock.

In the one building remaining of the former royal palace, known as the Alcáçova, you can see Roman and Islamic tombstones. For a more detailed survey, borrow a pair of binoculars. Open every day from 9 a.m. till sunset, the castle may be visited without charge.

THE CATHEDRAL (SÉ): Even the tourist literature admits that the cathedral is not very rich. Characterized by twin towers flanking its entrance, it represents an architectural wedding of Romanesque and Gothic. The facade is severe enough for a medieval fortress, and like many European cathedrals, it has had so many different architectural fathers that it's a stylistic bastard. And then the devastation caused by the earthquakes of 1344 and 1755 didn't help either.

At one point in its history, the site of the present Sé was allegedly used by the Saracens as a holy mosque. When the city was captured by Christian Crusaders, led by Portugal's first king, Afonso Henriques, the structure was rebuilt. That early date in the 12th century makes the Sé the oldest church in Lisbon.

Inside are housed many treasures, such as the font where St. Anthony of Padua is said to have been christened in 1195. A notable feature is the Gothic chapel of Bartolomeu Joanes, constructed in the 14th century. Other interesting sidelights include a crib by Machado de Castro (the Portuguese sculptor of the 18th century who did the equestrian statue on Praça do Comércio); the sarcophagus of Lopo Fernandes Pacheco, dating from the 14th century; and the original nave and aisles.

To visit the sacristy and cloister requires a guide and a 5$ (8¢) admission ticket. The cloister, built in the 14th century by King Dinis, is of ogival construction, with garlands, a Romanesque wrought-iron grille, and tombs with inscription stones. In the sacristy are housed marbles, relics, valuable images, and pieces of ecclesiastical treasure from the 15th and 16th centuries.

Whether you're Catholic or not, you may want to attend a service here if for no other reason than to see the scarlet red robes of the priests, a miniature medieval pageant. If viewed in the morning, the stained-glass reflections on the floor evoke a Monet painting.

At Largo da Sé, the cathedral may be visited from 9 a.m. till 6 p.m. Although within walking distance of Praça do Comércio (Black Horse Square), it can be reached by taking streetcar 28 (Estrêla) or 11 (Graça).

Facing the cathedral is:

SANTO ANTÓNIO DA SÉ: St. Anthony of Padua was born in 1195 in a house that stood on this spot at Largo de Santo António da Sé. In the crypt, a guide will show you the spot where the saint was allegedly born. The original church was destroyed by the earthquake of 1755, and the present building was designed by Mateus Vicente in the 18th century.

Although buried at Padua, Italy, this itinerant Franciscan monk remains the patron saint of Portugal. The devout come to this little church to light candles under his picture. He is known as a protector of young brides.

As a saint, he also has a special connection with the children of Lisbon. To erect the altar at the church, the children of the Alfama built miniature altars with a representation of the patron saint on them to raise money.

June 12 of every year is designated as St. Anthony's Day, a time of merry-making, heavy eating, and drinking. In the morning there are street fires and singing, climaxed by St. Anthony's Feast on the following day.

2. Belém

At Belém, where the Tagus (Tejo in Portuguese) meets the sea, the caravels were launched on their missions: Vasco da Gama to India; Ferdinand Magellan to circumnavigate the globe; Dias to round the Cape of Good Hope.

Belém emerged from the Restelo, that point or strand of land from which the ships set sail across the so-called Sea of Darkness. As riches, especially spices, poured back into Portugal, Belém flourished. Great monuments, such as the Belém Tower and Jerónimos Monastery, were built and embellished in the Manueline style.

In time the royal family established a summer palace here. Much of the character of the district came about when wealthy Lisboans began moving out and erecting town houses. For many years Belém was a separate municipality, eventually, however, becoming incorporated into Lisbon as a parish.

Nowadays it's a major target for sightseers, as it's a virtual monument-studded museumland.

For most visitors, the first sight is:

THE TOWER OF BELÉM: This quadrangular tower on the Avenida Marginal is a monument to Portugal's Age of Discovery. Erected in the Manueline style between 1515 and 1520, the tower is the most classic landmark in Portugal, often used on documents and brochures as a symbol of the country.

It has been called a symbol of Portugal's great military and naval past. Erected in the reign of Manuel the Fortunate, the tower stands on or near the spot where the caravels set out.

Architect Francisco de Arruda blended a potpourri of styles: Romanesque, Gothic, even Moorish—all flavored by the Manueline style, characterized by such devices as twisting ropes of stone. The coat-of-arms of Manuel I rests above the loggia, and balconies grace three sides of the monument. The stone crosses along the balustrade of the loggia symbolize the Portuguese Crusaders.

However, the richness of the facade fades once you're inside. Gothic severity reigns. A few antiques are there, including a 16th-century throne graced with finials and an inset paneled with pierced Gothic tracery. To go inside, you'll cross over a drawbridge and enter through a Renaissance-style doorway. The tower is open daily from 10 a.m. to 5 p.m. (in summer, from 10 a.m. to 7 p.m.); an admission ticket costs 10$ (15¢).

If you scale the steps leading to the ramparts, you'll be rewarded with a panorama of boats along the Tagus and pastel-washed tile-roofed old villas in the hills beyond.

Facing the Tower of Belém stands a monument in commemoration of the first Portuguese to cross the Atlantic by airplane (not nonstop). The date was March 30, 1922, and the flight took pilot Gago Coutinho and navigator Sacadura Cabral from Lisbon to Rio de Janeiro.

At the center of the Praça do Império at Belém is the **Fonte Luminosa**, the Luminous Fountain. The patterns of the water jets, estimated at more than 70 original designs, make an evening show lasting nearly an hour if you want to see all of them.

MEMORIAL TO THE DISCOVERIES: Like a prow of one of the Age of Discovery caravels, this memorial stands on the Tagus, looking as if it's ready at any moment to strike out across the Sea of Darkness. The Portuguese call it **Padrão dos Descobrimentos.** Memorable explorers, chiefly Vasco da Gama, are immortalized in stone along the ramps.

At this point where the two ramps meet stands a replica of Henry the Navigator, whose genius opened up new worlds. The memorial was unveiled in 1960, and one of the figures in stone is that of a kneeling Philippa of Lancaster, the English mother of Henry the Navigator.

Other figures in the frieze symbolize the Crusaders (represented by a man holding a flag with a cross), navigators, monks, cartographers, and cosmographers. At the top of the prow is the coat-of-arms of Portugal at the time of Manuel the Fortunate. The museum is at Praça da Boa Esperança.

READER'S SIGHTSEEING TIP: "The space in front of the Padrão dos Descobrimentos is remarkable in that the floor of the map of the world is in multicolored marble, with the dates of the discoveries set in metal—that is, '1412' near the Azores. The map of the continents is in reddish marble, the oceans a gray-blue, the figures of the years of discovery in metal set in. Pictures of the caravels are in yet another color to be set off against the blue-gray marble of the sea" (Mrs. A. Stockhausen, Toronto, Ontario, Canada).

JERÓNIMOS MONASTERY: "Here, frozen forever in stone, is the blazing noontide of empire. Stylized hawsers writhe in the arches. Shells and coral and fish entwine in every column. Sanctuary lamps glow red above carved African lions." Or so wrote Howard La Fay.

In an expansive mood of celebration, Manuel the Fortunate ordered this monastery built to commemorate the sailing of Vasco da Gama to India. The style of architecture to which the king contributed his name, Manueline, combines a flamboyant Gothic with the dawn of the Renaissance in Portugal.

Opening onto Praça do Império in Belém, the monastery was founded in 1502, part of it financed by the spice trade that was to grow following the discovery of the route to India. Originally, a small chapel dedicated to St. Mary had been built on this spot by Henry the Navigator, and although the earthquake of 1755 damaged the monastery, it didn't destroy it. Extensive restoration, some of it ill-conceived, was carried out.

Outstanding is the decorated southern doorway. Inside, the most interesting architecture is to be seen in the cloister. Every pillar is different, as each craftsman vied with the others in exuberance of his motifs. From the cloister, doors lead to cells where the monks lived in a confined area about seven feet long and four feet wide. You walk across the unmarked tombs of unmarked ghosts. Other bodies were buried in the walls, the tombs designated by the markings you see today. On the second tier of the cloisters, approached by stairway, monks of old walked in meditation.

The interior of the church is divided into a trio of naves, noted for their fragile-looking pillars. Some of the ceilings, such as those in the monks' refectory, have a ribbed barrel-vault ceiling. The "palm tree" in the sacristy is also exceptional.

Many of the greatest names in Portuguese history are said to be entombed at the monastery, but none is more famous than Vasco da Gama. The Portuguese also maintain that Luís Vas de Camõës, is enshrined here. Camõës, of course, was the national poet of Portugal, author of *Os Lusíadas* (The Portuguese), in which he glorified the triumphs of his compatriots. Both tombs rest on the backs of lions.

Camõës' epic poetry is said to have inspired a young Portuguese king, Sebastião, to dreams of glory. His remains were allegedly entombed in a marble shrine built in the 16th century in the Mannerist style. The foolish king—devoutly, even fanatically, religious—was killed at Alcácer-Kibir, Morocco, in a crusade against the Mohammedans in 1578. Those refusing to believe that the king was dead formed a cult. Known as Sebastianism, it rose to minor influence, and four men tried to assert their claim to the Portuguese throne. Each maintained steadfastly, even to death, that he was King Sebastião.

Finally, the romantic poet Garrett (1800–1854) is buried at Jerónimos, as are two former Portuguese presidents, Sidónio Pais and Oscar Carmona.

Open from 8 a.m. to 7 p.m. daily, the monastery charges no entrance fee. Take bus 12 from Praça Pombal or 14 from Praça Figueira.

Sheltered in a wing of the abbey is the:

ETHNOLOGICAL MUSEUM: This museum covers a panoramic scope, from the dawn of history until more recent centuries. Standing out from the prehistoric ages are the remains of megalithic graves and villages from early metal ages, as well as the remarkable materials unearthed from Iron Age graves and villages in southern Portugal. It's pre-Roman and Roman jewelry is exceptional. The Roman era in Portugal is also recalled by the ancient mosaic floors displayed. Some of these remains were discovered in the Algarve. Dating from the second or third centuries A.D., "The Muses," a Roman mosaic, depicts robed figures, some of whom are holding masks in their hands.

One of the most valuable pieces is an elaborately carved Roman sarcophagus from the third century A.D., unearthed at Vila Franca de Xira in Ribatejo.

A large ceramic display complete with Greek and Roman terracotta vases is also interesting, as is the small but well-arranged Egyptian collection, complete with mummies.

The museum may be visited daily, except Monday, from 10 a.m. to 12:30 p.m. and from 2 to 5 p.m. for a 10$ (15¢) entrance fee.

Off to the side of Jerónimos Monastery is:

THE NAVAL MUSEUM: The pageant and the glory that was Portugal on the high seas is evoked for posterity in this maritime museum, one of the most important in Europe. In the most appropriate environment, it is installed in the west wing of the Monastery of Jerónimos, the 16th-century monument built by King Manuel I to thank the Lady Mary in commemoration of Vasco da Gama's voyage. The royal galleys recreate the age of opulence that never feared vulgarity. Dragon heads drip with gilt; sea monsters coil with abandon; and, of course, a large crew was no problem for kings and queens in those days.

Surely Cleopatra sailing down the Nile on her barge would have recoiled with jealousy at the sight of the galley Queen Maria I ordered built for the marriage of her son and successor, Crown Prince João, to the Spanish Princess Carlota Joaquine Bourbon in 1784. Eighty wax-dummy oarsmen, elaborately attired in scarlet- and mustard-colored waistcoats, represent the crew.

The museum contains hundreds of models of 15th- to 19th-century sailing ships, the transition from sail to steam, 20th-century warships, merchant marine vessels, fishing boats, river craft, and pleasure boats. In a section devoted to the East is a pearl inlay replica of a Dragon Boat used in maritime and fluvial corteges in the Orient. Other models include a large reproduction of the frigate *Ulysses,* dating from December 15, 1792, and an early 20th-century destroyer with two torpedo tubes.

Wax dummies model a full range of Portuguese naval uniforms, from one worn at a military outpost in Mozambique in 1896 to a model worn as late as 1961. In a special room can be seen the queen's stateroom as it was on the royal yacht of Carlos I, the Braganza king assassinated at Praça do Comércio in 1908. It was on this craft that his son, King Manuel II, and the queen mother, Amélia, escaped to Gibraltar, following the collapse of the Portuguese monarchy in 1910.

Historical exhibits include a letter from Lord Nelson (Brontë Nelson), dated October 24, 1799, earnestly desiring "that your Excellency will not think of quitting Malta till I have a proper force to relieve you." A large map traces the trail of Brito Capelo and Roberto Ivens through the African continent in 1884–1885.

The Naval Museum also honors some of the early Portuguese aviators. On display is the aquaplane *Santa Cruz,* the first aircraft to cross the South Atlantic. The date was March 30, 1922 (*"Aventura Magnifica"* hailed the press), and the captain was Commander Sacoduro Cabral and the navigator Admiral Gago Coutinho, who invented a new sextant for use by airmen. The flight was from Lisbon to Rio de Janeiro, with stopovers en route. Also displayed is a 1917 airplane, the first one used by Portuguese aviators.

The museum charges 7$50 (12¢) for admission every day except Wednesday when it's free (children 8 to 16 pay half price). Known as the **Museu de Marinha,** it is open daily, except Monday, from 10 a.m. to 5 p.m.

Annexed to the Naval Museum, the **Calouste Gulbenkian Planetarium** is open Wednesday from 3 to 4:15 p.m. for students; Saturday and Sunday from 4 to 5:30 p.m. for the general public. The sessions are in Portuguese unless a previous request has been made for English. Admission is 20$ (31¢) for adults and 10$ (15¢) for children during weekends. It is free on Wednesday.

Those too rushed to see the above-mentioned attractions somehow find time for:

THE COACH MUSEUM: Visited by more tourists than any other attraction in Lisbon, the Coach Museum at Belém's Praça Afonso de Albuquerque is considered the finest of its type in the world. It's housed in what was originally an 18th-century riding academy connected to the Belém Royal Palace.

Around the turn of the century, Queen Amélia, wife of the painter king Carlos I, founded the museum. Amélia, however, fled to England with her son Manuel II upon the collapse of the monarchy.

The coaches stand in a former horse ring, and most of them date from the 17th to the 19th centuries. Drawing the most interest is an opulently decorated

106 DOLLARWISE GUIDE TO PORTUGAL

trio of gilded baroque carriages once used by the Portuguese ambassador to the Vatican at the time of Pope Clement XI (1716). Also displayed is a 17th-century coach in which the Spanish Hapsburg king, Philip II, journeyed from Madrid to Lisbon to see his new possession.

Other coaches include the processional chariot of "Our Lady of Cabo," the coach of King João V, of Queen Maria Ana de Austria, as well as Queen Maria's berlinda. Portuguese and foreign harnesses and trappings, all the gala livery, are exhibited on the second floor.

The portrait gallery belonged to the House of Braganza, which collapsed in 1910. Pictured are such notables as Maria I and a host of minor royalty.

The museum is open from 10 a.m. to 5 p.m. daily, except Monday and holidays. During summer it is open from 10 a.m. to 6:30 p.m. It charges 15$ (23¢) admission, except on weekends, when it's free.

Opening onto the Avenida Marginal is:

THE MUSEUM OF POPULAR ART: Nowhere are the folk arts and customs of the Portuguese displayed more dramatically than here. Regional crafts and costumes are grouped according to provinces. The walls are painted by contemporary artists, some of the best in Portugal, including Manuel Lapa and Thomaz de Mello. Their work is supplemented by enlarged photographs of the people of the provinces, each region of which maintains its separate personality.

From the fertile Minho district in the northwest (considered by many the most beautiful part of Portugal) and from the slopes of the Douro Valley (where grapes for port wine are grown) comes a collection of sun clocks, ceramic plates and pottery, a Matósinhos chest, a 19th-century bride's hat, musical instruments, and hand-painted harnesses used for oxen.

Trás-os-Montes, in the severe mountains of the northeast, is represented by an exhibition of fire blowers, masks, spinning wheels, black earthenware (which you can purchase along the roadside if you travel there), and a large handmade rug collection.

In the museum, it's a short trip from Trás-os-Montes to southern Portugal and the Algarve, the region that evokes the landscape of North Africa. On display are the line-cut chimneys from Loulé (in shops you can buy miniatures of these), a water cart, cork objects, palm baskets, and fishing nets.

The Beira room reproduces the interior of a country house of Monsanto, once voted the "most Portuguese village in Portugal." Blacksmith artifacts, ox harnessess, hand-embroidered linen bedspreads, boats from Aveiro, and wicker and straw baskets round out the offerings.

The central tourist district of Estremadura and the plains and pasturelands of Ribatejo are represented by dogs of the hearth, painted dolls from Estremoz, a pilgrimage cart from Elvas, fishermen's "popcorn" sweaters from Nazaré, cork sculptures, and a wax dummy modeling the garb of the *campino*. This Ribatejo cowboy is a herdsman who looks after the bulls on the plains.

The museum is open daily, except Monday, from 10 a.m. to 5 p.m. and charges 10$ (15¢) admission, except on Thursday and Sunday when it's free. Buses 12 and 14 go there.

If you have a car, drive up to **Restelo Chapel** before heading back to Lisbon. It was at this point that priests held masses, praying for the success of such epic voyages as that of Vasco da Gama. A chapel in the Manueline style stands on the spot. A belvedere overlooks the Tagus, offering good views of Belém Tower and Jerónimos Monastery.

3. Museums and Galleries

Although most of the museums of Lisbon are at Belém, two major attractions are found in the city: the National Art Gallery and the Gulbenkian Center for Arts and Culture, described below. For a survey of yet two more museums, the St. Roque gallery of ecclesiastical art and the Archeological Museum in the ruins of the Carmo Church, refer to "The Churches of Lisbon," immediately following.

NATIONAL ART GALLERY: The country's greatest collection of paintings is housed in this art gallery, including many notable paintings, such as *The Temptations of St. Anthony* by Hieronymus Bosch.

At 95 Rua das Janelas Verdes, the museum is open from 10 a.m. to 1 p.m. and from 2:30 to 5 p.m. every day, except Monday (on Thursday and Sunday until 7 p.m.) A 15$ (23¢) entrance fee is charged, except on admission-free Saturday and Sunday.

An important part of the museum, and actually its oldest building, the Church of the Carmelite Convent of S. Alberto contains an exhibition of sculpture, painted and gilt-carved wood, and glazed tiles (azulejos) of the 16th, 17th, and 18th centuries, with which the chapel is decorated.

In the 15th century Nuno Gonçalves painted a series of panels for the Convent of S. Vicente de Fora. Not only was the polyptych the masterpiece of Gonçalves, but it has remained the most celebrated of all Portuguese artworks. It depicts a red-robed and scarlet-hooded saint (whose body was said to have been carried to Lisbon by ravens) holding a Bible, and surrounded by about 60 people.

Another notable painting is a *Salomé* by Lucas Cranach, showing the curiously attired creature holding the disembodied and open-eyed saint's head on a plate. Also attributable to Cranach is a *St. Catherine*.

Other memorable works are by Velázquez, Anthony Vandyck, Sir Joshua Reynolds, Gustave Courbet, Andrea del Sarto (a self-portrait), Magnasco (a Venetian scene standing on an easel), Pieter Brueghel (*Charity Works*), Memling, Murillo, Joos Van Cleef, Dürer (*St. Jerome*), Hans Holbein (*Virgin and Saints*), Zurburán (an entire salon), Poussin, Pontormo (*Alessandro di Medici*), and Frei Carlos, a well-known painter of the Flemish-Portuguese school (first half of the 16th century).

The collection of antique jewelry is remarkable. Gil Vicente created a custodia or monstrance for the Jerónimos Monastery at Belém in 1506 with the first gold that Vasco da Gama brought back from the East. Exceptional also is a processional cross once used at the Monastery of Alcobaça. The Germain brothers created a famous 18th-century silver plate weighing at least a ton—ordered by King João V.

The outstanding sculptor of the 18th century, Machado de Castro, is well represented. Other exhibits include a collection of rare china, both Oriental and European; an exhibition of old Portuguese ceramics; rare antiques, some dating from the 15th century; Flemish tapestries; 16th-century Persian carpets; a rich assemblage of vestments; Italian polychrome works; and the Patiño Room, lined with 18th-century French-designed rocaille boiseries from the Paar Palace in Vienna, and decorated with furniture and a Savonnerie carpet of the same century.

GULBENKIAN CENTER FOR ARTS AND CULTURE: Lisbon's newest museum, inaugurated in 1969, is also one of its best. The Armenian oil tycoon

Calouste Gulbenkian willed to the foundation an outstanding collection of art, considered by many to be among the best in the world in private hands.

This multi-million-dollar center was erected on what was formerly the private estate of the Count of Vilalva. At 45 Avenida da Berna, it is open on Tuesday, Thursday, Friday, and Sunday from 10 a.m. to 5 p.m.; from 2 to 8 p.m. on Wednesday and Saturday. The museum closes on Monday. Except on admission-free weekends, the entrance fee is 10$ (15¢).

Gulbenkian, a long-term art connoisseur, purchased some of his most notable acquisitions from the Hermitage at Leningrad, a feat requiring almost superhuman negotiating skill.

Some of the best known paintings displayed are Rembrandt's *Figure of Age;* Rubens's *Portrait of Helena Fourment;* and Renoir's *Portrait of Madame Claude Monet Lounging.* Other outstanding works include Guardi's scenes of Venice; Gainsborough's *Portrait of Mrs. Lowndes-Stone;* Anthony Vandyck's *Portrait of a Man;* Degas's *L'homme et le pantin,* plus a self-portrait; Mary Cassatt's *Motherly Care;* and Monet's *The Break-up of the Ice.*

The displays also include 15th- and 16th-century French antiques; gold and silver tea service and candelabras; René Lalique glassware and jewelry; and Luca della Robbia ceramics. In the Egyptian wing, the bronze cats are exceptional, as are many of the Greek and Roman exhibitions, including a head attributed to Phidias from the fifth century B.C.

The museum also has a rich collection of art of the Middle East, particularly ceramics and textiles of Turkey and Persia.

MUSEUM OF DECORATIVE ART: Once a private palace belonging to a banker, this Alfama museum is devoted to the decorative arts. Many of the furnishings inside date from the 17th and 18th centuries. The museum stands at the Largo das Portas do Sol, one of the most attractive belvederes in Lisbon.

You are conducted through by a guide every day except Monday, from 10 a.m. to 1 p.m. and from 2 to 5 p.m. (on Sunday from 1 to 5 p.m.). The admission charge is 30$ (46¢), except on Sunday when it's free.

Run by the Fundação Ricardo do Espírito Santo Silva, the museum displays the banker's rich collection of art objects, tapestries (many Flemish ones), rare Oriental china, engravings, and a crystal and silverplate collection. One exhibit is a rare Flemish tapestry dramatizing the sea route of Vascô da Gama to India.

A visit to this Azurara Palace is usually followed up by a tour of the **Fundação Ricardo do Espírito Santo Silva,** 90 Largo das Portas do Sol. This is really a factory—but what a factory! Naomi Barry exclaimed, "Every other nook and cranny of the palace is an atelier humming with a kind of activity that has almost disappeared from the world."

In the two dozen workshops, you'll find woodcarving experts, iron forgers, metal engravers, Arraiolos carpet weavers, silversmiths, and bookbinders who work in gold leaf and can reproduce with accuracy characteristic bindings from the 16th century up to the romantic period.

One of these workshops was responsible for the restoration of Madame Du Barry's library at Versailles. Many of the furnishings in the suites at the Ritz and at the Palácio de Seteais at Sintra were reproduced in the workshops here.

Whatever you want reproduced, including anything you see at the palace, can be turned out. However, money and time should be no object.

LISBON: SIGHTS

MUSEUM OF CONTEMPORARY ART: Don't expect anything at this museum to be very contemporary or very exciting. Still, for the art connoisseur, especially one with traditional tastes, it displays works of leading romantic Portuguese painters of the late 19th and early 20th centuries.

The gallery is an old museum, dating from 1911 when it was probably considered avant-garde. Some of the paintings, such as a portrait that Sousa Lopes did of his mother, are intriguing. The Porto-born sculptor Teixeira Lopes is represented by several works, but you'll see better examples of his style if you visit his home city.

Occasionally, a foreign piece, such as a Rodin bronze, will creep in, or else a rare nude by Sousa Pinto. Perhaps the best known painter represented is Columbano, who lived from 1856 to 1929. The gallery offers an entire room filled with his canvases, chiefly his portraits. Other works are by José Malhoa, Velozo Salgado, Carlos Reis, and Eduardo Malta.

At 6 Rua Serpa Pinto, the museum is open daily except Monday, from 10 a.m. to 5 p.m., and charges 10$ (15¢) for entrance, except on admission-free weekends. Buses 12 and 27 from Praça Pombal, or bus 14 from Praça Figueira will take you there.

NATIONAL ARMY MUSEUM: This museum was built on the site of an early foundry 800 yards west of a naval shipyard, which existed in the reign of Dom Manuel I (1495-1521). Later a new foundry was erected, producing gunpowder for the ships sailing on their missions of maritime discoveries. A fire damaged these buildings and the 1755 earthquake destroyed them completely.

King Joseph I (1750-1777) ordered the construction of new buildings and an additional arms warehouse. The present building, therefore, was not at all planned as a museum. For that reason, paintings by Portuguese masters from the past three centuries coexist with beautiful tiles and pieces of gilt carved wood. These are but a backdrop, of course, for bronze cannons of various periods and light arms of artistic and historical value. One of the cannons is from Diu, weighs 20 tons, and bears Arabic inscriptions. Some iron pieces date to the 14th century.

Light weapons, such as various guns, pistols, and swords, are displayed in cases. One of the prize exhibits is a gorget worn by Francis I, king of France. Other exhibits include the swords of King John I and Nuno Alvares Pereira, both of the late 14th century. Yet another display is a two-handed sword once belonging to Vasco da Gama.

The museum is at Largo do S. Apolónia, in front of the railway station of Santa Apolónia, a short walk from the Terreiro do Paço.

The National Army Museum is open daily, except Monday, from 10 a.m. to 4 p.m., charging 10$ (15¢) for admission. It's free on Sunday.

RAFAEL BORDALO PINHEIRO MUSEUM: Rafael Bordalo Pinheiro was a ceramicist and caricaturist in the 19th century, and this museum at 382 Campo Grande honors his memory. Actually, it's one of the most esoteric museums in Lisbon and is of little interest to the average North American visitor, unless he or she is faced with a rainy day in the city with nothing else to do.

But if one knew more about Bordalo Pinheiro's day—that is, 19th-century Portuguese life—if one were aware of the scandals of the literati, then the kindly artist could be more appreciated. In his caricatures he poked fun at some of the most distinguished people of his day.

Bordalo Pinheiro's crustacean and reptilian ceramics are of interest, perhaps intentionally bordering on caricature. Search out the portrait that Columbano, the outstanding Portuguese painter who died in 1929, did of Bordalo Pinheiro.

You can visit the museum (no entrance fee) any day, except Monday, from 10 a.m. to 5 p.m.

4. The Churches of Lisbon

"If you want to see all of the churches of Lisbon, you'd better be prepared to stay here for a few months," the guide told a tourist. What follows is the pick of the litter.

THE PANTHEON CHURCH OF ST. ENGRÁCIA: Generations came and went, but it looked as if St. Engrácia would never be built. The old church that stood on this spot was wiped out in the earthquake of 1755, but workmen in the 18th century started the task of rebuilding in the baroque style. The job bogged down, and it wasn't until the 1960s that the church was finally completed.

The effect today is austere, befitting a Pantheon of such heads of state as Sidónio Pais, assassinated in 1918, and the general, António Oscar de Fragoso Carmona. The latter was president of Portugal from 1928 until his death in 1951.

The church, built in the form of a Greek cross, with four square towers, also contains memorials to such personages as Henry the Navigator, Luís Vas de Camões, author of *Os Lusíadas;* Almeida Garrett, the 19th-century romantic poet; Vasco da Gama; and Pedro Alvares Cabral, the explorer who discovered Brazil. You can visit daily, except Monday, from 10 a.m. to 5 p.m.

CARMO CHURCH (THE ARCHEOLOGICAL MUSEUM): Standing in its ruins today, you can only imagine the glory of this former convent of the 14th century. On the morning of November 1, 1755, the church was crowded for All Saints Day. The roof cracked and buckled. It was the Lisbon earthquake. When the debris was cleared, only a Gothic skeleton remained. For some reason, the Carmo Church was never reconstructed.

Silhouetted against the Lisbon sky are the chancel, apse, and the Great Door, a section of which has been converted into an **Archeological Museum.** The meager treasures inside include a Roman sarcophagus, a numismatic collection of rare medieval coins, a window removed from the Jerónimos Monastery at Belém, some skeletons resting under glass, and a few 16th-century tombs. The museum is at Largo do Carmo, best reached by taking the Santa Justa elevator from the Rua do Ouro below. The hours are from 10 to noon and 2 to 5 p.m. daily, except Monday. Entrance fee is 10$ (15¢).

ST. ROQUE CHURCH AND MUSEUM: Go here to see a fabulous collection of baroque-style silver sculpture. For example, a pair of silver and gold torchères, designed by Gagliardi, weighs about 840 pounds, one of the finest in the world. Among the treasures is gold embroidery dating from the 18th century. The church was built in the late 1500s in what has been called Jesuit-style architecture.

The museum adjoins the church and is usually visited first. Among the treasures, aside from those already mentioned, is a vestment said to have been worn by the pope 200 years ago in the sacrament of St. John's Chapel in Rome. Most of the religious art came from Italy in the reign of João V. Specific gems include a Gigli-designed chalice, iconographs of St. John the Baptist, portraits from the 16th century (notably one of the wedding ceremony of Manuel the Fortunate, plus portraits of João III and Catherine of Austria).

In the church, under a painted wood ceiling, is one of the best known chapels in Lisbon, that of St. John the Baptist. It was built in Rome in the 18th century, completely dismantled, then shipped to Lisbon and reassembled in its entirety, with alabaster, lapis lazuli, and other materials. João V ordered the chapel in 1740. The mosaics in marble resemble an oil painting.

In the sacristy are paintings depicting events in the lives of Jesuit saints.

The church and museum at Largo Trindade Coelho may be visited from 10 a.m. to 5 p.m. daily, except Monday, for a 10$ (15¢) admission fee. There is no charge on Sunday.

ST. VINCENT OUTSIDE THE WALLS: In this Renaissance church, the greatest names and some forgotten wives of the House of Braganza were placed to rest. It's really a Pantheon. Originally a convent from the 12th century, the church was erected between 1582 and 1627. At that time it was outside the walls of Lisbon, although the sprawling city has long ago incorporated it. On the morning of the earthquake of 1755, the cupola fell in.

The Braganzas, one of whom is still a pretender to the throne of Portugal, assumed power in 1640. This one family then ruled until 1910, when the Portuguese monarchy collapsed and King Manuel II and the queen mother, Amélia, fled to England.

The body of Manuel II was subsequently returned to Portugal following his death. Amélia, the last queen of Portugal, died in 1951 and was also entombed here. Her husband Carlos I, the painter king, and her son, Prince Luís Felipe, were both killed by an assassin at Praça do Comércio in 1908. Their bodies were also interred here.

Aside from the royal tombs, one of the most important reasons for visiting St. Vincent is to see its azulejos (the glazed earthenware tiles), some of them illustrating the fables of La Fontaine. Although I suspect no one's officially counted them, their number is placed at one million. In the sacristy the architect chose Portuguese marble to line the walls and combined it with jacaranda wood from Brazil. Look for a curious ivory statue of Christ, carved in the former Portuguese province of Goa in the 18th century.

The church, at Largo de S. Vicente, may be visited only from 1 to 7 p.m. for 15$ (23¢) admission. Closed Sunday.

CHURCH OF MADRE DE DEUS: One of the outstanding characteristics of Portuguese churches is the architectural device of lining the walls with azulejos, glazed earthenware tiles. Delft blue and white usually predominate in the color scheme, crowned by baroque carved gilt wood, framing a rich collection of 17th- and 18th-century oil paintings. The small sacristy is lined with polychrome azulejos (Portuguese work), and there you can also see the retable of Sta. Auta, of the 16th-century Flemish school. For some of the finest azulejos decoration, visit this former convent founded by Queen Leonor in 1509.

Near the riverside, at 4 Rua Madre de Deus, it is open from 10 a.m. to 5 p.m. every day, except Monday, and charges no admission. Generally, a guide will conduct you on a tour of the precincts.

5. A Bullfight Spectacle

Bullfighting in Portugal was once the sport of noblemen. Today, the art form still draws a crowd, although the "aristocrats" are now the spectators.

Unlike the Spanish, the Portuguese do not kill the bull, a prohibition decreed in the 18th century by Prime Minister Marquês de Pombal, following the death in the sport of the son of the Duke of Arcos.

Critics in the last few years have been mounting an attack against this limitation. A Lisbon commentator Jaime Saraiva was quoted in the press: "A bullfight without a kill is a great lie; it is not serious."

However, Marvine Howe wrote: "With the elimination of the death stroke, the Portuguese bullfight lost most of its excitement only to become one of the most beautiful equestrian displays in the world."

At the start of the *corrida*, the matadors parade in, attired in their suits of light, based on the same style worn in the 18th century. They are followed by *cavaleiros*, the men who fight the bull on horseback, eventually placing darts in his neck.

Trailing are the *moços de forcado*, a team of tacklers who grapple with the bull, some in face-to-face combat! The *forcados* wear olive-colored trousers separated from their gold jackets by a red sash. Their calves are covered with white stockings, and traditionally a green cap, trimmed in red, rests on their heads (many of the tacklers have now abandoned this garb).

When the trumpet sounds, the *cavaleiro* and the bull enter the ring. The horseman and his steed race toward the bull, swerving just in time to avoid a head-on collision. As he passes the animal, the cavaleiro thrusts three or four darts into his neck.

Before the fight ends, a phalanx of eight tacklers advances toward the bull, the leader shouting: "*Eh, Touro! Eh! Touro!*" Using nothing but their bare hands, the *forcados* tackle the bull. For many, this is the most exciting aspect of the game. However, the horns are padded with leather bandages known as *emboladas*.

You can attend one of these pageants from Easter until around mid-October. The 8500-seat **Campo Pequeno** (reached on the Metro) in Lisbon is the largest ring in the country, and usually presents fights on Thursday and Sunday afternoons in season. These *corridas* and the names of the stars (or lack of them) are announced well in advance, so your hotel concierge can be of help to you (many arrange tickets).

Another major bullring is the **Monumental de Cascais**, at Cascais, the resort lying west of Estoril on the Costa do Sol. You can take the electric train from Lisbon which ends its run in Cascais; from the station, an inexpensive taxi will take you to the bullring itself, just outside the center of town.

When a major star isn't appearing, the average price for one of the best seats is 750 ($11.48) to 1200$ ($18.36)—that is in the *sombra* (shade) section. For *sombra y sol,* you'll pay around 400$ ($6.12), and your seat will be in the shade for half of the fight, in the sun for the remainder.

6. Other Sights

Those sights in and around Lisbon that could not be categorically listed elsewhere are highlighted below. Certain of these attractions reveal much about the nation's natural resources, geography, climate, inhabitants, and lifestyle, and it is the knowledge of these things that makes you far more than just a tourist passing through. For example:

THE SPECTACLE OF THE MARKET: The big market of Ribeira Nova is as close as you can get to the heart of Lisbon. Near the Cais do Sodré, where trains are boarded for the Costa do Sol, an enormous roof shelters a collection of produce stalls, where you'll see, in its native state, the produce you'll be eating later at one of Lisbon's finest restaurants.

Foodstuffs are brought in each morning in bulging wicker baskets filled with oversize carrots, cabbages big enough for shrubbery, and stalks of bananas. Some of the produce arrives by donkey; some of it by truck; some balanced on top of the heads of Lisboan women in the Mediterranean fashion—all from yesterday's field. The rich soil produces the juiciest of peaches, the most aromatic tomatoes.

"Seeing-eye" fishing boats, many believed to have been based on Phoenician designs, tie up at the dock at dawn with their catch. The fish are deposited on long marble counters; cod, squid, bass, hake, swordfish. Soon the *varinas* (fishwives) take wicker baskets of the fresh catch, balancing them on their heads, and climb the cobbled streets of the Alfama or the Bairro Alto, selling the fish from door to door.

At the market, mounds of vegetables, fruit, and fish are hovered over by hearty, friendly, outgoing Portuguese women gaily clad in voluminous skirts and calico aprons. On cue the vendors begin howling out the value of their wares, stopping only to pose for an occasional snapshot.

Adjoining the market, away from the river, cutstone streets are flanked with shops selling inexpensive Portuguese clothing. The best buy, if you can locate one, is a distinctively styled cape from the Alentejo district. In three tiers, these capes are often capped with red-fox collars.

Finally, we know of no better way to cap your Lisbon sightseeing adventure than by heading to:

THE GREENHOUSE: The Portuguese call it their **Estufa Fria**. It's in the handsomely laid out Edward VII Park, named after Queen Victoria's son, to commemorate his three trips to Lisbon. Against a background of streams and rocks, the tropical plants grow in such profusion that some writers have called it a "sylvan glade." It is even more than that, so luxuriant is its growth that it evokes a rain forest.

The park lies at the top of the Avenida da Liberdade, crowned by a statue of the Marquês de Pombal, with his "house pet," a lion. There's a 10$ (15¢) admission charge to the greenhouse, which is open from 10 a.m. to 6 p.m.

READER'S RECOMMENDATION: "For a good view of the harbor and a place to sip a drink leisurely, go to the **Esplanada in Topo** in the Parque Eduardo VII. The drinks are cheap, and there is food available, although it didn't look too inviting. The strangest part of it was that there weren't any other tourists there during our visit. You can sit outside under umbrellas on top of this nice hill and just look. A lot of students were there with their books studying" (Mrs. Bob Lowdon, Fort Worth, Tex.).

JARDIM ZOOLOGICO: The Zoological Garden, with a collection of some 2000 animals, enjoys a flower-filled setting in the 65-acre Park of Laranjeiras, about a ten-minute subway ride from the Rossio, on the Estrada de Benefica. The Children's Zoo, with its miniature houses in small gardens, is exceptional.

There are also a small train, rowboats, a roller skating rink, elephant and pony rides, films, and puppet shows presented on Sunday. It's open from 9 a.m. till sunset. Admission is 70$ ($1.07) for adults, 10$ (15¢) for children 7 to 10. You can reach it on the Metropolitan or else take bus 15, 31, or 46, leaving from the Rossio.

BRITISH CEMETERY: Up the Rua da Estrêla at one end of the Estrêla Gardens lies the British Cemetery. It's famous as the burial place of Henry Fielding, the English novelist (*Tom Jones*) and dramatist. A sick man, Fielding went to Lisbon in 1754 for his health, and the story of that trip is narrated in the posthumous tract *Journal of a Voyage to Lisbon*. Reaching Lisbon in August, he died two months later. A monument was erected in 1830, honoring him.

Chapter IX

NIGHTLIFE IN AND AROUND LISBON

1. The Fado Clubs
2. The Capital After Dark
3. Estoril by Night
4. The Clubs of Cascais

UNLESS YOU HAVE experienced the nostalgic sounds of fado, the songs of sorrow, you will not know Portugal. Certainly not its soul. The fado is Portugal's most vivid art form; and no visit to Lisbon should be planned without at least one night spent in a local tavern, where this traditional folk music is heard.

Originating in the lowly dock area, fado rose to embrace the hearts of the Portuguese people. A rough translation of *fado* is fate, from the Latin *fatum*, meaning prohpecy. The quintessence of *saudade*, fado usually tells of unrequited love, jealousy, a longing for days gone by. As one expert put it, it speaks of "life commanded by the Oracle, which nothing can change."

Fado found its earliest fame in the 19th century with Maria Severa, the beautiful daughter of a gypsy who took Lisbon by storm, singing her way into the hearts of the people, and especially the heart of the Count of Vimioso, an outstanding bullfighter of his day. Legend has it that she is honored by present-day *fadistas* who wear a black-fringed shawl in her memory.

In this century the most famous exponent of fado is Amália Rodrigues, introduced to American audiences at an unheralded appearance in the 1950s at the New York club, La Vie en Rose. She was discovered while walking barefoot and selling flowers on the Lisbon docks, near the Alfama. Fado is also sung by men, who are called *fadistas* as well.

Clutching black shawls around themselves, the female fadistas pour out their emotions, from the tenderest whisper of hope to a wailing lament of life's tragedies. As they sing accompanied by a guitar and a viola, they seem to lose all contact with the surrounding world, standing against a black gas street lamp, without benefit of theatrical spots, makeup, or other scenery—just standing there. They seemingly outdo the Rhine's Lorelei in pulling you into their world of tenderness and fire.

Even though a great deal of enjoyment is derived from understanding its poetic imagery, a knowledge of Portuguese is not essential. The lyrical power, the warmth of the voices, the personality of the singer can go a long way in communicating.

Don't go to hear fado and plan to carry on a private conversation. It's considered very bad form. Most of the authentic fado clubs are clustered near each other in either the Bairro Alto or in the Alfama, between St. George's Castle and the docks, and you can "fado hop" between these two typical quarters.

Alfama-bound hoppers can ask the taxi driver to deliver them to the **Largo do Chafariz,** a small plaza a block from the harbor, and Bairro Alto devotees can get off at the **Largo do S. Roque.** Most of our recommendations lie only a short walk from either of these squares.

The cafés offer regional Portuguese dinners, although it's customary to go and order drinks only (usually a two-drink minimum). The music begins between 9 and 10 but it's much better to arrive after 11 p.m. Many of the clubs stay open till 3 a.m.; others, till dawn.

1. The Fado Clubs

Lisboa à Noite, 69 Rua das Gáveas (tel. 36-85-57). Electricity fills the air—the tempestuous Fernanda Maria is about to make her first appearance of the evening. Tossing down a shot of whiskey offered by a waiter, she stands quietly, tensely clutching her black shawl. Then she comes forward, pauses, scans the audience, and pours forth all the fiery intensity of fado. You, too, may fall under her spell. Success has come to Fernanda—she owns the club.

The 17th-century-style setting is rustic, yet luxurious (once this Bairro Alto club was a stable). Creating its present ambience are thick stone-edged arches, heavy hand-hewn beams, blue and white tiled walls, a round well with its original bucket, a collection of old engravings, antique guns, and pewter and copper. When it's cold, scented eucalyptus logs crackle in a high fireplace. In the rear is an open kitchen and charcoal grill, with an assemblage of spices, sausages, garlic pigtails, and onions hanging from the beams.

House specialties include dry codfish Fernanda Maria, 400$ ($6.12), and steak Lisboa à Noite flambé, 600$ ($9.18). A soup à alentejana at 110$ ($1.68) can begin your meal. Minimum is 500$ ($7.65).

"A Severa," 49-57 Rua das Gáveas (tel. 36-40-06). Good food and careful selection of fadistas make this the perennial favorite. Before he became president, Mr. Nixon selected it for a night on the town with his wife, leading a conga-like line between tables, warbling the refrain, "Severa . . . Severa . . . Severa." Every night top singers, both male and female, appear at the Bairro Alto nightspot, accompanied by guitar and viola music. Alternating are folk dancers who perform in regional costumes. In a niche you'll spot a statue honoring the club's namesake, Maria Severa, the legendary gypsy fadista of the 19th century. After midnight tourists seem to recede a bit in favor of loyal Lisbon habitués, who request and sometimes join in on their favorite fado number.

The club is owned by Julio Barros and his wife Maria José. He keeps everything running smoothly out front, and she takes care of the kitchen, turning out regional dishes based on recipes from the north of Portugal. For dinner don't miss chicken cooked and served in a clay pot for 400$ ($6.12) per person. Her green cabbage soup goes for 125$ ($1.91). Another house specialty is stuffed squid, 325$ ($4.97), as well as steak of the house, fried in a clay dish, 340$ ($5.20). Closed Thursday.

Adega Machado, 91 Rua do Norte (tel. 36-00-95), has won the test of time and is today one of the favored fado clubs of Portugal. In days of yore you could spot perhaps Edward G. Robinson or Vittorio de Sica listening to the incomparable Amália Rodrigues. Alternating with its fadistas are folk dancers, whirling, clapping, singing their native songs in colorful costumes. The evening dinner hour starts at 8 p.m. and the doors don't close till 3 a.m. when the last fadista aficionado trails out humming his favorite song.

Dinner is à la carte, and the cuisine is mostly Portuguese, with any number of regional dishes. House specialties include chicken in a pot 250$ ($3.82); stuffed squid, 300$ ($4.59); steak Machado, 380$ ($58.14); roasted baby goat, 300$ ($4.59); and pork with clams, 320$ ($4.90). A simple dessert to follow might be almond cake made with nuts from the Algarve, 100$ ($1.53). If you drop in just for the show, you pay a minimum of 250$ ($3.82) for a drink.

Guests often join the singers and folk dancers, carrying arched garlands of flowers, as they parade around the crowded tables, singing the "Marcha do Machado."

Parreirinha da Alfama, 1 Beco do Espírito (tel. 86-82-09). Seemingly, every fadista worth her shawl has sung at this oldtime café, just a one-minute walk from the dockside edge of the Alfama. It's fado and fado only that enthralls here, not folk dancing. You can order a good regional dinner beginning early, but it's suggested that you go toward the shank of the evening . . . and stay late. It's open all night. In the first part of the program, the fadistas get all the popular songs out of the way, then settle in to their own more classic favorites.

Drinks average around 275$ ($4.21) for hard liquor, half that for soft drinks. You can order a filling dinner for 550$ ($8.42), and the menu includes specialties from nearly every region of Portugal. The atmosphere is self-consciously taverna, with all sorts of Portuguese provincial oddments along with photos of famous people who've been here. One can forgive the too-cute reproduction of a village, with its mock doors and windows. However, the singers selected by the management are first rate.

O Poeta, 22 Travessa de San Miguel (tel. 86-85-52), is a showcase for Maria da Fé, a Portuguese recording artist and fadista. Newer than the clubs recommended previously, it is air-conditioned. Madame da Fé performs against a backdrop of a Lisbon photo mural. Portuguese floor shows are staged nightly between 10 p.m. and 3 a.m. The minimum is 350$ ($5.36), which, incidentally, is the cost of an average drink.

2. The Capital After Dark

Fado outshines other nighttime entertainment in Lisbon. However, for a change of pace, we've included suggestions for most tastes: vaudeville houses; nightclubs for conventional drinking and dancing; and disco for those of limber limb.

On a more cultural note, opera and ballet buffs may want to attend a performance at the **Teatro Nacional de São Carlos,** at Largo de São Carlos, created in the 18th century and booking top companies from different countries. The season begins the latter part of January, extending through June. In addition, there are several theaters presenting plays from autumn through spring, but only in Portuguese. Recitals and concerts are held at various places in Lisbon, especially the Greenhouse in Edward VII Park. Motion pictures are shown in their original language. To obtain information on any of the above, consult a copy of *What's On in Lisbon,* available at most newsstands, although your hotel concierge is also a good bet for information, since one of his duties is reserving seats.

THE DISCOS: **Stone's,** 1 Rua do Olival (tel. 66-45-45), is the most exclusive and expensive disco in Portugal, and it's held this position for some time. The patrons are attractively dressed, the atmosphere is clubby, and the drinks are good. Stone's charges the highest door charge in all of Lisbon, 1500$ ($22.95), but you are permitted to use this up in ordering drinks, which cost, by the way, from 250$ ($3.82) to 388$ ($12.24). It's most fashionable here to arrive late.

Ad Lib, 28 Rua Barata Salgueiro (tel. 56-17-17), is a posh disco dreamed up by a clique of chaps who wanted an elegant place to have a bash. On the top floor of a modern building, it doesn't call attention to itself with a sign outside. A uniformed attendant at the formal entrance checks on the intercom system to weed out undesirables. If you're well groomed and not drunk, you stand a good chance of scaling the citadel; even so, it's wise to telephone in advance.

Upstairs, you'll enter a penthouse with a bar on one level, tables and a dancing area on another. A plant-filled terrace provides a view of Lisbon by night. The decor is that of the East, with fine stone Buddhas from Macão, mirrors, and candles in red bowls. Playing the newest continental and American records is a disc jockey. There's a minimum of 800$ ($12.24), with a whiskey costing around 300$ ($4.59) per drink; soft drinks, 200$ ($3.06).

Carrousel, 77 Rua Castilho, lives up to its position in the Ritz compound, overlooking Edward VII Park. Entered via a private doorway, it caters to well-heeled post-25 couples out for a night on the town. A carousel theme is suggested by stripes of red, white, and blue against walls of black infinity. Off center a disc jockey flips and plays an eclectic collection of international recordings.

The club is good for sound. The Carrousel imposes a 550$ ($8.42) minimum, with scotch going for 250$ ($3.82), rye for 280$ ($4.28). Although the doors open at 10:30 p.m., no one seems to appear until after midnight. Once there, couples often stay till 3:30 a.m., squatting on grasshopper chairs, sipping, dancing, or gazing at the "man in the moon" and the simulated stars. Closed Sunday.

Whispers, Edificio Aviz, 35 Avenida Fontes Pereira de Melo, next to the Sheraton Hotel (tel. 57-54-89), is run by the R. R. Club, or Rolls-Royce, in Cascais. So successful was the Costa do Sol version of this chic disco, that its managers brought it to the heartland of Lisbon as well. The minimum is 400$ ($6.12), including service and tax. Most whiskeys begin at 180$ ($2.75), and Whispers is open nightly.

THE NIGHTCLUBS: **Maxime,** 57 Praça da Alegria (tel. 36-53-66), is a nightclub of long standing, offering continental entertainment as well as folk dancing and fado. Its entrepreneurs have tried to carve a niche as an international showplace with the sexiest show in Lisbon, which is staged at 1 a.m. and again at 3 a.m.

The early part of the evening starts at 8 for dancing, the second part at 10 and 11 p.m., when a showcase of Portuguese folklore dances and fado is presented, the performers regionally garbed. The minimum charge is 1000$ ($15.30) per person, and you can order dinner from a menu that includes such dishes as steak Maxime, 500$ ($7.65); a chateaubriand for two, 1000$ ($15.30); and banana flambé, 250$ ($3.82).

O Porão da Nau, 1 Rua Pinheiro Chagas (tel. 51-501), is a disco-nightclub, featuring Brazilian music, fado, and sometimes a drag show in their nightly cabaret. The action takes place in the hold of a simulated Portuguese man-of-war of the 15th century. You descend to the lower levels at the centrally located

Residência A Ponte. You get the feeling that the gangplank will be lifted, the sails hoisted.

Around a circular marble dance floor, tables are set on different levels. The main beams are time-aged, the wall planked, and there are rope railings, a gun collection, an early map charting Portuguese possessions, a finely carved wooden figure used on the bow of a sailing vessel, and a spherical globe. A minimum of 300$ ($4.59) is charged, including service. At 5 a.m. you're tossed overboard. Whiskey costs 225$ ($3.44).

BARS IN LISBON: Procopio, 21-A Alto San Francisco. Forget about maps! Ask someone how to find this place. It's worth the search, one of my favorite bars in the Portuguese capital. Deep into nostalgia, the atmosphere is turn of the century. Your host is Alice Pinto Coelho, who makes the bar like a living room and is a devotee of art nouveau and a film buff. A tiny projector shows silent-screen masterpieces on the wall, as guests sit on red tufted velvet. The bar has many faithful habitués who enjoy its stained and painted glass and its ornate brass hardware. Whiskey costs from 170$ ($2.60). Tasty snacks are available. Procopio is open from 6 p.m. to 3 a.m. except Sunday.

Metro e Meio, 174 Avenida 5 de Outubro (tel. 77-59-97), is spotted easily. A giant yellow ruler forms its facade. In the renovation, the management discovered several grotto-like rooms which had been hidden for decades. Now guests have a choice of a maze of rooms, with a central fireplace. The decor is formed by hand-loomed wall hangings, gilt mirrors, statues, hanging lamps, Victorian fringed shades, and contemporary paintings. Recordings are piped in. Whiskeys begin at 150$ ($2.30), and you can order an omelet or club sandwich for 130$ ($1.99). A taxi ride from the center of Lisbon, the bar stands near the Gulbenkian Museum.

A BAWDY CRAWL ALONG THE DOCKLAND: Remember those movies of port cities, showing red neon lights flashing, drunken sailors staggering down labyrinthine narrow streets, a mixed bag of human flotsam unmatched since Jean Genet wrote of his "whores, thieves, pimps, and beggars." These rip-roaring scenes live on in Lisbon, in the little streets near the dock area, where sailors hang out at bars named after Western American states: Arizona, California, Texas.

The most popular, occasionally drawing some of the slumming Ritz and Palácio crowd, is the **Texas Bar,** 21 São Paulo, a gutsy tavern under a bridge. A singer and seedy combo are suspended from the ceiling, usually warbling a Portuguese version of an old country and western hit.

If you're a man alone (if you're a woman alone, stay away), you'll be surrounded on entering by the wildest assemblage of Gravel Gertie look-alikes this side of Barcelona or Marseilles. "Speak English?" is the typical query. One young man trying to escape answered a resounding, "No, Svenska," But a girl was found who spoke lilting Swedish. The Texas Bar accommodates all.

When the fleet's in, and some fleet from some port is likely to be in all the time, this waterfront hotspot can be very rowdy.

READER'S ENTERTAINMENT SUGGESTION: "For adventurous visitors in Lisbon who have done all the museums, sightseeing, fado, and coffeehouses you recommend so well, there is still the **Parque Mayer,** off Avenida da Liberdade between the Rossio and Hotel Tivoli, where at least one live theatrical experience is still to be enjoyed. Non-Portuguese speakers will not know what the audience is laughing about (rather sharp satirical satire), but where on Broadway or in West End London can you buy a ticket for less than $5 (U.S.), best seats, for an extravaganza with about a dozen changes of scenery, gorgeous costuming on the pretty dancing girls, toe-tapping live music, and live fireworks on stage (behind a fireproof shield)? Ticket-buyers should show the ad from the daily Lisbon paper to get to the right theater so they won't be misdirected to the pornographic skin flicks in the same area" (Mrs. H. S. Stokes, Lagos, Portugal).

For much tamer fare, we strike out for nighttime fun along the Costa do Sol.

3. Estoril by Night

GAMBLING: The **Casino** (tel. 26-45-21) at Estoril is the glamor hub for international society. Occupying a position on the rise of a hill, it opens onto the formal gardens of the Parque Estoril which sweep toward the water. The glass walls suggest an international museum of modern art, and enclose an inner courtyard, with tiled paths, a fountain and pool, and borders of lilac-colored petunias and red carnations.

Off the main lobby are various bars, a nightclub, a motion-picture theater, an art gallery, and groups of boutiques. The five-star magnet, of course, is the Casino, which accepts your mad money between 3 p.m. and 3 a.m. (passport required). An adjoining salon is for one-arm bandits. In the main room you can take your chance at roulette, French bank, chemin de fer, baccarat, blackjack/21, craps, and slot machines. A tourist pass is given for 60$ (92¢).

Other diversions include the **Grand Salon Restaurant,** really a supper club offering a limited 750$ ($11.48) dinner for light eaters, beginning at 9 p.m. Many prefer to go for drinks only, paying a minimum or 350$ ($5.36), 400$ ($6.12) on Friday and Saturday. The extravaganza stage show commences at 11:30 p.m. On the arena stage, leggy, feathered, and bejeweled showgirls strut their wares to good advantage in billowing trains and bespangled bras. Another cabaret-style show begins at 1 a.m. in the **Wonder Bar,** where the house minimum is also 350$ ($5.36) on weekdays, but 400$ ($6.12) on Saturday.

A small movie theater shows films daily, the matinee costing 100$ ($1.53); the nighttime showing 120$ ($1.84). It's the same on weekends and holidays. There's also an art gallery selling contemporary paintings, and a few boutiques offering women's apparel and souvenirs.

DINING AND DANCING: A **Choupana,** on the coastal road at S. João do Estoril (tel. 26-30-99), is the best supper club along the Costa do Sol. It offers a good sound for dancing nightly in a setting on the edge of a cliff, with views of lights from fishing boats and ocean liners, the sound of the surf, and the sight of sunsets. A Choupana, which means hut or shack in Portuguese, is the territory of five partners. One rules in the kitchen, winning bravos from such an elite crowd as South American embassy officials, the Spanish royal family, the Count of Paris, even actors such as Ray Milland and Raymond Burr.

The main room is on two levels, with enough waterside window space to provide everyone with a good seat. On the bill of fare, you can order such dishes as partridge stewed in a casserole, 420$ ($6.43); duck with orange sauce, 450$ ($6.89); and a mixed grill Choupana, 440$ ($6.73). Two exceptional fish dishes are lampreys, Portuguese-style (only in season), 450$ ($6.89), and a Marseilles-style bouillabaisse, 410$ ($6.27). In season, strawberries from Sintra at 150$ ($2.30) make an exciting finish.

Last but not least is the top-notch trio. Music for dining begins at 9:30 p.m., for dancing at 10 p.m., and continues until closing at 3:30 a.m. It's possible to order drinks only, for which you'll pay a minimum of 300$ ($4.59).

ESTORIL: NIGHTLIFE

Frolique, Avenida Clotilde (tel. 26-12-19), is both a disco and a first-class restaurant. If you want dinner, you can go early, at least from 7 p.m. on. Featured are such items as chateaubriand at 340$ ($5.20) and sole meunière with prawns at 360$ ($5.51). If you're just in the mood for dancing, the best hours are between 10 p.m. and 3:30 a.m. You're charged a minimum of 300$ ($4.59). Whiskeys are priced at 200$ ($3.06).

A FORTRESS DISCO: Forte Velho (Old Fort), São Pedro Cadaveira, S. João do Estoril, is where the very young meet in a very old setting. On the sea, the disco was ingeniously conceived by José Dias Pegado, who captured a 17th-century fortress built on a cliff above the ocean. It's built of solid rock and offers a central room with fireplace and walls papered with magazine cutouts, all dominated by a hanging metal fish casting reflections from the psychedelic spotlights.

Dancing is to records only, and there's an adjoining bar with stools and cozy banquettes, ideal for hand-holding couples. For a change of pace, drinks are carried out on the terrace to the parapet, where imbibers gasp at the steep drop to the surf below. The fun commences at 10 p.m., although it doesn't really warm up till around midnight. The Old Fort rides the crest until closing at 3:30 a.m. every night. You pay a minimum charge of 300$ ($4.59) nightly. For scotch, the price is 170$ ($2.60), only 120$ ($1.84) for beer or soft drinks.

BARS IN ESTORIL: Bar Galito, Estrada Marginal, is handy for those who want an easy and inexpensive evening of fado, without having to make the trek into Lisbon. Within sight of the Hotel Cibra, it is near the station and next door to the Banco de Alentejo. Inside, it consists of two adjoining rooms, the gap bridged by fadistas and their guitarists. The decor is contrived taverna, with brass-studded leather chairs and crude stools. There's a house minimum of 240$ ($3.67) after 10 p.m., and it's a friendly and pleasant place, easy to while away an hour.

The most popular bar is the **Pickwick Pub,** 3 Avenida Biarritz. The Pickwick is decorated like an old English pub, complete with carpeted floor, mugs hanging over the bar, and plenty of cozy nooks and crannies where you sit in subdued lighting. Soft music is provided from a disc jockey sitting in an adjoining room. You can play darts, have light meals, and while away a couple of hours chatting with the locals and foreigners. It's open from noon to 2 a.m. A pint of English ale goes for 100$ ($1.53), a half pint for 75$ ($1.15). Whiskey is 200$ ($3.06).

A BOÎTE AND BAR IN MONTE ESTORIL: Ronda, 3 Avenida Sabóia. Disco addicts are fickle, flitting from one hot spot to another, then on to the next even before the season is over. Apparently, one exception to the rule is this perennially popular boîte. Perched on a hill above the coastal highway in Monte Estoril, it offers an unobstructed view of the bay of Cascais, and a smartly and comfortably outfitted interior in red. It provides the latest recorded music for dancing. The records start spinning at 10 p.m. There is a 240$ ($3.67) minimum. You pay 110$ ($1.68) for a beer, 200$ ($3.06) for whiskey, plus taxes. Open nightly, it closes at 3:30 a.m.

Ray's Cocktail Bar & Lounge, 25 Avenida Sabóia (tel. 268-01-06), in Monte Estoril, is popular with American expatriates, many of whom make it their private club. It's a souped-up decorator extravaganza that belongs to a New Yorker in exile who is known simply as Ray. Inside, you're likely to find a completely catholic assemblage of elements—a fátima hand from Tangier, a glass ruby-colored newel post finial, chandeliers dripping with crystal, an ostrich fan (in black, no less), antique benches, provincial chairs, plus a heterogeneous mixture of modern art. Everyone seemingly enjoys Ray's drinks (many enjoy quite a few of them), and his minimum is a modest 50$ (77¢). Most strong drinks cost 150$ ($2.30). Hovering everywhere at once, even joining in a bit of the juicy gossip of the day, Ray is the perfect host. He is at home from 6 p.m.

4. The Clubs of Cascais

The **Van Gogo,** 9 Travessa Alfarrobeira, is a chic playground. Modestly hidden in a corner stone building, it was transformed from a simple fisherman's cottage into a disco. A doorman inside carefully evaluates those who would cross the threshold, using some inner radar we don't understand. If you are seemingly well-behaved and not on the prowl, then you'll be given the green light to go inside.

Behind its facade, you'll encounter a young crowd similar to the one at Juan-Les-Pins. On the inside, a seductive atmosphere is created by the black glass walls, and the customers can rock and roll. You pay 1500$ ($22.95) as an entrance minimum, with beer priced at 180$ ($2.75), whiskey at 260$ ($3.97). The Van Gogo opens its doors year round at 10 p.m., closing at 3:30 a.m.

Palm Beach, Praia da Conceição (tel. 28-08-51), is a hillside disco with a rather swank atmosphere—again with a doorman to weed out undesirables. As of this writing, the Palm Beach is riding the crest of the wave along the Costa do Sol, drawing a young, fun-loving crowd that's well mannered enough to please the management. The club is positioned below the coastal road, its wide windows overlooking the bay at Cascais. You lounge comfortably on banquettes and chairs when not dancing on the mini-size floor. The atmosphere is informal, not dressy, and only records are played. The minimum is 240$ ($3.67), with beer costing 90$ ($1.38), and hard drinks at 180$ ($2.75) to 250$ ($3.82).

Borsalino, 19 Rua Visconde da Luz (tel. 286-43-81), is a hub for an international crowd of young people, who drop in any time between 4 p.m. and 3:30 a.m. for drinks and talk. The excitement is generated partly by the head bartender, Luís Eduardo, and partly by the atmosphere. Art nouveau reigns. On quiet nights you're likely to find some twosome playing chess at one of the tables. You pay 50$ (77¢) for soft drinks, 75$ ($1.15) for a pint of beer, 140$ ($2.14) for gin or vodka, and 180$ ($2.75) for a regular whiskey.

Arreda, 3 Rua Alexandre Herculano (tel. 28-38-64), is a showcase for male fadista Julio Ribeiro. "I'm just an amateur," he confesses. However, we know he's been singing for 22 years. He takes special care to capture the nuance of the words and music of fado. His somewhat hard-to-find fado house is off the beaten path. The decorations are regional. Sometimes late at night he invites his friends to join him in fado singing. The atmosphere is spontaneous. The Arreda is open daily from 10 p.m. till 3:30 a.m. The price of one whiskey—that is, 200$ ($3.06)—is the only admission you have to pay.

Rolls-Royce, 6-B Travessa Fonso Sanches, is sometimes known as the R. R. Club. It's the latest craze in Cascais among disco dancers. Because of the blasting soundtrack, the atmosphere is supercharged. To get in, you're charged a minimum of 400$ ($9.18), including service and taxes. The average whiskey costs 225$ ($3.44). The Rolls-Royce runs every day, from 11 p.m. to 3:30 a.m.

READER'S NIGHTLIFE SUGGESTION: "We found a fado club which we enjoyed called **Kopus** at 3 Largo das Grutas in Cascais. It was a local fado. People of the country would sing, as would professionals. We only had wine here, but Portuguese sausage, sweet cookies, candy, and olives were served. It's open every night until 4 a.m." (Mrs. Rosanna Pastor, West Hartford, Conn.).

Beyond Lisbon and the Costa do Sol lies a series of one-day trips from the capital, previewed in the two chapters coming up.

Chapter X

SOUTH OF THE TAGUS

1. Azeitão
2. Sesimbra
3. Portinho da Arrábida
4. Setúbal
5. Palmela

THE WIDOW AND THE SPINSTER, the rheumatic and those plagued with "the vapors"—the bulwark of Victorian England's 19th-century continental travelers—crossed the Tagus by boat and headed for the scenic wonders on the left bank of Lisbon.

Chances are, under one arm they carried a gold-leafed copy of a work by Robert Southey, England's poet laureate. After all, this Lake poet, a much-traveled gentleman, did more than anyone to publicize the glories that awaited his compatriots on the other bank. He virtually made the trek famous when he wrote: "I have never seen such a sublime panorama as the Arrábida Mountains afford, which, constantly changing as we go our way, offer us new beauties at every turn."

Nowadays, the narrow isthmus south of the Tagus is fast booming into a major attraction, beefed up by foreign visitors who seemingly have never heard of, nor could care less about, what the son of an unsuccessful linendraper had to say about the district's natural beauties.

Behind the upsurge of interest is the Ponte 25 de Abril, the longest suspension bridge ever erected in Europe. It has speeded traffic and development to the area, and now it is possible to cross the Tagus in minutes, then head rapidly across good roads through pine groves to the vertexes of the triangle known as "The Land of the Three Castles": Sesimbra, Setúbal, and Palmela. Of course, traditionalists still prefer taking the ferry from Praça do Comércio (Black Horse Square) in Lisbon, docking in Cacilhas.

The isthmus, long cut off from the Portuguese capital, is wild, rugged, lush, and productive. The groves are heavy with the odors of ripening oranges and vineyards known for their grapes used to make muscatel. With craggy cliffs and coves in the background, the crystalline waters of the Atlantic are ideal for swimming and skindiving, or fishing for tuna, swordfish, bass, whatever. Sandy beaches double as the sites of fish auctions and leisurely sunbathing (some of the skimpy suits worn by North European beauties make aging black-shawled Portuguese varinas cross themselves). Farther up from the sardine-canning center of Setúbal, the coastline roughens where the Sêrra of Arrábida meets the sea, resulting in an abundance of caves, grottos, and precipitous crags.

The land possesses vivid reminders of its past, reflected in Moorish architectural influences, Roman ruins and roads, heritages from the Phoenicians, and Spanish fortresses. Mighty castles and humble fishermen's cottages alike shook on a November day in 1755 when the earthquake brought Lisbon to her knees. Signs of that catastrophe are still evidenced in the ruins of the hamlet of Palmela, and the lonely walls of Coina Castle.

The strip of land plummets toward the sea, stretches along for miles of sandy beaches, and rolls through fertile vineyards. It's a place of contrasts, natural beauty, and history.

Its proximity to Lisbon (Setúbal is only 25 miles from the capital) makes it possible for a one-day excursion. But its unusual inns and moderate tariffs mark it as a place where the dollarwise reader will want to linger.

1. Azeitão

This sleepy village lies in the heart of quinta country. In Portuguese, a quinta means a farm, villa, or country house. At its most meager, it is a simple farmhouse surrounded by lands. At its best, it is a mansion of great architectural style filled with art decorations. Azeitão boasts the best.

It is said that King Manuel I started the concept of quintas in the early 16th century when he built the **Quinta de Bacalhoa** at Vila Fresca de Azeitão. The king's mother once lived there. In time it was taken over by the son of Afonso de Albuquerque. At one point in its history, the building was owned by the Braganzas, eventually falling into disrepair, as many of its decorations, specifically its antique tiles, were carted off by vandals.

Before World War II, the mansion was purchased by an American woman who worked for years restoring it as much as possible to its original condition. The architecture is characterized by loggias, pavilions, half-moon domes that suggest a Moorish influence, and a trio of pyramided towers. One of the panels of 16th-century azulejos (tiles) depicts an innocent Susanna being hotly pursued by lecherous Elders. Some architectural critics have suggested that the palace betrays the first buds of the Renaissance in Portugal. Even though it is a private residence, you can sometimes obtain permission at the gate lodge to visit the topiary gardens.

On the other hand, the second 16th-century mansion, **Quinta das Torres**, can not only be visited, but you can stop over for a meal or even spend the night (see below). The third palace was erected at Vila Nogueira de Azeitão by the Dukes of Aveiro in a classically Renaissance style.

Azeitão makes a good base for trekkers, especially those who want to scale the limestone Sêrra of Arrábida by foot. Others settle for long walks through scented pine woods or silvery olive groves. To cap your day, you can order some Azeitão cheese and a bottle of local muscatel. The village lies 9½ miles north of Setúbal, 15½ miles south of Lisbon.

THE BUDGET RANGE: Quinta das Torres, 5 Estrada Nacional, Azeitão (tel. 228-00-01), is a 16th-century baronial mansion, which up until recently used only candlelight and kerosene lamps to illuminate its stately rooms at night. It's been kept intact on purpose for those desiring to live quietly, stepping back in time. It has been owned by the same family for many generations, and the present descendant, Dr. Bento de Sousa, perpetuates the old traditions.

The estate is approached through large gates and along a tree-lined driveway. Gradually, a pair of square peaked towers framing the entrance terrace comes into view. Ten bedrooms, all with private baths, have been set aside for paying guests. Each is quite different, ranging from smaller chambers to a ballroom-size suite dominated by princess-style brass beds, with a high tester and flouncy soft ruffles. Some of the rooms have high shuttered windows, time-mellowed tiled floors, antique furnishings, vases of fresh flowers, oil lamps, and niches with saints or madonnas. A double room, with breakfast, goes for 1900$ ($29.07), increasing to 2500$ ($38.25) in a suite.

The dining room of the Quinta has a coved ceiling, a tall stone fireplace where log fires are lit on chilly evenings, plus elaborate scenic tiles depicting "The Rape of the Sabine Women" and "The Siege of Troy." The rich-tasting, heavy cuisine is well recommended, and a meal will cost around 450$ ($6.89).

The windows open onto a pool where white swans glide by. Luncheon is often served near a tree-bordered ornamental fish pond filled with carp and containing a cupola. A five-minute walk through an olive grove leads to a large, spring-filled pool where guests dip and sunbathe.

2. Sesimbra

To the Portuguese, Sesimbra used to be a closely guarded secret. With justification, it is considered one of the most unspoiled fishing villages in the country. True, the hill-scaling Hotel do Mar has opened up, attracting a steady stream of international visitors; but the varinas and fishermen still go about their time-honored task of plucking their livelihood from the Atlantic.

Against a backdrop of rocky cliffs, sardines, shellfish, whiting, and the scabbard fish, with its whip-shaped body and dagger-like teeth, lie stretched out in the sun. When the fleet comes in, the day's catch is auctioned at a lota at the harbor (Porto Abrigo). Donkeys carry boxes laden with sea fruit, and saffron-colored nets are hoisted up into the sun to dry.

Far down the beach, beyond the boat-clogged harbor, is the 17th-century **Fortress of St. Teodosio,** built to fortify the region against the pirates who plagued and plundered, carting off the most beautiful women and young girls.

A walk along the ruined battlements of the five-towered **Castle of Sesimbra** reduces the village to a nearly immobile miniature. The castle was captured from the Moors in 1165 and rebuilt following the 1755 earthquake, which sent sections of its crenelated walls tumbling to the ground. Enclosed within is a church and a meager archeological display of artifacts removed from the ruins.

More recently, Sesimbra has been enjoying popularity as an angling center, attracting swordfish hunters. The resort lies about 19 miles south of Lisbon, 17 miles west of Setúbal. Sesimbra is connected by bus to Lisbon. You can also get to Sesimbra by taking the ferry from Praça do Comércio wharf for a fare of 10$ (15¢), then a bus from Cacilhas for 40$ (61¢).

THE TOP HOTEL: Hotel do Mar (tel. 223-33-26) is one of the most unusual self-contained beach resort hotels south of the Tagus, a beehive construction of luxury units spreading from a high cliff to the water below. Its architectural concept is perhaps the most creative of any hotel in Portugal. The passageways are like continuous art galleries, with good contemporary paintings and ceramic plaques and sculpture, and the main lobby houses a glassed-in aviary with tropical birds. The year-round hotel was the creation of three brothers, one of whom did the interior design. He is to be congratulated, especially for such features as creating an "undersea" boîte beneath the pool, and turning it into a haven for snug disco life. During the day, one can soak up sun at the beach or at the circular swimming pool.

The 120 bedrooms are stacked up adobe fashion, each with its own bath and private terrace, with a view of the ocean and gardens sweeping down the hillside. Furnishings are streamlined and well selected; the rooms are airy, with breakfast being served on an outer flower-filled terrace. Full pension for two costs $70 (U.S.) or $110, depending on the size of the rooms and time of year. Singles with all meals are $45 or $80, taxes included.

There are two dining rooms; one circular self-service, operating in summer; the other, on an upper ledge, warmed with wood-grain paneling and overlooking the sea. If you're stopping off on a day trip from Lisbon, you can order a luncheon for about $10. The before-dinner gathering point is a rustically styled bar; after-dinner guests congregate in a living room, with a white wall fireplace, and islands of red and black chairs and tables on Chinese red floors. The concierge will arrange for everything from fishing to hairdressing appointments to excursions by private boats. The hotel operates transfer services.

THE BUDGET RANGE: Espadarte Hotel, Esplanada Comandante Tenreigo (tel. 223-31-89), is home base for those addicted to fishing, especially for swordfish. *Espadarte* means swordfish in Portuguese. The walls of the reception room are lined with candid photographs of proud fishermen, standing beside their catch. The five-floor hotel stands securely, right on the esplanade, and below the incline ramp are boats and seamen mending their nets.

All bedrooms have a private bath or shower, central heating, radio, telephone, and most have private balconies overlooking the sea. The room furnishings are in a jazzy Portuguese style, and all is kept immaculately clean. In high season, the half-board rate is 1160$ ($17.75) per person daily. Lunch or dinner, ordered separately, costs 420$ ($6.43). Meals are simple—soup, fish or meat, plus dessert.

The desk clerk will provide you with the price list for fishing and the dates and the kinds of fish you can expect to catch. It's a serious sport and whether nightfishing for swordfish or group fishing for big fish such as shark, it's exciting.

READER'S PENSION SELECTION: "Special praise is deserved by the place where we stayed and ate many of our meals in Sesimbra, **Casa Mateus,** 13E Largo da Fortaleza (tel. 223-30-39), which you recommend for its food. Our room in the pension was large, clean, and well furnished. The cost, with bath and breakfast, is 800$ ($12.24) per night. On this basis alone, we would recommend staying there. However, our host made the stay special. At various times, he gave us tastings of Portuguese port and brandies, prepared special dishes for us, and suggested food which we might otherwise not have tried. On the day before we were to leave, we discovered that because of a mistake on our part, he was not aware that we were planning to stay an extra night. He informed us that he had already obligated the room for someone else and that his pension was full. When we explained our problem, that we were to fly to Paris the next day and it would be inconvenient for us to move to another hotel, he gave us his bed, and he and his wife slept at a neighbor's apartment. Moreover, his family moved all of our belongings to the new room while we were away. Needless to say, we were extremely grateful" (William Sanders, Palo Alto, Calif.).

WHERE TO EAT: Ribamar, 6 Largo da Fortaleza (tel. 223-31-07), a modern restaurant on an old square, is one of the best eating places in Sesimbra, serving quality Portuguese cooking. Perhaps its best dish is swordfish, costing 275$ ($4.21). The chef also specializes in a fondue bourguignonne at 750$ ($11.48), for two persons. As an appetizer, we'd suggest a skewer of shrimp and bacon, 250$ ($3.82), or perhaps you'll settle for a bowl of soup, 40$ (61¢). Grilled sole and mullet are good here, priced according to weight.

Another nearby possibility is **Casa Mateus,** Largo da Fortaleza, a simple place that nevertheless offers a good, presentable cuisine, rich in the treats of the sea, although you can get a fair roast chicken as well for 150$ ($2.30). Natural clams are a savory treat at 180$ ($2.75), and caldeirada (stew) at 150$ ($2.30) is also good. Most diners, however, prefer fresh fish, either grilled or fried, at 150$ also. For dessert, you can order flan at 30$ (46¢).

3. Portinho da Arrábida

The limestone Arrábida Mountains stretch for about 22 miles, beginning at Palmela and rolling to a dramatic end at Cape Espichel on the Atlantic. At times the cliffs and bluffs are so high that you must seemingly peer through clouds to see the purple waters of the Atlantic below.

A Swiss botanist once said the mountain range contained "the most amazing flora to be seen in Europe." The foliage that rims the cliffs and the surrounding areas is lush, subtropical, and wide ranging, with everything from holm oaks, sweet bay, pines, laurel, juniper, cypress, araucaria, magnolia, lavender, myrtle, and pimpernels. It's a riot of color and fragrance carpeting the mountains.

The sêrra is riddled with numerous caves and grottos, the best known of which is the **Lapa de Santa Margarida.** Of it, Hans Christian Andersen wrote: "It is a veritable church hewn out of the living rock, with a fantastic vault, organ pipes, columns, and altars."

Perched on a hillside like a tiara over Portinho da Arrábida, the **New Convent** dates from the 16th century. You can go to the gate and ring for the caretaker, who may or may not show you around the precincts.

Plummeting down to the sea, you arrive at Portinho da Arrábida, at the foot of the sêrra. This is a favorite oasis with many families from Lisbon who rent little multicolored cottages on the beach. Portinho da Arrábida, which can be approached from either Setúbal or Sesimbra, lies about 23 miles south of Lisbon. By public transportation, you must make bus connections in Sesimbra.

READERS' RESTAURANT SUGGESTION: "We had an excellent lunch at the **Beira Mar Restaurant** (tel. 208-05-44), which is on the water just at the end of the road which brings you down from the mountains into the bay area. We had fish soup from a local recipe, grilled sardines and fried sole, salad, vegetable, mineral water, and coffee for 580$ ($8.87). We dined outdoors on a deck jutting into the bay, with a view of the boats and the village. There is also an indoor dining room" (Sandra A. Ciullo and Gary R. Donner, Brookline, Mass.).

4. Setúbal

On the right bank of the Sado River, 25 miles south of Lisbon, lies one of Portugal's largest and most ancient cities, said to have been founded by the grandson of Noah. Motorists often include it on their itineraries because of an exceptional inn, the **Estalagem de São Filipe,** installed in a late 16th-century fort overlooking the sea (see below).

Setúbal is known as the center of Portugal's sardine industry and for the production of the most exquisite muscatel wine in the world. As far back as the days of the Romans and the Visigoths, the aromatic and hearty grapes of this region were praised by connoisseurs.

Orange groves (a jam is made from the fruit), orchards, vineyards, and outstanding beaches (a popular one, **Praia da Figueirinha**) compose the environs of Setúbal. And the white pyramidal mounds you see dotting the landscape are deposits of sea salt drying in the sun, another major commercial asset of this seaside community.

Many artists and writers have come from Setúbal, none more notable than the 18th-century Portuguese poet Manuel Maria Barbosa du Bocage, a forerunner of romanticism. At the Praça do Bocage, a monument honors him.

Across the Sado is the sand-dune-studded isthmus of **Tróia.** Ruins of Roman villas on the bank and occasional discoveries of Phoenician remains indicate a once-thriving port. Excavations began on the ruins in the mid-19th century, uncovering part of what was known to be Cetobriga, a city dating from the third and fourth centuries. A ferry or a launch will take you over and back. If the pursuit of antiquity isn't enough, you can relax at one of the beaches.

In Setúbal is the late-15th-century **Church of Jesus,** an example of the Manueline style of architecture. Of particular interest are the ornate decorations on the main doorway and the Arrábida marble columns. Each of the latter is actually three columns twisted together like taffy to form a cable or root-like effect. Somehow they don't seem to hold up the vaulted ceiling, but give the illusion of appendages grown down to the floor.

Raymond Postgate wrote that the columns "look as if they had been twisted and wrung by a washerwoman," and Hans Christian Andersen recorded that the monument was "one of the most beautiful small churches that I have ever seen." The church has been heavily restored, the latest wholesale renovation in 1969–1970. Adjoining is the unpretentious **Town Museum,** housing some early 16th-century Portuguese paintings, as well as some Spanish and Flemish works, coins, shards, and other artifacts from the sandy pit of Tróia. The church-museum is at the Praça Miguel Bombarda, off the Avenida 22 de Dezembro.

To reach this port, where windmills still clack in the countryside, roosters crow, and the "girls of the sardines" speak Portuguese with a seemingly Arabic accent, take the ferry from Lisbon to Barreiro. There, you can board a train for the rest of the way.

For accommodations, Setúbal offers two possible choices: one a hilltop castle, another a partially restored 16th-century convent. Modern hotels cater to more conventional tastes. If you're passing through for the day, the recommended luncheon stopovers are the Estalagem de São Filipe of the Club Naval Setúbalense.

THE MEDIUM-PRICED RANGE: Estalagem de S. Filipe, Castelo de S. Filipe (tel. 238-44). This fortress-castle, dating back to 1590, was built by an Italian architect who came to Portugal during the ill-fated reign of the young king Sebastião. The builder gave it a crowning perch on a hilltop overlooking the town and the harbor. You wind your way up a curving mountain road, passing through a stone arch, by towers to the belvedere. Rooms that once were for the soldiers and the governor have been tastefully and richly furnished with antiques and reproductions. In earlier days there were guns and ammunition, but they have given way to soft beds and ornate Portuguese crafted headboards. The walls of the chapel and the public rooms contain tiled dados, depicting scenes from the life of S. Filipe and the life of the Virgin Mary.

The bedrooms are individually treated, each with its own personality They are reached via what seems like miles of plant-filled corridors, up wide, worn stone steps. Doubles range from 2250$ ($34.43). Suites go for 3000$ ($45.90).

Dining is pleasant, sitting in Windsor-style armchairs. Six alcoved windows open onto a panoramic view. Against a background of tiled dado, a primitive tapestry, and photostated engraving, a luncheon or dinner, including many fish specialties, is served. Two set menus cost either 500$ ($7.65) or 650$ ($9.95). Most guests take this meal when they stop over on a day trip from Lisbon. The clients seem to gravitate to the medieval-style drinking lounge, with its coved and arched ceiling, pierced copper hanging lanterns, tiled bar, and husky brass-studded armchairs. The sitting rooms are also intimate, with tiled walls, antiques, bowls, engravings, chests, and copper artifacts in the niches.

Quinta de S. João, 18 Rua Almeida Garrett (tel. 226-81), is installed in a half-restored 16th-century monastery. Behind high walls, it sits on a street honoring Portugal's romantic poet of the 19th century. The convent was first used by nuns in 1529, and the granddaughters of João II came here. Neglected for centuries, it had been handed along to various proprietors before it came into the healing hands of Rafael Emidio Croner Torres and his wife. He is a collector of antiques—in fact, he has an antique shop in the city (we suspect he uses the convent to store surplus pieces). The long and arduous task of restoration has begun.

First, he furnished the bedrooms well and installed a bath with each one of them. The rooms vary in size and convenience, but they are all reached via long narrow flights of stairs, along many corridors. The price of a single is $1100 ($16.83), the tariff in a double graduating from 1400$ ($21.42) to 1800$ ($27.54). Those who prefer to live here as master of the quinta should consider suite no. 106 (one night it accommodated nine guests). The cost hovers around 2500$ ($38.25) for a party of four. Your parlor will have a red velvet settee and matching chairs, a grandfather clock, and several chandeliers dripping with crystal.

Breakfast is the only meal served—family-style at a long refectory table on one side of the loggia of the inner cloister. There's a cozy living room, with a valuable inlaid desk, open fireplace, time-mellowed chests, and a Victorian settee and chairs. Everything seems to open onto the cloister, with its overgrown and untidy garden, planted with plum trees, flowers, vegetables, wisteria, all growing around an aged carriage. In the chapel, tiled walls depict scenes from the life of John the Baptist, including one of Salomé asking for his head.

Esperança Hotel, 220 Avenida Luisa Todi (tel. 211-51), stands in the heart of Setúbal, on the main inner street. It's a very modern dove-gray, six-story hotel, with basic amenities, a clean-cut beige and brown lounge, plus a reception area with streamlined furnishings, all in a restrained design. Each bedroom has built-in headboards, a dressing table, with pastel colors, bedside lighting, and all tiled bath. Singles are 1250$ ($19.13); doubles 1500$ ($22.95). There are two dining rooms, one more informal for light meals, the other on the top floor with all glass windows, providing a panoramic view of the area, including the Sado River. The hotel also has a bar and nightclub.

YOUR OWN APARTMENT: Rio Azul Hotel Apartamento, Tróia (tel. 44-151), is an island resort, a tourist development reached by hourly Hovercraft service across the harbor from Setúbal. It's an architectural venture of Torralta, a high-rise complex with striking contemporarily designed rooms and apartments. Against a white background, most of the rooms have strong colors, wide, low white couches and lounge chairs, white globe lights, large paintings, and dining room areas and complete kitchens. Bedrooms are stark but attractive. Each apartment will house two to four persons, and the daily cost is 1500$ ($22.95) for two persons in summer, increasing to 2000$ ($30.60) for four occupants. In spring and autumn, tariffs are reduced to 900$ ($13.77) for two, 1250$ ($19.13) for four. Adjoining is a Roman ruin. The view of the coastline is special, and there are encircling sandy beaches. It's complete with all the resort amenities.

WHERE TO DINE: Restaurante Naval Setúbalense, 300 Avenida Luisa Todi (tel. 236-74), is especially noted for its tempting array of *acepipes* (hors d'oeuvres). In a creaky, once-private home, you dine in the old-fashioned living room. Favored by many Portuguese navy officers, the restaurant offers acceptable food at low prices. The proprietor, Laureano Rocha, came from Vigo, Spain, nearly a half century ago.

For only 325$ ($4.97), he offers a well-prepared four-course meal, beginning with a selection of 18 hors d'oeuvres, including "whatever the best things are on the market that day." The best things are likely to include "knives" (a particular kind of shellfish), oysters both stuffed and natural, curried rice, two kinds of sardines, squid, garbanzos, and a type of black-eyed pea known as "the man with two faces." The second course always includes fish, perhaps sole or turbot, followed by beef with french-fried potatoes and green beans, then cheese and dessert. It's one of the best food buys in Setúbal. The service is polite and the ambience is homelike, enhanced by walls covered with dime-store-modern paintings.

Caranguejus, 62A Avenue Alexandre Herculano (tel. 292-63), opposite a park, is housed on the ground floor of a simple little apartment building. At first, you may think you've come to the wrong address. However, Caranguejus is favored by some diners as the finest and most sophisticated restaurant in Setúbal. For an appetizer, you have several choices, including onion soup at 75$ ($1.15). The menu is varied and imaginative, borrowing freely from the international repertoire—fondue bourguignonne, 450$ ($6.89) for two persons; pepper steak 250$ ($3.82); or veal scallops with Madeira, 150$ ($2.30)—although the chef seems equally pleased to prepare a more prosaic roast chicken, 140$ ($2.14). For dessert, you can order a chocolate mousse at 40$ (61¢).

O Beco, 24 Largo da Misericórdia (tel. 246-17), in the center of town, is entered through a narrow passageway which leads to two dining rooms, decorated in a typical style with old ovens, regional artifacts, and a fireplace. The service is friendly and helpful, the food excellent, although the quantities could be smaller and nobody would leave hungry. Shellfish soup is the classic opener at 120$ (1.84). Pork chops are from the acorn-sweetened variety in Alentejo, costing 240$ ($3.67), and a special beefsteak is offered for 290$ ($4.44). Cabrito (goat) is also good, 270$ ($4.13). Two more recommendable regional dishes include a Portuguese stew, cozido, 270$ ($4.13), and paella, 250$ ($39.78). More adventurous seafaring palates will order the grilled squid, 270$ ($4.13). A typical dessert is the rice pudding, 60$ (92¢).

From Setúbal, it's only 5½ miles north to:

5. Palmela

The village of Palmela lies in the heart of a wine-producing region, in the foothills of the Arrábida Mountains. It is famous for its fortress, from which at a vantage point of 1200 feet, you'll be rewarded with one of the most extensive and varied views in all of Portugal. Over sienna-hued valleys and vineyards heavy with grapes, one sees the capital to the north, the estuary of the Sado to the south.

The position of **Palmela Castle** has long been a strategic point in securing control of the lands south of the Tagus. It was from Palmela that Afonso Henriques, the first king of Portugal, drove out the Moors and established his new nation's domination in the district. The fortress was built in the 12th century, and was, in its day, a splendid example of medieval military architecture. It is further believed that the Celts founded a castle on the spot in 300 B.C.

Shades of 1755 still haunt the once-mighty fortress today. Its stones, covered with saffron-colored moss, are dislocated from their foundations, and gaping cracks appear in the walls. Indeed, the denizens of Palmela claim that much of their little hamlet was constructed with pieces of the fortress.

Of special interest is the Roman road discovered behind the castle by archeologists. It is the only such road to be unearthed in Portugal, and makes for speculation as to its relationship with the Roman beach colonies of Tróia, off Setúbal. You can scale the hill to the castle any time of the day.

A Pousada

Pousada of Palmela (tel. 235-12-26), a converted nunnery in the 1000-year-old Castle of Palmela, has been opened by the government and is an instant success. The conversion was done skillfully and nonintrusively, preserving, miraculously, the feel and look of a classic cloister. Its position is on the high crest of a hill, overlooking the valley and sea in the distance. It's traditional in design, a huge, square building opening into a large courtyard. The lower-level arches have been glassed in and furnished with lounge chairs.

The dining room, where once soft religious chants were sung, is now stately yet informal. Each of the bedroom cells has been opened up, enlarged, and given a glamorous up-to-date ambience. The rooms have private baths and are furnished in the Portuguese manner, with hand-carved pieces, fine fabrics, and tiled baths. Most of them open onto views. The price of a double and bath is $51.50 (U.S.), including breakfast. Meals are $10 if simple, and $15 for a larger repast.

The tourist circuit belt between Óbidos and Nazaré unfolds in the next chapter.

Chapter XI

ESTREMADURA

1. Óbidos
2. Caldas da Rainha
3. Berlenga Islands
4. Alcobaça
5. Aljubarrota
6. São Martinho do Pôrto
7. Nazaré
8. Batalha
9. Fátima

THE BLACK-SHAWLED WOMEN of Nazaré traced against the darkening sea . . . the phenomenon of Fátima . . . the sedate charm of the antique town of Óbidos . . . the curative waters of Caldas da Rainha . . . the jagged granite islands of Berlenga. . . the rolling plains near Alcobaça . . . the sandy beaches along the way.

The first flowers of empire bloomed in these lands north of Lisbon hundreds of years ago, and the beauty has not been diminished by time. Like the once-white limestone of Battle Abbey (Batalha), this land has been gilded in the sunlight of the passing years.

Estremadura is a land of contrasts. Stories apocryphal, real, and living still inspire the burial hall of kings, empty niches never filled, and broad squares and green plains where faith has been restored and fate decided. Deaths and royal intrigues, castles rising in the air, all are woven together, the warp and woof inextricably bound up in the whole fabric.

The Atlantic smashes the coast at Guincho, while further up it can hardly muster a ripple in the snug cove of São Martinho do Pôrto. These coastal regions are teeming with seafood: nursery-bred lobster, shrimp, crabs, squid, tuna, barnacles, and albacore. The sea is never far from any spot in Estremadura. From many a village's bastion, its shimmer can be seen, a reminder of the source of the land's bounty. In the many examples of Manueline architecture, especially at Batalha, the tie with the sea remains unbroken. The basic nautical designs—ropes, cables, armillary spheres, seascape effects—acknowledge the debt.

If it is impossible for you to spend several days exploring Estremadura, you can dip into it on one-day trips from Lisbon: first to Óbidos, 58 miles from Lisbon; then to Alcobaça, 67 miles from Lisbon; on to Nazaré, 81 miles from Lisbon; back to Batalha, 73 miles from Lisbon, and finally, a stop at Fátima,

87 miles from the capital. Traveling to these five major targets will take you through the heartland of Estremadura.

1. Óbidos

Years after Afonso Henriques drove the Moors out of Óbidos, the poet king, Dinis, and his saintly wife Isabella of Aragón passed by the battlemented walls of this medieval borough and were struck by its beauty. The queen likened the village to a jewel-studded crown, with its extended walls and gleaming plaster-faced houses. Anxious to please, Dinis made her a present of this gem-like village ribboned by a defensive wall. A tradition was established. Instead of giving precious stones, Portuguese royal bridegrooms presented Óbidos to their spouses—and it didn't cost them a penny. And what queen could complain at getting such a gift?

Entered through a tile-coated gatehouse, Óbidos rises on a sugarloaf hill, above a valley of vineyards. Its golden towers, its ramparts (rebuilt in the 12th century and subsequently restored), and its crenellated battlements contrast with bright white houses and the rolling countryside where windmills clack in the breeze.

Inside its confines, you will have traveled back hundreds of years. The narrow streets are either cobbled or made of roughly hewn flagstones. Green shoots lodge in the crannies of the walls, and vines climb the sides of tile-roofed houses. A loom hums in a candlelit vaulted workshop. It's a living piece of history.

In the baroque **Parish Church of Santa Maria**, Afonso V, at the age of ten, exchanged marriage vows with his cousin, only eight. Inside, the church is lined with blue and white azulejos (tiles). Pause long enough to admire a Renaissance tomb and the paintings of Josefa of Óbidos, a 17th-century artist. In the Chapel of St. Lawrence are contained relics of saints' hands.

The castle has been converted into a tourist inn (pousada). From its ramparts you can bask in views of Estremadura, the scene so unspoiled one can imagine Afonso Henriques' retinue marching over the hills.

Save some time for browsing through the shops, searching out thick-woven fabrics, regional rugs (both hand- and machine-made), raffia and hand-made bags, and the local lace.

This well-preserved national monument village lies 59 miles north of Lisbon. Trains leave the Rossio station in Lisbon.

In accommodations you have a choice of a converted castle, a convent, or a hostelry outside town.

THE BUDGET RANGE: Pousada do Castelo (tel. 951-05). This Manueline-trimmed stone palace lodged on the ramparts of the walls of Óbidos is firmly rooted in Portugal's history, and today, with the supervision of the government, it is one of the best run pousadas (tourist inns) in the country. Reached via twisting cobblestone streets through the village, the entrance is through a thick Gothic archway. You ascend further, into a wide sunny forecourt, and up a grand stone stairway to the main hall.

There are several well-furnished lounges, but regrettably, only six bedrooms. Three of these contain private baths, the occupants of the others making use of corridor plumbing. Most wayfarers stop off just for the day, partaking of the 650$ ($9.95) luncheon or dinner. Try for a table near one of the view windows. The dining room is in the Portuguese quinta style, almost grand, yet nicely provincial, with old oak beams, tiled dado, a fireplace, wrought-iron chandeliers, and leather chairs. If you're not staying at the pousada, call ahead for summertime dining reservations.

The fortunate few snare the rooms, enjoying the character of the bedchambers, furnished with antiques or fool-the-eye reproductions. Deeply set windows have tiny monk ledges, where you can squat to enjoy the view of the surrounding countryside. Homelike cretonne fabrics cover the beds, and a few rooms contain desks with brass church lamps, armchairs, and ecclesiastical wall plaques.

For half board, the rate ranges from 2250$ ($34.43) for a single, increasing to 2850$ ($43.61) for two persons. Fellow guests gather in one of two drinking lounges for sundown libations.

Estalagem do Convento, Rua Dom João Ornelas (tel. 952-17), is an old village nunnery turned inn. Outside the town walls, it is owned by a chemist, Luís de Sousa Garcia. The reception lounge is surely the tiniest on the Iberian peninsula, with a fireplace, 17th-century chest, torchéres, and a pair of gilt angels. He has utilized his ingenuity in furnishing the 13 rooms, employing furniture to complement the structure. Although the beds are old, the mattresses are more recent, and tiled bathrooms have been sneaked in. The bedchambers open off rambling corridors with chests and benches large enough to hold the trousseaux of a dozen brides. The cost for one person is 1700$ ($26.01) with breakfast; a double, with sitting room and breakfast, is 1800$ ($27.54).

Since this is primarily an inn and the food is good, it's wisest to pay the extra 1000$ ($15.30) for two meals a day. Guests from outside are welcomed as well, and can order a 600$ ($9.18) table d'hôte or else specialties from the à la carte menu, including French onion soup, pepper steak, and crêpes suzette. The dining room decor consists of heavy black beams, an open corner stone fireplace, and a brick oven. On sunny days, guests dine on the rear patio, in a garden with a moldy stone wall and tangerine and orange trees. In addition to a bar with hand-hewn beams, there's a living room with leather armchairs, old paintings, an 18th-century desk, and a brass-studded chest dated 1827. A curiosity is the converted wine cellar, now a typical pub.

About 3½ kilometers out of Caldhas on the road to Óbidos is a pleasant hostelry called **Mansão da Torre** (tel. 952-47). You drive under a stone archway down an entry some 100 feet long and come to a hacienda-type building, flanked by a large stone tower. Inside, there's a foyer with a large painting of Portuguese galleons, an old clock, model sailing ships, and two globes on a chest. There are only six rooms, but they have a homey charm about them. A double with breakfast costs 1400$ ($21.42), and singles go for 950$ ($14.54). In the rear is a pleasant ranch-style bungalow, where some of the rooms are located. The Mansão is open all year.

READER'S HOTEL SELECTION: "We found suitable accommodations at the **Residêncial Martim de Freitas,** (tel. 9-51-85), outside the walls on the road that leads to Alcobaça. We had an enormous double with sitting area, furnished with Manueline-style pieces. Everything was spotless in this small family-run 'residencia,' including the bathroom down the hall. There's plenty of hot water. Breakfast is the only meal served. Rates are quite reasonable, 1100$ ($16.83) for a bathless double" (Carole L. Chiaro, Middleburg Heights, Ohio).

READER'S BAR SELECTION: "The desk clerk at the pousada at Óbidos, Louis da Silva, is a charming man and very interesting to talk to (in his good English and our very hesitant Portuguese). We discovered that Louis and his very pleasant wife, Maria, have a tiny bar just outside the city wall on the Rua Boquinho, **Bar Abrigo do Boquinho.** We visited in the early evening, and it is a delightful little place, all whitewashed. The building it very old, dating back to the 15th century. The bar is on several levels; the first has the liquor supply and refrigerator and the usual bar and stools. One level down is equipped with a balcony for fadistas, tables, and chairs; another level has a large table made from an old mill stone, with padded kegs for stools. There is a fireplace, two fountains built into the walls, and a tiny courtyard with tables and benches that can be used in summer. It is done with imagination, and the warmth and friendly greetings make one feel very welcome. We stayed and visited with Louis and Maria and some of the village people who dropped in, and left feeling that we would certainly like to tell our friends about it" (Mrs. Dale N. Timbrook, Saratoga, Calif.).

READER'S SIGHTSEEING TIP: "A spectacular site to visit, 24 kilometers east of Óbidos and three miles east of Peniche is the **Cabo Carvoeiro**, which offers breathtaking views of the surf smashing into incredible rock formations hundreds of feet below the road, from which people fish. The view ranks with that at the Grand Canyon in many ways, yet few people go there. A seaside village with a whitewashed church is pleasant, and there is a four-star restaurant at the *farol* (lighthouse) at the end of the Cabo road. You'll see some interesting windmills on the road from Óbidos. The whole trip takes about 40 minutes and is worth it" (Robert M. Levine, Long Island, N.Y.).

2. Caldas da Rainha

After a bad night's sleep, the sister-queen of Manuel the Fortunate one day set out from Óbidos to Batalha. Passing through a small village en route, the rheumatic Leonor is said to have seen peasants bathing in fetid pools off to the side of the road. When told of the therapeutic value of these springs, she had her ladies-in-waiting clear the area to protect her modesty. A screen of fabric was draped around her, and she descended partially dressed into a foul sulfur bath.

So great was her relief from her long-suffering ailment that she returned to Caldas da Rainha again and again—in fact, she hocked her personal wealth in rubies and gold jewelry (many gems given to her by her deceased husband, the Perfect Prince, João II) to construct a hospital and an adjoining church. The chapel, **Nossa Sanhora do Pópulo**, was built at the dawn of the 16th century in the Manueline style, then at its apex, and is graced with a well-executed landmark belfry. Inside are handsome 300-year-old glazed earthenware tiles in buttercup yellow and marine blue. Today, a classic green bronze statue of Leonor stands at Largo do Conde de Fontalva; and the town has been a spa ever since, enjoying a particular chic in the 19th century.

Caldas da Rainha is also noted for its ceramics, especially the cabbage leaf designs on soup tureens and accompanying bowls. Inside the town and outside along the road to Alcobaça you can stop at many roadside stands and purchase these ceramics at far cheaper prices than you'd pay in Lisbon. However, you'll have to carry them back to the capital with you and arrange shipment there. These primitively painted reproductions of cabbage, fruit, shellfish, and lizards are made from the local clay, and many of them, especially the reptilian and crustacean specialties, evoke the designs of the ceramist and caricaturist Rafael Bordalo Pinheiro. He had a studio at Caldas da Rainha during its heyday as a 19th-century resort.

Caldas da Rainha is also a thriving market town, the activity centering on the Praça da República where you'll see what surely must be the world's largest cabbages. Women with weather-beaten faces sell wild hares in the shop stalls, and at day's end, trudge wearily home. In winter, men in fur-trimmed coats walk around clutching red hens, much to the pleasure of camera-snapping tourists.

The town is some 60 miles north of Lisbon, and is usually visited after Óbidos, four miles away.

3. Berlenga Islands

The Berlenga Islands, granite rocks set in the Atlantic, are an island hideaway. Eight miles out in the ocean, a medieval fortress once stood sentinel over the Portuguese coastline.

Drawn especially to the isles in summer are skin divers and fishermen, intrigued by the undersea fauna, the long-finned tunny (albacore), jackfish, and varieties of marine crustaceans. Equipment is available at Peniche, 57 miles north of Lisbon. From this port town jutting out into the Atlantic like a tongue, a launch goes to the Berlenga Islands. The trip, likely to be rough over choppy waters, takes about an hour.

You can visit the islands just for the day, exploring on your own and returning in the late afternoon. The launch leaves Peniche weekdays at 10:30 a.m., coming back at 6 p.m. On Sunday, the ferry departs twice in the morning, at 9:30 and again at noon, returning at 4 and 6 p.m. If the sea is bad, the ferry schedule is altered or abandoned.

Once on the island, you can enjoy a good and freshly cooked meal at the **Abrigo Para Pescadores** (tel. 99-021), which is run by the pousadas of Portugal. In tasteful surroundings, enjoying friendly service, you can order a complete meal for about 425$ ($6.50). I'd suggest the fresh sardinhas na brasa, or the caldeirada (fish stew) à Berlenga.

4. Alcobaça

At the apex of its power in the Middle Ages, this Cistercian monastery was one of the richest and most prestigious in Europe. Begun around 1152, it was founded to honor a vow made by Portugal's first king, Afonso Henriques, should he be victorious over the Moors at Santarém. Alcobaça, at the confluence of the Alcoa and Baça Rivers, was built to show his spiritual indebtedness to St. Bernard of Clairvaux, who inspired (others say goaded) many Crusaders into battle against the infidel.

Today, the monastery, in spite of its baroque facade and latter-day overlay, is a monument to simplicity and majesty. Somehow a sense of otherworldliness pervades as you walk down the 350-foot-long nave. Tall chalk-white clustered columns, like trees, hold up a vaulted ceiling nearly 70 feet high.

The transept of Alcobaça shelters the Gothic tombs of two star-crossed lovers, the Romeo and Juliet of Portuguese history. They were Pedro the Cruel and the ill-fated Spanish beauty, Inês de Castro, his mistress and (later perhaps) his wife. The work of an unknown sculptor, their sarcophagi (although damaged) are considered the greatest pieces of sculpture from 14th-century Portugal.

The oval-faced Inês is guarded and protected by angels hovering over her. Her tomb rests on sculpted animals with human faces, said to represent the assassins who slit her throat. Pedro captured two of them, personally ripping out and eating their hearts. Inês was buried at Alcobaça during a torchlight parade, following a ghoulish ceremony in which her decaying body was exhumed. The king had his courtiers kiss her rotted hand and honor her as "the queen of the realm." Around the tomb are panels depicting scenes from the Last Judgment.

Pedro hoped to rise on that day of Resurrection to greet Inês emerging from her sleep of centuries. On a wheel of fortune at his tomb, a sculptor, following his mandate, carved the words *ate o fim do mundo,* meaning "until the end of the world." Guarded over by angels, his feet nestled on a dog, Pedro was buried in a tomb supported by lions, symbols of his timeless rage and vengeance.

There is much to see at Alcobaça, certainly the Cloisters of Silence, with their delicate arches, favored by Dinis, the poet king. He sparked a thriving literary colony at the monastery, the monks busily engaged in translating ecclesiastical writings. But aside from the tombs and cloisters, the curiosity is the kitchen, through which a branch of the Alcoa River was routed. As in most Cistercian monasteries, the reason for a flowing brook was one of sanitation. Chroniclers have suggested that the friars fished for their dinner in the brook, later washing their dishes in it. In the huge chimneyed pit, five or six steers or oxen were roasted at the same time. A six-ton marble table resting here would probably have accommodated Gargantua and Pantagruel.

In the dining room are found niches where the monks prayed while the hierarchy ate. In honor of an old tradition, Queen Elizabeth II was feted at a luncheon here. In front of the dining room is a fountain, where Portuguese girls wet their fingers, putting the water to their cheeks. The old women of the village predict that by so doing the young girls will soon get married.

Finally, in the 18th-century Salon of Kings are niches with sculptures of some of the rulers of Portugal (many fell from their resting places and were damaged in the 1755 earthquake). An air of melancholy is lent to the scene by the empty niches left waiting for the rulers who were never sculpted. The tiles in the room depict, in part, Afonso Henriques' triumph over the Moors.

After your visit, you can explore the nearby market, said to sell the best fruit in all of Portugal, especially succulent peaches grown in surrounding orchards originally planted by the Cistercian monks. Many stalls also sell the blue and white pottery of Alcobaça.

Trains depart from Lisbon's Rossio station, 67 miles away.

5. Aljubarrota

Against a backdrop of mountain scenery, the extensive green fields on the Aljubarrota plateau are considered "the birthplace of Portugal." Between Alcobaça and Batalha, on August 14, 1385, near the village of Aljubarrota, Portuguese independence was secured. João I, the founder of the Aviz dynasty, and his young captain, Nuno Álvares—fortified by scythe- and shovel-bearing peasants and some English archers—defeated the Castilian sea of soldiers.

A story of the battle relates how during the heat of conflict the king and his army were consumed by thirst under a blazing sun. He vowed that never would a voyager pass this way again without access to water. Today, outside of the village, a small chapel offers a pitcher of fresh water in a niche in honor of that ancient commitment.

6. São Martinho do Pôrto

This seaside village nestles between pine-covered foothills and the ocean. Its main attraction is an almost landlocked sandy beach, brightly scalloped into the terrain. The waters are calm and clear, the days gently descending from May to October.

For many, São Martinho do Pôrto makes a good base for touring: Óbidos is 12½ miles away; Alcobaça, 11; Fátima, 28; Batalha, 22; and Caldas da Rainha, 9½. It is 72 miles by rail from Lisbon, and only a short run north to the fishing village of Nazaré. A coastal road skirts the village, and buses run regularly into Nazaré.

In hotels, there is the following recommendation:

THE BUDGET RANGE: Parque Hotel, Avenida Maréchal Carmona (tel. 9-85-05), is old-fashioned and gracious, set in its own small private garden. Ideal for families who want to live pleasantly and inexpensively near the beach, it is surrounded by trees, with summer furniture set out for periods of relaxation. It's especially favored by economy-minded English tourists who like an atmosphere of large-size bedrooms and homey furniture.

Open only from the first of July to the first of October, it has installed private baths in its 40 bedrooms. They cost from 800$ ($12.24) to 1000$ ($15.30) in a single, from 1500$ ($22.95) to 2100$ ($32.13) in a double. A continental breakfast is included.

You breakfast in a turn-of-the-century hall, with an elaborate ceiling and an old chandelier. In all, the hotel is a world of polished floors, well-scrubbed rooms, and old-style servants. On the grounds are two tennis-courts.

7. Nazaré

What strikes one immediately about the people of Nazaré is their self-containedness. The inhabitants of Portugal's most famous fishing village live in a unique, tradition-bound, ageless world. Many have never been to Lisbon; indeed, many have never left their village, except perhaps to make the pilgrimage to nearby Fátima.

The people remain insular, even though their village blossoms into a resort in summer. White tents filled with international visitors dot the crescent-shaped beach. Yet the natives go about their time-honored tasks, perhaps pausing to pose for camera fans. Nazaré was originally discovered by writers and painters; but in the 1960s seemingly everyone arrived.

Don't expect stunning architectural styles or historic sights. The big attraction is its people and their boats. Claiming descent from Carthaginian and Phoenician ancestors, many of the natives are characterized by aquiline noses and dark brows, a gentle, hard-working folk whose classical features are marked and lined by sad, yet noble, countenances.

The clothes of the villagers are patch quilts of sun-faded colors. The rugged-looking men appear in rough woolen shirts and trousers, patched in kaleidoscopic rainbow hues, resembling Scottish plaid. Although the origin of this apparel remains unknown, one explanation ventured is that the fishermen picked up the designs from Wellington's troops who passed this way during the Napoleonic wars. On their heads, the men wear long woolen stocking caps, in the dangling ends of which they keep their valuables—a favorite pipe, even a crucifix.

The women are mostly barefooted, wearing embroidered handmade blouses and pleated skirts also made of plaid woolens patched many times. It is customary for the women to don black as a traditional sign of mourning—black tasseled shawls, black capes or cowls; whereas the unmarried girls of the village are traditionally attired in seven petticoats. The government has made it illegal to count these petticoats, as many tourists were fond of doing in the 1950s.

The boats of the fishermen are Phoenician in design, elongated, slender, and decorated in bold colors. Crudely shaped eyes often appear on the high knife-like prows, eyes supposedly imbued with the magical power to search the deep for fish and to avert storms. Powered by oars, the boats contain lanterns for the dangerous job of fishing after dark. During the gusty days of winter, or at high tide, the boats are hauled in and lined up along the waterfront promenade.

While the men are at sea, the women wait, passing their time mending nets, drying sardines on the beach, perhaps nursing children, darning socks, or sewing patches on articles of clothing. At sundown they squat in circles, waiting on the somber shore. When their men come in, the business of sorting out the fish begins. The women trudge up toward the shoreline with heavy baskets balanced precariously on their heads. Some hang nets to dry in the night air; some slice entrails from the silver bodies upon the beach; others chase away pestering children . . . and some wait.

Nazaré is divided into two sections, the fishing quarter and the Sítio, the latter being the upper town which is almost exclusively residential. Near the beach, you'll find handicraft shops, the markets, restaurants, hotels, and boarding houses. The main square opens directly onto the sea, and narrow streets lead to the smaller squares, evoking a Medina in a Moorish village. Simple shops hang objects outside their doors, indicating what they sell (for example, a carved wooden cow head indicates the butcher shop). At the farthest point from the cliff and square are the vegetable and fish markets, where auctions are held.

Jutting out over the sea, the promontory of the Sítio is awesome, a sheer drop to the ocean and the beach below. It is reached either by a funicular or else a goat-steep cobblestoned pathway. At the Sítio the Virgin Mary supposedly appeared in 1182. A young horseback-riding nobleman, Faus Roupinho, was pursuing a wild deer dangerously near the precipice, shrouded in mist. The fog lifted suddenly to reveal the Virgin and the chasm below. In honor of this miracle, the nobleman built the Chapel of Memory. Today, near the spot, you can go inside the 18th-century structure honoring that long-ago event.

About 8 miles from Alcobaça, Nazaré lies 82 miles north of Lisbon. From the capital, take the three-hour train ride to the nearest station of Valado, where bus connections into Nazaré can be made. Coaches depart from Lisbon's Rossio station.

In accommodations, Nazaré offers the following:

TWO MODERN HOTELS: Hotel da Nazaré, Largo Afonso Zúquete (tel. 463-11). Such *moderno* as this hotel offers is a contrast to the fishing village. Six streamlined floors of contemporary design are set on a tiny plaza, a two-minute walk from the waterfront and beach. The facade is a sun-reflecting white and yellow, with a private balcony and all-glass picture windows for the front bedrooms. A rooftop terrace for the sun-lounging life puts the beauty of Nazaré and the clifftop Sítio in your lap.

The dining room underneath also opens onto window walls peering out over the village housetops, the rugged cliffs, the harbor where tomorrow's sardines are being hauled in. The dining room (open to the public in general) serves fish dishes. The set lunch for 500$ ($7.65) includes a soup course such as Alentejana gazpacho, followed by grilled sardines, then a meat selection—perhaps pork in the style of the Algarve. Assorted cakes from the dessert trolley pass by, topped by a choice of seasonal fruit. On the à la carte menu, the specialties on which the tab changes daily include lobster thermidor, grilled crab, shrimps, natural clams, or clams in a savory sauce.

Those staying over will find functional but well-furnished bedrooms, some with carpeting in the Nazaré plaid design. The tariffs vary according to the size and view, with doubles ranging from $40 (U.S.), and singles going for anywhere from $22. Importantly, the hotel provides parking places in space-starved Nazaré. There is both a main-floor lounge and a duet of drinking bars, all brightly modern, with bold solid color schemes, a nautical tapestry, murals, and paintings of the local fishermen. It's open all year.

Hotel Praia, 39 Avenida Vieira Guimaraes (tel. 464-23), is the leading competitor. An 80-bedroom, six-floor hotel, it is decorated in a contemporary style, all rooms equipped with private bath, the front ones opening onto the ocean. It is well positioned, opposite the Mercado (open market) and only a three-minute walk to the sandy beach where the fishing boats and bathing cabins lie. Touches of the village spirit abound in the decor. A room-long photo mural of the Phoenician-inspired fishing boats rests in the dining room. Even the colors of the lounge furnishings, cardinal red and spring green, match some of the sea-going craft.

The bedrooms are streamlined with Nordic-inspired furnishings. Depending on the size and the view, a single rents for 1800$ ($27.54), a double from 2400$ ($36.72), and a triple from 3600$ ($55.08).

AN OLD-FASHIONED INN: Pensão-Restaurante Ribamar, 9 Rua Gomes Freire (tel. 461-58), is a genuine old-fashioned village inn, with a traditionally styled dining room where candlelit meals are served at night. It's exactly on the water, with most of its rooms opening onto a balcony seat from which guests watch the beaching of the sardine-filled boats. Or you can watch (without being caught staring) the multipetticoated women or the tasseled stocking caps of the men.

Even if you're passing through just for the day, you may want to try a regional meal in the oak-beamed dining room. A meal is offered for 520$ ($7.96) and includes specialties such as cream of shellfish soup, fish stew (caldeirada) in the Nazaré style, and roast kid. The atmosphere is genial, with ornate tiles, forest green chairs and draperies, and stark white cloths.

A twisting stairway in the rear leads to the old-style bedrooms, down halls of muted cream, with rattan baskets of pine cones on each landing. Some rooms are simple, perhaps too much so for the average traveler. But they are maintained immaculately; the beds are good, the linen fresh. All of the 22 rooms contain private baths. Two persons can stay here, taking all three meals, at prices that range from 2900$ ($44.37) to 3800$ ($58.14) per day, depending on the season. All taxes are included.

WHERE TO DINE: Mar Bravo 75 Praça Sousa Oliveira (tel. 461-80). Of the dozens of restaurants and boarding houses in this bustling village, one of the most frequented is Mar Bravo, on the corner of the town's busy square overlooking the ocean. The decor is simple tile, with a huge photo of the Nazaré beach covering the back wall. A complete meal costs only 400$ ($6.12) and consists of soup, followed by a fish or meat dish, and bread. There's a menu in English. À la carte specialties are bass caprice, 260$ ($3.98); fish stew Nazarena, 210$ ($3.21); and a charcoal-grilled pork, 210$ also. Dessert might be a soufflé for 120$ (1.84), a fruit salad for 75$ ($1.15), or an orange pudding for 60$ (92¢).

Even on a rainy winter Sunday the restaurant attracts many locals, which is the best proof of the pudding (or the caldeirada). Upstairs is a second dining room, with an oceanside view. Connected with the Mar Bravo is a three-star boarding house, the **Pensão Madeira,** simple but adequate. A single with shower and breakfast costs 1000$ ($15.30); a double with the same amenities, 1500$ ($22.95).

READER'S RESTAURANT SUGGESTION: "The **Beira Mar** is a restaurant directly on the beach at 40 Avenida da República (tel. 4-64-58). It's a fairly new building, and it also provides a good residential accommodation. I had a nice lunch there for 500$ ($7.65)" (Mrs. A. Stockhausen, Toronto, Ontario, Canada).

8. Batalha

The founder of the House of Aviz, João I, vowed on the plains of Aljubarrota in 1385 that if his underequipped and outnumbered army defeated the powerful invading Castilians, he would commemorate his spiritual indebtedness to the Virgin Mary. The result is the magnificent Battle Abbey, Batalha. Designed in the splendid Gothic-Manueline style, it appears as an imposing mass of steeples, buttresses, and parapets when approached from its western facade. Although much restored, it is a jewel case of fine cut gems in stone.

The western porch, ornamented by a tangled mass of Gothic sculpture of saints and myriad figurines, is capped by a stained-glass window of blue, mauve, and amber. The hue of the limestone has supposedly changed through the ages; today it is a light burnished beige, similar to the color of the facade of the Convent of Christ at Tomar. Napoleon's irreverent Gauls used the stained-glass windows for target practice, turning the nave into both a latrine and a bordello.

In the Founder's Chapel, completed in 1435, João I and his English queen, Philippa of Lancaster, daughter of John of Gaunt, lie in peaceful repose, their hands entwined. Near that of his parents is the tomb of Prince Henry the Navigator, whose fame eclipsed their own even though he never sat on the throne, but spent a great part of his life at the School of Navigation at Sagres, on the southern coast of Portugal. Henry's sculpted hands are clasped in prayer. Three of the other princes are also entombed here under a ceiling resembling snow crystals. The Royal Cloister, considered by many the most outstanding feature at Batalha, is attributed to Afonso Domingues. These cloisters reveal the beginnings of the nautically oriented Manueline architecture. (Still a second cloister, called the Meditation Cloister, dates from the 15th century.)

The magnum opus of the monastery is the Chapter House, a square chamber whose vaulting is an unparalleled example of the Gothic style, bare of supporting pillars. When originally built by a French architect it collapsed, but a Portuguese redesigned it and slept under it for eight days to prove its soundness. The two tombs of Portugal's Unknown Soldiers from World War I are guarded by sentinels and the glow of an eternal flame. In one part of the quadrangle is the Unknown Soldiers Museum, housing gifts to the fallen warriors from the people of Portugal and from other countries, including a presentation from Maréchal Joffre. Beyond the crypt are the remains of the old wine cellars.

The filigree designs ornamenting the coral-stone entrance to the seven Unfinished Chapels is stunning. The Capelas, under an inconstant "sky ceiling," are part of one of the finest examples of the Manueline style of architecture, a true extravaganza in stone. It seems a pity that construction was abandoned here so that workers and architects for Manuel I could help build his Monastery at Belém. Originally, the chapels were ordered by Dom Duarte, the son of João I, but he died before they could be completed.

Outside in the forecourt, a heroic statue was unveiled in 1968 to Nuno Álvares, who fought with João I on the plains of Aljubarrota. Batalha stands 73 miles north of Lisbon, reached by taking a train to Valado where bus connections are made to Batalha.

9. Fátima

This is a world-famous pilgrimage site. Thorny bushes, dwarfed holly, gnarled and twisted olive trees, a stray oak—the terrain around Fátima is wild, almost primitive, with an aura of barren desolation hanging over the countryside. But if you should go on the 13th of May or the 13th of October, the drama that unfolds is remarkable. Beginning on the 12th of each of those months, the roads leading to Fátima are choked with pilgrims traveling in donkey-pulled carts, on bicycles, or in automobiles. Usually, however, they go on foot, some even walking on their knees in penance. They camp out till day breaks. In the central square, larger than St. Peter's in Rome, a statue of the Madonna passes through the crowd. In the breeze 75,000 handkerchiefs flutter, like thousands of peace doves taking flight.

Then, as many as are able crowd in to visit a small slanted-roof shed known as the Chapel of the Apparitions. Inside stands a single white column marking the spot where a small holm oak had once grown. It is alleged that an image of the Virgin Mary appeared over this oak on May 13, 1917, when she is said to have spoken to three shepherd children. The oak has long ago disappeared, torn to pieces by souvenir collectors; many of its fragments now rest in the homes of peasants where they are viewed as sacred religious relics. The oak that now stands near the chapel existed in 1917, but was not connected with the apparition. The original chapel constructed here was dynamited on the night of March 6, 1922, by skeptics who suspected the church of staging the so-called miracle.

While World War I dragged on in Europe, the trio of devoutly faithful children—Lúcia de Jesus and her cousins Jacinto Marto and Francisco—claimed they saw the first appearance of "a lady" on the tableland of Cova da Iria. Her coming had been foreshadowed in 1916 by what they would later cite as "an angel of peace," who is said to have appeared before them.

Although attempts were made to suppress their story, news of it spread quickly, eventually generating worldwide enthusiasm, disbelief, and intense controversy. During the July appearance, the lady was reported to have revealed three secrets to them, one of which prefigured the coming of World War II, another connected with Russia's "rejection of God." The final secret, recorded by Lúcia, was opened by church officials in 1960, but they refused to divulge its contents.

Acting on orders from the Portuguese government of the time, the mayor of a nearby town threw the children into jail and threatened them with torture, even death in burning oil. Still, they would not be intimidated, sticking to their original story. The lady was reported to have made six appearances, the final one on October 13, 1917, when the children were joined by an estimated 70,000 persons who witnessed the famous Miracle of the Sun. The day of October 13 had broken to pouring rain and driving winds. Observers from all over the world, many of them journalists and self-professed atheists, testified that at noon "the sky opened up" and the sun seemed to spin out of its axis and hurtle toward the earth. Many at the site feared that the Last Judgment was upon them. Others later reported that they thought the scorching sun was crashing into the earth and would consume it in flames. Many authorities, and certainly the faithful pilgrims, agreed that a major miracle of modern times had occurred. Only the children reported seeing "Our Lady," however.

In the influenza epidemic that swept over Europe after World War I, both Francisco and Jacinto died. The oldest, Lúcia, is still alive, living as a Carmelite nun in a convent at the university city of Coimbra. Lúcia returned to Fátima to mark the 50th anniversary of the apparition. The pope flew in from Rome.

A cold, white, pristine basilica in the neoclassic style was erected at one end of the wide square. If you want to go inside, you may be stopped by a guard if you're not dressed to suit him. A sign posted outside reads: "The Blessed Virgin Mary, Mother of God, appeared in this place. Therefore, women are asked not to enter the sanctuary in slacks or other masculine attire." Men wearing shorts are also excluded.

Outside of Fátima, in the simple and poor village of Aljustrel, you can still see the houses of the three shepherd children.

Fátima lies 36 miles east of Nazaré and about 88 miles north of Lisbon. A train from the capital arrives near Fátima. From the rail station, coaches connect with the pilgrimage site.

When you arrive, everything at first seems to be either a souvenir shop, a pension, or a hotel. But in accommodations, Fátima is disastrously equipped on the days of the major pilgrimages (it's virtually impossible to secure a room unless you've reserved months in advance). Those visiting at other times of the year may find the following recommendations suitable:

LODGINGS: Hotel de Fátima, Cova da Iria (tel. 977-51), is a leading hotel, rated three stars by the government. Many of its 69 rooms and nine suites overlook the sanctuary. The ever-increasing invasion of pilgrims to the shrine forced the hotel to enlarge, branching out into a new part. All rooms have natural wood furnishings in the provincial Portuguese style, with private baths, central heating, and telephones. The building has three floors, serviced by two elevators. For half board, the price for two persons is 2900$ ($44.37), taxes included. On the main floor is a cozy little sitting room with a brick fireplace, a reception lounge, a large sitting room, plus a dining room where you can order a two-course table d'hôte luncheon or dinner for 500$ ($7.65).

Hotel Os Três Pastorinhos, Cova da Iria (tel. 976-29), is translated as the Inn of the Three Shepherd Children. The building is designed in a holiday style, with its most recently added bedrooms opening onto private balconies overlooking the sanctuary.

All rooms are newly furnished with modern facilities. All of them contain private bath, although one group offers showers instead of tubs and is cheaper. One person pays from 1300$ ($19.89) for a room with bath; two persons are charged from 1900$ ($29.07). Breakfast is included. If you're just passing through, you can come in for a multicourse meal costing 500$ ($7.65). The lounge and dining room open onto raised sun terraces, edged with pots of flowering plants.

Hotel Pax (tel. 974-12) is modern, perched atop a hill near the shrine. It is only rated as two stars, but for quality and comfort it should certainly be three. Among its many facilities are a large souvenir shop; a clean, large but ascetic dining room; and simple but comfortably appointed rooms. The hotel has its own chapel as well as a small bar. A single is 800$ ($12.24); a double, 1200$ ($18.36). Lunch or dinner by itself is 480$ ($7.34). Complete board costs an extra 700$ ($10.71) per person.

Pensão Exercito Azul, adjacent to the sanctuary grounds (tel. 972-00), can be seen from miles around because of its towering blue-colored Byzantine cupola. It is a boarding house with a story. Twenty-nine years ago, Monseignor Colgan, an American from Plainfield, N.J. (who died in 1972), founded an organization called the Blue Army to promote Fátima. The organization runs this 55-room hotel as well. Among the facilities are a large conference hall seating 500, a Byzantine chapel, containing the "Our Lady of Kazan" icon which the organization bought six years ago for $1 million, a small bar, and a no-frills restaurant. At the entrance to the building is a large white statue of the Virgin, with a golden crown on her head and a rosary in her right hand. Rooms at the hotel (also known as Pilgrim House) cost 775$ ($11.86) for a single, 1200$ ($18.36) for a double, and 1650$ ($25.25) for a triple. Most rooms by the way, have only a shower. Full board is 850$ ($13.01) per person extra. Special rates are given for groups of more than 15 persons. To get to the hotel, follow the Blue Army signs posted all over town. You may have no chance of finding a room here, however, because the hotel is rented regularly by large groups on pilgrimages to Fátima.

Pensão-Restaurant Zeca (tel. 972-62) is a modern, clean hotel set in a large garden at the entrance to town and serving the best food in Fátima, with the biggest portions. You sit in a friendly dining room with picture windows facing a garden, wood and tile wall decorations, cloth napkins, and tablecloths. À la carte specialties are a mixed salad, 60$ (92¢); a sausage omelet, 140$ ($2.14); and fish and meat dishes, from 250$ ($3.82).

You can stay at this 40-bedroom boarding house for 1400$ ($21.42) for two persons.

THE THREE CAVES CIRCUIT: Just eight miles from Fátima, the caverns in and near the village of Mira de Aire offer visitors a glimpse at another kind of miracle: the miracle of nature. The first of these subterranean marvels are the **Alvados Caves,** which are a series of caverns natrually segmented into many smaller caves dotted with lakes. The favorite of these is the Lake of Pearls, with rock formations unique in Europe, including even the remains of an ancient stag preserved in stone. The **Mira de Aire Caves,** opened in 1974, boast the only Portuguese cavern with an underground river. Its "Great Lake" is decorated with no fewer than 14 luminous fountains. Effective use of stereophonic sound and 3000 hidden lamps make this underground paradise come alive with dancing waters and constantly changing rock formations.

Saint Anthony's Cave, opened in 1969, was the first Portuguese cave to become a tourist attraction. Its main feature is a single chamber about the size of a football field whose walls, ceiling, and floor are covered with unusual rock formations. Sound and light equipment are used here as in the other caverns to make the tour both enjoyable and educational. Atop the cave is a restaurant whose windows offer a panorama of the rolling hillsides around Mira de Aire. Hours for all three caves are from 9 a.m. to 9 p.m. from April through September, closing at 7 p.m. during the winter months. Separate admission to each of the caves is 60$ (92¢). For information, telephone 049/223-89.

Chapter XII

THE ALGARVE

1. Sagres
2. Lagos
3. Portimão
4. Praia da Rocha
5. Silves
6. Armação de Pêra
7. Albufeira
8. Praia de Quarteira
9. Vilamoura
10. Vale do Lobo
11. Faro
12. São Brás de Alportel
13. Olhão
14. Monte Gordo

IN THE ANCIENT MOORISH town of Xelb (today called Silves), a handsome and sensitive vizier is said to have once lived. During one of his sojourns into northern lands, he fell in love with and won the hand of a beautiful blond-haired Nordic princess. Marrying her, he brought her back to the Algarve.

Soon the young princess began to pine, finding no solace in the Moor's rose castle. Her young husband finally learned, after much coaxing, that his new bride's melancholy came from her longing for the snow-covered hills and valleys of her native land.

Issuing a decree, the vizier demanded that thousands of almond trees be planted throughout his realm. From that day on, pale white almond blossoms have blanketed the Algarve in late January and early February. The sight acted as an anodyne to the heart of the young princess. On seeing the blossoms, she found she could finally fulfill her marital duties and lived happily ever after in her vizier's sun-drenched kingdom with its sweet-smelling artificial winters ... or so the story goes.

The maritime province of the Algarve, often called the Garden of Portugal, is the southwesternmost part of Europe, its coastline stretching a distance of 100 miles, all the way from Henry the Navigator's Cape St. Vincent to the border town of Vila Real de Santo António, fronting a once-hostile Spain.

THE ALGARVE

Called Al-Gharb by the Moors, the land south of the sêrras (hills) of Monchique and Caldeirão remains a spectacular anomaly that seems more like a transplanted section of the North African coastline. The temperature in winter averages around 60 degrees Fahrenheit, increasing to an average of 74 in summer. During the day the sky is a pale blue, deepening in the evening to a rich cerulean. The countryside abounds with growth: almonds, lemons, oranges, carobs, pomegranates, and figs, the latter sending their branches crawling across the ground like the tentacles of an octopus. The road from Lagos to Sagres is lined with giant geraniums.

Expanses of sun-drenched golden sands contrast harmoniously with sinuous scored rock passageways that open up into high-ceilinged grottos and sea caves with natural pillars supporting ponderous arches above inrushing waters. The variety of the coastline provokes wonder: sluggish estuaries, sheltered lagoons, low-lying areas where the cluck of the marsh hen rises into the air, long sandy spits, pine woods breaking upon a pounding surf, and promontories jutting out into the white-capped aquamarine foam.

Even though most of the towns and villages of the Algarve are more than 150 miles from Lisbon, the great earthquake of 1755 was felt here as well. Entire communities were wiped out; however, there remain many Moorish (even Roman) ruins. In the character of its fret-cut chimneys, mosque-like cupolas, and cubist houses, a distinct Oriental flavor still prevails.

The marketplaces in the shaded arcades of Algarvian villages sell esparto mats, copper work, pottery, and almond and fig sweets, sometimes shaped like birds and fish. Through the narrow streets comes the fast sound of little accordions pumping out the rhythmical *corridinho*.

Many small fishing villages dot the Algarvian coast, their names tongue twisting: Carvoeiro, Albufeira, Olhão, Portimão. The black dress of the varinas (with embroidery on their apparel, a flower-studded hat on their head), the healthy ruddy faces of the "bullfighters of the sea," the fishing craft—all create a living bridge with tradition in a land known to Phoenicians, Greeks, Romans, Visigoths, Moors, Christians, and now foreign visitors of every hue.

A NEW RIVIERA: Clearly a new Riviera is in the making.

The accommodation outlook is one of exceptional, although government-regulated, growth. New construction is planned so as not to spoil the natural beauty of the coastline (Spain's Costa del Sol is a painful nightmare for what can happen with an unchecked hotel boom).

Excellent accommodations are provided in nearly all price levels, the list topped by luxury hotels (two of which have their own 18-hole championship golf course). The hotels scattered along the coast from Monte Alvor to the Vale do Lobo, have reciprocal meal arrangements. Others are at Praia dos Três Irmãos, Praia de Rocha, and Albufeira.

Budgeteers seek out bargains in the pensions and estalagems, some of them in converted mansions and villas. The government owns two pousadas—one on the sea at Sagres, the other in the mountains (São Brás de Alportel). In July and August the Algarve peaks in popularity.

The flight from Lisbon to the Algarvian airport at Faro takes about 30 minutes. There are daily flights all year leaving Lisbon, with two daily return flights also. You can go by one of three daily trains. Take the ferryboat at Praça do Comércio in Lisbon, disembarking at Barreiro on the opposite bank of the Tagus, where Algarve-bound trains can be boarded. Three times a week there's a first-class-only special run. A daily motorcoach also leaves from Barreiro to the Algarve, and a drive in your own rented car takes about five or six hours.

ALONG THE WAY—SINES: On the somewhat barren route from Lisbon to the Algarve, attractions are rare. However, 99 miles south of the capital, almost exactly midway between there and Cape St. Vincent, sits the little fishing village of Sines. The side road to the promontory of Sines runs through a land swept by sea breezes. Along the 11-mile route from the cutoff point at Santiago do Cacém, pine forests rise along the horizon, the scent from the resin-filled barrels permeating the air.

The origin of Sines is lost. Many of the natives, like those at Nazaré, trace their ancestry to the Phoenicians. The village sits upon the crest of a high inclined surface, its little houses trimmed in cobalt blue blending into the sky. Below the residential district, a natural rock looms over the tiny harbor. Off the coast is a small island, Pessegueiro, on which the crumbled ruins of a fortress remain.

Vasco da Gama was born at Sines in 1469, and his house, long ago torn down, has been reconstructed in the original style. Even the local cinema is named after the great explorer. Anglers are attracted to Sines because of the bass and swordfish. Sand dunes rise along the extensive beaches, which are private, remote, seldom sharing their tranquil beauty with the Algarve-bound motorist.

SANTIAGO DO CACÉM: On the main road to the Algarve, the village of Santiago do Cacém, dedicated to St. James, is crowned by the ruins of a castle built by medieval knights upon the foundation of a Moorish fortress. At the castle walls there is a fine view of the sea and the cypress-studded countryside, from which a low hum and clack of windmills can be heard.

Two Pousadas

Algarve-bound vacationers or returning suntanned tourists like to stop off for a luncheon at the **Pousada de São Tiago,** Estrada Nacional (tel. 224-59). This salmon-pink hilltop villa is approached via a climbing road through pine and fir trees, seemingly like a private estate. Guests walk around the terraced garden or take a dip in a pool surrounded by lawns and rows of cypress trees, plus a classic piece of sculpture in a coved niche.

In the chalet-style dining room (or on a wide terrace where tables are set under an arbor of magenta bougainvillea), you can order table d'hôte luncheons at 500$ ($7.65), including a hobnail glass carafe of the local wine and crusty homemade bread. You get a bowl of soup from the tureen, fish caught that day at Sines, meat with vegetables, then seasonal fruit. You can take coffee in the lounge in front of a 15-foot inglenook, sinking into the soft sofa. This combination lounge and dining room is decorated in the provincial style, with a collection of handmade ceramic figures and jugs.

Seven bedrooms are furnished comfortably with antiques or good reproductions. Four contain private baths; three in the annex, hot and cold running water. Rooms with bath cost 1600$ ($24.48) in a single, 1800$ ($27.54) in a double. Suites go for 2900$ ($44.37).

Continuing south, we come upon the **Pousada Santa Clara,** opened in 1971, at the Barragem Marcello Caetano of **Santa Clara-a-Velha** (tel. Santa Clara-a-Velha 522-50), overlooking the large lake and dam of the Rio Mira. The charming pousada is a most convenient stopover on the Lisbon–Sagres road to the Algarve. There are six pleasant double rooms with bath. A twin-bedded room with private bath and breakfast included rents for $35 (U.S.). If you stop for just a meal, the tab comes to $15. An ideal place for swimming and fishing, the inn has spacious lounges and good food, such as roast kid done to a turn or fish freshly caught from the lake.

1. Sagres

At the extreme southwestern corner of Europe, Sagres is a rocky escarpment jutting out into the Atlantic, the ocean beating itself into an aquamarine froth upon the steep cliffs. It was here that Henry the Navigator, the Infante of Sagres, "dreamed dreams no mortal ever dared to dream before." He also proved that they could come true, launching Portugal and the modern world upon the seas of explorations. At Sagres, Henry, son of João I and Philippa of Lancaster, established his School of Navigation.

He died (1460) before the great discoveries of Columbus and Vasco da Gama, but those explorers owed a debt to him. A virtual ascetic, he assembled the best navigators, cartographers, geographers, scholars, sailors, and builders he could muster, infusing them with his rigorous devotion and methodically setting Portuguese caravels upon the Sea of Darkness.

Today, at the reconstructed site of his windswept fortress upon Europe's Land's End (nicknamed that after the narrowing westernmost tip of Cornwall, England), you can see a huge stone compass dial which he is alleged to have used in the naval studies pursued at Sagres.

At a simple chapel here, restored in 1960, sailors are said to have prayed for help before setting out into uncharted waters. To the left of the chapel is the villa where Henry lived (inquire at the Tourist Office nearby if you want to visit the interior). On what is believed to have been the site of the School of Navigation, a youth hostel has been installed. In the Auditorium of Sagres, a film is shown daily depicting the story of Henry the Navigator; the English-language version (it costs 10$) is shown at 3:45 p.m. daily.

Three miles away is the promontory of **Cape St. Vincent.** The cape is so named because, according to legend, the body of St. Vincent arrived mysteriously here on a boat guided by ravens. Others claim that the body of the patron saint, murdered at Valencia, Spain, washed up upon the shores of Lisbon. A lighthouse stands here. Sea gulls glide upon the air currents; and on the approach, a few goats graze on a hill where even the trees are bent from the gusty wind.

Both the cape and Sagres (especially from the terrace of the pousada), offer a view of the sunset. To the ancient world, the cape was the last explored point, although in time the Phoenicians pushed beyond it. Many mariners thought that when the sun sank beyond the cape, it plunged over the edge of the world. To venture around the promontory was to face the demons of the unknown.

Sagres lies 174 miles south of Lisbon; from Lisbon's Praça do Comércio, you can take a ferry across the Tagus to Barreiro. From there, it's possible to make connections with the Southern Line Railway on its run to Lagos. At Lagos, buses ply back and forth between that town and Sagres. The accommodations at Sagres are limited, but good.

ACCOMMODATIONS: Hotel da Baleeira (tel. 642-21) is a first-class whaleboat, its name in Portugal. It enjoys a ship's bow position, spread out as it is above the tiny fishing port, with boats tied up in the harbor. Rising on the crest of the hill like a building on the North African coast, it affords a view of the shoreline. Even its angular saltwater swimming pool is thrust out on a ledge, surrounded by a flagstone terrace. It's almost like swimming in the ocean, only you're perched high on a cliff. The largest hotel on this land projection, it offers 114 bedrooms and three suites, all with private baths and sea-view balconies.

The hotel has nearly doubled the number of its bedrooms in recent years, although the older ones are quite small (as are the baths) and are furnished with dated modern pieces. The bedrooms are on the lower level. In high season, you pay 3200$ ($48.96) for full board based on double occupancy, 2000$ ($30.60) for one person.

If you're exploring the Algarve and are in Sagres just for the day, you can stop off and order a 700$ ($10.71) luncheon or dinner in a dining room cantilevered out toward the sea, with everyone getting view seats. The chef has his own private lobster tanks (no frozen lagosta here); and the meals are well prepared and served in an efficient manner.

The atmosphere is that of a private world, as the hotel has its own sandy beach, car park, cocktail lounge, and nearby hairdresser.

Pousada do Infante, Ponta da Atalaia (tel. 64-222), seems like a one-time monastery built by ascetic monks who wanted to commune with nature—the rugged beauty of the rocky cliffs, the pounding surf, the sense of the infinity of the ocean. The glistening white-painted government-owned tourist inn with a tiled roof is spread out along the edge of a cliff, protruding rather daringly over the sea. It boasts a long colonnade of arches with an extended stone terrace set up with garden furniture, plus a second floor of bedrooms with private balconies.

The public rooms are generously proportioned, gleaming with marble and decorated with unusually fine tapestries depicting the exploits of Henry the Navigator. Large gold velvet couches flank the fireplace with tall brass floor lamps. In the dining room, the walls are lined with azulejos (tiles), and in the corner rests a cone-shaped fireplace with a mounted ship's model. Sitting in Portuguese provincial chairs, guests can order the traditional bargain luncheon or dinner of the pousadas, costing 550$ ($8.42), and including homemade bread, homemade soup from a tureen, a fish course, meat with vegetables, and dessert.

There are 21 bedrooms, and each has a private tiled bath and is furnished with traditional pieces. You pay 2250$ ($34.43) for a double room.

Have a predinner drink on the terrace, and watch the ocean-going vessels make their way around the point, heading for faraway ports of call.

Residência Dom Henrique, Sítio Da Mareta (tel. 641-33), is a sun-pocket, two- and three-story hotel with a restaurant, situated dramatically on the *promontorio,* the viewpoint above the beach. Rather motel-like, it is a white stucco building, stretched along a small garden. Each room has a sun balcony. There are regular rooms, apartments with three rooms, a balcony, two baths, plus a living room and kitchen. A single room with a private shower goes for 600$ ($9.18) daily; and doubles, either with private showers or baths, range from 850$ ($13.01) to 950$ ($14.54). Lunch or dinner is another 450$ ($6.89) per person.

Owner Alberina Martins da Cunha can arrange for boats, waterskiing, and bike rentals. It's also an informal place for afternoon tea, where you can sample some of the regional cakes.

ON THE OUTSKIRTS: Casa Fajara (tel. Bordeira 76123) lies just north of Carrapateira, between Lagos, Vila do Bispo, and Cape St. Vincent. Immediately after the village of Carrapateira, turn right onto an unpaved lane (a left turn will take you to the beach), passing palm trees and following the lane to Casa Fajara.

Once there, an English couple, Jeffrey and Diana Honour, will welcome you to their small café and restaurant, which is also a guest house, costing 1000$ ($15.30) per night for two persons, including a continental breakfast. The inn is open all year, although it's closed on Thursday in the winter months. Originally the building was an old granary before its conversion. Now an outdoor swimming pool has been added, and there are sandy beaches nearby. The area along the coast is well known for bird watching.

If you're stopping in for a meal, you'll find such appetizers as prawn soup at 60$ (92¢) or cream of lettuce soup, 40$ (61¢). Main courses include grilled robalo at 280$ ($4.28); filet steak, 300$ ($4.59); and goat prepared in the provençal style, 250$ ($3.82). In season, you can round off your meal with strawberries and fresh cream, 75$ ($1.15). Lunches, teas, and dinners are served daily, and on the first Sunday of every month a special chicken curry meal is offered (on other Sundays, special three-course luncheons are served).

Casa de Cha da Fortalez do Beliche (tel. 64124) stands in the vicinity of the lighthouse on the road to the cape. Although it rents out a few modestly priced rooms, it is primarily a restaurant and teahouse. The restaurant is in the middle of the ancient fort, right close to the cliff's edge, and it offers a complete menu—soup, fish, meat, and dessert—for only 500$ ($7.65), although you can order à la carte as well.

2. Lagos

What the Lusitanians and Romans called Locobriga, and the Moors knew as Zawaia, was to become, under Henry the Navigator, a private experimental shipyard of caravels. Edged by the Costa do Ouro (Golden Coast), the Bay of Sagres at one point in its epic history was big enough to allow 407 warships to maneuver with ease.

An ancient port city (one historian traced its origins back to the Carthaginians three centuries before the birth of Christ), Lagos was well known by the sailors of Nelson's fleet. From Liverpool to Manchester to Plymouth, the sailors spoke wistfully of the beautiful, green-eyed, olive-skinned women of the Algarve. Eagerly they set into port, looking forward to drinking the heady Portuguese wine and carousing.

Actually, not that much has changed since Nelson's day, and few go to Lagos wanting to know of its history. Rather, the mission is to drink deeply of the pleasures of table and beach.

In winter, the almond blossoms match the whitecaps on the water, and the climate is warm enough for sunbathing.

In town, the **flea market** sprawls through narrow streets, the vendors selling such articles as rattan baskets, earthenware pottery, fruits, vegetables, crude furniture, cutlery, knitted shawls, and leather boots.

Less than a mile down the coast, the hustle-bustle of market day is forgotten as the rocky headland of the **Ponta da Piedade** (Point of Piety) appears. This beauty spot is considered by many the best on the entire coast. Dotted among the colorful cliffs and secret grottos carved by the waves are the most flamboyant examples of Manueline architecture.

Much of Lagos was razed in the 1755 earthquake, at which time it lost its position as the capital of the Algarve. Today, only ruins remain of its former walls of fortification. However, traces of the old are still to be discovered on the back streets. On the Rua Silva Lopes, just off the waterfront, sits the 18th-century **Igreja de Santo António** (Church of St. Anthony). Decorating the altar are some of the greatest rococo gilt carvings in all of Portugal. Begun in the 17th century, they were damaged in the earthquake, but subsequently restored. What you see today represents the work of many artisans—at times, each of them seemingly pursuing a different theme.

Attached to the church is the **Museu Regional de Lagos,** containing replicas of the fret-cut chimneys of the Algarve, three-dimensional cork carvings, 16th-century vestments, ceramics, 17th-century embroidery, ecclesiastical sculpture, a painting gallery, weapons, minerals, and a numismatic collection. An oddity is a sort of believe-it-or-not section, displaying among other things an eight-legged calf. In the archeological wing are Neolithic artifacts, along with Roman mosaics found at Sagres, fragments of statuary and columns, and other shards of antiquity from excavations along the Algarve. Charging an admission of 5$ (8¢), the museum is open daily, except Monday, from 9:30 a.m. to 12:30 p.m. and from 2 to 5 p.m. (tel. 623-01).

In the old **Customs House** on the Praça Infante, Dom Henriques stands as a painful reminder of the Age of Exploration. The arcaded slave market, the only one of its kind in Europe, looks peaceful today, but under its four Romanesque arches captives taken from their homelands were sold to the highest bidder. The house opens onto a peaceful square, dominated by a statue of Henry the Navigator.

Lagos is 21 miles east of Sagres, 164 miles south of Lisbon, and 49 miles west of Faro. To reach it by rail from Lisbon, take the ferryboat at Praça do Comércio across the Tagus to Barreiro. There, connections to Lagos can be made on the Southern Line Railway.

In accommodations it is well stocked, beginning with my favorite:

THE UPPER BRACKET: Hotel de Lagos, 1 Rua Castilho (tel. 620-11), is a 20th-century castle with its own ramparts and moats (two swimming pools). This first-class hotel is spread out over three acres of hilltop overlooking Lagos, so no matter which room you're assigned, you'll have a view, even if it is one opening upon a sun-trap courtyard with semitropical greenery. The main room evokes a hacienda atmosphere, with a background of bone-white plaster walls, enlivened by sunny colors. Guests gather here in one of the clusters of soft built-in sofas set on carpets. In a corner logs burn in a fireplace in chilly weather. Excellent meals are served in an expansive harbor-view room, decorated in wood paneling.

A few bedrooms with patios are on the ground level, but most of them are on the upper six floors, each containing a private bath. The rooms, both single and double, even the suites, offer a choice of standard and deluxe. In high season (June through September), the half-board rate for one person ranges from 2700$ ($41.31) to 3200$ ($48.96); for two persons, from 3400$ ($52.02) to 4800$ ($73.44). The average bedroom has a background of stark white walls contrasted with warm Oriental colors in shades of burnt orange, gold, lime, sun yellow, and bronze. The furnishings emphasize the slimline upholstered look, with most rooms opening onto a wedge-shaped balcony where you can eat breakfast. Amenities include a boîte (the Zum-Zum Room), a poolside bar, two lounge bars, and complete air conditioning.

The Hotel de Lagos also owns **Duna Beach Club** on Meia Praia Beach, with a heated saltwater swimming pool, daily buffets, and a private clubhouse. Guests of the hotel are given a free membership during their stay. A private motor coach makes regularly scheduled trips to the beach club, only five minutes from the hotel.

Arrangements can be made for tennis only a short distance from the hotel; for golf at any one of the international courses in the Algarve; for skindiving and sports fishing in the waters along the coast; for horseback riding through nature's garden; for sailing in the bay; and for international floorshows and gambling in the Algarve's casinos.

THE MEDIUM-PRICED RANGE: Hotel Sa Cristovão, Rossio de S. João (tel. 630-51), may have been a simple inn at one point, but that is now history. The rather modest beginnings have given way to an avant-garde stylishness, the interior seemingly inspired by a latter-day Frank Lloyd Wright. At the edge of town, almost within sight of the harbor, the hotel sits on a busy parkway junction of the coastal highway and the road to Lisbon. There is a rooftop solarium. Owned and run by Torralta C.I.F., the first-class hotel is maintained on a personal basis.

The bedrooms are inviting in their uncluttered design. Shafts of fine-grain wood are used in a Mondrian fashion at the windows, beds, and headboards. The walls are likely to be sky blue, with deeper hued carpets and draperies. Each room opens onto a private terrace and is priced according to size and placement. The price of a single is 900$ ($13.77) in low season (October to March) and 1500$ ($22.95) in high season. Doubles cost 1000$ ($15.30) in low season, 2200$ ($33.66) in high season. Breakfast is included in the tariffs quoted, and you can order lunch or dinner for 350$ ($5.36).

Opening off the reception are several public lounges. The largest uses natural pine slats for the ceiling, cube lighting, and pillars. One part on a lower level makes for intimate seating around a free-standing black fireplace. Before-dinner drinks are available in the cocktail lounge, which opens onto an inner patio with a fountain waterfall.

Hotel Meia Praia, Meia Praia (tel. 620-01), means halfway to the beach. Edging up to the ruins of an old fortress, this first-class hotel is for those who want sand, sun, and good food rather than an exciting decor. The hotel, containing 66 bedrooms, all with private bath, was built as the Greeks preferred: at a point where a hill begins its rise from the sea. Surrounded by private gardens, it fronts railway tracks and a wide sandy beach, four miles long. The guests play tennis on two professional hard courts, linger in the informal garden where white iron outdoor furniture is scattered under the olive and palm trees, or loll by the large pools, one for adults, another for children. The hotel is three kilometers from the center of Lagos and one kilometer from the Palmares golf course.

The oceanside bedrooms have balconies with partitions for sunbathing. The furnishings in the rooms are uncluttered, functional, and modern. The most expensive rooms have sea views and two balconies; the medium-priced rooms, a sea view and one balcony; and the cheapest rooms have no balconies and overlook the hills. For full board in high season, a single pays 2400$ ($36.72) nightly; two persons, from 3900$ ($59.67) to 4500$ ($68.85). Rates are reduced off-season. Across the entire all-glass front of the hotel is the dining room lounge and cocktail bar.

The hotel is run by the Torralta group and is open all year.

Hotel Riomar, 81 Cándido dos Reis, (tel. 630-91), is a modern structure in the center of town. It has a pleasant downstairs lounge, a cozy bar, and a tasteful decor. Its rooms are closed in the winter. In low season, singles rent for 1500$ ($22.95), doubles for 2100$ ($32.13). In high season, the tariffs rise to 2100$ ($32.13) in a single, 2600$ ($39.78) in a double, breakfast included.

Casa de São Gonçalo da Lagos, 73 Rua Cándido dos Reis (tel. 621-71). This exquisite pink town villa, with its fancy iron balconies, dates back to the 18th century. Until recent times, it was the private family house of a gracious English-speaking Portuguese woman. Mr. and Mrs. Da Cunha now run it as a hotel. He was the general manager of the Alvor Praia Hotel for five years. At the core of Lagos, close to restaurants and shops, the antique-filled home is a near-undiscovered gem. Most of the public lounges and bedrooms turn, in the Iberian fashion, to the inward peace of a sun-filled patio. Here, surrounded by bougainvillea climbing up balconies, guests order their breakfast, sitting under a fringed parasol and enjoying the splashing and gurgling of the fountain.

All the furnishings are individualized: no bedroom is like another. Delicate hand-embroidered bed linens are color coordinated to the counterpanes and blankets, and you're apt to find period mahogany tables, silver candlesticks, chests with brass handles, inlaid tip-top tables, old desks, fine ornate beds brought from Angola, pewter and brass lamps, even crystal chandeliers. In high season, June 1 to September 30, a twin rents for $47 (U.S.), a single for $39. During other months, a twin goes for $35, a single for $27. In the restoration of the house, modern amenities were added, so that each room contains a private bath.

The luxury pension is in a rambling casa (house), with various stairways leading to corridors with fine old prints, engravings, and Portuguese ceramic bowls of flowers set on aged hand-carved chests. Guests enjoy get-togethers in the large living room with its comfortable armchairs drawn up around a fireplace. Here, again, the furnishings are personalized, with a preponderance of antiques, including an English spinet piano, a gilt Italian mirror and console, a statue of a saint, and bronze torchères.

WHERE TO DINE AND DRINK: The Bar Barroca, 1 Travessa da Senhora do Graça (tel. 621-85), is a Portuguese tavern, dispensing healthy-size drinks and regional meals. It's placed at the top of a slight incline and narrow street, close to the waterfront. The atmosphere is relaxed, conducive to dining and drinking. Guests dine under a high beamed ceiling. On a busy night, the tables in the rear or on the mezzanine are popular. It is closed on Friday in winter only.

The food is well prepared, the portions generous, the cuisine Portuguese. The chef's specialty is caldeirada Barroca, an Algarvian fish stew costing 300$ ($4.59). Others prefer bife Barroca, 325$ ($4.97), or the chicken Barroca, 340$ ($5.20). To begin your meal, try the caldo verde (potato and greens soup), 60$ (92¢).

Os Arcos ("The Arches"), 32 Rua 25 de Abril, only a block from the fishing harbor, is a friendly restaurant and bar, under English management. The accent is on informality and good food. A central meeting place, the restaurant has excellent bar snacks and economical lunches. A lunch averages 160$ ($2.45); bar snacks, around 100$ ($1.53). At night international specialties are featured, a dinner (served between 7:30 and 10:30 p.m.) averaging around 750$ ($11.48). Specialties include homemade pâté, duck prepared with peaches, and apple pie. The restaurant shuts down in November.

Pouso do Infante, 11 Rua Alfonso d'Almeida, is a pleasant tavern-type restaurant, with an iron chandelier, walls decorated with local craftwork, and rustic-type chairs painted green with straw seats. A vegetable soup costs 55$ (84¢); a shrimp cocktail, 150$ ($2.30); veal scallopine with spaghetti, 270$ ($4.13); sole with banana, 290$ ($4.44); chicken curry with rice, 220$ ($3.37); lamb in wine sauce, 225$ ($3.44); and almond cake, 50$ (77¢).

Lagosteira, 20 Rua 1 de Maio (tel. 624-86), has long been a mecca for knowledgeable diners in Lagos. Its decor is simple, with tiles running up half of the wall, the rest painted in a deep maroon color. There's a small bar on one side. On an à la carte menu, you can order the fish soup, 100$ ($1.53); clams

Lagosteira style, 350$ ($5.36); sirloin steak, 350$ also. Custard is 60$ (92¢). The restaurant is open from noon till 2 a.m., except Monday. It also shuts down from November 1 until March 31.

O Trovador, Largo do Convento da Senhora da Gloria (tel. 631-52), is run by a young German couple, Marion and Bernhard, who have lived for ten years in the States and in Bermuda. It's especially nice off-season when comfortable chairs are placed around a log-burning fireplace. But at any time of the year you get a pleasant atmosphere, friendly service, and good food. The location is up the hill behind the Lagos Hotel. The cuisine is international. Among the recommendable appetizers are homemade chicken liver pâté at 120$ ($1.84) and an octopus cocktail, a specialty of the house, at 150$ ($2.30). The chef also prepares goulash soup Trovador at 75$ ($1.15) and escargots bourguignonnes, 275$ ($4.21). Main courses include quails fried in butter (when available), 240$ ($3.67), and spare ribs Trovador, 280$ ($4.28). You might also enjoy Portuguese swordfish at 275$ ($4.21). The desserts are good, including a homemade cheesecake (not baked) at 70$ ($1.07) or coupe Trovador, 100$ ($1.53). It's open nightly from 7 p.m., although it's closed on Thursday.

Restaurante-Bar Alpendre, Rua Barbosa Viana (tel. 627-05), has one of the most elaborate and sophisticated menus along the Algarve. Service and food are first rate. Your evening might begin in the downstairs bar where you can have a before-dinner drink, sampling crunchy Algarvian almonds and olives. Later, you can order your menu, selecting among excellent soups, such as onion au gratin at 200$ ($3.06), following with one of the house specialties, such as pepper steak, 1500$ ($22.95) for two persons, or filets of sole with caviar sauce, 600$ ($9.18). Flambé dishes are done with style and flair. A favorite is the filets of sole with a vermouth sauce, costing 1500$ ($22.95) for two persons. Two dessert features are the mixed fruits flambé, 600$ ($9.18) for two, or crêpes flambés with coffee, 750$ ($11.48) for two. Go for dinner, but make a reservation first. You'll be welcomed with consideration.

READERS' RESTAURANT SUGGESTIONS: "A Gruta de João de Sousa e Castro, 9 Rua do Ferrador (tel. 625-85). Of all the kind and warm Portuguese I've met and known, Don João is unrivaled. His warmth, goodness, and sincerity are indeed a rarity anywhere today. And it was this radiating kindness which came straight from the heart that drew us like a magnet over and over again for the ten days we spent here in Lagos. I cannot do justice to this gracious man by writing you about him, but only ask that your readers find out for themselves, as we did by visiting his little restaurant-bar. Gruta is Portuguese for cave, hence the caveman amid the pots and pans. But please don't expect a restaurant with a 'cavelike' atmosphere—as there is none. This place is a small, simple, family-like restaurant, with some of the best food I've eaten in all my travels. We ate there daily, ordering soup, a main course, fruit, and a liter of wine, with meals costing from 300$ ($4.59 to 450$ ($6.89). Soups are as low as 30$ (46¢); desserts, 40$ (61¢); wine, 85$ ($1.15) by the bottle. The fish especially is delicious. You can eat quite well for very little if you don't drink the way we do (we usually had a couple of brandies). Closed on Thursday. But the most fantastic thing about the place—and I cannot emphasize this enough—is Don João" (Mary Helen Hernandez, San Antonio, Tex.).

"We discovered **A Capoeira,** the Chicken Coop restaurant, 76 Rua 25 de Abril. The specialty is broiled chicken and chips. Other main dishes include cold roast beef plate, pork chop, and ham salad plate. Salad is served with the chicken or pork chop. A complete à la carte meal costs from 400$ ($6.12). The restaurant is very small, seating about 16 people. The decor is simple, with red-checkered tablecloths with a white overlay and flowers on each table. The atmosphere is spanking clean. All the food is good, with everything cooked to order by the owner's wife. The husband, John Cooper, is bartender, waiter, and bus boy. The only drawback is the small selection on the menu, a choice of five main dishes. Unless you really dig chicken, which is the best, after two or three meals you have exhausted the menu. But, on the other hand, 'good things come in small packages'" (Mrs. William W. Lederer, Hartsdale, N.Y.). . . . "For those who, like me, are always glad to have access to good Chinese food wherever they are, I recommend the **Mandarin Chinese Restaurant** at Lagos, on the road to Meia Praia just outside the town. In a charming building with elevated views of the surrounding countryside, two delightful Chinese sisters serve authentic and very tasty Chinese food. Their Peking duck with five spices is the best I have tasted anywhere, and when I inquired about an unfamiliar and intriguing vegetable, they told me with pride that they have it especially flown in from Taiwan by their mother" (H. L. Goodman, London, England).

PRAIA DONA ANA: About a mile west of Lagos, this tiny cove contains rock formations that appear as a painted desert in the sea and sand. The grottos, arches, caves, and grotesques have been carved and colored by the weather and water in subtle hues of reds, ochres, golds, and scarlets. An island at its mouth landlocks the lagoon where scarred cliffs, reflecting amber, burgundy, russet, plummet into the deep-blue waters. This cove is a rare experience and one of the most scenic spots along the Algarve.

Hotel Golfinho (tel. 620-81) is modern and built near the swimming cove of this idyllic little retreat. It's been such a success that more rooms have been added as well as a swimming pool. For those who enjoy sun and sea, it brings a sophisticated touch. The lounges and bar, however, have a starkly contemporary background which the nautical paraphernalia doesn't offset.

The bedrooms, each with a private bath, are in a restrained style, crisp and neat. Sitting terraces with rattan furniture are an added attraction. The prices vary according to the view, with a twin sea vista being the most favored. In high season, two persons can stay here on half-board rates that begin at 4000$ ($61.20). Singles in the same arrangement are charged from 2800$ ($42.84).

Meals are served by candlelight, casting shadows on the rough white plaster walls with large jewel-like inserts. At dinner, the tab for the table d'hôte is 600$ ($9.18) per person. There are two bars where guests congregate—one semipaneled in pine is a focal point for expatriates who've built sea-view villas along the nearby cliffs.

3. Portimão

Go here only if you prefer the life of a bustling fishing port instead of a hotel perched right on the beach. Ever since the 1930s, Praia da Rocha, two miles away, has snared sun-loving traffic. But the Algarve is so popular in summer that Portimão has developed a base of tourists.

The wafting aroma of the noble Portuguese sardine permeates every street and café nook. As a fish-canning center, Portimão leads the Algarve, but it doesn't top Setúbal in production. Still, for a change of pace, this town, on an arm of the Arade River, makes a good stopover center (it also has some fine dining recommendations). Stroll through its gardens, its shops (especially noted for their pottery), drink the wine of the cafés, and roam down to the quays where you will see sardines roasting on braziers. The routine activity of the Algarvians is what gives the town its charm. On its left bank the little whitewashed community of **Ferragudo** is unspoiled, but tame, with a castle.

Fish, fruit, and vegetable **markets** are held every morning except Sunday in the market building and open market square, closing at 2 p.m. On the first Monday of every month, a day-long, gigantic regional market is held with gypsies selling local artifacts, pottery, wicker, even snake oil. Boutiques offering the Algarve's best selection of hand-knit sweaters ($14 U.S.), socks ($4 U.S.), hand-painted porcelain, and pottery abound.

Between 9:30 and 10:30 a.m., the fishermen can be seen unloading their boats by tossing up wicker baskets full of freshly caught fish.

PRAIA DONA ANA/PORTIMÃO 157

Many of the buildings in the old quarter of town date back to the mid-18th century when the town was rebuilt after the devastating earthquake of 1755. Roaming the streets, you can peer into delightful hidden courtyards, some with bread ovens built into the three-foot-thick walls, blacksmith stables, tinsmiths, sardine-canning factories where sardines are still cleaned and packed by hand, and carpenters' shops.

Portimão is a perfect escape from the summer rush of visitors (mostly European) in the oceanfront towns, and room rates are considerably cheaper. A bus to the beach at Praia da Roche, mentioned above, is only 12¢ (U.S.) or a taxi, $1. Buses or trains leave Portimão for all parts of the Algarve and Portugal. An express bus to Lisbon costs around $12, including a light snack and drink served on the bus during its 4½-hour run.

In accommodations Portimão is limited.

THE MEDIUM-PRICED RANGE: Hotel Globo, 26 Rua 5 de Outubro (tel. 221-51), is an island of contemporary living in the heart of the old town. A first-class hotel, it is recommended for its clean-cut, well-thought-out design. Snug modern balconies overlook the tiled rooftops crusted with moss. In 1967 the owner-manager Faustino Pereira de Carvalho imported an uninhibited architect to turn his inn into a top-notch hotel. Each of the 74 bedrooms, all with private baths, enjoys good taste in layout and furnishings. The decor is highlighted by parquet floors, matching ebony panels on the wardrobes, built-in headboards, living room chairs and tables, and a marble desk with a black stool. Depending on the season, singles range from 1250$ ($19.13) to 2000$ ($30.60), and doubles range from 1700$ ($26.01) to 2500$ ($38.25).

On the ground floor is an uncluttered, well-furnished lounge, again with comfortable pieces in warm fabrics and woods. There is an adjoining lounge and bar, with a stylized cut-out mural of fine food and drink, neat zigzag table nooks, and a rich marble-topped bar.

Crowning the top floor is a dining room, the Aquarium. Encircled by four glass walls, permitting unblocked views of the harbor, ocean, or mountains, the restaurant is inviting, its tables set with crystal stemware and flowers.

A MOTEL IN THE ENVIRONS: Motel Parque Algarvio, nine kilometers outside Portimão and one kilometer from Lagoa on the main highway (tel. 522-65), is good for overnighting on the route along the Algarve. There are 42 rooms furnished simply and functionally, each with a small terrace and plastic chairs. The rustic room has a vaulted roof, with tile-decorated walls. Prices are in the three-star range. The motel has a pleasant pool. Single prices in low season are 1250$ ($19.13), going up to 1700$ ($26.01) in high season. Depending on the season, doubles range from 1400$ ($21.42) to 2150$ ($32.90). Breakfast is included, although you pay 550$ ($8.42) per person extra for half board.

THE BUDGET RANGE: The Dennis Inn & Bar, 10 Rua 5 de Outubro (tel. 242-73), is a very homey inn created from a 275-year-old converted town villa. Lunches costing from 400$ ($6.12), offering homemade chili, shepherd's pie, salads, and meat pies, are served in the pub and on the flower-filled garden patio. Charcoal-broiled giant hamburgers are available in the summer evenings under the stars. The Pub comes alive with piano and guitar playing and nightly sing-alongs. All rooms have private baths, hand-painted Alentejo furniture, and original Portuguese oil paintings. Guests are served breakfast in bed or on the patio. The atmosphere is one of friendly hospitality. Doubles cost 950$ ($14.54), including breakfast and tax.

The **Roma Pensão**, 34 Rua Júdice Fialho (tel. 242-73), is one of the best bargain-hunter pensãos in the Algarve, with 18 rooms, all with private bath. The bedrooms are functional and clean, and at 650$ ($9.95) for a double (less off-season) or 330$ ($5.05) for a single, the price is hard to beat. It's in the oldest quarter of town, surrounded by cafés and restaurants and is just one minute from the harbor.

WHERE TO DINE: Alfredo's Restaurant (tel. 229-54), near the waterfront in Portimão, 10 Rua Pé de Cruz, fills an important gap along the Algarve: a top-notch restaurant operating outside of a hotel dining room. It is in the old tavern style, on the ground floor of a modern building. Against a backdrop of chalk-white walls, provincial artifacts are used decoratively, the new combined with the old. From the dining room, you can see an ornately tiled open kitchen, with a charcoal grill, crocks of lobster, baskets of mushrooms, cabbage, salad greens, even a glass case of fresh fish.

You dine on high-back chairs with rush seats, where you can see the carved refectory table laden with cheeses, baskets of fruits, special desserts, and a tall scale. A candle in a brass holder is lit by the waiter, and you make your choice from an à la carte menu. Recommended are the fish soup at 75$ ($1.15); ameijoas à Alfredo's, 550$ ($8.42) for two; pescada (hake) à marinheira, 420$ ($6.43); and tournedos Rossini, 480$ ($7.34). A light and creamy chocolate mousse costs 60$ (92¢).

Cesar, on the Rua do Pé da Cruz, a few feet from Alfredo's, is a fine choice for the budget. It's like a bistro, with a counter-bar at the entrance containing an espresso machine, and then there are two rows of tables, with high-back chairs. Soft lights adorn the green walls, as do plates and pictures. The daily specials might be a fish soup for 75$ ($1.15); shrimp cocktail, 210$ ($32.13); or grilled steak, 280$ ($42.84). After dinner you can have your coffee and brandy in the small corner lounge in the back of the restaurant.

Lucio, 1 Largo Francisco A. Mauricio (tel. 242-92), is as simple as can be, but serves the best seafood in town at low prices. The rooms command a view of the port and the sea gulls circling the fish boats, even a less romantic gas station. The dining room is small, triangular in shape, with no frills, tiny tables, and tiled walls. This is where knowledgeable locals go, too. Fresh clams cost 225$ ($3.44); lagostas, 315$ ($4.82); shrimp, 220$ ($3.37). A fried or grilled sole goes for 375$ ($5.74); sardines, 180$ ($2.75); and squid, 315$ ($4.82).

READER'S RESTAURANT SUGGESTION: "An excellent, inexpensive restaurant in Portimão is called **Mirarocha**, standing in a small square several blocks from the bridge in the fishing beach area. I think the name of the street is Rua de Cándido dos Reis. The service is attentive, and both waiters we encountered spoke some English. The specialty of the restaurant is tableside cooking, and menu items with the word *blaze* in them are all cooked at your table. These include selections such as steak au poivre, sole blaze, spaghetti Bolognese blaze, and, for dessert, crêpes suzette or bananas blaze. The menu also includes many seafood items and other fine choices such as pork cutlets and a type of wienerschnitzel. Salads are fresh and tasty, and the soups we tried were all good. The price is under $8 (U.S.) a head for a main course with salad, vegetable, roll, and dessert. There is a good choice of inexpensive wines" (Linda H. Underwood, Rochester, N.Y.).

A RESORT COMPLEX: Just a couple of miles outside of Portimão, on the coast, **Torralta Alvorbeach** (tel. 202-11) is a complex still in the course of expanding (telephone the Torralta Club International at 517-48 in Lisbon for more information before striking out for it). The facilities, both natural and man-made, include more than three miles of fine sandy beach, a nearby golf course, swimming pools, riding facilities, tennis courts, nautical sports, fishing, several bars and restaurants, including self-service snackbars.

The self-contained and comfortably furnished studios, apartments, and villas are handsome. In studios and apartments, the cost for two persons in high season comes to 2250$ ($34.43). Ranging upward, six clients are accommodated in a villa for 4700$ ($71.91). These tariffs include water, gas, electricity, a change of linen, and daily cleaning. Breakfasts are 110$ ($1.68), with a complete lunch or dinner going for 475$ ($7.27).

EXCURSIONS FROM PORTIMÃO: An excursion can be made from Portimão via a winding 15-mile road north to **Monchique, Foia,** high in the hills at an altitude of 2700 feet. In Roman days the soldiers discovered this little spot and turned it into a spa.

Where to Stay and Eat

The **Estalagem Abrigo de Montanha** (tel. 921-31) is a small inn set amid such scenery as a botanical garden. With all those camellias, rhododendrons, mimosa, banana palms, and arbutus blooming, plus the tinkling waterfalls, you'd never believe the hot Algarve coast was only a couple of miles away. The inn has five double rooms and six suites, each complete with bath. On chilly evenings guests gather before a fireplace in the lounge. In the attractive restaurant, good food is served. For two persons, the daily rate is 1750$ ($26.78) in a room, 2500$ ($38.25) in a suite. Full pension charge for two persons is 3300$ ($50.48) in a room and 3800$ ($58.14) in a suite. Otherwise a main meal, if ordered separately, costs 450$ ($6.89). Breakfast is included, however.

ON THE OUTSKIRTS: **O Leao de Porches,** in Porches, a small village on the way to Lagoa (tel. 523-84), is a 17th-century farmhouse which has been converted into a restaurant of charm and style. Operated by H. V. Coles, this dining room is good for either lunch or dinner, when an international and Portuguese menu is featured, including some English dishes in honor of the owner's homeland. Everybody has heard of duck soup, although many have never tried it. You can try it here for 75$ ($1.15), or the cold prawn and cucumber soup at 180$ ($2.75) may lure you, or perhaps the smoked fish pâté at 140$ ($2.14). Main courses include such delectable selections as quail à la Portuguêsa, 320$ ($4.90); steak-and-kidney pie, 280$ ($4.28); ox tongue with sweet-and-sour sauce, 340$ ($5.20); and chicken curry, 370$ ($5.66). Desserts, costing from 120$ ($1.84), include American lemon cheesecake, banana butterscotch, and fresh strawberries with cream. The restaurant is closed on Sunday, and reservations are necessary.

4. Praia da Rocha

This creamy yellow beach has long been the most popular seaside resort on the Algarve. The beauty of its rock formations led English voyagers to discover it around 1935. At the outbreak of World War II, there were only two small hotels on the Red Coast, interspersed with a few villas, many built by wealthy Portuguese. Nowadays, Praia da Rocha is booming, as many have fallen victim to the spell cast by its shoreline and climate.

It is named the Beach of the Rock because of the sculptural formations of the rock, the best known one suggesting bears, twin brothers, and a triumphal arch. Some have seen a seaside cathedral; others, surrealistic sculptures. At the end of the mussel-encrusted cliff, where the Arade flows into the sea, the ruins of the **Fort of St. Catarina** lie, the location offering many views of Portimão's satellite, Ferragudo, and of the bay.

Praia da Rocha is endowed with accommodations in all price ranges, the leader of which is the **Algarve Hotel,** Praia da Rocha (tel. Portimão 240-00), which is strictly for those who love the glitter and glamor of the lush life. With a vast staff at one's beck and call, a guest is ensconced in luxury within an elongated block of rooms poised securely on the top ledge of a cliff. On a lower terrace is an overscale kidney-shaped heated swimming pool (plus another one for children), with a sundeck cantilevered out over still another cliff, projecting above rugged rocks, caves, and a sandy cove.

The main lounge is like a sultan's palace: gold velvet chairs, Oriental carpets, brass and teak screens, antique chests, and sink-deep sofas set around a copper-hooded fireplace. The corridors are graciously styled, with white marble, patterned blue tiles, carved figures and chests, plus lamps and stone slab consoles. The bedrooms have white walls, colored ceilings, intricately tiled floors, mirrored entryways, indirect lighting, balconies with garden furniture, and baths with separate showers, double basins, and heated towel racks. Everything is air-conditioned and centrally heated. In low season, singles on the half-board rate pay 4200$ ($64.26), the tariff going up to 6700$ ($102.51) in a double. In spring and autumn, these same tariffs are 4600$ ($70.38) in a single, 8200$ ($125.46) in a double. From July through September, only doubles are accepted at a half-board rate of 8500$ ($130.05) daily. Costing more, of course, are three spectaculars, a decorator's tour de force in originality, the Yachting, Oriental, and Miradouro Suites.

In the formal dining room, with its waterside windows, chinoiserie ceilings and pillars, you can order dinner. Two French chefs, with Brazilian backgrounds, provide gourmet-level meals on the à la carte menu. Buffet luncheons in season are served down by the swimming pool. A one-of-a-kind nightclub books top-flight entertainers (even Amália Rodrigues), in addition to their regular troupe of folk dancers. The club is like an Oriental grotto dug out of a cliff, with three stone walls and a fourth allowing for an oceanic backdrop.

Extra services include a sauna, hairdresser, barbershop, manicurist, laundry and dry cleaning, babysitting, boutiques, and complete room service. There's even a social director who plans personalized activities such as fishing parties on the hotel boat (with seafood stews), games of bridge, barbecues on the beach, mini-golf, volleyball, tennis competitions, plus waterskiing and deep-sea fishing.

Tarik Hotel (tel. 221-61) is a high-rise, 600-bed resort hotel on the edge of a cliff, with a stairway winding down to its wide sandy beach. It attracts sun-seekers, as each room or apartment has a balcony and an all-glass solarium extended into the room, with garden furniture. It's considered a luxury apartment hotel, complete with a restaurant, snackbar, and nightclub. The rooms have European contemporary furnishings, strong colors for furniture set against white walls. You can get either a single, with sofa bed, a twin-bedded room, or a small suite for three or four persons, a studio for two persons with a small kitchen, or studio suites for three or four occupants. Rates are based on the season. High season is June through September, mid-season is April, May, and October, and low is November through March. In high season, a single ranges in price from 2500$ ($38.25) to 2900$ ($44.37), and doubles jump from 3500$ ($53.55) to 4000$ ($61.20). Suites for three to four persons range from 4000$ ($61.20) to 7500$ ($114.75) per day.

Hotel Bela Vista, Praia da Rocha (tel. 240-55), is an old mansion built during the last century by a wealthy family as a summer home. Since 1934 it's been a special kind of hotel, ideal for those who respond to the architecture of the past. Rated first class, it's lodged in an oceanside position, atop its own palisade, with access to a sandy cove where you can swim. The villa is white, with an ornate tower and terracotta tiled roof, a coastal landmark spotted by fishermen bringing in their boats at sundown. It's flanked by the owner's home and a simple cliff-edge annex shaded by palm trees.

The attractive structure and its decorations have been preserved, although plastic furniture has been sneaked into the public lounges. The entry hallway has an art nouveau bronze torchères and a winding staircase, with walls amost covered with blue and white tiles. The tile decorations are on most of the lounge walls as well. Guests enjoy get-togethers around a baronial fireplace with a tiled facade. In the high-ceilinged dining hall are more tiled dados, plus high-back carved chairs. Meals combine Portuguese cuisine with a continental flair.

The bedrooms, all with bath, are priced according to size, plumbing, view, and placement. Those facing the sea, the former master bedrooms, are worth the additional money asked. The main house is preferable to the annex. For room and breakfast in high season, one person pays 1500$ ($22.95); two persons, from 1750$ ($26.78) to 2300$ ($35.19). Although each room has character, most of them contain tiled dados. Decorations vary from a tiled inset shrine of the Virgin Mary to crystal sconces.

WHERE TO DINE: Safari, Rua António Feu (tel. 235-40), overlooks the sea near the Hotel Jupiter, as well as the Pensão Sol opening onto the Praia da Rocha. José Francisco Continho, your host, offers a variety of fresh fish daily, and at the same time he features a number of African-inspired dishes. Real charcoal is used in his grill. In addition, he offers a good variety of wines from his well-stocked cellar. Most people seem to order the pepper steak which, at 300$ ($4.59), is really good, although other palates seem to prefer rabbit Safari at 280$ ($4.28). Another specialty is curry Safari at 250$ ($3.82) or swordfish at 220$ ($3.37). For a beginning, I'd suggest fish soup Safari at 60$ (92¢), and you might follow with large shrimps Safari, 380$ ($5.81). In fact, it might be best to go Safari all the way, finishing with pudding Safari at 60$ (92¢). Attaching the name "Safari" to the specialties means that the chef has prepared dishes based on original recipes. Go for dinner. Reservations are recommended.

PRAIA DOS TRÊS IRMÃS: Go here for the beach, nine miles of burnished golden sand, broken only by an occasional crag riddled with arched passageways. Just west of the better known Praia da Rocha, the Beach of the Three Brothers has been discovered by skin divers who explore its undersea grottos and shoreside caves.

Its neighbor is the whitewashed fishing village of **Alvor,** where Portuguese and Moorish arts and traditions have mingled since the Arabs gave up their 500 years of occupation. Alvor was a favorite coastal haunt of King João II.

The gambling casino, the **Casino de Alvor,** is modest in size compared to the one at Estoril, but it does feature roulette, blackjack, and craps. You pay 100$ ($1.53) for a two-day pass, 250$ ($3.82) for a week. A restaurant features an 800$ ($12.24) set menu, and also offers a floor show at 11 p.m. and 1 a.m. Those going just for the show pay a minimum of 500$ ($7.65).

Staying in Praia dos Três Irmãos

Alvor Praia, Praia dos Três Irmãos (tel. Portimão 240-21). "You'll feel like you're loved the moment you walk in the door," said a well-dressed woman visitor from the Midwest. This citadel of hedonism seemingly has more joie de vivre than any hotel on the Algarve. Its position is ideal, as are the building, bedrooms, decorations, service, and food.

On a landscaped crest, the luxury hotel has many of its bedrooms and public rooms exposed to the ocean view, the gardens, and the free-form Olympic-size swimming pool. Gentle walks (or else an elevator) lead down the palisade to the sandy beach and the rugged rocks which rise out of the water.

The accommodations are quite varied, everything from a cowhide-decorated room evoking Arizona's Valley of the Sun, to *típico* Portuguese accommodations with provincial furnishings. Many of the rooms contain private balconies where guests take breakfast facing the backdrop of the Bay of Lagos. In low season, the hotel charges from 2800$ ($42.84) to 3500$ ($53.55) in a single, that rate going up in high season to anywhere from 3500$ ($53.55) to 4000$ ($61.20), the latter price for a location overlooking the sea. Low-season doubles run from 3500$ ($53.55) to 3700$ ($56.61), depending on the view. In high season, doubles range from 3800$ ($58.14) to 4500$ ($68.85). Half board is an extra 1100$ ($16.83) per person. The rooms contain oversize beds, plenty of clothing space, a long desk and chest combination, and well-designed baths with double basins and lots of towels.

The hotel is so self-contained you may never stray from the premises. Inside, a wide, domed airborne staircase leads to a lower level, encircling a Japanese garden and lily pond. The main dining room is on two levels, with three glass walls so that every guest has an ocean view. The Maisonette Grill is considered separately as a restaurant recommendation (see below). Like an exclusive club, the main drinking lounge is equipped with deep leather chairs and adorned with a cubistic modern ceiling.

The concierge will arrange for fishing excursions on the hotel's 14-ton hull boat, the *Caturra,* brought here from Holland. In addition, he can get you reduced greens fees on a nearby 18-hole golf course. Other sports include horseback riding, waterskiing, and tennis. On the lower level of the hotel are boutiques, a newsstand, hairdressers, and the "only authentic Finnish sauna in Portugal."

Dining in Praia dos Três Irmãos

The **Maisonette Grill,** Hotel Alvor Praia, Praia dos Três Irmãos (tel. 242-01), takes its rightful place alongside other distinguished restaurants connected with luxury hotels, such as the Ritz Grill in Lisbon. It has become the smartest place for gourmet cuisine along the restaurant-poor Algarve coast.

The Grill, in spite of its spaciousness, has an intimate aura, allowing you plenty of time to peruse the à la carte menu. You might begin your meal with vichyssoise at 160$ ($2.45). Entrees include poached turbot in court bouillon for 420$ ($6.43), and a rib of beef, 1000$ ($15.30) for two persons. The dessert menu has such delicacies as Rothschild soufflé, 240$ ($3.67), and crêpes suzette, 300$ ($4.59). All taxes are included.

MONTES DE ALVOR: The **Penina Golf Hotel,** Montes de Alvor (tel. Portimão 220-51), between Portimão and Lagos, was founded by a group of hotel entrepreneurs, the first deluxe hotel on the Algarve. Nowadays, of course, it's getting competition from the other luxury choices. Golfing fans remain loyal to the Penina, however, as it is a major sporting mecca. A 36-hole championship golf course was designed by Henry Cotton between the hotel and the sea.

Most of the bedrooms contain picture windows and honeycomb balconies providing views of the course and swimming pool. The less expensive rooms open onto vistas of the Monchique hills. Singles with a Monchique view cost $99 (U.S.). Golf-view singles go for $110. Doubles with a Monchique view rent for $84 per person all year. With a golf view, doubles cost $90 per person. All these terms include breakfast and dinner, plus greens fees for golf. The standard bedrooms are furnished in a pleasant style, combining traditional pieces with Portuguese provincial spool beds. The rooms are spacious enough for off-the-course relaxation, and contain good-size beds and tiled baths.

Those not sunning themselves by the pool are transported to the hotel beach, with its own snackbar and changing cabins. The ground level of the Penina is devoted to changing rooms, lockers, and a golf school and shops. Other facilities include a sauna, billiard room, a beauty parlor, and a barbershop. Two hard tennis courts are offered. The main lounges have more practical comfort than style. Guests enjoy cocktails in the longest bar in the Algarve, then proceed to either the Grill Room or the dining room (table d'hôte meals in the latter) for a well-prepared repast, capped by dancing.

PRAIA DO CARVOEIRO: One of the beaches along the Algarve coast has been turned into an expatriate colony. Often a chic crowd of people settle here. If you're honored with an invitation inside one of the whitewashed villas, don't be surprised to find, say, a couple of original Dufys on the walls. Lying about three miles south of the wine-rich town of Lagoa, the sandy beach nestles between two rock masses, creating a solarium. The shadows of the cliffs are cooling, the sea calm.

Incidentally, before venturing down to the little commune of Praia do Carvoeiro, you may want to stop off at **Lagoa,** on the main coastal highway. If you announce yourself at the door to the big warehouse here, chances are you'll be allowed to visit the wine cellars.

Dining in Praia do Carvoeiro

A Galeria, Estrada do Farol (tel. Lagoa 571-33), is a unique island of good food, offered in the fishing village "living room" of the friendly Portuguese couple. A parade of discerning visitors, as well as American and English expatriates who live in the nearby villas, are drawn to this little place.

They set three tables in their pleasant living room: one in front of the sofa, another by the window, a third in front of the fireplace where they keep gnarled knots burning slowly on cool nights. Hot rolls pop out of the oven in the evening and are placed on your white tablecloth along with country-churned butter. A table d'hôte menu is offered for 420$ ($6.43), and might include a vegetable soup, moussaka, homemade cake, coffee, and even brandy. On the à la carte menu, you can order Italian spaghetti at 175$ ($2.68). It's also possible to drop in for the afternoon ordering tea or coffee with a sandwich for 105$ ($1.61). At the counter, they always keep a homemade cake, perhaps banana layer, or a pie made with tart apples, to tempt you.

A short drive north from Lagoa takes you to:

5. Silves

When you pass through the Moorish-inspired entrance of this hillside town, a strange feeling hovers in the air. Silves is unlike the other towns and villages of the Algarve. It lives in the past, recalling its heyday when it was known as Xelb, the seat of Moslem culture in the south before it fell to the Crusaders.

Christian warriors and earthquakes have been rough on Silves. But somehow the **Castle of Silves**, crowning the hilltop, has held on, although it's seen better days. Once the blood of the Moslems, staging their last stand in Silves, "flowed like red wine," as one Portuguese historian put it. The cries and screams of women and children resounded over the walls: decapitation was swift. Nowadays, the only sound you're likely to hear is the loud rock music coming from the gatekeeper's house.

The red sandstone castle may date back to the ninth century. From its ramparts you can look down the saffron-mossed tile roofs of the village houses, down the narrow cobbled streets where roosters strut and scrappy dogs sleep peacefully in the doorways.

Inside the walls, the government has planted a flower garden, adorning it with golden chrysanthemums and scarlet bracteal poinsettia. In the fortress, water rushes through a huge cistern and a deep well made of sandstone. Below are dungeon chambers and labyrinthine tunnels where the last of the Moors hid out before the Crusaders found them and sent them to their deaths.

The 13th-century Gothic **Cathedral of Silves**, down below, is disciplined but foreboding. Its walls are cracked and split, and the evidence of decay and neglect hang over it. On the interior, it is bleak. The Christian architects who originally built it may have torn down an old mosque. Still in all, the cathedral is considered one of the most outstanding religious monuments in the Algarve.

Outside the main part of town, near an orange grove (one of the local Silves boys will surely volunteer as your inexpensive guide), a lonely open-air pavilion shelters a 15th-century stone lacework cross. This curious ecclesiastical art work is two-faced, depicting a pietà (the face of Christ is destroyed) on one side, the Crucifixion on the other. It has been declared a national monument of incalculable value.

6. Armação de Pêra

Squat fishermen's cottages make up the core of this ancient village. It rests almost at water's edge on a curvy bay that edges up to its Golden Beach, one of the largest along Portugal's southern coast. In the direction of Portimão are rolling low ridges, toward Albufeira's rosy cliffs.

Once Armação de Pêra was utilized by the Phoenicians as a trading post and stopping-off point for cruises around Cape St. Vincent. Near the center of the village is a wide beach where fishing boats are drawn up on the sands—a sight when a fish auction (*lota*) is held. The **Casino**, however, is dull—no gambling, only occasional dancing, and during the day women often come here with their embroidery.

While at the resort, you may want to walk out to the desolate **Nossa Senhora da Rocha** (Our Lady of the Rock), a Romanesque chapel on a 95-foot-high stone that sticks out into the ocean like the prow of a boat. Underneath are the cathedral-size **Sea Grottos** (Furnas). To visit these, you have to call at the Tourist Office and make arrangements to go out in a boat, but they're certainly worth the effort. Unique in the Algarve, the sea caves are entered through a series of arches that frame the sky and ocean from the inside. In their galleries and vaults, where pigeons nest, the splashing and shouting reverberate in the upper stalactite-studded chambers.

The nearest railway station is at the village of Alcantarilha, five miles away.

ARMAÇÃO DE PÊRA

A DELUXE CITADEL: Vilalara, Praia das Gaivotas (tel. 553-33), is a luxury apartment complex on a cliffside, with a sandy beach and two pools—all in all, a self-contained miniature resort one mile west of Armação de Pêra. International magazines have acclaimed the high taste level, which has attracted diplomats, movie stars, members of royalty, as well as business executives. Curving with the contour of the coast, the apartments are built in a serpentine fashion, two floors of one-, two-, and three-bedroom units, each with a private sun-pocket terrace balcony. That balcony is, in fact, an outdoor living room, furnished in bamboo and rattan. A long continuous flower box softens the look at the railing. Just at the edge of the cliff, nestled into a small canyon, is the silver-blue swimming pool complex, with an adjoining bar and restaurant facilities. It's an informal life, casually chic. Each apartment is spacious and delightful, with a furnished living room, a fully equipped kitchen, a veranda with a southern view, and each attractive bedroom has its own tiled bath. One-bedroom apartments for two persons rent for 4800$ ($73.44) daily in high season, rising to 7500$ ($114.75) daily for four persons in a two-bedroom unit. Six persons can stay here in a three-bedroom unit for 10,000$ ($153) daily in high season. Off-season reductions are granted. An orchestra plays in a small nightclub, and perhaps you can hear some fado.

THE UPPER BRACKET: Hotel do Garbe, Armação de Pêra (tel. 551-94), is a self-contained resort dominating the top of a cliff, with a sandy beach at its feet. Stone steps lead up through the terraced palisade to the hotel, built block fashion, its white walls, bedroom balconies, and public terraces shining in the summer sun.

The gracious public rooms, built on several levels, are modern, but warmed by a use of color and natural wood. In the main sitting room, with its open fireplace, furnishings are grouped with an eye to the sea view; likewise, the dining hall turns to the sea. If you're just passing through, you can order a luncheon or dinner for 600$ ($9.18).

The bedrooms combine Scandinavian and Algarvian features. Often a room will have stone and plaster built-in end tables and window seats; beds set on pine frames; an occasional white skin throw rug; a red parasol on a private patio; and leather-toned tile floors. Room rates vary according to placement, size, and view, the higher tariffs for one of the four luxury or nine junior suites. The high-season, full-board rate for one person ranges from 2300$ ($35.19); for two persons, from 3800$ ($58.14) to 5000$ ($76.50)—taxes and service included.

WHERE TO DINE: A Grelha, 2 Rua do Alentejo (tel. 552-45), is a typical Portuguese restaurant decorated in the regional style. The location is near Fisherman Beach. It's run by the friendly, helpful João Alberto Prudencio Da Silva, who speaks English. Every Wednesday and Friday from 9:30 p.m. he offers a program of fado, although you must call ahead to reserve a table. His fish dishes are excellent, as are his arrangements with local fishermen to keep him constantly supplied with the freshest catch. For an appetizer you might select either his fish soup at 40$ (61¢) or else fresh clams at 175$ ($2.68). Chef's suggestions offer a number of Portuguese dishes (changed daily) in the 125$ ($1.91) to 400$ ($6.12) range. Specialties include Cataplana (a special casserole with clams, pork, and tomato sauce done in the local style), 325$ ($4.97); prawn curry, Angola style, 325$ also; fish casserole à la Fragateira, 250$ ($3.82); and special steak with mushrooms, 425$ ($6.50). Lobster and fresh crayfish are also featured, and the price on this changes almost every day.

Restaurant Pipa, 1 Rua Gavotes, stands on the main town street leading down to the beach. Mr. Greenshields, its owner, offers a repertoire of both Portuguese and international cuisine. Most guests begin their meals with his boiled shrimp with chili sauce at 180$ ($2.75) or else a soup of the day at 45$ (69¢). Shrimp can also be ordered as a main course at 425$ ($6.50). He invariably features fresh grilled sardines at 200$ ($3.06) and chicken Hawaiian style, 325$ ($4.97). All dishes include a vegetable of the day, although the Pipa salad costs an additional 75$ ($1.15). In his cellar he keeps an unusual assortment of the "green wines" of Portugal. The atmosphere is pleasant, and the service is good.

From Armação de Pêra, it's a 6½-mile drive east to:

7. Albufeira

This cliffside fishing village is the St. Tropez of the Algarve. The lazy life, sunshine, beaches, and cheap food make it a haven for young people and artists, although the villagers haven't quite made up their minds as to what they think of the invasion that began in the late 1960s. Some of them, however, open the doors of their cottages to those seeking a little tuck-away cell for a few escudos a night. Those without the money often sleep in a tent on the cliff, or under the sky.

The village retains characteristics more readily associated with a North African seaside community. Its streets are steep, the villas drunkenly staggered up and down the hillside. Albufeira rises above a sickle-shaped beach that shines in the bright sunlight. A rocky grottoed bluff separates the strip used by the sunbathers from the working beach, where brightly painted fishing boats are drawn up on the sand. Access to the beach is through a tunneled rock passageway.

In accommodations, the resort is well supplied, although the tariffs in many of the establishments are more suited to the middle-class pocketbook than that of the young people who favor the place so much. Outside of the village at the **Praia Maria Luísa** sits a Dutch-owned hotel, one of the finest on the Algarve but for a luxury market only. We'll lead off with this recommendation, following with the lower-priced establishments in the village proper.

AN AVANT-GARDE LUXURY HOTEL: Hotel da Balaia, Praia Maria Luísa (tel. 52-681). When you walk into the domed entrance hall, you might think you're in Manhattan's Guggenheim Museum, or maybe one of the leading department stores of Paris. Tiers of roughly hewn balconies rise sky high, making the Hotel da Balaia the most exciting establishment, decoratively and architecturally, on the Algarve. The public rooms seem to flow one into another, with connecting passageways.

The architect, a Portuguese named Conceição Silva, designed the hotel like a $ sign, so as to give more rooms a view of the sea. His wife, Carmo Valente, did the interior decoration, using overscale contemporary paintings on stark white walls. The large-scale, colorful furnishings were selected by her.

Above the central core, corridors lead to 186 bedrooms and six deluxe suites. The bedrooms are fashion-plate examples of taste; every room is uncrowded, with fine furnishings coordinated with simple textured fabrics, and often utilizing silkscreen hangings of fishermen. In high season, the rate in a single room is $75 (U.S.), increasing to $92 for two persons, usually in a twin-bedded room (these tariffs include breakfast, service, and tax). Near the main building are 12 attractive bungalows, each having a three-bedroom suite, a complete home with a kitchenette and private terrace, renting for $155 daily for anywhere from two to six persons. Half board is an additional $23 per person daily.

The general manager, António Machaz, runs the hotel as if it were his own estate. To set the mood, he offers new arrivals welcoming cocktails. In addition, he has lined up a number of social and sporting activities arranged through the concierge, everything from waterskiing to clay pigeon shooting (also, an 18-hole golf course is nearby). Most guests, however, like to lounge by the heated swimming pool, enjoying a cold buffet luncheon.

The drawing rooms and salons are too numerous to itemize. The dining room, in brown and white, provides a stunning setting; whereas the grill relies on cardinal red linen and white carpeting, a background for dinner nightly (except Monday). Also on the premises is a disco, featuring occasional fado and folklore entertainers. A whiskey costs about $5.

The resort is four miles east of Albufeira, on about 40 acres of hilly land, encompassing a shoreline of rugged rock formations and a series of near-private coves for surf swimming.

A Range of Hotels

Hotel Sol e Mar (tel. 52-121), has captured the prime position within the village. The leading first-class hotel is Albufeira, it deceives you with its two-story entrance on the upper palisade. You suppose you're entering a ranch-style inn. Not so. When you walk across the spacious, sun-filled lounges to the picture windows and look down, it's a six-story drop. Hugging the cliff are bedrooms and a wide stone terrace with garden furniture and parasols. On still a lower level is a sandy beach.

There are 74 bedrooms, only six of which are singles. Most contain private balconies, and a knowing decorator's touch is manifested. For example, the streamlined twins have overscale black and white plaid covers. South American wooden headboards, locally painted seascapes, slimline armchairs, and plenty of wardrobe space. In high season, the room rate is 3200$ ($48.96) for a double, 2500$ ($38.25) for a single. Breakfast is included, and a table d'hôte luncheon or dinner is priced at 750$ ($11.48).

Guests, a continental crowd with a sprinkling of Americans, enjoy the sunsets from the main living room. Diners take their meals in a two-level room. On the opposite side is a drinking lounge, bright and lively, and a room for card players. There is also a television room decorated with prints of uniformed soldiers. After-dinner concerts are played on the electric organ till long past midnight.

During the day, guests take the elevator to the lower sun terrace, to find swimming, sunbathing, and the Esplanade Café, designed as a Portuguese tavern with Madeira stools, decorative tiles, hanging anchors, and waiters in checked plaid shirts in the Nazaré style.

Every night except Monday, guests dance at the O Pescador boîte to the latest records, paying a minimum of 250$ ($3.82).

Estalagem do Cêrro, Rua B (tel. 52-191), happily captures Algarvian charm, yet doesn't neglect all the contemporary amenities. It's appropriately named the Inn of the Craggy Hill, and is the inspiration of a young architect helped by the proprietor, an old navy commodore. An oldish, regional-style building was joined to a more modern structure and provided with central heating and an elevator, while maintaining its original character. They are connected by a two-story open solarium with trailing vines. Making for a lush setting are the little patios, filled with waist-high geraniums, fig trees reaching across balconies, towers, and paved walks through spice and rose gardens.

The bedrooms, all with private baths, are regionally inspired, each maintaining its own character. The decorations include reed and rattan chairs, built-in window seats, esparto mat headboards, fireplaces (in some rooms), hanging basket lamps, hand-woven draperies, tiled walls and niches. In high season, the bed-and-breakfast rate is $22 (U.S.) per person daily, rising to $30 for half board. In the low season, bed-and-breakfast terms drop to just $9.50 per person daily or $15.50 for half board.

The villa-size dining room, built on several levels, with arched windows, parquet floors, and provincial reed chairs, provides good meals, combining regional Portuguese dishes with an international cuisine. Before and after dinner, guests gather in a comfortable, modernized, air-conditioned bar or in a living room, with its armless leather chairs, wooden slat ceiling, and wall of decorative tiles. A fado show is presented weekly with folklore dances by a group which has won several international competitions. Guests of any age can join in these popular Algarvian dances.

Mar a Vista, Cêrro da Piedade (tel. 52-154). From the crow's nest vantage point of this estalagem, you can gaze out over the rooftops of the village below, the beach dotted with bright tents for bathers. The rooftop dining room of this first-class inn, decorated in a provincial style with blonde paneling, takes advantage of the view. Regional dishes are the fare, mixed with an international cuisine. Off the reception area, the petite salon blends hues of bronze, gold, and maroon, where guests may watch television if they wish. Still another place for guests to gather is the bar, whose muted tones of soft brown and amber panels, marble tables, and sofas create a pleasant ambience for drinks and conversation.

The rooms, 84 beds in all, mostly contain private balconies. The walls are hung with interesting prints; the furnishings, although not sumptuous, are typical and comfortable. On the half-board plan, single rates range between 1500$ ($22.95) and 2000$ ($30.60), the latter in high season; doubles range from 2400$ ($36.72) in low season to 2900$ ($44.37) in high, including taxes.

Hotel Boa-Vista, Rua B (tel. 52-175). Built in the Algarvian style, and set high above the sea outside the village center, the Residence of the Good View offers two different modes of living: one in its amenity-loaded main building, another in its block of furnished efficiencies across the street. The style, the welcome, the high level of taste are set by an Englishman, Alfred Worth, the hotel's owner who once managed the well-known Santa Isabel in Funchal, Madeira. A special feature is a temperature-controlled swimming pool with an encircling moat.

The decor of the reception area and lounges exudes an easy sophistication. The view of the bay from the dining room complements the fine meals served, and in either of the two bars, the waiter will quickly learn your favorite drink. The rooms open onto balconies, from which you can look down upon the whitewashed, orange-tile-roofed cottages to the bay below. The private baths are superb, in gray and white with marble. Leather banquettes and Carmen-red fabric add an attractive note. For half board, a single person is charged 1350$ ($20.66) off-season, 2250$ ($34.43) in season; two persons, 2400$ ($36.72) and 3000$ ($45.90), taxes included.

For a real bargain, consider the nearby apartments, ideal for the family trade. Each of the 15 suites contains a kitchen, dining room, lounge, and balcony. Each can accommodate up to four persons and is furnished with twin beds, double settee, sofa, armchairs, refrigerator, stove, and marble-topped sink. The apartments range in price from 750$ ($11.48) to 900$ ($13.77), the cheaper rate for one person, the higher tariff for occupancy by four.

Villa Recife, up the hill from Sol e Mar, on the street leading into and out of town (tel. 52-047), is an old villa converted into a hotel. Many of its 23 rooms look down on a garden with palm trees where guests sip drinks in the evenings sitting on white metal lawn furniture, shaded by cool arbors and purple bougainvillea. There's also a large adjoining garden, plus an old-fashioned sitting room as well. The high-ceilinged bedrooms are homey, some commanding a view of the town. Upstairs is a terrace for sunworshipers. A double with breakfast costs 1400$ ($21.42) off-season, rising to 1800$ ($27.54) in season. Five double rooms without bath go for only 1000$ ($15.30) to 1200$ ($18.36), depending on the season. Singles without bath rent for 700$ ($10.71) to 900$ ($13.77) with bath, from 900$ ($13.77) to 1250$ ($19.13). The house is open all year.

Montechoro (tel. 526-51) occupies an impressive setting atop a hill overlooking the fishing village below, with a complete view of the coastline. It's a fully equipped resort complex, a four-star hotel with ample facilities such as a pair of swimming pools, professional tennis courts, a sauna and gymnasium, as well as a panoramic view from the dining room and bar lounge. You might get lost here, as it contains 362 air-conditioned bedrooms and nearly 50 well-furnished suites. Singles cost 2500$ ($38.25) daily; twins, 3000$ ($45.90); and triples, 3500$ ($53.55). A suite for two persons is rented at 4000$ ($61.20). Each meal is an additional 750$ ($11.84), with an American breakfast carrying a supplement of 200$ ($3.06). The decorative theme throughout the rooms is tasteful, with bright colors contrasting against stark white. All units have room-wide picture windows, and the baths are tiled. In addition to main meals in the restaurant, specialties are served in the à la carte grill room. Guests are faced with a choice of four bars and a disco. Lots of regional merchandise is also sold at shops within the precincts.

Hotel da Aldeia (tel. 520-31) is a complete holiday complex, where you have the advantage of an apartment or villa. It's in the holiday village of Areias de São João, near Golden Beach, about a mile from Albufeira. You'll find adequate recreation facilities offered—a tennis court, mini-golf, and two adjoining swimming pools with spacious sun terraces. Across the road is a restaurant if you don't want to cook a meal in your own kitchen. The apartments have one and two bedrooms, accommodating a maximum of six guests, and the villas have two to four bedrooms, housing as many as ten guests, although that might be extremely crowded. All units have fully equipped kitchens; maid service includes dish washing, cleaning, and making of beds, as in a hotel. Suites and apartments are handsomely decorated, using strong colors and natural wood furniture with rattan and bamboo. Built-in headboards hold telephones and provide background music and light switches. You have a choice of sea or mountain view, and you can even have half- or full-board rates if desired. A double room peaks at 1700$ ($26.01) daily, a suite costing 2000$ ($30.60). Each extra bed carries a 500$ ($7.65) supplement. Lunch or dinner is 450$ ($6.89), or you can ask for full board, 850$ ($13.01) in addition to your room costs. A continental breakfast is included in the room tariffs, and off-season discounts are granted.

Aparthotel Auramar, Praia dos Avelros (tel. 533-07), at the edge of Albufeira sits on a low cliff overlooking a sandy beach, like a friendly fortress facing the ocean. Close to the sea cliff is an outstanding recreation area, with the finest swimming pool in the area. There's an informal snackbar, although the main building has a restaurant providing Portuguese and an international cuisine. Essentially an apartment house, the Auramar offers meals as well as a bar lounge. The 282 fine apartments have living-room furnishings in addition to a kitchenette and a terrace for sunbathing. Single occupancy costs 1800$ ($27.54) in April, May, and October, daily. In high season, only double rates are in effect, these going for 3450$ ($52.79) daily, with an extra bed for 1250$ ($19.13). A continental breakfast is included in the daily rates.

Hotel Baltum, Avenida 25 de Abril (tel. 521-06), is a one-minute walk from the main beach strip. The hotel and its nearby annex offer modern accommodations. In the main building, the Baltum offers 26 rooms, each with central heating, private bath, telephone, and balcony (except for three rooms). Cozy sitting areas—furnished with armless leather chairs, blonde coffee tables, and overstuffed couches—are available to those willing to spend a few more escudos.

The tariff ranges from 700$ ($10.71) in a single in high season to 1350$ ($20.66) in a double, with breakfast included. The solarium-terrace with its little bar has music for dancing nightly.

The annex, called the **Anexo Baltum,** Rua Cándido dos Reis (tel. 523-06), is in the center of the village, near the Cine Pax. The lobby is dominated by a circular staircase (the walls of which are carousel-lined from floor to ceiling with decorative tiles). The rooms here are similar to those at the Hotel Baltum, being even newer, and equipped with showers instead of tubs. You'll have to do your soaking in the Atlantic. Some of the streamlined bedrooms have balconies, although others open onto an uninspired view of the central air shaft. The rates are slightly lower here than at the main hotel. A single with breakfast costs from 650$ ($9.95) daily in high season. Doubles rent from 1250$ ($19.13), depending on the view and whether or not a sitting room is included.

Apartamentos Albufeira Jardim, Cêrro da Piedade (tel. 520-85), is becoming increasingly popular with visitors who like to anchor into one place for a while before resuming their touring. Standing on a hill overlooking the resort, it has attractively furnished studio apartments for rent which are ideal for families. Units include a fully equipped kitchen. The good news is that you don't have to do your cleaning, as the management provides daily maid service. Winter rates are only $25 (U.S.) a day, going up to perhaps $35 or more in summer. Balconies from the apartments open onto the ocean and a view of Albufeira. As a further enticement, there's a heated swimming pool.

READER'S LODGINGS SELECTION: "**Residêncial Atlantica,** 13 Rua Padre Semedo de Azevedo (tel. 521-20), nestles onto the slope of the hill. It is a new building, and all bedrooms have baths. I had a lovely room with a balcony looking out over the city, getting the morning sun. The house has very simple but adequate furniture and friendly people. In peak season, a double bedroom with bath, plus breakfast, rents for 900$ ($13.77). The owner, who worked in Labrador for a number of years, speaks English" (Adele Stockhausen, Toronto, Ontario, Canada).

WHERE TO DINE: **Restaurante Alfredo,** 9-11 Rua 5 de Outubro (tel. 520-59), serves what are really banquets, in an attractive atmosphere. Just a minute's stroll from the market square, it is housed in an old building that looks as if it's always been an inn. It's full of atmosphere: crude wooden tables and chairs just made for leisurely drinking.

The restaurant's on the second floor, a heavily beamed room furnished with antiques, such as a grandfather clock, a gilt mirror, faded oil paintings, and silver candelabra. There's an open fireplace with a pair of cherub torchères, plus a kitchen open to the full view of diners who watch their meals being grilled in a ten-foot-wide fireplace, or simmered in copper pots and pans.

ALBUFEIRA

To begin your meal, a shell dish of black olives, country pâté, and crusty bread is set before you. On the menu you'll find cod, 280$ ($4.28); fish filets, also 280$; a mixed grill, 300$ ($4.59); tournedos, 590$ ($9.03); roast chicken, 300$ ($4.59); a mixed salad, 85$ ($1.30); and melon, also 85$. Alfredo's is open daily from noon for lunch, from 7 to 10 p.m. for dinner. It's closed on Wednesday.

O Cabaz da Praia (The Beach Basket), 7 Praça Miguel Bombarda (tel. 521-37), near the Hotel Sol e Mar, sits on a colorful little square, opposite a little chapel that is now used as a museum. It is owned by an Englishman, David H. Shean, who emigrated from Surrey to this eternally sunny spot. He has transformed a fisherman's cottage into a friendly place at which to order homemade meals. So inviting is the ambience that it has lured guests from nearby hotels who have already paid for their meals en pension.

Mr. Shean has given the place a marine look and set up tables on the sheltered terrace overlooking the main beach, which is unique in the area, giving one a sea view while dining. The specialty is an international cuisine with an emphasis on French cooking. A favorite local dish is freshly caught Algarve sole served meunière with fresh vegetables, of which there is an abundance in the area. Two popular dishes are the soufflé omelet, 220$ ($3.37), with tomatoes, onions, pimientos, and cheese, and lemon meringue pie, 90$ ($1.38). Each day there is a special dish, such as boeuf bourguignonne, 350$ ($5.36), or perhaps chicken jambalaya, 310$ ($4.74).

O Cabaz da Praia is firmly established and one of the most popular restaurants in the Algarve.

La Cigale, Olhos de Agua (tel. 52-607), stands right on the beach, with a terrace that makes this a romantic choice at night. Here is your cliché of the sunny southern coast of Europe. Fortunately, the food matches the atmosphere, enough so that the place draws a lot of diners who have villas on the Algarve—hence, reservations are important. The wine list is fairly distinguished, in keeping with the impressive food. The management seems to operate everything with amiable efficiency. Expect to spend from 750$ ($11.48)—a rock-bottom quotation—and perhaps a lot more for your meal here.

Franguinho, at Branqueira, about 1½ miles to the east of Albufeira, on the highway between Faro and Vilamoura, is the place to go to sample the celebrated Algarvian charcoal-grilled chicken. The restaurant is open every evening except Thursday. And if you grew up in the Depression South believing in "chicken every Sunday," you can also come here and order a lunch between 1 and 3 p.m. on that day. There is also take-away service. The most unimaginative palate will order it plain (actually it's quite good that way), but the most adventurous fowl-fancier will ask for it with piri-piri, a hot sauce best for an asbestos-lined mouth. I tend to prefer the tandoori chicken, and the barbecue's not bad (but likely to be different from the sauce you're used to "down home"). The atmosphere is plain and simple, but also clean. Along with your chicken, you're served an array of fresh salads and crisp french-fried potatoes, a fit accompaniment. Your bill is likely to be under 500$ ($7.65), and you get good value for your escudo here.

Sleeping Donkey, Olhos de Agua, stands on the same beach as the previously recommended La Cigale, but it's quite a different establishment. The location is east of Albufeira, out past the Hotel da Balaia, already recommended. Sleeping Donkey translates into Portuguese as *De Slapende Ezel,* but everybody seems bilingual around here. Frans and Chris welcome you in whatever language at this friendly Anglo-Dutch restaurant, where you're served a host of regional specialties, along with fresh seafood and tender steaks prepared as you like them. The setting has been likened to that of a bistro, a comparison a little far-fetched. It has its own style and charm. The food is good, the prices reasonable, with meals beginning at 750$ ($11.48) per head. Never show up on Friday. The staff takes a well-deserved day of rest then.

Café Doris, Aldela Turistica (tel. 524-55), is a rotisserie-crêperie, German operated, which does some well-prepared specialties, especially in crêpes, home-baked cakes, and ice creams. Ice cream comes in many flavors, including one delectable cup with fresh strawberries, 100$ ($1.53). To begin your meal, a rich-tasting soup is always offered. I always gravitate to the goulash meat soup at 100$ ($1.53). The crêpe Bombay at 325$ ($4.97) is a savory concoction, accompanied by a mixed salad with cream sauce and herbs, 110$ ($1.68). Doris also makes a side order of baked tomatoes topped with cheese, also 110$. In addition, she has an unusual selection of hot drinks, including coffee Algarve (with Medronho), 100$ ($1.53). You can visit any time between 11:30 a.m. and 11 p.m. Doris runs this pleasant little place with her husband, Horst Hewer.

Fernando, on the main square (tel. 521-16), with a large terrace temptingly displays low-priced tourist menus. Soup is 55$ (84¢); sole 320$ ($4.90); fish filets, 250$ ($3.82); and steak 375$ ($5.74). Desserts range in price from 55$ (84¢) to 100$ ($1.53). There's a pleasant indoor dining room as well.

Oasis, Rua Largo Eng. Duarte Pacheco, right on the town's main square and opposite the market, is a favorite budgeteer's haunt, owing to its pleasant location, outside terrace, and low prices. Although this is the south, you can order north Portugal's classic caldo verde at 45$ (69¢), followed by fried squid for 240$ ($3.67). The best dish prepared here is perhaps porco Alentejana, 230$ ($3.52), followed by a cream caramel at 40$ (61¢). You can sit outdoors under shady trees, or indoors at candlelit tables.

A Ruina, Cais Herculano (tel. 520-94), sits right opposite the fish market. From the arcaded dining room, with its long wooden, candlelit tables, you can peer out at the fishermen mending their nets. Another cave-like room has more tables and a bar. The decor is simple and unpretentious, but the seafood is fresh. Specialties include grilled tuna for 300$ ($4.59). A tomato soup goes for 45$ (69¢); cutlets for 300$ ($4.59). The house specialty is a caldeirada at 325$ ($4.97). Custard is 75$ ($1.15); mousse, 50$ (77¢). The prices are posted behind the counter near the entrance.

Snack Bar O Isca, 10–12 Rua Cándido dos Reis (tel. 520-75), despite its name, is a pleasant little restaurant with a varied menu and no frills. Spaghetti bolognaise costs 200$ ($3.06); pork with clams, 265$ ($4.06); and a prawn omelet, 240$ ($3.67). There are high-back wooden chairs set at tables and a bar on one side.

READERS' RESTAURANT SELECTIONS: "Just beside the supermarket, upstairs in a new building, we found a 'restaurant Français,' called **l'Ecu de France,** on Rua Cêrro Grande (tel. 526-08). The owners, Monsieur et Madame Hamon, originally from Paris, do all the work: he cooks and she serves. The food is excellent and an appreciated change. My husband had the menu of the day for 300$ ($4.59), consisting of soup, main course of half a chicken and french fries, delicious French apple pie for dessert. We paid more the second time around but had a good steak (very tender) in wine sauce, two half bottles of wine, two beers, onion soup, salad, bread, and coffee, for about 450$ ($6.90) per person" (Mrs. Nicole Jodoin, Gatineau, Quebec, Canada).... "We dined at **O Alexandre,** 17 Rua Alves Correia (tel. 521-31), twice during our week-long stay. The establishment is very clean, with new-looking, unfinished furniture in the dining areas. The restaurant describes itself as serving *cozinha típica portuguêsa,* and we had excellent frango em tomate for only 150$ ($2.30) per entree. Prices for grilled chicken are about 170$ ($2.60), and Portuguese pork costs about 200$ ($3.06). Waiters are friendly and courteous. If I were ever in Albufeira again, I would certainly return to this restaurant" (Kathleen M. James, Phoenix, Md.).... "An interesting new restaurant is **The Beefeater Carvery,** 87 Rua 5 de Outubro (tel. 543-34). The owner, Jim Ashwell, a charming, ruddy-faced Englishman, is a true host in the best sense, greeting each customer, visiting each table to see that all is well, and personally carving the three specialties: roast beef, roast pork, and turkey breast. All come with an array of side dishes, such as fresh vegetables, potatoes, Yorkshire pudding, apple sauce, and salad. The food is well prepared and the portions generous" (Nathan J. Strauss, New York, N.Y.).

THE LOCAL PUB: Sir Harry's Bar, on the market square, is in the center of the village. Sir Harry (Warner) can be distinguished by his beaming smile and RAF-type moustache. His fashionable bar is a gravity point for any bloke who has abandoned his Cotswold tweeds for the lighter threads of the Algarve. Converts swear that Sir Harry's is their Algarvian "local," and after 15 years it has earned the reputation of being the Algarve's most popular international rendezvous. The bar merges the ambience of a black and white timbered village pub with the coziness of a Portuguese fisherman's cottage.

Beneath the low natural beams, a comfortable array of Savonarola chairs, crude tables, and wooden settles are found on two levels, divided by wrought-iron railings. The collection of rifles, steins, gleaming copper pots and pans, and earthenware water jugs provides the genuine ye olde touch. A bar of herringbone brick and timbers has heel-propping stools, attracting those drawn to the center of the action. Most drinks, such as a rum Coke, go for 90$ ($1.38), and beer for 30$ (46¢). Hearty sandwiches are served as well. It's open daily all year.

READER'S BAR SELECTIONS: "A bar with unusual decor and free-form walls is **Friday's Bar,** where a large beer is 65$ (99¢). In addition, **Cava Vinho do Porto** on Travessa da Liberdade serves a variety of port wine drinks as well as beer and cocktails. The exterior is uninteresting, but the interior is very pleasant, containing a number of brick arched rooms and walls of stored wine bottles" (Clair Kinney, San Jose, Calif.).

8. Praia de Quarteira

With its miles of sand dunes, Quarteira may one day be billed as the Atlantic City of the Algarve, but that isn't likely to happen soon.

Between Albufeira and Faro, this once-sleepy fishing village used to be known only to a handful of artists who provided amusement for the local fishermen and their varinas. Now with the invasion of outsiders, the traditional way of life is upset.

Golfers who don't want to pay the high tariffs at Vale do Lobo or Vilamoura (both of which have 18-hole golf courses) can stay inexpensively in Quarteira at one of the accommodations listed below. The above-mentioned courses are only a ten-minute drive away, and Quarteira lies about seven miles from the Faro Airport.

Hotel Beira Mar, Avenida Infante de Sagres (tel. 651-32). One of the tallest buildings to grow up in Quarteira is a second-class, 51-bedroom hotel. It is functional, efficient, and has a fine location. With a single bound from the front entrance, a long-legged sprinter will land right on the sandy beach. All bedrooms contain immaculately kept private baths and sun porches, from which guests can see the Phoenician-inspired prows of the fishing boats 150 yards down the beach.

The rooms have up-to-date furnishings, many utilizing decorative blue and white tile configurations. For a room plus breakfast, the single tariff is 1800$ ($27.54); the two-person tab, 2500$ ($38.25). In off-season, a single with bath is 1500$ ($22.95); a double with bath 2000$ ($30.60). The lounges and reception make use of walnut-colored slat facings and ceilings. The brown tile floors, especially at the entrance, are highlighted by the whiteness of the walls and stark plaster pillars. Before-dinner drinks and evening get-togethers may be enjoyed in the hotel bar, walled with tiles of a golden-grain.

Hotel Quarteirasol (tel. 654-21) is a big land development of apartments and villas, as well as a core-block hotel with 90 twin rooms and 150 junior suites, plus 18 apartments, some of which are furnished in a jazzy style. Each contains full air conditioning and private tiled baths. For bed and breakfast, singles pay 1500$ ($22.95) daily, the rate rising to 2200$ ($33.66) in a double or twin. Half board is an extra 500$ ($7.65) per person daily, all taxes included. The hotel block is set back from the beach, and is built in a somewhat bizarre design, with arches, coved ceilings, and a grotto-like disco. At the center of the hotel is an open courtyard, with bedroom balconies overlooking a central fountain with splashing water and a lily pond.

The Quarteirasol Apartments (tel. 654-21) are like a village, some of which evoke North African design. Buildings are placed around a community swimming pool, and there's a three-tiered red-tiled Chinese restaurant, the Lotus House, plus a disco and other shops and facilities. The apartments have dramatic dining-room areas, with Persian rugs and high-back chairs. Bedrooms have ornate Portuguese spindle-style beds, and units contain complete kitchens, as well as balconies. Studios range in price from 1800$ ($27.54) for two to 4000$ ($61.20) for six persons. Villas cost 4500$ ($68.85) for two persons daily, going up to 6000$ ($91.80) for six persons. Breakfast and dinner are an additional 550$ ($8.42) per person daily.

Hotel Dom José, Avenida Infante de Sagres (tel. 343-10), provides 134 rooms, mostly seafront, with a wide sandy beach as its front yard. Each room is provided with a private bath, central heating, telephone, radio, and piped-in music. Half of the lodgings have oversize glass doors opening onto private balconies. Half-board rates range from $25 (U.S.) in a single, from $48 in a twin, taxes included. Lunch or dinner is $9. The Portuguese bill of fare, incidentally, is excellent, with an emphasis on sea fruits. Adding to the hotel's resort aura are a heated swimming pool, two solariums, an open-air, sea-view dining room, two bars, souvenir shops, and a disco. A windsurf course is available.

READERS' RESTAURANT SELECTION: "We feel special mention should be made of the restaurant, **O Pescador,** in Largo Cortés Real. We will remember this restaurant for the best asparagus we have ever had. A veritable feast is available for 450$ ($6.89), and the owner, Martin, is eager to please. The restaurant is usually crowded, and service is slow by American standards, but all dishes arrive freshly made and piping hot. Fresh seafood is, of course, the specialty. O Pescador is beside the fish market, west of the straw market" (Mr. and Mrs. Raymond Hyde, Alexandria, Va.).

A HOLIDAY VILLAGE: Between Albufeira and Quarteira, in a delightful pinewood, the **Aldeia das Açoteias,** Pinhal do Concelho (tel. 662-67), is the most recently developed holiday village, designed in the typical Moorish style of the Algarve. For rent are fully equipped and furnished small studio apartments, bungalows, and large family villas. The resort is operated under the aegis of the **Touring Club of Portugal,** which accepts bookings at its main office in Lisbon at 258 Avenida Almirante Reis (tel. 71-91-81). The village offers a supermarket, restaurant, nightclub, two swimming pools, and a conference room. Golf and riding facilities are nearby. Apartments in low season cost 900$ ($13.77) for one person, 1000$ ($15.30) for two, 1200$ ($18.36) for three, 1400$ ($21.42) for four. Villas range from 1800$ ($27.54) for five persons to 3000$ ($45.90) for ten. In high season, the price for apartments is 1200$ ($18.36) for one, 1500$ ($22.95) for two, 1750$ ($26.78) for three, and 2000$ ($30.60) for four. Five persons in a villa will pay 3000$ ($45.90). The cost ranges upward to 4500$ ($68.85) in a villa for ten persons. The breakfast price is 110$ ($1.68) in the restaurant. Lunch or dinner costs 500$ ($7.65). Included in the tariffs are beach facilities, a daily cleaning service, and babysitting.

Adjoining the fringes of Praia de Quarteira is:

WHERE TO DINE: O Barão (tel. 627-19) stands in the pines, about two miles from Quarteira on Estrada de Loulé. Margaret Ding presents an international cuisine, specializing in Russian and Oriental dishes. The menu changes nightly, so what is presented below should only suggest the type of cuisine offered. Usually there's a rich good-tasting soup for 80$ ($1.22), or else you might begin your meal with smoked swordfish which looks like smoked salmon but, to me at least, tastes even better, 350$ ($5.36). Her Chinese sweet-and-sour chicken at 390$ ($5.97) is excellent, as is the leg of lamb Madrileño (roasted Madrid-style with sherry and garlic), 350$ ($5.36). Hopefully, you'll be there the night she offers Korean beef (filets of sirloin marinated in soya, sesame, and pepper, then charcoal grilled), 460$ ($7.04). Try, if possible, the Tifteli at 320$ ($4.90). This is beef filet, finely minced, with herbs and red wine, briefly deep fried, and served with a tomato-flavored Russian sauce and sour cream. An almond tart at 80$ ($1.22) should round it off nicely. The restaurant opens nightly except Monday at 8 p.m., and it's closed from New Year's to Easter.

9. Vilamoura

Although the remains of a Roman villa were discovered when builders were working on a marina, the history of this settlement is yet to be written. At a central point on the Algarve coast, only 11 miles from Faro Airport, Vilamoura is an expansive land-development project. Plans call for a city larger than Faro, a protected harbor sheltering 1000 boats, and an interior lake linked with the bay and ocean by two canals. One can sum up the Vilamoura situation by comparing it to the weather of New England: "If you don't like it now, wait a minute!"

The **Vilamoura Casino** is the second of the Casinos do Algarve. It is close to the Vilamoura Golf Club. The casino features a gambling salon with roulette, blackjack, French banque, and baccarat. A separate salon is devoted to slot machines. Featured also is a 250-seat supper club, with two floor shows nightly.

Admission to the slot machines is free, but a small entrance fee to the main gambling room is charged, beginning at 100$ ($1.53) for two nights. The casino is open from 5 p.m. to 3 a.m. every day of the year. Tourists must present their passports.

More than 100 hotels are projected but at the moment you'll have to make do with a more limited selection in:

THE UPPER BRACKET: Hotel Dom Pedro (tel. 354-50) is a large hotel of first-class comfort, right in the tourist complex of Vilamoura. The 261-room center stands next to the beach, although there is a choice of three swimming pools as well, including one for children. The four-star Dom Pedro also has its own 18-hole professional golf course adjacent to the hotel. The public rooms are sleekly styled, often in a futuristic modern, and the private rooms are pleasantly furnished and carpeted, with private terraces. In April, May, June, and October, doubles rent for $37 (U.S.), singles for $25. Summer tariffs rise to $50 in a double, $37 in a single. Three tennis courts are available, and after a game guests can enjoy a bar overlooking the pool. Other facilities include a sauna, massage, and hairdresser. The staff at the hotel arranges for guests to go deep-sea fishing or else riding from its fine stable of horses. The Dom Pedro is part of the Saviotti chain which also owns hotels in Machico in Madeira, Povoa de Varzim, in the north of Portugal, Guamares, and Braga.

THE MEDIUM-PRICED RANGE: Vilamoura Hotel (tel. Quarteira 323-21) is for golf enthusiasts who like to sleep, swim, and dine close to the links.

The hotel features a cluster of cubistic rooms, built around a swimming pool and terrace. These rooms contain their own tiny patios, and all of them are equipped with tiled baths. For two persons at the golf club, the high-season cost of lodgings ranges from 2200$ ($33.66) to 2500$ ($38.25), the latter rate for a twin-bedded room classified as a superior suite. The single rate is 1750$ ($26.76) daily, all tariffs including breakfast, service, and tax. In one of the terrace houses, two persons pay 2000$ ($30.60) in a studio complete with kitchenette, telephones, and maid service. Four persons are housed for 2700$ ($41.31); six persons, for 350$ ($53.55). Full board is an additional 1200$ ($18.36) per person daily.

Motorists passing through for the day can stop off and enjoy an excellent meal at the golf club restaurant, where à la carte luncheons or dinners are served.

Estalagem da Cegonha, Centro Hípico de Vilamoura (tel. 661-80), stands at Poço de Boliqueime, Vilamoura, about 2½ miles from the golf course, casino, marina, and beach, on the national road between Portimão and Faro. The inn lies in a setting that is peaceful and quiet, adjoining the riding stables (which charge very reasonable rates, incidentally). There are only ten rooms, but they are large and cozily decorated, each containing a private bath. For a double room with breakfast, the charge is 1200$ ($18.63) per person, the cost rising to 2200$ ($33.66) for half board. The decoration is in a *típico* style. The chef at the inn has won an award for regional food. Before or after dinner, you can enjoy drinks in one of the comfortable bars. A horse-jumping contest is held every year in September.

AN AFTER DARK COMPLEX: Viking Vilamoura (tel. 652-51) is a complex that contains a luxury restaurant, a beer tavern, and a *belle époque* nightclub. Albio Pinto, who owns the Pink Panther disco in Vale do Lobo, created it, and Tony Couto runs it. When he's not managing the complex, Madeira-born Mr. Couto plays a very good piano to entertain guests. The restaurant is attractively stylized, and the service is among the best in the Algarve. You can peruse the menu in a pleasant bar, deciding between the shrimp cocktail or the shrimp-stuffed crêpes as an appetizer, perhaps selecting lobster thermidor as a main course. The seafood dishes are fresh and well prepared, and a number of good meat dishes are offered as well. A specialty is the steak Viking (prepared with cream), topped with sliced mushrooms and chopped ham. A window in the dining room reveals what is happening in the kitchen. Depending on what you order, your meal is likely to cost 1400$ ($21.42).

Downstairs is the beer tavern which is open until the early hours of the morning. Even if you've been somewhere else that night, you can drop in here past midnight and order not only beer but a snack. Seating is at trestle tables, and the waitresses wear Germanic dress.

The nightclub is like an Edwardian music hall. Go here at 12:30 a.m. or 2:15 a.m. for a 45-minute stage show which might include anything from ballet to striptease. A minimum consumption of 500$ ($7.65) is levied. The entire complex shuts down on Sunday.

10. Vale do Lobo

The name Valley of the Wolf suggests some forlorn spot, set amid bleak terrain. Hardly likely! The Vale, west of Faro, about a 20-minute drive from the airport, is the site of a golf course designed by Henry Cotton, the British champion. Some of the holes are played by the sea, resulting in many an anxious moment when a shot may hook out over the water a precarious distance from the green. To play costs 400$ ($6.12) a day for visitors, 250$ ($3.82) a day for hotel guests. Recently another nine-hole course and a nine-hole par-three course, a putting green, and driving range have been installed.

Reached through fig orchards, cork forests, and a valley of tufted pines, the seaside strongly evokes Carmel, California. Pale golden cliffs jut out over sandy beaches that stretch brilliantly in the distance until they evaporate into a faint haze.

A DELUXE GOLF HOTEL: Hotel Dona Filipa, Vale do Lobo, Almansil (tel. 941-41). With such touches as gold-painted palms holding up the ceiling, the Dona Filipa is a citadel of ostentatious living. The grounds are impressive, embracing 450 acres of rugged coastline with steep cliffs, inlets, and sandy bays.

The exterior of the hotel is comparatively uninspired, but a greater dimension was brought to the interior by Duarte Pinto Coelho. Green silk banquettes, marble fireplaces, paisley-covered pillars, Portuguese ceramic lamps, old prints over baroque-style love seats—the flair is lush. Aside from a Chinese room for card playing, the most popular meeting point is the Gothic Bar, with its cathedral-like stools, wooden decorations, and matching floor and upholstery fabric in azulejos patterns.

There are 130 air-conditioned rooms—all with bath, most with balcony. In summer, a single rents for $90 (U.S.), rising to $135 in a double. In winter these tariffs are reduced to $42 in a single, $60 in a double. A meal in the restaurant averages around $23. All prices include service and taxes. Greens fees at the Vale do Lobo championship 27-hole golf course are reduced for hotel guests.

Dining is formal and gracious, with a knowledgeable maître d'hôtel and wine steward guiding you on your selections. At the beach is a disco, where international records are played for dancing (occasionally, folk artists and fadistas perform).

A RESORT CENTER: Quinta do Lago, near Almansil, ten miles west of Faro, is a sprawling 1600-acre estate, which is selling private plots within it. Already open are: a riding center, one of the best in southern Europe; a 27-hole golf course, designed by American course architect William F. Mitchell, and recognized among the top six in Europe; two tennis courts; **Pony's,** the Algarve's sophisticated disco; the luxurious **Casa Velha Apartamentos** (tel. 943-58), overlooking the seawater lake and provided with every modern comfort; and the superb **Casa Velha** restaurant (tel. 942-72), renowned for its fine food and impeccable service. Its dining room is built in a simple rustic style. You sit along divans with cushions. Adjoining is a swimming pool for those who want to take a dip into the water before plunging into the meal. It has recently been enlarged with a grill room and a pergola at the pool edge. Recommended are chateaubriand for two persons, 1000$ ($15.30); a rack or saddle of lamb persillé, also for two persons, also 1000$; délices of sole Casa Velha, 750$ ($11.48); sea bass Quinta do Lago, 600 ($9.18); steak, Portuguese style, also

600$; fishermen's soup, 200$ ($3.06); and smoked swordfish with horseradish sauce, 400$ ($6.12). The dessert specialty is crêpes Casa Velha, 290$ ($4.44).

11. Faro

Flowers brought in from the countryside are plentiful. In the blue lagoon sailing enthusiasts glide by. A *típico* old quarter flanks the ruined ramparts that proved all too vulnerable in the past. At the yacht harbor starlings and sparrows flutter nervously, while children run noisily to the pastry shops to buy stuffed figs and almond cakes. Beyond the waterfront lie the tree-studded avenues and cobbled alleyways of the city.

Once loved by the Roman and later by the Moor, Faro is the capital of the Algarve. Sit at a café sampling the wine and you'll watch yesterday and today pass by. An old man walks ahead, pulling a donkey on which a parasol-shaded girl in a white dress is sitting. Brushing past is a German student in short pants, his white skin turned golden by the sun.

Faro is a hodgepodge of life and activity: it's been rumbled, sacked, and "quaked" by everybody from Mother Nature to the Earl of Essex (Elizabeth's old favorite).

Since Afonso III drove out the Moors for the last time in 1266, Faro has been Portuguese. On its outskirts an international jet airport brings in thousands of visitors every summer. The airport has done more than anything else to speed tourism not only to Faro but to the Algarve in general, as jet planes make it possible to reach Faro from Lisbon in 30 minutes.

The most bizarre attraction is the **Capela d'Ossos** (Chapel of Bones), entered from the rear of the **Igreja de Nossa Senhora do Monte do Carmo do Faro,** via a courtyard. Erected in the 19th century, this chapel is completely lined with the skulls and bones of human skeletons, an extraordinary ossicular rococo. In all, it's estimated there are 1245 human skulls.

The church, built in 1713, contains a gilded baroque altar. Likewise, its facade is baroque, with a bell tower rising from each side. Topping the belfries are gilded mosque-like cupolas, connected by a balustraded railing. The windows of the upper levels are latticed and framed with gold, with statues standing in each of the niches on either side of the main portal.

Other religious monuments include the old **Sé** (cathedral), built in the Gothic and Renaissance styles (originally a Moslem mosque stood on this site); the **Church of St. Francis,** with panels of glazed earthenware tiles in milk white and Delft blue, depicting the life of the patron saint; and the **Convent of Our Lady of the Assumption,** declared a national monument and noted for its Renaissance portal and cloister.

But most visitors don't come to Faro to look at churches, regardless of how interesting. Rather, they take the harbor ferry to the wide, white sandy beaches called the **Praia de Faro,** on an islet. The ride (available only in summer) costs 30$ (46¢) for a round-trip passage. The beach is also connected to the mainland by bridge, a distance of about 3½ miles from the town center. Once there, you can waterski and fish or just lounge in the sun, renting a deckchair and umbrella.

The accommodations, however, tend to be disappointing, except for the following recommendations:

Eva, Avenida da República (tel. 240-54), dominates the harbor like a fortress. This eight-floor modern hotel occupies an entire side of the yacht-clogged harbor, providing direct sea views from most of the bedrooms. It's recommended mainly for overnighting. Bedrooms are air-conditioned and are furnished in a very restrained style, containing private tiled baths. The twin-bedded rooms rent for around $60 (U.S.) daily. The Eva's best feature is a penthouse restaurant and rooftop swimming pool, supported on 16 posts, with sun terraces and a bar. Dancing is offered at the hotel's disco, Scheherazade, five nights a week, with a folklore show on Thursday. Other facilities include a snackbar, three cocktail bars, hairdresser, and a boutique.

The **Hotel Faro,** Praça D. Francisco Gomes (tel. 220-76), is a first-class B hotel with 52 rooms (eight with shower) opening right onto the bustling harbor, a prime position. The lobby—a cool, tasteful, and contemporary design, with splashes of greenery—sets the tone: that is, all the conveniences with very little fanfare. The furnishings in the rooms are comfortable but uninspired, and many contain balconies opening right onto the square and its bird concerts.

For full pension, you pay anywhere between 1950$ ($29.84) and 2580$ ($39.47) for one person, between 2825$ ($43.22) and 4310$ ($65.94) for two persons. Taxes are included. The least expensive rooms contain shower baths. The suites have a small sitting room with a bed sofa, suitable for a third person. In a light and spacious room, the restaurant serves French and Portuguese dishes complemented by a well-coordinated wine list. The bar provides drinks, which you can order from the mezzanine while surveying the scene below.

Casa de Lumena, 27 Praça Alexandre Herculano (tel. 220-28), was once the town house of a reigning sardine family of Faro, but now it's an English-run pensão with telephones in the rooms, central heating, and a cozy bar where the British community often meets at lunchtime. It sits on a square shaded by jacaranda trees.

Built at the edge of the sidewalk with wrought-iron gratings at its windows, the Lumena offers eight double rooms, three singles, and a suite, each with private bath. A double room for two persons with breakfast is about 1500$ ($22.95). The restaurant is open in the evening.

The accommodations are shaped differently and furnished in part with pieces inherited with the casa. Throughout are antiques, carved chests, satinwood tables, painted dressers, and armoires. In summer, drinks and light snacks are also served in the courtyard at the rear, which is shaded by grapevines.

WHERE TO DINE: Al Faghar, 30 Rua Tenente Valadim (tel. 237-40), serves the best food in Faro. Installed in a classic 18th-century town house, the restaurant is on the first floor and reached by following a rather dark corridor which leads to a staircase. The dining room has high white walls with hanging lanterns and old prints scattered around. An oil lamp is placed on each table. There are overhanging balconies with flags hanging out from them. The gardens of the old Bishop's Palace have been opened. Classic Portuguese dishes are served, along with appropriate wines from the regions of Portugal. A complete dinner costs about 600$ ($9.18). The restaurant is open from 12:30 to 3 p.m. and from 7:30 to 11 p.m. It's closed on Sunday.

FARO AFTER DARK: The **Kon Tiki Nightclub,** Rua da Marinha, under the Hotel Faro, right off the harbor square, is considered the most elegant place in town. The table candles cast a dim, almost lurid, rose glow, reflecting off the white Moorish arches. The ceiling is low and dark, and the crude rattan and bamboo tables and low chairs are in the Polynesian style. Many are huddled in corners and secluded nooks, providing ideal spots for intimate conversations during breaks in disco dancing. There is no minimum, and drinks run around

150$ ($2.30) to 250$ ($3.82) for whiskey. Just off the harbor square, the Kon Tiki floats from 10 p.m. until 4 a.m.

Paddy's Bar, 1 Rua Oliveira Salazar, is snugly hidden in a lane. It is perhaps the friendliest bar in Faro, where meeting people is easy in a relaxed atmosphere, especially for those who like an occasional (or frequent) pint. The pub rooms are warmed by an open fire in winter, the knotty-pine walls and rough oaken beams hung with 19th-century prints and a collection of brass stirrups from the British Isles. Settled in any one of a multitude of handsome leather chairs, you can enjoy a whiskey for 150$ ($2.30), a bottle of beer or a brandy for 100$ ($1.53). Paddy's is open seven days a week.

A SIDE TRIP TO LOULÉ: Loulé, 9½ miles north of Faro, is a market town in the heart of the chimney district of the Algarve. If you ever thought that chimneys couldn't excite you, you haven't seen the ones here. From many of the houses and cottages, these fret-cut plaster towers rise. You may even see one on the house of a very discriminating dog! They resemble fine lacework or filigree in stone; others are as delicately contrived as forms of snow crystals blown against glass.

In Loulé, you may want to visit the Gothic-style **Parish Church,** which was given to the town in the latter 13th century, and the **Church of the Misericórdia,** looking like a wedding cake, especially its Manueline entrance. The town also contains the remains of a fortress-castle which Afonso III captured from the Moors.

12. São Brás de Alportel

Traveling north from Faro for 12½ miles, you'll pass through groves of figs, almonds, and oranges, through pine woods where resin collects in wooden cups on the tree trunks. At the end of the run, you'll come upon isolated São Brás de Alportel, one of the most charming and least known spots on the Algarve.

Far from the crowd on the beaches, it attracts those wanting pure air, peace, and quiet—a bucolic setting filled with flowers pushing through nutmeg-colored soil. Northeast of Loulé, the whitewashed, tile-roofed town rarely gets lively except on market days. Like its neighbor, Faro, it is noted for its perforated plaster chimneys. At the foot of the Sêrra do Caldeirão, the whole area has been labeled one vast garden.

The big attraction at São Brás de Alportel is:

A HILLTOP BUDGET POUSADA: Pousada de São Brás (tel. 423-05) offers a change of pace from the seaside accommodations. The government-owned inn is a hilltop villa, with a crow's-nest view of the surrounding sêrras. It's approached through a fig orchard in which stones have been painted with welcome in many languages. The fret-cut limestone chimneys perch over the potted plants and foliage of the grounds and an occasional antique wagon wheel, a sedate and tranquil scene.

Many visitors arrive just for lunch or dinner, returning to the coastline by night, but a knowing few remain for the evening. In the dining room, rustic mountain tavern chairs and tables rest on hand-woven rugs. The soft sofa before the wood-burning fireplace is a perfect place for lingering over a cup of coffee. The 500$ ($7.65) table d'hôte dinner offers soup, a fish course, a meat dish, vegetables, and dessert. Pleasant waitresses in blue and white pleated aprons edged with lace serve you the savory soup from a steaming tureen. The cuisine is plain, but good—the portions generous.

After dinner you may want to retire to the beamed-ceilinged sitting room to watch the embers of the evening's fire die down. Then trundle upstairs, past the large ornamented tasseled donkey collar for a night's sleep in cozy beds in a room cooled by highland breezes. The bedrooms are decorated in inventive regional styles, and all of them contain private baths. The full-board bill is 2300$ ($35.19) in a single, 3100$ ($47.43) in a double.

In addition to Loulé and São Brás de Alportel, do see:

ESTÓI AND MILREU: Two broken capitals and some fluted columns stand on ground blanketed by buttercups. In classical times, the Roman soldiers, seeing the gardens of the Algarve in spring, decided that a Temple of Venus was in order. **Milreu** was turned into a spa, and numerous fragments, mosaics, baths, even water pipes are in evidence. Archeologists have claimed that some of the ruins are those of a Christian church built in the third century A.D., making it one of the earliest in the world. There is no admission, no guard, just a lonely field and an old deserted farmhouse adjoining.

From Milreu, you can see **Estói**, a former Roman town five miles from Olhão. Tourists are still greeted with interest around here; old women stare at them from behind the curtains of their little houses, but begging children are likely to follow them about. Estói is an unspoiled village, where women can be seen washing their clothing in a public trough. Its garden walls are decaying, its cottages well worn by the time and the weather.

In Estói is the 18th-century villa, the **Palácio do Visconde de Estói**, with a salmon-pink facade. It is made up of formal gardens, Italian marble statues, fountains, belvederes, and stairways rising by cypresses and patches of lavender.

13. Olhão

If you approach this fishing village by the road from Estói, you'll pass a small aqueduct, a creaking watermill, and sheep grazing in the fields. Along the way, gypsies trudge by, some riding in gaily painted carts pulled by mules (known as *carrinhos de molas*).

Then Olhão appears, a living recreation of a Georges Braque collage with all the skillful shading and color modulations of Cézanne. This is the famous cubist town of the Algarve, so long beloved by painters. The brilliant white blocks stacked one upon the other, with flat red tile roofs, and exterior stairways on the stark walls, evoke the aura of the casbahs of North African cities.

We hope that you'll be able to attend the fish market near the waterfront when a *lota* (auction) is under way. Olhão is also known for its bullfights of the sea, in which fishermen wrestle with struggling tuna trapped in nets and headed for the smelly warehouses along the harbor.

For the best view, climb **Cabeça Hill**, its grottos punctured with stalagmites and stalactites, or perhaps **St. Michael's Mount**, offering a panorama of the Casbah-like Barreta. Finally, for what is perhaps the most idyllic beach on the Algarve, take a ten-minute motorboat ride to the **Ilha de Armona**, a nautical mile away. Olhão is 6½ miles west of Faro.

Most tourists visit just for the day, although an estalagem is there for those wanting to soak up color.

Hotel Caíque, 37 Rua General Humberto Delgado (tel. 721-67), in a village hard pressed for suitable overnight accommodations or restaurants, is an easy winner. The Kayak Inn is open all year; its 40 bedrooms come equipped with private baths. The rooms are small and uninspired, but they're clean and comfortable. Prices are from 1650$ ($25.25) for full board for one, from 2500$ ($38.25) to 2700$ ($41.31) for full board for two. To be quoted en pension terms, you must stay a minimum of two days.

Guests on full board may have picnic lunches packed for day excursions at no extra charge. Also, the hotel provides a launch service to the beach on Armona Island, and will arrange fishing and sightseeing expeditions. The hotel also offers a lounge, a fine regional restaurant serving 400$ ($6.12) table d'hôte meals, a bridge room, a bar, solarium, and three sitting rooms, one on each floor. From the rooftop terrace is a view of the village.

TAVIRA: An Algarvian gem, sleepy Tavira sits like a town of the past century. It's approached through green fields studded with almond and carob trees, the latter producing a dry pod of hard seeds in sweet pulp (eaten by both people and animals). Sometimes called the Venice of the Algarve, Tavira lies on the banks of the Ségua and Gilão Rivers, which meet under a seven-arched Roman bridge. In the town square, palms and pepper trees rustle amid the cool arches of the arcade.

A tunny fishing center, Tavira is cut off from the sea by an elongated spit of sand, the **Ilha de Tavira,** which begins west of Cacela and runs all the way past the fishing village of Fuzeta. On this sandbar, reached by motorboat, are two beaches: the Praia de Tavira and the Praia de Fuzeta. Others prefer to go to the beach at the tiny village of **Santa Luzia,** about two miles from the heart of town.

Tavira is festive looking with floridly decorated chimneys topping many of the houses, some of which are graced with emerald-green tiles and wrought-iron balconies capped by finials. Many doorways are adorned with fretwork. The liveliest action, however, centers on the fruit and vegetable market on the river esplanade. The town lies about 19 miles east of Faro.

READERS' RESTAURANT SELECTION: "One of the best meals we had in Portugal was eaten at the **Imperial** 24 Rua José Pires Padinho, a small restaurant off the main square in Tavira. We were served vegetable soup, a heaping platter of pork and clams with french fries, and a rich egg and almond dessert, plus a bottle of sparkling green wine. Our bill was 450$ ($6.89) per person. A patron at the restaurant insisted on helping us choose a *típico* Portuguese meal" (Mr. and Mrs. James Borland, Frankfort, Ind.).

14. Monte Gordo

Monte Gordo is the last in a long line of Algarvian resorts, lying as it does directly west of the frontier town of Vila Real de Santo António. Its wide beach, one of the finest along the southern coast of Portugal, is backed by lowlands studded with pines. The resort lies at the mouth of the Guardiana River.

The fishing village goes on as before (except the varinas urge their sons to take to the hotels instead of the sea, fishing for tips instead of tunny). Wives in housecoats emerge from newly built houses to receive the best of the fresh catch from fishermen who ride bicycles through the streets delivering orders. The village is small, filled with squat houses predominantly colored robin's egg blue or coral.

For such a small resort, Monte Gordo is well supplied with hotels.

Hotel Vasco da Gama, Avenida Infante Dom Henriques (tel. 321), is the most expansive and impressive modern hotel built at the eastern end of the Algarve. Its entrepreneurs know what their northern guests seek—lots of sun-

TAVIRA/MONTE GORDO 183

bathing and swimming. Although it enjoys a position on a long, wide, sandy beach, it also offers an Olympic-size swimming pool with high-dive board, and nearly an acre of flagstoned sun terrace.

Inside is a sky-high oceanfront dining room, with additional tables on the mezzanine, plus several well-furnished lounges with many groupings of chairs for that quiet conversation. Other conveniences include two drinking bars, and a boîte where it's possible to dance to records or combos several nights a week.

While the hotel is geared to large groups, individual guests are welcomed as well. For full board in high season, the rates range from 3000$ ($45.90) to 3800$ ($58.14) in a single, and from 5800$ ($88.74) to 9000$ ($137.70) in a double. The prices of the 182 rooms vary according to size and exposure. In all cases, the furnishings are excellent and conservative. Glass doors open onto balconies, and the baths are tiled.

Families who want to anchor in by the beach should consider booking one of the flats in the block of efficiency apartments overlooking the sea. The **Hotel Apartamendo Guadiana,** Avenida Infante Dom Henriques (tel. 422-69), rents units in high season for 2000$ ($30.60) for two persons, increasing this to 2500$ ($38.25) for four persons. A real bargain is an apartment for six guests, costing only 3200$ ($48.96).

Just a block away, also overlooking the pine woods and ocean, is a small, less expensive hotel owned by the Vasco da Gama (guests are allowed to use the facilities of the more expensive sister). Rated first-class B by the government is the **Hotel das Caravelas,** Monte Gordo (tel. 459). It's modern and simpler, with eight floors of rooms, and a roof terrace attracting sun-seekers. Its 87 bedrooms have little balconies, private baths, and attractive and comfortable furnishings. For full board, a single person pays from 2300$ ($35.19) to 2600$ ($39.78); two persons, 3100$ ($47.43) to 3500$ ($53.55). The dining room on the top floor opens onto a good view in many directions.

Hotel dos Navegadores, Rua Gonçalo Velho (tel. 451). Its glaring white facade belies the niceties found inside. All 103 rooms come with private baths and terraces, opening onto the pine woods and the sea, a short haul from the sands. The furnishings are inspired by provincial designs, most inviting, especially the black-cushioned rattan armchairs. There is a warm-water swimming pool. The full-board rate for two people is 3600$ ($55.08).

Black and gold ladderback chairs are foils for the creamy interior of the dining area, where fine international and regional dishes are served. What could better satisfy the sun-soaked bather than a chilled bowl of gazpacho, followed by an omelet with savory bits of smoked ham, then grilled mutton chops, and an iced bowl of fresh fruits? Dinners are even more elaborate. The chef doesn't believe in attracting weight-watching guests.

Pensão Residência Catavento, Rua Projectada (tel. 424-28), is the best bargain in Monte Gordo, rated by the government as a luxury boarding house. This Inn of the Weathervane is owned by Manuel Dias and Fernando Lagaro, who maintain a simplicity and cleanliness that have won them many repeat customers. Their rooms are so pristine they're almost monastic. Room and breakfast for one is 1000$ ($15.30) to 1200$ ($18.36); for two, 1200$ ($18.36) to 1600$ ($24.48). Breakfast only is served.

Inside the Catavento, the walls are hung with wooden cutouts and atmospheric prints of fishing boats. The lounge is highlighted by a two-tone wooden dado, and the breezy dining room serves a varied local and international cuisine. The beach is but a minute's walk from the front door, and for 30$ (46¢) you're permitted the use of a shower, an umbrella chair, and the toilets there.

Albergaría Monte Gordo, Monte Gordo (tel. 421-24), is a modern, streamlined structure, open to sea and sky, emulating Pueblo architecture. It is across the road from an immense sweep of beach, clean and colorful with the local fishing boats. Each room has a private bathroom, and a double with terrace and sea view costs 1400$ ($21.42) in summer, 800$ ($12.24) in winter, with breakfast. The atmosphere is informal, the staff friendly and helpful. Many speak English. Sylvia de Almeida, who manages the inn, has added a decorative touch to the public rooms with her fabric and needlework hangings. There is a lively bar-disco and an excellent restaurant, known for its soups, local fish dishes, and mini-plate meals. Nonresidents may enjoy its sea-view location and good service. The peaceful winter atmosphere makes this a place ideal for writers, painters, or people looking for the simple life. Special prices can be made for long winter stays.

For a final stopover, about two miles east of Monte Gordo, there is:

VILA REAL DE SANTO ANTÓNIO: Twenty years after the Marquês de Pombal rebuilt Lisbon, after the great earthquake of 1755, he sent the architects and builders to Vila Real de Santo António where they reestablished the frontier town on the opposite bank from Spain. Separated from its Iberian neighbor by the Guadiana River, Vila Real de Santo António offers a car-ferry between Portugal and Ayamonte, Spain.

Pombal's reason for wanting a town here was motivated by jealousy of Spain. It took only five months to build. Much has changed, of course, although the Praça de Pombal remains. An obelisk stands in the center of the square, which is paved with inlays of black and white tiles radiating like rays of the sun, and filled with orange trees.

A long esplanade, the Avenida da República, lines the river, and from its northern extremity you can view the Spanish town across the way. Gaily painted horse-drawn carriages take you sightseeing past the shipyards, the lighthouse, or to the bullfights in July and August.

A short drive north on the road to Mertola takes you to the gull-gray castle-fortress of **Castro Marim**. This formidable structure is a legacy of the old border wars between Spain and Portugal. The ramparts and walls watch Spain across the river. Afonso III, who chased the Moors out of this region, founded the original fortress, which was brought to its knees by the 1755 earthquake. Inside the walls are the ruins of the Church of São Tiago, dedicated to St. James. The best way to visit the castle is to take the road through the marshes on a carriage known as a trem.

From the Algarve, we continue directly north to two provinces whose culture, architecture, and customs make them unique.

Chapter XIII

ALENTEJO AND RIBATEJO

1. Évora
2. Beja
3. Vila Viçosa
4. Elvas
5. Marvão
6. Castelo de Vide
7. Estremoz
8. Vila Franca de Xira
9. Santarém
10. Tomar

THE ADJOINING PROVINCES of Alentejo and Ribatejo are the heartland of Portugal. But while Ribatejo is a land of bull-breeding pastures, that of Alentejo is characterized as a plain of fire and ice.

Ribatejo is the country of the river, where the Tagus, coming from Spain, overflows its banks in winter. It is famed for blue grass, Arabian horses, and black bulls. The most striking feature, however, is a human one: the *campinos,* in their stocking caps, the sturdy horsemen of the region. Theirs is the job of harnessing the Arabian pride of their horses and searching out the intangible quality of bravery in the bulls.

Whether visiting the château of the Templars, rising in the middle of the Tagus at Almourol, or attending an exciting *festa brava,* when the hooves of horses and rumble of bulls reverberate in the streets of Vila Franca de Xira, you'll marvel at the passion of the people of Ribatejo. Their fadistas have long been noted for intensity.

The cork-producing plains of Alentejo (literally, beyond the Tagus) compose the largest province in Portugal—so large, in fact, that the government has divided it into Alto Alentejo in the north (capital: Évora), and Baixo Alentejo in the south (capital: Beja). Even today it's difficult to reach. Take the Ponte 25 de Abril across the Tagus via Setúbal, or go all the way north to Vila Franca de Xira, then head east.

In Alentejo the locals have insulated themselves in whitewashed houses with tiny windows that keep in heat in the cold winters, coolness during the scorching summers. The least populated of Portuguese provinces, Alentejo possesses seemingly endless fields of wheat, and is the world's largest producer of cork (the trees can be stripped only once in nine years).

In winter the men are a dramatic sight in their characteristic capes, which are long brown coats with two short tiered capes, often adorned with a red fox collar. The women are even more of a spectacle, especially when seen working in the rice paddies or wheatfields. Their skirts and patterned undergarments are short so they can wade barefooted into the paddies. Over a knitted cowl, with a "peek through" for their eyes, is a brimmed felt hat usually studded with flowers.

1. Évora

The capital of Alto Alentejo is a historical curio. Considering its size and location, it is something of a phenomenon, a mélange of styles, its builders freely adapting whatever they desired from mudéjar to Manueline, from Roman to rococo. Évora lives up to its reputation as the Museum City. As it lies only 96 miles from Lisbon, it is most often visited on a day trip from the capital.

Nearly every street in Évora is filled with 16th- and 17th-century houses, many with tiled patios. Cobblestones, labyrinthine streets, arcades, squares with bubbling fountains, whitewashed houses, a profuse display of Moorish-inspired arches characterize the town, all of which used to be enclosed behind medieval walls.

Évora today is a sleepy provincial capital—perhaps self-consciously aware of its monuments. One local historian actually recommended to an American couple that they must see at least 59 monuments. Rest assured that you can capture the essence by seeing only a fraction of that number.

Many conquerors have passed through, and several have left architectural remains. To the Romans at the time of Julius Caesar, Évora was known as Liberalitas Julia. Perhaps its heyday was in the 16th century, during the reign of João III, when it became the Montmartre of Portugal, and then avant-garde artists congregated under the aegis of royalty. Included among them were Gil Vicente, sometimes known, not too accurately, as the Shakespeare of Portugal.

The major monument in Évora is the **Temple of Diana,** in the central plaza, directly in front of the government-owned pousada. Dating from either the first or second centuries A.D., it is a light, graceful structure, with 14 Corinthian granite columns topped by marble capitals. Of course, no one can prove that it was actually dedicated to Diana (the goddess of the moon and of hunting), but with her fine physique, she's a better choice than most. Incidentally, it withstood the earthquake of 1755, and there is evidence that it was once used as a slaughterhouse. Don't fail to walk through the garden for a view of the Roman aqueduct and the surrounding countryside. A short stroll leads to the:

Sé (cathedral): Bulky and heavy, the mother church of Évora was built in the Roman-Gothic style between 1186 and 1204, although notably restored and redesigned over the centuries. The stone facade is flanked by two square towers, both topped by cones, one surrounded by satellite spires. The interior consists of a nave and two aisles. The main altar, from the 18th century, is the finest in town, made of marble in tones of pink, black, and white.

At the sculptured work, *The Lady of Mothers,* young girls pray for fertility. A French couple, whose marriage had produced no children, prayed here, and the wife found herself pregnant by the time she returned to Paris. The next year the couple returned to Évora, bringing their new child.

The museum, charging an admission of 10$ (15¢), is open from 10 a.m. to 12:30 p.m. and 2 to 5 p.m., except Monday. It houses treasures from the church, the most notable of which is a 13th-century Virgin carved out of ivory (it opens to reveal what at first appears to be her innards, but is really a collection of scenes from her life). A reliquary is studded with 1426 precious stones, including sapphires, rubies, diamonds, and emeralds. The most valuable item is a piece of wood said to have come from the True Cross.

In the 14th-century cloister, the medallions of the Apostles include the Star of David, incongruous in a Catholic church. A cross in the ceiling, called the Key of the Cloister, marks the last stone to be set into place.

Facing the Temple of Diana is the **Church of St. John the Evangelist.** Next door to the government-owned pousada, this private Gothic-mudéjar church is connected to the palace built by the Dukes of Cadaval. However, it is open to the public—in fact, is one of the gems of Évora, although seemingly little visited. It contains a collection of azulejos (glazed earthenware tiles) from the 18th century. A guide will show you a macabre sight: an old cistern filled with neatly stacked bones removed from tombs. In the sacristy of the chapel are some paintings, including a ghastly rendition of Africans slaughtering a Christian missionary. A curiosity is a painting of a pope that not only has moving eyes, but moving feet. In addition, you can see part of the wall that once completely encircled Évora.

The **Royal Church of St. Francis** is visited by those wanting to see its ghoulish **Chapel of Bones.** The chancel walls and central pillars are lined with human skulls and other parts of skeletons. Costing an admission of only one escudo, the stone chapel dates from the 16th century. Alternate legends have it that the bones came either from soldiers who died in a big battle, or from plague victims. Over the door is the sign: "Our bones who stay here are waiting for yours!" The church itself was built in the Gothic style with Manueline overtones between 1460 and 1510.

The **Church of Our Lady of Grace** is viewed chiefly for its baroque facade, with huge classical nudes dangling their legs over the pillars. Above each group of lazing stone giants is a sphere with a flame atop. These pieces of sculpture are often compared to works by Michelangelo. The church was built in Évora's heyday in the reign of João III. The central window shaft is flanked by columns and large stone rosettes, the lower level supported by ponderous neoclassic columns.

Finally, you may want to visit the **Ancient University.** In 1559, as a natural outcropping of the cultural flowering of Évora, a university was constructed and placed under the tutelage of the Jesuits. It flourished until the Jesuit-hating Marquês de Pombal closed it in the 18th century. The baroque structure is double tiered and built around a large quadrangle. The arches are supported by marble pillars, the interior ceilings constructed with Brazilwood. The inner courtyard is lined with blue and white tiles. Other azulejos representations throughout depict women, wild animals, angels, cherubs, and costumed men contrasting with the austere elegance of the classrooms and the elongated refectory. The compound is no longer used as a university, although pupils (the equivalent of high-school students in America) attend class here.

Estalagem Monte das Flores, four kilometers outside Évora on the road to Alçacoves (tel. 254-90), is out of the ordinary. One of Portugal's leading bull-breeders converted what formerly were adjoining stables and servants' quarters into a well-decorated hotel, with a rustic lounge, a roaring fire, easy chairs, and country artifacts. The dining room is pleasant and spacious, featuring another "walk-in" fireplace. Outside, a large dining terrace, surrounded by hedges, overlooks the open countryside, a delight in summer. The bedrooms contain private baths and are decorated with hand-painted bedsteads and closets.

The hotel's good for those who like the sporting life. There's a large swimming pool, plus plenty of lawn, a tennis court, horseback riding, and a private lake three kilometers away. If you've ever wanted to live on a hidalgo's private estate, here's your chance to do so. Two people pay 2870$ ($43.91), a single costing 1960$ ($29.99).

An à la carte dinner or luncheon goes for anywhere from 400$ ($6.12) to 600$ ($9.18). On one recent occasion, and for the latter price, I enjoyed a soup à alentejano (a clear bouillon with croutons, perfumed with herbs and garlic), plus a large portion of beef à la Flores, consisting of a steak with french fries and tomato sauce, followed by apricots, coffee, and a large bottle of Mondego wine.

Pousada dos Lóios, Évora (tel. 240-51), is one of the finest government-owned tourist inns in Portugal. It was built as a convent in the 15th century, undergoing further adaptation and enlargement during the 18th century, and culminating in the mid-20th century with the installation of heating and private baths in every bedroom. Its position in the museum-like center of Évora is prime, between the cathedral and the ghost-like Roman Temple of Diana.

Even if you're not bedding down for the night, like a pilgrim of old, you should at least stop for a regional meal of Alto Alentejo. There are 27 double rooms and one suite, now unrecognizably luxurious when compared to the quarters of old. They're traditionally furnished in a provincial style, with a blending of antique reproductions. Rooms cost 2200$ ($33.66) a day. A cardinal-like suite for splurgers rents for 2800$ ($42.84) for two persons. Taxes, service, and breakfast are included in all these tariffs. During the peak summer season, wayfarers are sometimes housed in the simpler, top-floor "chauffeur rooms," which are smaller. Ask for a room in the interior. Otherwise, the front rooms can get noisy at night, as young men roam the street, talking and making a lot of racket with their motorcycles and cars.

There's a salon in white and gold (a one-time private chapel), with an ornate Pompeian-style decor and frescoes. Now it's formal, with antique furnishings, hand-woven draperies, crystal chandeliers and sconces, and painted medallion portraits. A portion of the old kitchen has been converted into a small bar for drinks and snacks. In addition, there's a vaulted stone-pillared tea veranda where you can order four o'clock tea between June 1 and September 30, relaxing in rattan chairs and enjoying a view of a palace built by a count.

In winter meals are served in the main dining hall, with its heavy chandeliers. But in fair weather most guests dine in and around the cloister, at tables set under the Manueline fan-vaulted ceiling and an ornate Moorish doorway leading to the Chapter House. You pay 700$ ($10.71) for a complete luncheon or dinner. For this, you get a basket of freshly baked bread and butter, a bowl of hot soup, followed by a fish dish, such as sole prepared in a herb-flavored tomato sauce and accompanied by mashed potatoes. For your main course, try the acorn-sweetened pork cooked with clams in the manner of Alentejo. For dessert, a trolley of assorted pastries is wheeled by.

Hotel Planície, Rua Miguel Bombarda (tel. 240-26), is Évora's leading modern hotel, furnished with Nordic-style pieces. However, it nods briefly to the past (for example, in its boîte for drinks and dancing it has built an imitation Gothic ceiling; and out back a little boy porter will show you the remains of a Roman cistern). Although the street entry reception room is pocket-size, the lounges and bar on the second floor are spacious and comfortable. In the late afternoon, guests seek out the roof terrace, with its view of the cathedral.

The lounges are laden with leather and wood chairs and lots of marble from Borba. Luncheons and dinners, generous in portions, are served in the low-key restaurant, with its black parquet floor; a complete four-course meal goes for 600$ ($9.18). The bedrooms are consistent with the hotel's up-to-date idiom, and contain fully tiled baths. For two persons, the rate range is from 1750$ ($26.78) to 1850$ ($28.31), depending on the view, size, and plumbing (the cheaper rooms contain showers instead of tubs). The best single rents for 1200$ ($18.36). Full board for one person is 1000$ ($15.30) extra.

O Eborense, 1 Largo da Misericórdia (tel. 220-31), is a budget boarding house with a touch of grandeur in the form of a stone staircase leading up to an entrance lined with plants and decorated with tiles. As you come up to the first-floor terrace, you're greeted by a caged parrot and your host Senhor Barreto, who speaks English. He offers 25 rooms in this building, and an additional 17 in the annex where accommodations range from only 350$ ($5.36) in a single to 450$ ($6.89) in a double. The more expensive rooms, in the main building, cost 450$ ($6.89) for a single, 625$ ($9.56) for a double. All rooms are clean, a bit old-fashioned, and quite pleasant. You can sit on the terrace nursing a drink and peering through the cloister-like, mullioned veranda. An adjoining rooftop garden-café attracts sunworshipers. Breakfast is included.

WHERE TO DINE: Cozinha de St. Humberto, 39 Rua da Moeda (tel. 242-51), is the most atmospheric restaurant in Évora. Hidden away in a narrow side street leading down from the Praça do Giraldo, it is rustically decorated with old pots, blunderbusses, standing lamps, a grandfather clock, and kettles hanging from the ceiling. Carnations stand on each table, and you sit in rush chairs or on divan-settees. In warm weather, you can enjoy a gazpacho Alentejana for 65$ (99¢), followed by fried fish with tomato and garlic, 165$ ($2.53), or else pork Évora style (a real meal in itself), 240$ ($3.67), topped off by regional cheese, costing from 55$ (84¢). A half bottle of Borba wine is 75$ ($1.15). Each meal comes with an appetizer, consisting of cheese and a portion of the local saucisson.

READER'S RESTAURANT SUGGESTION: "We had the best dinner in all of Portugal in Évora at a restaurant called **Fialho**, 16 Travessa das Mascarenhas (tel. 230-79). Don't be misled by the seedy outer appearance. A very nice dining room is off to the side. We had an excellent dinner, with wine, four appetizers, hearty entrees (I had the partridge), and also dessert, for $12 (U.S.) for the two of us" (Mrs. S. Mattes, Glencoe, Ill.).

2. Beja

The capital of Baixo Alentejo, founded by Julius Caesar and once known as Pax Julia, rises like a pyramid above the surrounding fields of swaying wheat, only 116 miles from Lisbon. The women of Beja still cook on braziers on their front doorsteps, and timid donkeys draw blue carts through the narrow streets. Clothes hang on lines strung between the castle ramparts and olive trees, and children scuffle in a soccer game under the shadow of the fortress wall.

The fame of Beja, however, rests on what many authorities believe to be a literary hoax. In the mid-17th century, in the Convent of Conceição, a young nun named Soror Mariana Alcoforado is said to have fallen in love with a French military officer, identified as the chevalier de Chamily. He was believed to have seduced her, then to have left Beja never to return again.

The girl's outpouring of grief and anguish found literary release in the *Five Love Letters of a Portuguese Nun*. Published in Paris in 1669, they created a sensation and have remained an epistolary classic of self-revelation and remorse ever since. However, in 1926, F. C. Green, author of *Who Was the Author of the 'Lettres Portugaises'?* claimed their true writer was the Comte de Guilleragues.

The mid-15th-century convent has been turned into a **Regional Museum** (Museu Rainha D. Leonor), at the Largo da Conceição. It houses a varied assortment of artworks, artifacts, and historical curios, including Roman axes, sarcophagi, Roman amphorae, statuary of Florentine marble, Chinese porcelains from 1541, paintings of Saints Jerome, Augustine, and Bartholomew assigned to Ribera, delicate silverwork, vestments, and dummies dressed in regional Alentejo costumes, 17th-century Spanish and 15th-, 16th-, 17th-, and 18th-century Portuguese paintings.

One of its most unusual exhibits is a grille through which the nun and the Frenchman were supposed to have exchanged intimacies. Also displayed are copies of early editions of the literary classic, even an engraving of the count; revealing him to be chubby cheeked.

A modern Portuguese study, by the way, has submitted evidence that the *Lettres Portugaises* were actually written by Mariana Alcoforado, a nun in the convent.

The walls, especially those of the cloister, are profusely decorated with antique tiles, some blue and white, others emerald green. There are sacred relics as well, along with elaborate candelabra, and a gilded baroque altar with marble inlay work in pink, black, gold, and gray. The museum is open from 9:30 a.m. to 1 p.m. and from 1:30 to 5 p.m. daily, except Sunday. The regular admission is 10$ (15¢), except Saturday when it's free.

Crowning the town is the **Castelo de Beja**, which King Dinis built in the early 14th century on the ruins of a Roman fortress. Although some of its turreted walls have been restored, the defensive towers are gone, save for a long marble keep. Traditionally the final stronghold in the castle's fortifications, the old keep appears to be battling the weather and gold fungi. The walls are grown over with ivy, the last encroachment upon the structure's former glory. From the keep, you can enjoy a view of the provincial capital and the outlying fields. The castle opens onto the Largo Dr. Lima Faleiro.

THE BUDGET RANGE: Santa Bárbara, 56 Rua de Mertola (tel. 220-28), is a little gem in a town that has a lack of suitable accommodations. The residência is a bandbox building still shiny clean and immaculately kept. It's all small scale, with only a whisper of a reception lobby and elevator. The sitting room, however, is warm and personalized, with furniture arranged on the various hand-loomed or goatskin rugs. The decorations consist of an antique English desk, gilt mirrors, and cherubs, plus tiled dado around the walls.

The 26 compact rooms are adequate, with soft carpeting, good beds, tiled baths with showers, and central heating in the winter. The cost of staying here is low: 750$ ($11.48) to 900$ ($13.77) for one person, 1100$ ($16.83) to 1400$ ($21.42) for two. No meals are served except a continental breakfast which is included in the price.

Residência Coelho, 15 Praça da República (tel. 240-31), is simple and unpretentious, with small, unassuming rooms, somewhat cramped, but clean and modern. Some rooms have balconies overlooking the square with its large potted flowers. Singles cost 575$ ($8.80); doubles, 850$ ($13.01).

WHERE TO DINE: Beja is rather lacking in first- or even second-class restaurants. However, at the **Luís da Rocha,** Rua Capitão João F. de Sousa, on the same street as the Tourist Office, you can sit downstairs in the café where the whole town seems to congregate for coffee and pastries, or go upstairs where you'll find two spacious neon-lit dining rooms, featuring a tourist menu for 245$ ($3.75) to 420$ ($6.43).

SERPA: Languishing in the Middle Ages, Serpa is a walled town with defensive towers. All this medieval stone once had a purpose. Serpa lies only 20 miles west of Vila Verde de Ficalho (the Spanish frontier). Today the town has become a stopping-off point (for lunch or just a rest) for travelers on the way to or from Spain.

Silvery olive trees surround the approaches to the town. The whiteness of the settlement is in contrast to the red-brown of the plains. To the east at a distance of 18½ miles lies Beja; but many motorists prefer to spend the night at Serpa rather than the provincial capital because of the following hilltop pousada:

Where to Stay

Pousada de São Gens, Alto de São Gens (tel. 52-327). In keeping with the Portuguese love of vistas, this budget-range government-owned tourist inn is set at the crown of the hill of São Gens. On clear nights guests can see all the way to Spain. Although a long way from the Algarve, the architecture is Moorish inspired, almost a Pueblo-style villa with stark white walls easily seen as you ascend the winding road past olive trees.

The pousada is family run and has a homelike atmosphere. All the 18 bedrooms have private baths, tiled in aqua and white. The furnishings are modern, making use of bold colors. A room rents for 1500$ ($22.95) for one person, 1600$ ($24.48) for two.

Dining in winter is in a salon with a coved ceiling, overflowing in the warmer months onto the wide veranda. A Portuguese cuisine is offered, with many dishes of the region featured. A complete meal, including soup from a tureen, a fish course with potatoes, a meat dish with vegetables, and dessert goes for 600$ ($9.18). There are two servings for dinner. Before dinner you can have a drink in the gold and white bar, or in one of the stark-white living rooms.

3. Vila Viçosa

This borough was the near-private dominion of the Dukes of Braganza, the last royal rulers of Portugal. Thirty-four miles northeast of Évora, Vila Viçosa has been a ducal seat since 1442. But what cast it into worldwide prominence was when one of its members journeyed to Lisbon in 1640 to be declared the head of a new royal dynasty. Ruling as João IV, he freed Portugal from 60 years of Spanish domination.

Ironically, one of the last of the Braganza kings, Carlos I, spent his last night dining under his favored antler chandeliers before making the journey to Lisbon. His staff, lined up at the Terreiro do Paço, waved him and his older son good-bye. But when they arrived at another Terreiro do Paço (this one in Lisbon), the reception was less friendly. Both died by an assassin's bullets.

The **Paço Ducal de Vila Viçosa** remains as a memorial to the Braganzas. You'll see pictures of the last king, Manuel II, who fled with his mother, Amélia, into exile in 1910. The uniforms of Carlos I are here as well. Perhaps the most remarkable personal exhibit is a gallery of Carlos's (otherwise known as the painter king) paintings and watercolors. As one critic put it, he was a better artist than a king.

The inside of the palace and its furnishings are a collage of faded mementos, foreign art influences, and nostalgic specters of a once-royal life. As with a fine tapestry, separating the diverse treasures is difficult. The trappings include a frescoed Salon of Hercules; tapestries based on Rubens's cartoons; 16th-century Persian carpets; 17th-century armor; a Pompeian-style oratory; a Medusa chamber; Louis XVI furnishings; a 17th-century Holy Cross with 6500 precious stones (rubies, diamonds, pearls, and emeralds); hand-carved armoires; a chapel faced with pink marble; a sword and shield collection (even spears from Angola); and cloisters dating from the 16th century. The kitchen is filled with copper pots and utensils used by the royal family (a spit for roasting the big game Carlos I was fond of bagging), and a Coach Museum, containing about a dozen carriages, some from the 17th century, and a sedan chair. After your visit, you can stroll through the Garden of the Ladies.

In the archives you can see the bequest of Manuel II: his priceless library of printed books from the 15th and 16th centuries, including the first edition of *Lusíadas* by Luís de Camões. The music archives contain what remains from the Schola Cantorum instituted by the dukes in the 17th, 18th, and 19th centuries. The palace is open daily, charging an admission of 25$ (38¢).

Today, the white town of Vila Viçosa rests unchanged in the midst of the olive-green carpeted marble hills which are spotted with orange trees. The town is guarded by a walled castle dating from the 14th century, with a quartet of tall towers and crenellated walls. It is a natural extension of the museum in the palace. There is also an archeological museum with artifacts from Paleolithic, Neolithic, Iron Age, and Roman civilizations found around Vila Viçosa. Admission to the castle is 20$ (31¢). There are 22 churches in Vila Viçosa, many almost casually containing treasures, but only the most dedicated of visitors seek them out.

WHERE TO DINE: The **Restaurante Fromar,** 35 Praça da República (tel. 95), is where the local people gather for an inexpensive meal or coffee. In the heart of town facing a square of potted flowering plants, it's modern, with an all-glass facade. Past the coffee- and brandy-drinking Alentejo "cowboys" up front is a miniature dining area, with just four tables set on a platform.

A set luncheon or dinner is offered for 500$ ($7.65), including a bowl of soup from a tureen (perhaps a rich stock with turnips, greens, and red beans). For a second course, a sweet, lightly fried white fish is presented, accompanied by rice with sweet red peppers and a mixed salad. The main course is likely to be a platter of thinly sliced fried veal with lemon wedges and puffed potatoes. For dessert a big basket of fresh fruit is placed on the table.

There are many good à la carte selections as well, including regional dishes such as the typical soup of Alentejo for 55$ (84¢). The house specialty is febras de porco (a leg of pork simmered in wine and flavored with garlic), costing 190$ ($2.91) for one person. You pay 55$ (84¢) to 85$ ($1.30) for a small carafe of wine.

BORBA: The town that marble built, Borba lies only a short drive from Vila Viçosa. On the way there, you'll pass quarries filled with black, white, and multicolored deposits. In the village, donkeys pulling carts loaded with chips and slabs attest to the fact that marble is king. Along the streets many cottages have door trimmings and facings of marble, and the women get down on their hands and knees to scrub their doorways, a source of special pride to them.

On the Rua S. Bartolomeu sits a church, also dedicated to S. Bartolomeu. It contains a groined ceiling; walls lined with azulejos in blue, white, and gold; and an altar in black and white marble. The richly decorated ceiling is painted with four major medallions, one depicting decapitation. As Portuguese churches go, this one isn't remarkable. What is remarkable, however, are eight nearby antique shops (amazing for such a small town) which are filled with interesting buys. Borba is also a big wine center, and you may want to sample the local brew at a café (or prehaps at the pousada at Elvas).

On the outskirts is a remarkable sight, the **Museu de Cristo,** on the main road to Estremoz at Villa Lobos. It lies three kilometers from Borba and nine kilometers from Estremoz. The entrance is inauspicious, on a farm by the side of the road. In front is an antique shop filled with a hodgepodge of oddments, including many fine pieces from Alentejo. In the rear, the museum is the most intimate and personal one in Portugal. It's owned by the Lôbo family.

Started more than four decades ago, the collection includes 3000 crucifixes. One would suspect that this figure will change, as the Museum of Christ is an organic and growing thing. The father of the family started collecting primitive crucifixes from the country people, bartering his excess farm produce, picking up more figures in his travels to North Africa, Angola, and Spain.

The present collection spans about 13 centuries, 42 countries, and countless artistic traditions. For one of the rarest crucifixes, dating from the eighth century, a museum in Philadelphia offered $15,000, but was spurned. Some of his figures were hollowed out to hide money in the 16th century. One of the finest is from 18th-century Florence, showing a skull and crossbones at the bottom. In the other rooms of the museum are regional artifacts and furnishings. The museum may be viewed from 9 a.m. to 9 p.m. in summer (till 6 p.m. in winter).

4. Elvas

This city of the plums, known for its crenellated fortifications, is less than ten miles from Badajoz, Spain. The walled town is characterized by narrow cobblestoned streets (pedestrians have to duck into doorways to allow automobiles to inch by), and is surely an anachronism, so tenaciously does it hold on to its monuments and history.

Lining the steep hilly streets are tightly packed gold- and oyster-colored cottages topped by tiled roofs. Many of the doors leading to the houses are only five feet high. In the tiny windows are numerous canary cages and flowering geraniums. From the little plaza wells dotting the town, both men and women draw water in large copper and pottery jugs. The water is transported to Elvas by the four-tiered **Amoreira Aqueduct,** built in the 16th century.

In the Praça D. Sancho II (honoring the king who reconstructed the town) stands the **Sé (cathedral),** forbidding and fortress-like. Under a conically shaped dome, it is decorated with gargoyles, turrets, and a florid Manueline portal. The cathedral opens onto a black-and-white-diamonded square. A short walk up the hill to the right of the cathedral leads to the Largo D. Santa Clara, a small plaza on which was erected an odd Manueline pillory, with four wrought-iron dragon heads.

In accommodations there's a good pousada, which is often fully booked.

THE BUDGET RANGE: Pousada de Santa Luzia (tel 221-94), is not only a link in the government-inn circuit, but it's also an antique emporium, where nearly everything is for sale. Hopefully, the former occupant of your room didn't purchase that hand-carved bed. The bone-white stucco villa, facing the fortifications, sits on a hill, commanding a view of the town and countryside, especially from its terraces and dining room. The entire ground floor is devoted to a living room, an L-shaped dining salon, and a bar—all opening through thick arches onto a Moorish-style courtyard with fountain, lily pond, and orange trees.

Although there are some bedrooms on the upper floor, it's more interesting to be housed in the nearby annex, a villa with a two-story entrance hall and an ornate staircase. Here, the bedrooms are furnished with antiques and decorative accessories. (*Tip:* Ask to be let into the dungeon crypt by a seven-inch iron key, the door clanking open to reveal an antique dealer's paradise—carved wooden cherubs, tapestry-covered jewel chests, Chippendale chairs, gilt candelabra.)

Depending on the plumbing, doubles go from 1600$ ($24.48). A table d'hôte luncheon costs 450$ ($6.89), a dinner going for 600$ ($9.18). The menu is extensive. Noteworthy are the fish dishes, including grilled red mullet and natural oysters.

5. Marvão

This ancient walled town, lying close to Castelo de Vide, is well preserved and is visited chiefly for its views. Near the Spanish frontier, the fortified medieval town clusters around a castle at the foot of a peak of the Sêrra de São Mamede. The castle, which is inside the town walls, dates from the end of the 13th century.

The population is very small. If you arrive in the afternoon, you may think you're in a ghost town. Most of the inhabitants are working in the fields outside the walls.

THE BUDGET RANGE: The **Pousada de Santa Maria** (tel. Marvão 10-11) contains only nine double rooms (two without bath). Singles with bath rent for 1500$ ($22.95). Doubles with bath go for 1800$ ($27.54). Breakfast is included, and you need pay only 600$ ($9.18) for dinner, if you're just stopping by. For full board, one person pays 1000$ ($15.30). The rooms which face the street are poor. Mine opened onto a vacant lot with broken wine bottles. But, as compensation, the food is good.

6. Castelo de Vide

At an altitude of 1800 feet, this spa town lies at the foot of a castle. Nature has endowed Castelo de Vide with therapeutic waters. Inside its walls stand whitewashed houses, some on squares little changed since the 15th and 16th centuries. A view of chestnuts, pine woods, and oak trees gives the town a resort aura.

Cromlechs in the area testify to the ancient origin of the town. It was conquered by the Romans in A.D. 44 and destroyed by Vandals in 411. The Arabs who later occupied it rebuilt the castle in 1299. At this fortress the contract for the marriage of King Dinis to Dona Isabella of Aragón (later Saint Elizabeth of Portugal) was signed.

MARVÃO/CASTELO DE VIDE/ESTREMOZ

The Judiaria, or Jewish Quarter, is a sector of narrow alleyways and small homes, housing the richest collection of ogival doors in Portugal. This quarter also abounds with cats. A medieval synagogue has been restored.

It is said that the people who settled the Azores originated from this part of Portugal, as the populace speaks a similar dialect.

7. Estremoz

From the ramparts of its **castle**, dating from the 13th-century reign of King Dinis, the plains of Alentejo are spread before you. Although one 75-year-old British lady is reported to have walked it, it's best to drive your car to the top of the Upper Town, bringing it to a stop on the Largo de D. Dinis. The stones of the castle, the cradle of the town's past, were decaying so badly that the city fathers pressed for its restoration in 1970.

The large imposing keep, attached to a palace, dominates the central plaza. Dinis's saintly wife, Isabella, died in the castle. Isabella was unofficially proclaimed a saint by her local followers, even in life. However, one of her detractors wrote, "Poor Dinis!"

Also opening onto the marble- and stone-paved largo are two modest chapels and a church. As in medieval days, soldiers still walk the ramparts, guarding the fortress.

Rising from the Alentejo plain like a pyramid of salt set to dry in the sun, fortified Estremoz is in the center of the marble-quarry region of Alentejo, 108 miles east of Lisbon. Cottages and mansions alike utilize the abundant marble in forming windows and apertures or in fashioning balustrades and banisters.

With enough promenading Portuguese soldiers to form a garrison, the open quadrangle in the center of the Lower Town is called the **Rossio de Marquês de Pombal**. The **Town Hall**, with its twin bell towers, opens onto this square, and the walls of its grand stairway are lined with antique azulejos in blue and white, depicting hunting, pastoral, and historical scenes. In front, you can buy the characteristic earthenware pottery of the region.

A LUXURY POUSADA: Pousada da Rainha Isabel (tel. 226-16) is one of the best of the government tourist inns. Within the old castle dominating the town, and overlooking the battlements and the Estremoz plain, it is a deluxe showcase. In perfect style, comfort is provided within the framework of history. Therefore, do not be surprised that prices differ from those of the less regal pousadas.

There are 17 twin-bedded rooms, one double, two singles, and three suites (twin beds and a double), all with bath. Singles, including service charges, are 2150$ ($32.90); twins and the double, 2250$ ($34.43). Full board for one person ranges from 1125$ ($17.21). For a dinner, 650$ ($9.95) is charged.

THE BUDGET RANGE: Pensão Residência Carvalho, 27 Largo da República (tel. 227-12), is clean, simple, and inexpensive, just what you may be looking for in an emergency. A double with hot and cold running water rents for 600$ ($9.18), breakfast included. The Carvalho is a possible stop in case the pousada is full, and you're tired, two likely possibilities.

WHERE TO DINE: Aguîas d'Ouro, 25 Rossio do Marquês de Pombal (tel. 221-76). The Golden Eagles faces the largest square in Estremoz, its mosaic and marble balconied facade suggesting a doge's palace. On the second floor are several connecting dining rooms that combine contemporary and regional design. Rough white plaster walls rest under ceramic brick ceilings; heavy sumptuous black leather armchairs are set around white-draped tables. The waiters are well trained, placing a dish of homemade pâté with crusted rye bread before you.

À la carte dishes only are offered, including a large bowl of spinach and bean soup with crispy croutons floating on top, 75$ ($1.15). Main dishes include stuffed partridge at 410$ ($6.27) and pork and clams at 350$ ($5.36). The chocolate mousse at 75$ ($1.15) is the featured dessert.

Either en route to Évora or Estremoz, you may want to stop at:

ARRAIOLOS: This small village has been famous since the 13th century for its carpets—the early designs in imitation of those from Persia. The intricate patterns continued to develop and expand until the 18th century. After that, the crafts people seemed to suspend their originality, and the present rugs follow the old designs religiously. The rugs are made of heavy wool (the yarns tinted by natural dyes), are handmade, and often contain elaborate needlework. Many of the most elegant are displayed at the Museum of Antique Art in Lisbon. Even if you can't stop off at Arraiolos, you may want to see a wide-ranging display for sale at the **Casa Quintão** on 30 Rua Ivens in Lisbon.

PORTALEGRE: Portalegre is just 22 kilometers from the recently opened border post at Marvão, providing motorists with the shortest route between Lisbon and Madrid. Five kilometers away lies the mountain of São Mamede. The town, a center for cork production, is filled with baroque mansions, particularly on Rua 19 de Junho. In the 16th century, it was known for its tapestries. The workshops can be visited, and Portalegre merits a stopover.

We'd suggest the **Hotel D. João III,** Avenida da Liberdade (tel. 211-92), which is better than anything else around. It has a contemporary decor, although it widely uses native materials, including stone. The bedrooms are spacious and adequately equipped, and each one has a small balcony which looks out onto a town park. A single rents for 1200$ ($18.36), the cost going up to 1800$ ($27.54) in a double. The dining room, on the top floor, offers a fine view of the town and the amphitheater of hills in the distance.

8. Vila Franca de Xira

Vila Franca de Xira is the Pamplona of Portugal. Twice a year, the frenzied community ordeal of the *festa brava,* the running of the bulls, is staged. The Red Waistcoat is held the first week of July, and the Annual Fair the first week of October. Bullfights are also held at these events. In the countryside around Vila Franca, 20 miles north of Lisbon, are pasturelands that are breeding grounds for the black bulls. There's a modern speedway to take you there. The toll is 25$ (38¢). It costs a 10$ (15¢) toll to cross the bridge.

At the festivals, a herd of black bulls, fresh and primed for the rings of Lisbon or Cascais, are let loose in the main street of town. With the smaller side streets heavily barricaded, the *corrida* is ready to begin. When the *campinos* (Ribatejo cowboys with their traditional stocking caps) first turn the bulls loose in the streets, they appear bewildered and confused.

The crowds hoot and holler, trying to make the massive animals break rank. When one inevitably does, melees and frantic dashes follow, with occasional displays on the part of some young aspirant matador of virtuosity with the cape. The cape, incidentally, is likely to be an old piece of sack cloth or a quilt. The bulls are rarely intimidated by those who taunt them. Many a hopeful matador has been pulled by his arms to the safety of a spectator-filled wrought-iron balcony. Numerous injuries result, and the hospital staff is reinforced by recruits from Lisbon.

This blending of festive levity and grim reality, such as a critical injury, has made bull baiting an intriguing custom down through the ages. Although attacked and criticized by some who consider it barbaric, the pagan custom is well preserved on the streets of Vila Franca de Xira on at least two occasions of the year. Otherwise, there isn't much reason to go there, except to have a good meal at an inn.

THE BUDGET RANGE: Estalagem do Gado Bravo, Estrada do Cabo-Camarão (tel. 231-24), lies across the toll bridge on the other side of the Tagus. It's a roadside inn, encircled by a garden, right in the heart of the bull-breeding district—hence, its name, Brave Bull. You park your car under a bougainvillea arbor and walk past lemon trees. The emphasis is on the dining rooms, which bear a strong regional stamp. On goatskin rugs, the tables are draped with brightly colored, hand-woven cloths. Every diner has a view of one of the two brick and stone fireplaces. Around the walls are plastered bullfight posters, engravings, and prints.

The table d'hôte luncheon or dinner at 500$ ($7.65) is well prepared, with many Ribatejo specialties. The chef's favorite dish is linguado (sole) à brasileira. From most of the bedroom windows there's a view of the plains, and occasionally a stray bull noses up to the nearby fence. The room furnishings are modern but provincial, making for comfort. There are only eight bedrooms, five of which contain private baths. In a double the tariff is 1900$ ($29.07); in a single, 950$ ($14.54)—including breakfast.

Estalagem de Lezíria, Rua Palha Blanco (tel. 221-29), is a country inn set back from the busy highway by a tiny front garden with a bougainvillea arbor and rose bushes. It offers two old-world dining rooms, usually filled (especially during the running of the bulls) with those who appreciate regional dishes. The front room is more interesting, with tables set under a row of four wide plastered arches, an oak-beamed ceiling, and an open fireplace. The service is courteous and attentive.

True to the region, the cuisine features many Ribatejo dishes appearing on the table d'hôte dinner for 500$ ($7.65). The specialties please gourmets, many of whom drive up from Lisbon to sample enguias fritas (fried eels) or ensopado de enguias (eel stew). Not only eels, but much of the fresh fish comes from the nearby Tagus, earning for the estalagem the title, the Inn of the Marshland.

There are 15 rooms, six of which contain private baths. A double with bath is 1300$ ($19.89); without bath, 950$ ($14.54). A single without bath is a bargain at 650$ ($9.95). Breakfast is included.

9. Santarém

The Portuguese use the words "noble" or "Gothic" in describing this town, 49 miles north of Lisbon. The garrison here, set on a spur of land overlooking the river, has always been a key fortification. Afonso Henriques, the country's first king, drove out the Moors in 1147, and ordered the construction of the Cistercian monastery at Alcobaça to commemorate that feat.

Santarém still overlooks the low-lying lands devoted to cattle, vineyards, olive groves, even corn. It seems as if the whole of Ribatejo is spread out before one's eyes from the vantage point of the **Portas do Sol** (the Gates of the Sun), a park of tiled fountains, flowering plants and bushes, statuary, red benches, and globe lamps. At times the river is so shallow that sandy islets appear; at other moments, it overflows its banks. The gardens are reached by heading out the Avenida 5 de Outubro.

One of the main squares is **Praça de Sá da Bandeira,** lying right off the Garden of the Republic. Opening onto the largo is the **College of the Patriarchal See,** whose multiwindowed, niched, and statuary-studded facade takes up an entire side of the plaza. Inside, the main altar is decorated with marble and alabaster inlays, and flanked by four serpentine columns. Alabaster statues of saints, azulejos, and a baroque trompe l'oeil ceiling add to the lushness. Across the way from the seminary (entrance at the end of the Rua Cidade da Covilhã) sits the octagonal, domed **Chapel of Our Lady of Pity,** whose neoclassic style is enhanced by trompe l'oeil paintings.

One of the town's most interesting churches, **St. João de Alporão,** right off the R. S. Martinho, en route to the Portas do Sol, has been converted into an **Archeological Museum.** Built in the Romanesque-Gothic style, probably in the 12th century, it is graced with a rose window and multiple-arched doorway. Inside is the elaborate tomb of D. Duarte de Menezes, built by his wife after he died at the hands of the Moors. So badly mutilated was the body that the remains consisted of a lone tooth. The collection of Roman sarcophagi is more interesting.

Nearby, the Gothic **Church of Graça,** dating from 1380, has a rose window carved from a single stone. At the corner of Calçada da Graça and the Rua Vila de Belmonte, it has been completely restored and contains some carved tombs, and an architecture characterized by simple arches.

For either rooms or meals, the following establishment is recommended:

THE BUDGET RANGE: Hotel Abidis, 4 Rua Guilherme de Azevedo (tel. 220-17). Rated second class, Abidis is a place at which to order meals or enjoy a night's sleep. Although the reception area is small, the bedrooms are personalized, with old-style furnishings given a feminine touch with matching fabrics at the windows, on the beds, and at the dressing tables. Only six of the 27 bedrooms contain private baths. The cost of a double with bath is 1750$ ($26.78), 1200$ ($18.36) in a single.

The dining room is decorated in the Ribatejo tavern style. Noted for its attentive service and cuisine, it offers a table d'hôte luncheon or dinner for 450$ ($6.89). A typical meal is likely to include a bowl of onion soup, followed by turbot cooked with pimiento rice, a main course of roast kid, a carafe of good wine, cheese, and fresh fruit. The waiters, in kelly green, urge you to take second helpings. The setting is winning: a blue and white tiled dado, ox-yoke chandeliers, and provincial chairs.

10. Tomar

Tomar was integrally bound to the fate of the notorious quasi-religious order of the Knights Templar. In the 12th Century these militant monks of wealth and power established the beginnings of the **Convent of Christ** on a tree-studded hill overlooking the town. Originally a monastery, it evolved into a kind of grand headquarters for the Templars. These knights, who swore a vow of chastity (but didn't always keep it!), had fought ferociously at Santarém against the Moors. As a result of their growing military might, they built a massive walled castle at Tomar in 1160. The ruins, especially the walls, can be seen today.

By 1314 the pope was urged to suppress their power, as they had made many enemies, and their great riches were coveted by others. King Dinis allowed them to regroup their forces under the new aegis of the Order of Christ, of which Henry the Navigator became the most famous of the grand masters, using much of their money to subsidize his explorations.

From its inception, the convent underwent five centuries of inspired builders, including Manuel I (the Fortunate). It also saw its destroyers, notably the overzealous troops of Napoleon in 1810 who turned it into a barracks. What remains on the top of the hill, however, is one of the most brilliant architectural accomplishments in Portugal, an amalgam of styles.

The portal of the Templars Church is like a lacy valentine in the Manueline style, depicting everything from leaves to chubby cherubs. Inside, you enter an octagonal church with eight columns, said to have been modeled after the Temple of the Holy Sepulchre at Jerusalem. The effect is like a mosque, linking Christian tradition with Moslem culture, as in Córdoba's Mezquita. Howard La Fay called it "a muted echo of Byzantium in scarlet and dull gold." The damage done by the French troops is much in evidence. On the other side, the church is in the Manueline style with rosettes. Throughout you'll see symbols of the insignia of the Templars.

The convent embraces eight cloisters in a variety of styles. The most notable one, a two-tiered structure built in 1557 by Diogo de Torralva, exhibits perfect symmetry, the almost severe academic use of the classical form that distinguishes the Palladian school. A guide will also take you on a brief tour of a dormitory where the monks of old lived in cells.

The convent possesses some of the greatest Manueline stonework to emerge from that era. An example is the grotesque west window of the Chapter House. At first, you'll think that some effusive secretion has bubbled out the window; but a closer inspection reveals a meticulous symbolic and literal depiction of Portugal's sea lore and power. Knots and ropes, mariners and the tools of their craft, silken sails wafting in stone, recreate coral seascapes, all are delicately interwoven in this chef d'oeuvre of the whole movement.

The admission-free convent is open from 9:30 a.m. to 12:30 p.m. and from 2 to 6 p.m. (5 p.m. off-season). It is customary to tip the guide.

Tomar has many other sights of interest. On the way up the hilltop, you can stop off at the **Chapel of Our Lady of Conception,** crowned by small cupolas and jutting out over the town. Reached via an avenue of trees, it was built in the Renaissance style in the mid-16th century, and its interior is a forest of white Corinthian pillars.

In the heart of town, the **Church of St. John the Baptist** opens onto the Praça da República, built by Manuel I, with black and white diamond mosaics. Dating from the 15th century, the church contains a white and gold baroque altar (a chapel to the right is faced with antique tiles).

In and around the church are the narrow cobblestoned streets of Tomar, where shops sell dried codfish, and wrought-iron balconies are hung with bird cages and flower pots.

Divided by the Nabão River, historic Tomar lies 85 miles from Lisbon, 40 from Santarém.

Hotel dos Templários (tel. 331-21) is a modern 84-room hotel incongruously placed in such a small town. Pooling their know-how, five local businessmen created this five-floor structure placed on the banks of the river. Facilities include wide sun terraces, a riverside swimming pool fed by a fountain, two tennis courts, even a greenhouse.

The interior is spacious, including lounges. There is a terrace-view dining room. The bedrooms are suitable, containing private baths, plus air conditioning and heating. In high season (April 1 to October 31) doubles rent for as low as 1500$ ($22.95) or as high as 2000$ ($30.60). Singles go for 1200$ ($18.36) to 1700$ ($26.01). Most guests have breakfast either in their room or in a sunny salon overlooking the river. In the evenings they gather around the living room fireplace for drinks. If you're passing through, you can stop in for a table d'hôte luncheon or dinner for 600$ ($9.18).

Estalagem de Santa Iria, Parque do Monchão (tel. 324-27), lies on a three-acre island filled with sycamore and maple trees, right in the center of town. Just a 30-second walk across the bridge removes you from the bustle of town activity and plants you on the doorstep of a country inn. Regrettably, the place is old, the paint peeling, and it's in dire need of maintenance—so if you check in, you've been duly warned. However, there's such a limited choice of accommodations, you may have to "make do" for the night.

The ten bedrooms are small, often dimly lit, and the beds cot-like. Furnishings are in the provincial style, all hand-painted with figures and flowers. Many windows overlook the river, and you'll be lulled to sleep by the slow rippling of the water. A double with private bath rents for 1400$ ($21.42), 900$ ($13.77) for a single. Even cheaper are three accommodations with hot and cold running water only, with a double going for 1200$ ($18.36).

Regional meals are served in the park-view dining room, costing 450$ ($6.89) for a complete luncheon or dinner. In the summer months tables are set outside. The food is good, and you'll eat too much since second helpings are encouraged. After lunch you can go rowing around the island under weeping willows and past old water wheels.

WHERE TO DINE: Bella Vista, corner Rua Marquês de Pombal and Rua Ronte do Choupo (tel. 328-70), is, as its name indicates, a restaurant with a pretty view of the town and a small canal. You can dine outside, under a bower, or in rustic dining rooms decorated with plates, flowers, plants, and racks to hang your hat on. Meals are simple but plentiful, the prices low. A bowl of homemade vegetable soup costs 55$ (84¢); fried trout or sole, 230$ ($3.52). Chicken curry with rice is 200$ ($3.06), and pork chops with potatoes cost 310$ ($4.74). Round off your meal with some of the local cheese for 55$ (84¢) and a carafe of wine, also 55$.

The Beiras of Portugal unfold in the next chapter.

Chapter XIV

COIMBRA AND THE BEIRAS

  1. Leiria
  2. Figueira da Foz
  3. Coimbra
  4. Conimbriga
  5. Buçaco
  6. Curía and Luso
  7. Aveiro
  8. Caramulo
  9. Viseu
  10. Sêrra da Estrêla
  11. Castelo Branco
  12. Abrantes
  13. Guarda

FORTRESS TOWNS and feudal castles . . . undulating plains . . . steep wine-producing slopes . . . the mountain blocks of Estrêla . . . pinewoods and sand dunes . . . golden beaches . . . rice paddies and a lagoon . . . poplar-lined river banks . . . Roman ruins . . . a former royal forest . . . salt marshes . . . spas with radioactive springs . . . and water wheels sending rainbow-hued spray into the air.

  To many observers, the three provinces of the Beiras, encompassing the university city of **Coimbra**, are the quintessence of Portugal. Beira is a Portuguese word meaning edge or border. The trio of provinces includes **Beira Litoral** (coastal), **Beira Baixa** (meaning low), and **Beira Alta** (high).

  Embraced in the region is the **Sêrra da Estrêla,** Portugal's highest land mass and haven for skiers in winter, cool retreat in summer. The Mondego River, the mainstream of the region, is navigable, and the only major artery in Portugal that has its source within the boundaries of the country.

  The granite soil produced by the great range of sêrras blankets the rocky slopes of the Dão and Mondego River Valleys and is responsible for the wine of the region: the ruby red or lemon-colored Dão.

  In all, the Beiras are a subtle land, a sort of Portugal in miniature.

  Heading north from Estremadura, the first stopover is at:

1. Leiria

About 20 miles from Alcobaça, on the road to Coimbra, the town of Leiria rests on the banks of the Liz and spreads casually over the surrounding hills. From any point you can see the great **Castle of Leiria**, once occupied by Dinis, the poet king, and his wife, an Aragonese princess who became Saint Isabella. Tower-topped and imposing still, it has been extensively restored.

The castle lies on the summit of a volcanic outcrop, practically inaccessible to invaders. The Moors had their defense redoubt on this hill while they were taking possession of the major part of the Iberian Peninsula. The fortress was first taken for Portugal by its first king, Afonso Henriques, in the 12th century, and was twice recovered by him after the Moors had retaken it, the last recovery being definitive.

The church of the castle, as well as its palace, are pure Gothic. From an arched balcony, the city and its surroundings can be viewed.

To reach the castle, you may take either a car or a bus, right to the front door. On the way to the castle, you might also visit **St. Peter's Church**, dating from the 12th century. The fortress is open from 9 a.m. to 7 p.m. from July to September. During other months, it's open from 9 a.m. to 5:30 p.m. Admission is 15$ (23¢).

Around Leiria is one of the oldest state forests in the world. In about 1300 Dinis began the systematic planting of the **Pinhal do Rei**, with trees brought from Landes, France. He hoped to curb the spread of sand dunes which ocean gusts were extending deep into the heartland. The forest, still maintained today, provided timber used to build the caravels to explore the Sea of Darkness.

Many motorists find Leiria a convenient stopping point for the night. In the past, they lamented the town's lack of accommodations. That oversight has been rectified.

THE MEDIUM-PRICED RANGE: Hotel Euro Sol, Rua D. José Alves Correia da Silva (tel. 241-01), competes in position with the stone castle crowning the opposite hill. It's an 11-floor, well-styled hotel. All 52 bedrooms offer views, and compete successfully with any first-class hotel in the north. They are smartly simple, making use of built-in headboards and wardrobe walls of wood paneling. All of them contain private baths in forest green and white tile. In a single room, the half-board rate is 1700$ ($26.01); in a double, 2100$ ($32.13). Taxes and service are included.

The hotel is the social hub of Leiria, attracting business people to its rooftop lounge bar and dining room. Individual lunches or dinners cost $9.20 on the four-course table d'hôte. Lighter meals are offered in an adjoining snackbar. The restaurant entrance lounge is decorated with a museum-caliber contemporary wall hanging, depicting the story of the building of the castle. Time your visit to enjoy a dip and sunbathe in the open-air swimming pool, with its tiled terrace. There's a lower-level boîte for after-dinner diversions.

SÃO PEDRO DE MUEL: If you care to relax before plunging into the Coimbra heartlands, São Pedro de Muel is an undiscovered place. The bracing Atlantic breezes pervade the little village, perched on a cliff over the water. Although new villas have sprung up, the old quarter retains its cobblestoned streets.

The scattered rocks offshore create controlled beach conditions, rolling breakers and rippling surf. The beaches are white and sandy, running up to the

LEIRIA/FIGUEIRA DA FOZ

village's gray-walled ramparts. Paths border the cliffside, leading to the coastal lighthouse and a panoramic view.

The emerging resort is 14 miles west of Leiria and can be reached via a six-mile drive toward the sea from the glass-manufacturing center at Marinha Grande. Along the way you'll pass donkeys laden with twigs, the scent of pine mingling with salt air.

Staying in São Pedro de Muel

Hotel Mar e Sol (Sea and Sun), Avenida Marginal (tel. 591-82), is a three-story, modern hotel—starkly white, on a palisade above the beach at the residential edge of the village. This vantage point gives half of its 33 bedrooms views overlooking the ocean. It's for sun-and-sea addicts only, as there are no extravagant lounge facilities and only a minimum-size dining room. The compact bedrooms, all with private baths, are simply furnished with a mixture of contemporary and traditional pieces. The cost for one person, full board, is 1800$ ($27.54) in a sea-view room, 1600$ ($24.48) for the mountain vista. Two persons wanting full board pay 2600$ ($39.78) for the water-view rooms, 2400$ ($36.72) for the mountain vista. The second-class hotel, open all year, is immaculate and comfortable. (There is a 20% reduction in off-season, November to February.)

2. Figueira da Foz

Old villas on the sea compete with apartment houses. On the north side at the Beach of Brightness, Portuguese families frolic, the wealthier ones hitting the gambling casino at night. Back in the Old Town fishermen dry cod in the sun. Others make their living by reclaiming salt from the marshes, and having their wives scoop it up and carry it back to town in wicker baskets on their heads.

At the mouth of the Mondego River, Figueira da Foz literally means Fig Tree at the Mouth of the River, although how it got that name is long forgotten. North of Cascais and Estoril, Fig Tree is the best known and oldest resort along the Atlantic coastline of Iberia. Aside from its climate (city fathers claim that the sun shines 2772 hours annually), the most outstanding feature is the town's golden sandy beach, stretching for more than two miles. However, it's bordered by heavy construction equipment, and this creates a somewhat tawdry look.

Those who don't like the beach can swim in a pool sandwiched between the Grande Hotel da Figueira and the Estalagem da Piscina-Praia on the main esplanade. Should the beach crowds get you down, you can always go for a trek into the **Sêrra da Boa Viagem,** a range of hills whose summit is a favorite vantage point for photographers and sightseers.

Most visitors don't come to Figueira to look at museums, but there is one exceptional one, the **Casa do Paço** (tel. 221-58), the head office of the Associação Comercial e Industrial, a one-minute walk from the post office and esplanade. It contains one of the world's greatest collections of Delft tiles, numbering almost 7000 and most often depicting warriors with gaudy plumage (some blowing trumpets). The puce and blue tiles are detailed and subtly executed. The casa was the palace of Carlos I, who came here in the last century when Figueira was frequented by royalty, the equivalent of San Sebastian in Spain. The tiles may be viewed from 9:30 a.m. to 12:30 p.m. and from 2 to 5 p.m. all year (no admission is charged).

Bullfights are popular in season (remember, in Portugal the bull isn't killed and the animal's horns are padded). The old-style bullring operates from mid-July to September.

The **Grand Casino Peninsular,** open from May to October, features shows, dancing, a nightclub, and, of course, gambling salons.

Just two miles north of Figueira, bypassed by new construction and sitting complacently on a ridge near the sea, is **Buarcos,** a fishing village far removed from casinos and beaches. From the central square to the stone sea walls, it is pure and unspoiled. Cod dries in wire racks in the sun, streets faintly move with activity, and native girls with loaded baskets on their heads, arms akimbo, look out with bright eyes from under dark scarfs.

Figueira lies 80 miles south of Porto, 125 miles north of Lisbon, and 25 miles west of Coimbra. In accommodations it is well stocked in a number of price ranges beginning with:

Grande Hotel da Figueira, Avenida de 25 de Abril (tel. 221-46). This seven-floor modernized establishment stands right on the beach. Just walk across the esplanade and you have a clean sandy beach at your disposal, or go next door to the open-air saltwater swimming pool where you pay 35$ (54¢). The interior of the Grande is a world of marble and glass, more like a big city than a resort hotel. Some of the rooms on the sea (and these are preferable, of course) have glass-enclosed balconies similar to the miradores for which La Coruña, Spain, is known, but most have open balconies.

One English tripper called the furnishings in the rooms "sensible," and that seems fair enough. The 110 rooms contain private baths, with tariffs on the sea-view rooms set at 2900$ ($44.37) to 3350$ ($51.26) for half board for two persons, 2100$ ($32.13) to 2500$ ($38.25) for half board for one. The food is good and served in a lower-floor dining room. The price is 600$ ($9.18) for a table d'hôte luncheon or dinner. The hotel stays open all year, although you may be the only guest in the winter.

Hotel da Praia, 59 Rua Miguel Bombarda (tel. 220-82), is a first-class tourist hotel. It sits on a raised terrace along the beach esplanade, with its overscale, open-air swimming pool with three diving boards (one dubbed stairway to heaven). The 60 rooms and four suites contain private baths and are furnished with compact pieces, the draperies and counterpanes in Portuguese-designed fabrics. Depending on the size, placement, and plumbing, the full-board rate for two persons is from 2500$ ($38.25) to 3000$ ($45.90), while one person with full board pays 2000$ ($30.60) to 2400$ ($36.72). Meals are served in a walnut-paneled dining room, and there's a midget-size bar. The hotel is closed in winter.

Also opening onto the swimming pool and under the same management is the following recommendation:

Estalagem da Piscina, 7 Rua Santa Catarina (tel. 224-20). Totally modern, the estalagem of the swimming pool is a bargain. Here every bedroom has its own private bath and a balcony overlooking the water. Bright-patterned fabrics and herringbone floors enliven what would otherwise be a streamlined decor in the bedrooms. For full board, two persons pay 2500$ ($38.25) to 3000$ ($45.90), depending on the room; one person is charged from 1900$ ($29.07) to 2500$ ($38.25) for full board. Serving healthy-size and good-tasting meals, the dining room is wood paneled with indirect egg-crate lighting. A meal is 450$ ($6.89). Adjoining is a bar and sitting room overlooking the pool. Guests are welcomed from April to October 1.

IN BUARCOS—A BUDGET INN AND RESTAURANT: Restaurante-Pensão Teimoso, Estrada do Cabo Mondego (tel. 227-85), is a regional fish restaurant right on the shore, with a wing of modern rooms reserved for overnight guests. The Teimoso (a Portuguese word meaning stubborn or mulish) is family operated. The owner Antonio Perez Sanchez started many years ago with a simple waterfront restaurant. As business grew, he added more rooms. He attracts both visitors and locals alike who know of his bountiful meals. He's also known for his shellfish soup and regional entrees such as fresh bass baked in a tomato sauce and served with potatoes and other vegetables. In addition, he roasts kid and suckling pig. Fish soup is 20$ (31¢); fish stew (caldeirada), 180$ ($2.75). Clams go for 190$ ($2.91); roast veal, 220$ ($3.37); chocolate mousse, 25$ (38¢). The decor of the dining room is barren and aseptic, but the room has a fine view of the water.

There are 14 rooms, all with private baths. Tariffs range from 950$ ($14.54) to 1300$ ($19.89) daily. Some of the newer rooms, prettily decorated and equipped with private sun terraces overlooking the ocean, may go a little higher. It's hard to get in from July through September, so make reservations.

More charming, and a kilometer closer to town, is the **Tamargueira,** Estrada do Cabo Mondego (tel. 225-14), where you dine in an oval-shaped room with chandeliers made of ships' steering wheels. There's a fireplace at one end of the room, and the walls are decorated with typical plates and fishermen's nets. In good weather you can sit on the spacious terrace, from which you have a view of the sea. Menu specialties are caldeirada a mista a pescador, arroz de mariscos, (rice with shellfish), costela à Tamargueira, feijoada à Beirão. You can finish with a mousse or custard. Expect to pay from 400$ ($6.12) per person. There are also rooms available, furnished in simple New England style with bath. Doubles range from 1400$ ($21.42) to 1700$ ($26.01).

MONTEMOR-O-VELHO: Between Figueira da Foz and Coimbra, overlooking the fertile Mondego River Valley, is the historic village of Montemor the Old. Dating from the 12th century, the ruins of the **Castle of Montemor-o-Velho,** built by Sancho I, crown the hilltop. The main road runs scenically past villas, shrines, high walls, and churches. Narrow cobbled streets will lead you to the restored walls and ramparts, from which there is a fine vista of the valley.

The castle has witnessed many moments in Portuguese history—perhaps the most infamous being when Afonso IV sanctioned (according to historian Leonardo Coelho) the plot to kill Inês de Castro, mistress of the king's son. The castle is a moving medieval setting, especially when sparrows play among the air currents over its time-dated stones.

3. Coimbra

Black-caped students strumming guitars and violas and singing a serenade of their own *fado hilario* on narrow cobblestoned streets . . . tattered hems of fraying gowns that speak of heartbreak (some say conquest) . . . colored ribbons flying from the black student garb, signifying a young man's destined profession (but why violet for pharmacy?) . . . and a stream that "flows with the blood of the tortured Inês de Castro," who was crowned queen of Portugal, after her death. Coimbra, the most romantic city in Portugal, was the inspiration for the popular song "April in Portugal."

On the weather-washed right bank of the muddy Mondego, it is also the educational center of the country, its university the second oldest in the world, having been founded at Lisbon in 1290.

The students of Coimbra band together in republics, usually renting cramped buildings in the old quarters, some up many flights of winding stairs. An invitation to one of these student dormitories will give you an insight into Coimbra rarely experienced by the foreign visitor. Sometimes when they dart out in the morning in their black capes, they look like low-winging bats fleeing the belfry.

The republic isn't very democratic, run as it is on a strict seniority basis. A typical evening's bill of fare in a republic is likely to include grilled sardines, bread, and a glass of wine. If you do get an invitation, we hope the evening will be capped by the students presenting you with a fado concert. To show your gratitude, if you should happen onto an invitation, cigarettes are much appreciated.

Coimbra's charms and mysteries unfold as you walk up the Rua F. Borges passing under the Gothic **Arch of Almedina**, with its coat-of-arms. From that point, you can continue up the steep street, past antique shops, to the old quarter.

The focal point for most pilgrims, of course, is the **University of Coimbra**, entrenched in the town in 1537 on orders from João III. Among its alumni are Luís Vas de Camões (the country's greatest poet, author of the national epic, *Lusíadas*); St. Anthony of Padua (also the patron saint of Lisbon); even the late Dr. Salazar, once a professor of economics.

If you'll ignore the cold statuary and architecture on the Largo de Dom Dinis, you can pass under the 17th-century **Porta Pérrea** into the inner core of the academy. The steps on the right will take you along a cloistered arcade, the **Via Latina**, to the **Sala dos Capelos**, the site of graduation ceremonies. You can enter into a world with a twisted rope ceiling, a portrait gallery of Portuguese kings, walls of red damask, and the inevitable azulejos. Afterward, you can visit the **University Chapel**, decorated with an 18th-century organ, 16th-century candelabra, a painted ceiling, 17th-century tiles, and a fine Manueline portal.

Of course, the architectural gem of the entire town is the baroque **University Library** next door, with its chinoiserie motifs. It is one of the most elaborate (some say *the* most) decorative accomplishments in all of Portugal. Established between 1716 and 1723 and donated by João V, it shelters more than a million volumes. The interior is comprised of a trio of high-ceilinged salons walled by two-story tiers of lacquer-decorated bookshelves. The pale jade and sedate lemon marble inlaid floors complement the jeweled gold and emerald effect of the effusive gilt. The library tables are ebony and lustrous rosewood, imported from the former colonies in India and Brazil. Three-dimensional ceilings and the zooming telescopic effect of the room structure focus on the large portrait of João V, set against a backdrop of imitation curtains in wood. The side galleries, with their walls of valuable books in law, theology, and humanities of the 16th to the 18th century, the supporting pillars, the intricate impedimenta—all are dazzling, even noble. You may want to save the library for last; after viewing this masterpiece, other sights pale in comparison. Admission-free, it is open from 9 a.m. to 5:30 p.m.

To wind down after leaving the library, walk to the end of the belvedere for a panoramic view of the river—equal to scenes on the Rhine—and the rooftops of the old quarter. On the square stand a statue of João III and the famous curfew-signaling clock of Coimbra, known as "cabra," meaning goat.

A short walk down from the university square leads you to the **Machado de Castro Museum**, Largo Dr. José Rodrigues (tel. 237-27). Named after the greatest Portuguese sculptor of the 18th century, this museum is one of the finest in the north. Built as the Paço Episcopal in 1592, it houses a collection of ecclesiastical sculpture, especially polychrome, much of which dates from the 14th to the 18th century. The other exhibits include vestments, a relic of Saint Isabella (wife of King Dinis, the university's founder), paintings, antiques, coaches, silver chalices, old jewelry, embroideries, retables, and 16th-century ceramic representations of the Apostles and Christ. The museum is open from 10 a.m. to 1 p.m. and from 2:30 to 5 p.m., charging an admission of 30$ (46¢).

Across the way is the **New Cathedral (Sé Nova)**, but it isn't much admired. Dating from the 17th century, its interior is coldly neoclassic, although relief is provided by the baroque altars and a riot of angels playing horns atop the organ.

More interesting, however, is to walk down to the **Old Cathedral (Sé Velha)**. At the Largo da Sé Velha, the cathedral founded in 1170 enjoys associations with Saint Anthony of Padua. Crenellated and staunch as a fortress, it is entered by passing under a Romanesque portal. Usually a student is there, willing to show you (for a tip, of course) the precincts, including the restored cloister. The pride of this monument is the gilded Flemish retable over the main altar, with a crucifix on the top. To the left of the altar is a 16th-century chapel designed by a French artist, and containing the tomb of one of the bishops of Coimbra. The chapels house the sarcophagi of everybody from medieval kings to a lady-in-waiting to Saint Isabella, the patroness of Coimbra.

Reached by going up the Rua Visconde da Luz, the **Santa Cruz Church** is a former monastery, founded in the late 12th century when Afonso Henriques, Portugal's first king, ruled. However, its original Romanesque style gave way to Manueline restorers in 1507. The much popularized "Romeo and Juliet" story of Portugal, involving Pedro the Cruel and his mistress, Inês de Castro, reached its climax in this church. As mentioned, years after her murder at the hands of his father's assassins, Pedro, festering with vengeance, had her remains exhumed and set her upon a makeshift throne at Santa Cruz. The courtiers were forced to pay homage to her royal corpse, even kiss her hand.

The lower part of the walls inside are decorated with azulejos (tiles) sweeping along the walls like cutouts. Groined in the profuse Manueline manner, the interior houses the Gothic sarcophagi of Afonso Henriques, his feet resting on a lion, and that of his son, also a king, Sancho I. The pulpit nearby is one of the achievements of the Renaissance in Portugal, carved by João de Ruão in the 16th century. The choir stalls preserve, in carved configurations, the symbolism, mythology, and historical import of Portuguese exploration. With its twisted columns and 13th-century tombs, the two-tiered Gothic-Manueline cloister is impressive, with a fountain in the center.

The facade makes Santa Cruz one of the finest monuments in the land. Decorated like an architectural birthday cake, it is topped with finials and crosses, its portal top-heavy with a baroque porch, an unusual blending of styles. It's overadorned, but fascinating.

ACROSS THE MONDEGO: On the left bank lie four of the most interesting and least visited attractions of Coimbra. On the silt-laden banks of the Mondego stand the gutted, flooded, and crumbling remains of **Santa Clara-a-Velha,** a Gothic convent built in the 14th century. This church once housed the body of Coimbra's patron saint, Isabella, although her remains were transferred to the New Convent higher up on the hill. Rising out of the inrushing river, the Roman arches are reflected in the canals, evoking a Venetian scene. You can walk through the upper part only, as the river has already reclaimed the floor.

The former convent is reached by crossing the Santa Clara Bridge, and turning left down the cobbled street (Rua de Baixo).

Commanding a view of right-bank Coimbra, the **Convent of Santa Clara-a-Nova** provides a setting for the tomb of St. Isabella. Built during the reign of João IV, the convent is an incongruous blending of a church and a military garrison.

The church is noted for a rich baroque interior and Renaissance cloister. In the rear, behind a grille, is the tomb of the saint (usually closed except on special occasions). When her body was removed in 1677, her remains were well preserved, even though she died in 1336. Instead of regal robes, she preferred to be buried in the simplest habit of the order of the Poor Clares. At the main altar is the silver tomb (a sacristan will light it for you), which the ecclesiastical hierarchy considered more appropriate following her canonization.

At least for youngsters, the main attraction of Coimbra is **Portugal dos Pequenitos.** Called Portugal for the Little Ones, it is reached by crossing the Ponte de Santa Clara and heading out the Rua António Augusto Gonsalves. It's a mélange of miniature houses from every province of Portugal, including Madeira and the Azores, even the distant foreign settlements of Timor and Macão. It gives one the impression of a Dr. Lemuel Gulliver strolling across a Lilliputian world. The recreations include palaces, an Indian temple, a Brazilian pavilion (with photos of gauchos), a windmill, a castle, and the 16th-century House of Diamonds from Lisbon. From April to September, hours are from 9 a.m. to 7 p.m.; otherwise, from 9 a.m. to 5 p.m. Entrance to the garden is 20$ (31¢), but only 10$ (15¢) for the museum.

Farther up the road is the final attraction, the **Quinta das Lãgrimas** (the Garden of Tears; tel. 232-52). In "sweet Mondego's solitary groves," in the words of Camões, lived Inês de Castro, mistress of Pedro, and their three illegitimate children. Although the property of the Osôrio Cabral family since the 18th century, the gardens are visited by romantics from many countries. You can't go inside the house, but you can wander through greenery to the spring fountain, known as the Fonte dos Amores.

It was at the quinta on Camões "black night obscure" that the Spanish beauty was set upon by assassins hired by her lover's father. Pedro returned, finding her in a pool of blood, her throat slit. He would wait until he became king to seek his revenge.

So classic and enduring a Portuguese love story is it that who would want to suggest that it wasn't true, or that the murder didn't happen at the Garden of Tears? You can visit from 8 a.m. to 8 p.m. for an admission of 15$ (23¢).

HOTELS: Unfortunately, Coimbra is far better supplied with attractions than it is with hotels and restaurants. But there are the following recommendations.

The Medium-Priced Range

Hotel Bragança, 10 Largo das Ameias (tel 221-71), is a bandbox five-floor hotel, built next door to the railway station. Primarily catering to business people, it does a thriving trade in the summer season. A few of its bedrooms open onto balconies overlooking the main road. All of the 83 units contain private baths; the furnishings are utilitarian. The rooms vary in plumbing, size, and placement, as reflected by the tariffs. Two persons pay 1400$ ($21.42) to 2000$ ($30.60). Singles are priced at 1000$ ($15.30) to 1400$ ($21.42). Breakfast is included.

Astoria Hotel, 21 Avenida Navarro (tel. 220-55) on the river esplanade, overlooks the New Convent of Santa Clara on the left bank. Outside, it is decorative with an ornate dome—a crusted holdover from the 19th century.

The interior disappoints. Instead of potted plants or antiques, even reproductions, you're greeted with unfortunate modern. The overall impression of public and private rooms is that of being well worn. The beds too often have "army cot" springs, although the view from one of the balconies is pleasing. Furnishings are a bit tattered and sparse—don't forget to bring your own soap. In a double, the rate is $41.80 (U.S.). In a single with bath, the tariff is $39.50.

Meals in the corner dining room are appetizing; average cost, $13.60. The intimate bar in front of an open fireplace can be an attractive place for before- or after-dinner drinks. The bird-cage elevator, incidentally, can be temperamental.

READER'S PENSION RECOMMENDATION: "I'd like to recommend **Pensão Avis,** Avenida Fernão de Magalhaes (tel. 237-18), a ten-minute walk from the railway station. It is clean and centrally located. The cost is 545$ ($8.34) in a single room, with breakfast an additional 55$ (84¢). A hot shower is extra" (Mrs. Andrea Clerico, Napa, Calif.).

WHERE TO DINE: The **Dom Pedro,** 58 Avenida Emidio Navarro (tel 291-08), is an easily accessible first-class restaurant in the university town. Convenient for motorists, it has its own parking. English-speaking waiters will guide you through the menu of regional specialties, including such dishes as shrimp cocktail, 275$ ($4.21); tomato soup, 55$ (84¢); roast pork, 210$ ($3.21); veal caçador, 280$ ($4.28); and fruit tart, 65$ (99¢). To accompany your repast, why not order the regional vinho verde (the green wine)? The pleasant atmosphere is made even more so by the friendly and polite service.

Pinto d'Ouro (Golden Chicken), 68 Avenida João das Regras (tel. 250-08), is one of our favorite dining rooms in the district, offering a view from its perch on the other side of the Mondego. Alluring is a bar serving snacks or just a small coffee, a place for a rest. The little tables in the nook adjoining the dining room are preferred. A good dish is clams in a wine garlic sauce, costing 180$ ($2.75). On one recent occasion, I began a fine regional repast with caldo verde, followed by a very large portion of roast cabrito (goat) with french fries, rice, and fresh spinach, concluding with a huge amount of vine-ripened strawberries with sugar, as well as coffee. Vinho verde accompanied the meal, and, as an added surprise, I enjoyed fresh goat cheese as an appetizer. Service was fast and friendly, and the entire bill came to only 450$ ($6.89).

Café Nicola, 35 Rua Ferreira Borges (tel. 220-61), is a plain, but modern little second-floor restaurant over a delicatessen and pastry shop. It's spartan inside, even the flowers are usually wilted, but tradition is to be respected. Students gather here for strong coffee.

The window tables provide box seats for looking at the teeming street. The food is good but plain, and the platters of fish or meat are usually large enough to be shared by two. The cuisine, as might be expected, is regional. A nourishing bowl of the soup of the day costs only 30$ (46¢). Two favorite dishes include grilled cod with potatoes for 220$ ($3.37) and cutlets of pork, also with fried potatoes, for 210$ ($3.21). The house specialty is frango churrasco (barbecued chicken) with french fries, costing 200$ ($3.06).

Democratica, 7 Travessa do Rua Nova, is a stark budget restaurant popular with students and travelers on a shoe-string budget. A few steps off the main drag (make the first left on main street after passing the Café Santa Cruz), this place couldn't be simpler, with a little dining room, tiles on the walls, and the kitchen in the back. The servings are large. A soup costs only 25$ (38¢);

pescada (hake), greens, and potatoes go for 180$ ($2.75); and a rice pudding is 30$ (46¢). Wine costs 55$ (84¢) a bottle.

Mandarim, 13 Praça da República (tel. 268-26), near the university, serves simple local fare in a snackbar atmosphere. It's also popular with students, as are all cafés in the area. On a mezzanine is the dining room, serving soups for 30$ (46¢); trout meunière, 210$ ($3.21); salmonetes (red mullets), 260$ ($3.98); roast chicken with spicy sauce, 210$ ($3.21); pork chops, 180$ ($2.75); mousse, 40$ (61¢); and flan, 30$ (46¢).

A COFFEEHOUSE: Santa Cruz, Praça 8 de Maio, is an old-fashioned coffeehouse-restaurant, popular not only with young students, but with Portuguese gentlemen of yesteryear. The Santa Cruz appears to have been converted from a chapel belonging to the church next door. The bar and meat refrigerator counter are probably where the altar once stood. You sit on tooled leather and brass-studded chairs, drinking or dining at dark octagonal tables with marble tops. The walls are darkly paneled, and there is stained glass.

The mood is casual, with cigarette butts on the floor, but a lively spirit dominates. Students often sing fado here. It's a stronghold of Iberian tradition, holding out against modernization. The coffee is black and unblended, and the shots of cognac overflow the glass rim. Stick to the black coffee and don't eat the pastries. You can also have a meal here, ranging from 130$ ($1.99) to 270$ ($4.13) for a Santa Cruz steak.

READER'S SELECTIONS: "North of Coimbra is the little hamlet of **Mealhada,** a one-industry town devoted to selling roast suckling pig. We had a luncheon at **Pedro dos Leitoes,** and afterward saw the ovens in a separate building where the roasting is done" (Burton Ashford Bugbee, Brookfield, Conn.). [*Author's Note:* The town lies off the main road; the roast suckling pig appears on the menu in Portuguese as leitão assado, and can cost as little as 400$ ($6.12).]

4. Conimbriga

One of the great Roman archeological finds of Europe, the pre-Celtic village of Conimbriga lies less than ten miles southwest of Coimbra. Conimbriga was occupied by the Romans in the late first century. Since then and up to the fifth century A.D., the town knew a peaceful life. The site lies near a Roman Camp, but the town never served as a military outpost.

Roman mosaics of almost perfect quality have been unearthed in diggings in the area. The designs are triangular, octagonal, and circular—executed in blood-red, mustard, gray, sienna, and yellow. Motifs include beasts from North Africa and delicately wrought hunting scenes. Mosaics displaying mythological themes can be seen in one of the houses. Subjects include Perseus slaying the Medusa and the Minotaur of Crete in his labyrinth.

The diggings display to good advantage the complex functional apparatus of Roman ingenuity. Columns form peristyles around reflecting pools, and the remains of fountains stand in courtyards. There are ruins of temples, a forum, patrician houses, water conduits and drains. Feeding the public and private baths of the town were special heating and steam installations with elaborate piping systems. Conimbriga even had its own aqueduct.

The site is open from 9 a.m. to 1 p.m. and 2 p.m. till sunset, charging an admission of 20$ (31¢) on weekdays, free on Saturday and Sunday. If you don't have a car, you can reach the site by taking a bus from Coimbra to Condeixa. The bus, José Maria dos Santos Transports, leaves Coimbra at 9:30 a.m. and 1:30 p.m., returning at 1:50 and 6:10 p.m. Conimbriga lies about a mile away, reached either by walking (through an olive grove) or by hiring a taxi in the village.

5. Buçaco

The rich, tranquil beauty of the forests of Buçaco, 17½ miles from Coimbra, were initially discovered by a humble order of barefoot Carmelites, following dictates of seclusion as prescribed by their founder. In 1628, they founded a monastery at Buçaco, using materials from the surrounding hills. Around the forest they erected a wall further to isolate their lives and to keep women out.

These barefoot friars had a special love for plants and trees, and each year they cultivated the natural foliage and planted specimens sent them from distant orders. Buçaco had always been a riot of growth: ferns, pines, cork, eucalyptus, and pink and blue clusters of hydrangea. But the friars introduced such exotic additions as the monkey puzzle, a tall Chilean pine with branches so thick it confuses monkeys which climb in it.

The pride of the forest, however, remains its stately cypresses and cedars. Such was the beauty of the preserve that a papal bull, issued in 1643, threatened excommunication to anyone who destroyed a tree. Even though the monastery was abolished in 1834, the forest remains preserved. Filled with natural spring waters, the earth bubbles with many cool fountains, the best known of which is **Fonte Fria** (cold fountain).

The forest of Buçaco was the battleground where Wellington defeated the Napoleonic legions under Marshal André Masséna. The Iron Duke slept in a simple cloister cell right after the battle. A small, adequate **Museum of the Peninsular War** reconstructs much of the drama of this turning point in the Napoleonic invasion of Iberia. It's about a half mile from the hotel. The very slim museum consists of engravings plus a few pistols. Entrance is 20$ (31¢).

In the beginning of the 20th century, a great deal of the Carmelite monastery was torn down to make way for the royal hunting lodge and palace hotel of Carlos I and his wife Queen Amélia. He hardly had time to enjoy it, as he was assassinated in 1908. His son, the two-year monarch Manuel II, did use it as a hideaway for his affair with Gaby Deslys. Luigi Manini, an Italian architect, masterminded this neo-Manueline structure of parapets, buttresses, armillary spheres, galleries with flamboyant arches, towers, and turrets. After the fall of the Braganzas, wealthy tourists took their afternoon tea by the pools underneath the trellis hung with blossoming violet wisteria.

One of the best ways to savor Buçaco is to make the 1800-foot ride to **Cruz Alta** (high cross) by car through forests, past hermitages. At the summit is a view considered by many to be the best in Portugal.

LIVING IN DELUXE SPLENDOR: Palace Hotel do Buçaco, Mata do Buçaco (tel. Mealhada 931-01). "Good-bye forever," Queen Amélia said on her last visit to Buçaco in 1945. The government had permitted her a sentimental journey (in a limousine with ladies-in-waiting) to visit all the places where she had spent her reigning years before her flight to England in 1910. The palace is an architectural fantasy. The designer borrowed heavily from everyone: the Jerónimos Monastery at Belém; the Doge's Palace at Venice; the Graustark Castles of Bavaria.

Now a hotel, the palace is set in the center of a 250-acre forest. The structure is still intact and impressive, especially its grand staircase with ornate marble balustrades, 15-foot-wide bronze torchères, and walls of frescoes, some painted by Carlos. There are several drawing rooms and salons, a potpourri of architectural whims. Of course, many of the furnishings were removed, replaced with a mixture of antiques, reproductions, and modern and not-so-modern (the latter especially dominant in the bedrooms).

In 1910, the Swiss head of the kitchen, the king's cook, persuaded the government to let him run the palace as a hotel. For half board, two persons pay $97 (U.S.) to $108, depending on the room. For one person, half board costs $68 to $79. In some cases, the baths were once the adjoining rooms for a valet or maid. Now they have every convenience, sometimes including tubs on raised platforms.

The dining room is a theatrical success, the tables set with fine stemware and silver. Of note is the Gothic wooden ceiling and the view through two 20-foot-wide arched windows onto the gardens and the encircling neo-Manueline terrace. Even if you're not staying here, you should stop in for lunch or dinner, costing $15.50 for a table d'hôte. A typical repast: first, gnocchi, followed by sea bass with vegetables. For a third course, perhaps filet of veal, tender and sweet, will be served with a rosette of potatoes, topped by dessert, an assortment of cheese and crackers, and the fresh fruit of the season.

6. Curía and Luso

"Luso for the liver; Curía for the kidneys" goes the saying. Two of the most popular health resorts in the country. Curía and Luso lie in heartland Portugal. Thermal spa enthusiasts flock here generally from June 1 through October, some arriving on the mainline Sud-Express (Lisbon–Paris).

The spa at **Luso** is just two miles from Buçaco. The gold-colored facade of the Grande Hotel das Termas nestles in a valley in the midst of abundant foliage with a backdrop of rolling forests. Luso is known for the potency of its radioactive springs. In addition, the grounds feature tennis courts, indoor and outdoor swimming pools, hydrotherapeutic treatments, a radiation room, and laboratory facilities for all forms of analyses.

The secluded atmosphere and surroundings of **Curía** make for an enjoyable holiday. In the foothills of the Sêrra de Estrêla, Curía is in the winegrowing district of Bairrada, 7½ miles from Buçaco. Its waters have been compared to the famous ones of Vittel.

LUSO—A TOP SPA HOTEL: Grande Hotel das Termas, Rua dos Banhos (tel. 934-50), is a sprawling establishment offering 157 rather dated but roomy bedchambers, each with private bath. Habitués praise its thermal spa facilities. The emphasis is on good health. You can swim in a 150-foot Olympic pool, lounge and sunbathe on the surrounding grassy terrace, or relax under the weeping willows and bougainvillea arbor. There are hard tennis courts, mini-golf, and, at night, a boîte for dancing.

The accommodation is comfortable in well-proportioned bedrooms, with matching furnishings. Some of the rooms open onto private terraces, with views of the tree-covered valley. The bed-and-breakfast rate in a double room ranges from 1475$ ($22.57) to 1900$ ($29.07); in a single, from 1065$ ($16.30) to 1300$ ($19.89). Lunch or dinner is an extra 625$ ($9.56). The meals are large (the cuisine is both regional and international), and they are served in a muraled dining room. Guests are welcomed from May 2 to October 31.

CURÍA—A SPA HOTEL: Hotel das Termas (tel. 521-85) is imbued with the most festive air of any of the spa hotels. It is approached via a curving dirt road leading through a park-like setting with lacy shade trees—quiet and secluded.

Open all year, it offers facilities for health and relaxation, including a free-form swimming pool encircled with orange trees and umbrella tables. In the park a rustic wooden bridge leads over a lake to woodsy walks and the tennis courts.

The lounge is relaxed and casual, furnished with provincial pieces and hand-loomed rugs. The bar is actually a living room. The dining hall, with its parquet floors, brick fireplace, and overscale painting, is like a tavern, especially when filled with guests who aren't hesitant to chat from table to table. Even the bedrooms have a homey feeling, with lots of floral chintz, wooden beds, and walls of wardrobe space. Of the 39 rooms, 35 contain private baths. The cost of a room ranges in price from 850$ ($13.01) for a small single to 3000$ ($45.70) for a double suite.

7. Aveiro

The town on the lagoon, Aveiro is crisscrossed by myriad canals, spanned by low-arched bridges. At the mouth of the Vouga River, it is cut off from the sea by a long sand bar protecting clusters of islets. The architecture is almost Flemish, a good foil for a setting of low willow-reed flatlands, salt marshes, spray-misted dunes, and rice paddies. Oxen rigged with ornate harnesses trundle through the streets, passing racks of cod drying in the sun.

On the lagoon, brightly painted swan-necked boats traverse the waters. Called *barcos moliceiros,* these flat-bottomed vessels hold fishermen who harvest seaweed used for fertilizer. They are ever on the lookout for eels, a specialty of the region, which they catch in the shoals studded with lotus and water lilies. Outside the town are extensive salt pits, lined with pyramids, fog-white in color.

Houses built on stilts are often topped with finials and terracotta eagles. The surrounding lagoons and many secret pools dotting the landscape make a boat excursion (inquire at the Tourist Office) reminiscent of a trip into bayou country. Not only are the natural wonders unspoiled, but there is an uncommon wealth of artistic treasures as well.

The **Convent of Jesus,** at Praça do Milenário, is hailed as the finest example of the baroque style in Portugal. At the convent, the Infanta Santa Joana, sister of João II and daughter of Afonso V, took the veil in 1472. Her tomb, an inlaid rectangle of marble quarried in Italy, attracts many pilgrims. Its pale delicate pinks and roses lend it the air of a cherub-topped confection.

The convent, owned by the state and now the **Aveiro Museum,** displays a lock of the saint's hair, her belt and rosary, and a complete pictorial study of her life. A portrait of her, painted in intonaco, is exceptional. But what characterizes the convent is its carved giltwork, lustrous in the chapel, despite the dust.

In this setting is an assortment of 15th-century paintings, royal portraits of Carlos I and Manuel II (the last two Braganza kings), antique ceramics, and 16th-, 17th-, and 18th-century sculptures. There are also some well-preserved 18th- and 19th-century coaches and carriages. After viewing all this, you can walk through the cloisters with their Doric columns. The museum is open from 10 a.m. to 5 p.m., charging 15$ (23¢), except on entrance-free Saturday and Sunday. Closed Monday.

On the same square is the 15th-century **Church of St. Domingos,** with its blue and gold altarpieces and egg-shaped windows flanking the upper part of the nave. The facade, in the Gothic-Manueline style, is decorated with four flame finials. To the right (facing) is a bell tower. There are other churches as well, especially the **Chapel of Senhor Jesus das Barrocas,** built in the shape of an octagon in 1722.

After a meal of stewed eels and a bottle of the hearty Bairrada wine, you might wish to explore some of the settlements along the lagoon, specifically **Ilhavo**, three miles south of Aveiro. Here you can stop off at the **Municipal Museum of Ilhavo**, 13 Rua Serpa Pinto, an unpretentious gallery of the sea that offers an insight into a semiaquatic people. Inside you can see seascape paintings, boating paraphernalia, fishing equipment, ship models, and other exhibits.

From Ilhavo, drive along an avenue of olive trees to **Vista Alegre**, the village of the Vista Alegre porcelain works, which you enter during working hours through a gateway on a tree-shaded square. Founded in 1824, the establishment is noted for its delicate decorated china.

Back in Aveiro, the leading accommodations are the following:

THE BUDGET RANGE: Hotel Imperial, Rua Dr. Nascimento Leitão (tel. 221-41), is Aveiro's most important and most up-to-date hotel. It attracts the youth of the community who gravitate to the lower lounge social center for drinks and TV, or to the open and airy dining room with its two walls of glass. They look forward to their Sunday dates here—the 450$ ($6.89) dinners, or the drinks on the open terrace.

Many of the bedrooms and each of the lounges overlook the garden of the Aveiro Museum, the old convent described earlier. All the rooms contain private baths, as well as individually operated central heating. A double goes for from 1700$ ($26.01) to 1900$ ($29.07). A single rents for 1200$ ($18.36) to 1900$ ($29.07). The furnishings are in a satisfactory contemporary idiom, with many built-in features, and the color schemes are pleasant. A few suites are available, including a living room and a twin-bedded chamber with bath, costing 2250$ ($34.43).

The **Arcada Hotel**, 4 Rua Viana do Castelo (tel 230-01), enjoys an enviable position in the center of Aveiro, with a view of the river traffic in the canal out front. In the summer, you can see from your bedroom window the white pyramids of drying salt on the flats. Although the hotel has been modernized, the classic facade of beige and white has remained. Many of the rooms open onto balconies, and the rooftop is decorated with ornate finials.

The hotel occupies the second, third, and fourth floors of the old building. Based on the plumbing you require, the tariffs range between 1300$ ($19.89) and 1500$ ($22.95) in a double with bath, 950$ ($14.54) in a bathless double. A single with bath ranges from 900$ ($13.77) to 1050$ ($16.07). Breakfast, included in the rates, is the only meal served.

AN INN BETWEEN THE SEA AND THE LAGOON: Pousada da Ria, Bico do Muranzel, Torreira-Murtosa (tel 483-32), is a private world on a promontory, surrounded on three sides by water. Between the sea and the lagoon, it is a modern nearly all-glass building, with rows of balconies on its second floor. To reach the government-owned pousada, you can go by boat from Aveiro (boats are not for cars, only for passengers). Or take a long drive via Murtosa and Torreira until you reach the sandy spit. Along the way, you'll pass Phoenician-style boats in the harbor, sand dunes, pine trees, and houses on high-tide stilts.

The entrance to the inn has a long lily pond and planter with a stairway bridge leading to the marble-floored dining room on the upper level. The waterside terrace opens onto views of the brightly colored sails of the fishing craft or of the sunsets over the lagoon. The inn has a clubhouse atmosphere and is popular with holiday-seeking Portuguese families who quickly book the ten rooms.

Accommodation with full board is recommended: 3600$ ($55.08) for two persons, 2500$ ($38.25) for a lone traveler. The rooms are compact, furnished with space-saving built-in pieces—a semimodern decor with an emphasis on comfort. If you're stopping over for lunch or dinner (highly recommended), table d'hôte meals are priced at 450$ ($6.89) to 600$ ($9.18), plus service and tax. The chef's specialty is caldeirada a ria, a savory fish stew. A sunny Sunday is likely to be bedlam; otherwise, it's a peaceful haven.

AN INN IN THE VOUGA VALLEY: Pousada de Santo António, Mourisca de Vouga, Serém (tel. 522-30), is an overscale villa resting on a rise above the Vouga River. Near the main Lisbon–Porto highway, it is a fine location. The meadowlands and river valley are lush, filling the dining and living-room windows with the colors of three-dimensional postcards. Large natural flagstones make up the front courtyard, ushering you into a renovated villa decorated like a warm provincial inn.

All 13 rooms have their own baths and contain striped rugs and floral bedspreads. High headboards on the country-style beds and patterned stone floors give an air of simple comfort. The full-board tariff is 2100$ ($32.13) in a single, 2700$ ($41.31) in a double.

At dinner, whether you begin with a caldeirada or caldo verde, be sure to request (if available) the ovos moles (luscious egg sweets) typical of the area, along with fresh cheese from the mountains and the fruits of the valley. A lunch is 450$ ($6.89); dinner, 600$ ($9.18); and breakfast is included in the price of the room. The pousada is about 157 miles north of Lisbon.

8. Caramulo

Set against a background of mimosa and heather-laden mountains, this tiny resort is a gem. It is also a modern art center unique in Portugal. Founded by Dr. Abel de Lacerda, the bulk of the collection of the **Caramulo Museum** is made up of gifts from private donors. Many paintings, such as works by Salvador Dali and Picasso, were donated to the museum by the artists themselves. Other painters represented include Dufy, Léger, Chagall, Miró, and Graham Sutherland. Of special interest is a painting of St. John the Baptist by the 16th-century Portuguese artist, Grão Vasco, and a sultry nude by Henrique Medina (1934).

There is an assortment of modern and ancient sculpture, ranging from the matronly bovine *Maternidade* by José Clara (1955), to an ethereal *Lady of Fátima* (1946) by Canto de Maya, to a grimacing Chinese gnome (c. A.D. 386-577). The celebrated Tournai tapestries depict the trials of the Portuguese explorers in India. Other exhibits include enamel work, jewels and pendants, and fine 17th-, 18th-, and 19th-century Indian, Chinese, and English porcelain.

Adjoining is an **Automobile Museum**, housing at least 60 veteran and vintage cars, including a 1910 Benz, a 1909 Fiat, a 1927 Bugatti sports roadster, and a 1902 Darracq. These antique cars are restored to purring condition. A few early bicycles, one dating back to 1865, and motorcycles are also exhibited. In addition to the ground-floor car display area, workshop, and library, there is an upper gallery where more vehicles are arranged. Access to this is gained by a wide staircase at one end of the banister formed of crankshafts and camshafts from vintage engines. The admission is 20$ (31¢) to each museum. Both are open daily from 10 a.m. to 6 p.m.

These attractions are 50 miles north of Coimbra, midway between Aveiro and Viseu.

In accommodations Caramulo is provided with an inn.

Estalagem de S. Jerónimo (tel. 862-91) is placed high as an eagle's nest, near the crest of a mountain ridge. Its panoramic view is comparable to sights encountered in Switzerland and Austria. The inn is like a spread-out chalet, with a design not only aesthetically pleasing, but comfortable. You park your car and enter through a lower reception lounge, noticing a group of paintings casually hung. One is an original Dufy. You ascend to the reception, living, and dining rooms—with one salon flowing into another. In winter guests sit by the copper-hooded fireplace.

Beyond the wooden grille is a pleasant dining room, the window wall providing views of the hills. Dinner is candlelit, and guests sit on tall provincial chairs sampling the country-style cooking served by mountain girls. If you're just dropping in, a table d'hôte luncheon or dinner goes for 600$ ($9.18). There are five courses, and the helpings are generous.

The six double rooms are small but attractive, all with private bath. Portuguese antiques and reproductions are used—ornate iron headboards, a slab of wood as a console. Wide windows open onto vista-scanning private balconies. The cost for a double with shower is 1600$ ($24.48). Actually, it's more sensible for two persons to take full board at 2000$ ($30.60) to 2400$ ($36.72).

A POUSADA ON THE COIMBRA–GUARDA HIGHWAY: The **Pousada da Santa Bárbara**, at Povoa das Quartas–Oliveira do Hospital (tel. Oliveira do Hospital 522-52), is a most convenient stopover on the main Coimbra–Guarda highway. Not luxurious, it is suitable for those seeking a mountain spot. There are only 17 double rooms, but each comes equipped with a bath and phone. One person is charged 1500$ ($22.95) daily for a room with breakfast, and two persons pay 1600$ ($24.48). If you're motoring and would like to stop by for lunch or dinner, a set meal in the provincial dining rooms costs 450$ ($6.89) for luncheon, 600$ ($9.18) for dinner. For those staying over, a continental breakfast is included.

STAYING IN CANAS DE SENHORIM: The hotel at Urgeiriça is set amid the forested countryside near Canas de Senhorim, and is connected with all the major cities of Portugal by fine highways. The hotel lies about 25 miles from the Estrêla Mountains, popular with winter sports enthusiasts, and is 186 miles north of Lisbon, 102 miles from Porto, just 50 miles northeast of Coimbra, and 16 miles from the country town of Viseu.

Hotel Urgeiriça, Urgeiriça, Canas de Senhorim (tel. 672-67), is really more of a spread-out country club than a hotel. It's a place where nature lovers can live and dine in comfort and style, on 25 acres of vineyards and pine trees, without roughing it. The unique hotel is operated by João de Oliveira. Many discriminating guests know of this retreat, including Queen Elizabeth of England.

The bedrooms are in the grand style and are part of the reason for staying here. All individually decorated, they are often furnished with antiques, such as carved and tufted headboards (some reaching up to the ceiling), spinet piano desks, and Queen Anne chairs. For full board in a room with private bath, two persons pay 2700$ ($41.31) to 3800$ ($58.14), depending on the size, quality, and placement of the room. Around the impressive building are chalets where guests such as Sir Anthony Eden have stayed.

The lounge-bar is a favorite and there are many nooks and salons for conversation and rest. You can take your drinks in front of the wide granite fireplace, with its slow-burning chunks of pine root, or at the carved oak bar. Meals are served in the vast and impressive dining hall, lined with five palace-size portraits of English kings. Even if it's only for a meal, you should stop over. The cost of a table d'hôte is 400$ ($6.12); the bread is made on the premises; some of the wine is made with grapes grown in the farm vineyards; and much of the fruit comes from the hotel's own orchards. Of course, the bowls of freshly picked flowers are brought in directly from the garden.

The Urgeiriça is a winner for relaxing tired nerves. The more athletic are drawn to the tennis court, the rough nine-hole golf course, and the swimming pool.

9. Viseu

The capital of Beira Alta province, Viseu, is a quiet country town. But it is also a city of art treasures, palaces, and churches. Its local hero is an ancient Lusitanian rebel leader, Viriato. At the entrance of Viseu is the **Cova de Viriato,** where the rebel, a combination Spartacus and Robin Hood, made his camp and plotted the moves which turned back the Roman tide.

Some of the country's most gifted artisans ply their timeless trades in and around Viseu. Where racks creak and looms hum, the busy weaver women create the unique quilts and carpets of Vil de Moinhos. Local artisans of Molelos produce the region's provincial pottery, and women with nimble fingers embroider feather-fine, light bone lace.

There is much to see and explore at random in Viseu: the cubistic network of tiled overlapping rooftops and entwining narrow alleyways; the encroaching macadam streets; the river where the women pound out the day's wash upon smooth flat stones in the clear water. However, if your time is limited, head at once to the **Ardo da Sé,** one of the most harmonious squares in Portugal, often referred to as the showplace of Viseu. There you'll find the town's three leading buildings: a cathedral, a museum, and a church.

The severe Renaissance facade of the **Viseu Cathedral (Sé)** evokes a fortress. Two lofty bell towers, unadorned stone up to the balustraded summit with crowning cupolas, can be seen from almost any point in or approaching the town. The second-story windows at the facade, two rectangular and one oval, are latticed and symmetrically surrounded by niches containing religious statuary.

You can go first into the two-story Renaissance cloister on the right, adorned with classic pillars and arcades faced with azulejos. The interior of the Sé is basically Gothic, but is infused with Manueline and baroque decorations. Plain, slender Romanesque clusters of columns line the nave, supporting the vaulted Manueline ceiling with its nautically roped groining. The basic color scheme inside plays brilliant gilding against muted gold stone. However, the full emphasis is centered on the Roman arched chancel, climaxed by an elegantly carved retable above the main altar. The chancel makes ingenious use of color counterpoint, with copper, green gold, and brownish-yellow complementing the gilt work. The ceiling is continued in the sacristy.

Next door to the cathedral is the **Museum of Grão Vasco,** named after the 16th century painter, also known as Vasco Fernandes. The major works of this Portuguese master are displayed here, especially *La Pontecôte,* with the lance-like tongues of fire hurtling toward the saints, some devout, others apathetic.

Besides the works of this fine Portuguese primitive and his school of followers, the museum also has a moving and tender *St. Raphael* by the outstanding 18th-century sculptor Machado de Castro. Enameled reliquaries, Byzantine artifacts, liturgical apparel, a Manueline monstrance dating from 1533, and a chalice with vermeil pendants from 1626 are a few of the items on view.

Across the square from the cathedral is the palatial **Misericórdia Church** from the 18th century. Its pristine facade contrasts with the cathedral's baroque granite decorations, spirals, large windows and portal frames, balustrades, and matching towers.

In accommodations the town is well-equipped:

Grão Vasco (tel. Viseu 235-11) in the heart of town and surrounded by gardens and parks, is built motel fashion, with the bedroom balconies overlooking the swimming pool. After days of driving in the hotel-lean environs, it's a pleasure to check into this top-grade, sophisticated establishment, more suited to a resort than a provincial town. Popular with both business people and socialites, it also attracts tourists, especially in the summer months. The decor is colorful contemporary and elegantly designed.

The bedrooms are usually large, utilizing Portuguese traditional furnishings, enhanced by flowering chintz and softly muted colors. The price for a double starts at 2400$ ($36.72). For a single, the rate is 1500$ ($22.85). The dining room has Mediterranean-blue chairs, a baronial stone fireplace, plus a good cuisine, with many international dishes. If you're just dropping in you can sample an à la carte luncheon or dinner.

Hotel Avenida, 1 Avenida Alberto Sandaio (tel. 234-32), is a personalized small hotel right off the Rossio, the main plaza of town. Inside, it is the domain of the personable Mário Abrantes da Motto Veiga, who has combined his collection of antiques from Africa and China with pieces of fine old Portuguese furniture. He's created a friendly aura, bound to attract admirers of his eclectic taste. Each of the bedrooms varies in size, character, and price; and most of the 33 rooms have private shower or bath.

The nightly rate is 1050$ ($16.07) to 1200$ ($18.36) for one person, 1700$ ($26.01) to 2100$ ($32.13) for two. There's a nice room (210B) with a high coved bed and an old refectory table and chair, including an adjoining chamber with a wooden spindle bed and a marble-topped chest, like a nun's retreat. Meals in the plain, family-style dining room are well prepared and generous.

10. Sêrra da Estrêla

From January to May, the great granite Sêrra da Estrêla is the winter sports center of Portugal. In summer, campers, trout fishermen, and mountain climbers dominate. Once almost completely isolated from the rest of the country, the major points of interest in the Sêrra da Estrêla are now linked by roads.

The land is also the home of the Cão de Sena, or "dog of the mountain." The area is a major sheep-raising district as well and is infested with wild animals, especially packs of wolves. Reader A. Wayne Magnitzky writes: "The throats of the sheep dogs are protected from the teeth of wolves by an iron collar with long sharp spikes. Imagine the wolf's surprise when he attempts to throttle the dog and ends up with a long spike through his mouth!" The dogs survive by sucking ewes' milk.

One major auto route is from Covilhá to Seia via **Torre,** the latter the highest point in Portugal, at an altitude of 6500 feet. From its summit, a panoramic view unfolds.

SÊRRA DA ESTRÊLA/CASTELO BRANCO/ABRANTES

Covilhã is on the southern flank of the Sêrra, near the Zêzere Valley. A town of steep and narrow streets, it is known for its Monument to Our Lady of the Conception, a 25-foot statue of the Virgin Mary carved out of granite. Steps also carved out of granite lead to the statue. The sculptor was killed near this spot in a car accident, shortly after completing his work. The town is at its liveliest from June 22 to 25 when people from the neighboring hills come in for the Fair of São Tiago, and sell handicrafts.

Covilhá used to be known as the "dormitory" for the **Penhas da Saude** sports area, at 4500 feet above sea level.

Now Penhas da Saude has the most attractive hotel in the district, the **Hotel Sêrra da Estrêla** (tel. 240-91). Hand-woven fabrics, a copper-hooded fireplace (around which skiers gather in winter), modern paintings, and warm, natural colors—all these elements combine to create an outstanding first-class hotel in a remote district. A single room with breakfast rents for 1400$ ($21.42), increasing to 2000$ ($30.60) in a double. Even more expensive suites are available. The food is the finest in the district. A complete meal costs 450$ ($6.89). Although international dishes are offered, you may want to sample some of the regional specialties, especially the rabbit. Of course, the proper finish for any meal is the queijo da Sêrra, a strong cheese made from ewes' milk.

Instead of continuing to Seia, an alternate route is to go along the Rio Zêzere to **Manteigas**, a little town with several balconied 17th-century houses. It lies between mountain ranges. From there you can take an excursion to the **Poço do Inferno**, or Hell's Mouth. This is a gorge with waterfalls. The distance from Manteigas along an unsurfaced and narrow road is about four miles.

Near Manteigas the government runs a pousada, the **Pousada de São Lourenço** (tel. 471-50), a stone inn at an altitude of 5000 feet. It lies 9 miles to the north of Manteigas, 2 miles from Penhas Douradas, and 15 miles to the south of Gouveia. Rooms are comfortably rustic. A double with bath costs 1600$ ($24.48), breakfast included. If you're stopping over, you can order a country-style dinner for 600$ ($9.18), a luncheon for 450$ ($6.89).

11. Castelo Branco

The capital of Beira Baixa, Castelo Branco lies near the Spanish frontier. The city is beautiful and often filled with flowers. Shoppers may want to acquire some of the multicolored embroidery done by the women of the town. Some of the designs haven't been changed since the 17th century.

The gardens of the former Bishop's Palace are well kept and formal, with a statue-bedecked staircase, clipped box hedges, and numerous fountains. The statues are lifesize, depicting the Apostles, the kings of Portugal, as well as signs of the zodiac.

Adjacent are the ruins of a Moorish castle, rebuilt in the time of King Dinis.

The town takes about an hour to explore. Most motorists seem to stop just for a look at the gardens, then continue on to Abrantes.

12. Abrantes

After passing a dramatic view of the Tagus at Rodão, you arrive at Abrantes in central Portugal. The river must be crossed again to gain entrance to the town. Here, you see the ruins of a Roman bridge extending into the Tagus.

High on a hill, the old fortress was rebuilt during the reign of King Dinis. To reach the fortifications, you must go through a labyrinth of narrow streets. Once at its belvedere, a panoramic view of the valley unfolds.

The **Hotel do Turismo,** Largo de São António (tel. 256), overlooks the town on one side and the castle and the mountains on the other. An Olympic-size pool, belonging to the town but available at no charge to hotel guests, is adjacent to the Turismo. Room rates depend on location and view. Including breakfast, prices range from 1700$ ($26.01) to 2100$ ($32.13). The half-board range is from 2400$ ($36.72) to 3200$ ($48.96) for two persons. Reader A. Wayne Magnitzky writes, "This hotel serves the best bread I've eaten anywhere, certainly in Portugal." A complete meal is offered for 600$ ($9.18).

13. Guarda

Between Porto and Salamanca, a university city in Spain, Guarda is called "the highest town in Europe." Built at an altitude of some 3400 feet, it is some two-thirds of a mile above sea level, in the eastern foothills of the Serra da Estrêla. In the Beira Alta, it stands 28 miles from Vilar Formoso, 136 miles from Porto, and 212 miles from Lisbon. Today it is a pleasant summer resort.

Founded in the latter part of the 14th century, its **Sé (cathedral)** deserves some of your time. Originally the architects planned to build it in the Gothic style. However, by its completion in the mid-16th century, Renaissance, even Manueline, stylistic changes appeared in the plans. Betraying at least two different styles, the facade facing north is the best for viewing. Inside, you'll find a Renaissance altarpiece, a fine Gothic tomb, a "Last Supper" altarpiece, but more interesting than that is to take the stairs at the corner of the south transept. These will lead you to the rooftop of the cathedral where you'll have an excellent view of not only Guarda but the Sêrra da Estrêla.

Other sights include the Ferreiros Tower, an 18th-century Misericórdia Church, and from many vista points views of the Mondego and Zêzere Valleys below. There are also many ancient churches and old houses, some dating from the 16th century. You'll see many of these around Praça Luís de Camõës (Cathedral Square).

FOOD AND LODGING: Hotel de Turismo, Avenida Coronel Orlindo de Carvalho (tel. 222-06), is a first-class choice, centrally located in a traditional building. Rooms are well furnished and comfortable. Singles rent for $28 (U.S.), going up to $38 in a double. Children traveling with their parents can be housed in the same room for another $10. However, most guests prefer to stay there on the half-board plan, costing $40 in a single, $62 for two persons. A good Portuguese and international cuisine is featured.

READER'S LODGING SELECTION: "We stayed at **Residência Filipe,** 9 Rua Vasco da Gama (tel. 226-59). This was adequate, but there are no frills. It is right in the town, one block from the central plaza and cathedral and almost opposite the Ferreiros Tower. There is also a dining room which serves a good meal. A double with private shower rents for 1250$ ($19.13). Set dinner with wine is 450$ ($6.89)" (Dr. C. H. Chaffey, Dapto, Australia).

After this excursion into provincialism, a return to the atmosphere of a minor metropolis seems in order. Although Lisbon is the capital, denizens of Porto claim their hometown is the first city, the backbone of the country.

Chapter XV

PORTO AND ITS ENVIRONS

1. The Hotels
2. Where to Dine
3. What to See and Do
4. Exploring the Coast
5. Deep in the Environs

PORTUGAL'S SECOND CITY, Porto, is the home of port wine, traditionally drunk in tulip-shaped glasses. The grapes that produce the wine come from the vineyards along the arid slopes of the Douro River Valley, many miles inland. At harvest time in autumn, the hills echo with the trilling of flutes, the cadence of drums.

The wine is brought to lodges at **Vila Nora de Gaia,** across the river from Porto, where it is blended, aged, and processed. In the past it was transported on flat-bottomed boats called *barcos rabelos.* With their long trailing rudders and sails flapping in the breeze, these boats with tails skirted down the Douro like swallows. Nowadays, they have virtually given way to the unglamorous train or even the truck.

Porto not only gave its name to the port wine, but to the country, the word deriving from the old settlement of Portus Cale, which became Portugal. The Douro, from Rio do Ouro or river of gold, has always been the source of Porto's life blood. Although it enjoys many sunny days, at times Porto has been called a gray city of mist and rain.

It's set on a rocky gorge that the Douro cut out of a great stone mass. Of it, Ann Bridge wrote, "The whole thing looks like a singularly dangerous spider's web flung across space." Porto is most interesting in the old quarter, the **Alfândega.** Here the steep narrow streets, hardly big enough for a car to pass through, and the balconied houses evoke Lisbon's Alfama, although the quarter has its own distinctive character. The Alfândega preserves the timeless color of many of the old buildings and cobbled *ruas* lining the river bank.

Connecting the right bank to the port wine center of Vila Nova de Gaia and the lands south, is the **Maria Pia Bridge,** an architectural feat of Eiffel, completed in 1877. Two other bridges span the Douro, including the **Dom Luís I Bridge,** completed in 1866 by a Belgian engineer inspired by Eiffel. The other one is bright and contemporary, the **Arrábida Bridge,** totally Portuguese in concept and execution and one of the largest single-span reinforced-concrete arches in Europe.

Many write off Porto as an industrial city with some spectacular bridges, but that assessment is unfair. The provincial capital and university seat sits on the cover of its own artistic treasure chest, as we will soon see.

GETTING THERE FROM LISBON: At a distance of 175 miles from Lisbon, Porto is easily reached by train. TAP, the Portuguese airline, provides quicker connections between the two cities as well. There are daily flights all year.

1. The Hotels

There has long been a lack of top-rate accommodations in this, the capital of the north. Some so-called first-class hotels can only be recommended in the direst of emergencies. However, in recent years, the outlook was brightened considerably by the following top-notch establishments.

Dom Henrique, 179 Rua Guedes de Azevedo (tel. 257-55), is the biggest hotel in town. Eighteen stories high, and containing 102 rooms, this octagonal colossus towers over the whole city and provides some spectacular views from its 16th-floor bar-lounge and 15th-floor dining room. The decor, modern to the hilt, is somewhat impersonal and cold. The rooms are plastic and wood, all with terraces, rather narrow beds, and white furniture. What the hotel lacks in style it makes up for in conveniences. Somewhat away from the center, the Dom Henrique charges from 2100$ ($32.13) for a single room, from 2700$ ($41.31) in a double, breakfast included. Meals are à la carte, averaging around 700$ ($10.71) a repast. Clinton Gamble, Fort Lauderdale, Fla., writes: "Nowhere in Portugal will you find more kind personal attention and service."

Infante de Sagres, Praça D. Filipa de Lencastre (tel. 281-01), will coddle you in Edwardian comfort. Catering to those who prefer the glamorous old style, it gives its clients a chance to savor brass beds, crystal chandeliers, and personalized service. The reception lounge sets the pace, with its two-story-high stained-glass window and baronial staircase. Done in oak, the main-level bar is small enough to be intimate, large enough to be comfortable.

Breakfast is served in an Adam-style room, with ornate plaster work and shellback chairs. Dining in the main room is recommended, even if you aren't staying here. The large room is in the formal French tradition, with shimmering crystal, wood paneling, and service that is right in every detail. The food, both regional and international dishes, is among the best in the city; a complete luncheon or dinner starts at 750$ ($11.48) on the à la carte menu.

The bedrooms were created for large-scale living, a world of hand-loomed rugs, 19th-century furniture, and elaborate marble baths. The average double room rents for 3800$ ($58.14), increasing to 5000$ ($76.50) in a deluxe double. In all cases single occupancy costs 8% less.

Albergaría Miradouro, 598 Rua da Alegria (tel. 278-51), is like an eagle's nest, a slim 13-floor baby skyscraper built atop a hill outside the main part of the city. One of the newest hotels on the city's skyline, the Miradouro offers vista-scanning rooms (you can watch ships laden with port making their way to the open sea). Small-scale, the public rooms are tasteful, often dramatic. The lower bar, with its red velvet chairs, is decorated with wall tiles from Japan and Portugal. Two plush elevators whisk you to an upper bar, with walls opening onto a view, gold glass curtains, mosaic decorations, and fire-engine-red carpeting. The top-floor restaurant is fine enough to be featured separately in the dining recommendations detailed below.

The bedrooms are without fault. Even the most fastidious traveler usually responds to the streamlined style. The more expensive corner rooms are preferred, of course. In these, two walls have built-in wardrobes and chests (with a built-in pair of beds); the others are all glass, curtained with filmy draperies. In all the rooms, you'll find a vestibule, abundant luggage storage, a valet stand, desk, and sitting room. Bright colors are used without hesitation: golds, blues, and burnt orange. There are 30 rooms, all with private baths. One person pays from 1250$ ($19.13) to 1750$ ($26.78); two persons, 1500$ ($22.95) to 2300$ ($35.19). Breakfast only is served. The facilities include a subterranean garage.

Hotel Castor, 17 Rua das Doze Casas (tel. 286-91), is a personal statement, and a fine one. Maurício Macedo and his son have created a cultured, comfortable world, to be savored by those who enjoy individuality with style. The son, Doctor Francisco Macedo, is an enterprising decorator, managing one of the better antique stores in the north around the corner from his hotel. The hotel siphons off many of his best pieces, used well in the reception and lounge areas. In fact, the Castor is a glorified antique store, as every piece is for sale. In addition, a large salon has been set aside as an art gallery for contemporary painters, the artist contributing a painting for having been granted the premises.

The bedrooms have ornate antique or reproduction beds, original paintings, old mirrors, hand-screened printed fabrics covering the walls, centrally controlled-heating, and individual chimes for the maid. There are 62 rooms, all with baths, designed with tiled walls. Singles range from 1800$ ($27.54); doubles go for from 2000$ ($30.60) to 2700$ ($41.31).

Meals are well prepared by a talented cook. You sit in red, high-back Queen Anne chairs, enjoying well-prepared dishes and personal service. Predinner drinks are available in the stone-walled bar, with its troubador theme. The Castor has a disco in modern decor.

Albergaría S. João, 120 Rua do Bonjardim (tel. 216-62), is in a class by itself: the only hotel-residência of its type to be rated deluxe by the government. Such a designation shows what deep imprint human warmth can make upon a limited framework, especially when the owners have a high taste level, a certain flair, plus a concern for the welfare of their guests. Accomplishing this is the Baldaque family, who own the top floor of a modern building right in the heart of Porto. You ascend in an elevator and are greeted by a friendly receptionist.

The living room is inviting with its fireplace nook, deep sofa, and antiques, such as a grandfather clock. The main corridor leading to the bedrooms is like an art gallery, with old tapestries, high-back 18th-century chairs, engravings, and large copper bowls of flowers. The bedrooms—only 14 in all, each a double—combine modern with traditional furnishings, reserving a section for a sitting area. Every room contains its own pink and white marble bath. The tariffs are based on size and outlook. One person pays 750$ ($11.48) to 900$ ($13.77); two, 1000$ ($15.30) to 1200$ ($18.36)—including a continental breakfast.

Grande Hotel da Batalha, 116 Praça da Batakham (tel. 205-71), is highly favored by international buyers of port wine. A substantial business person's hotel, it has comfortable rooms and an excellent restaurant where one can order Portuguese specialties. Each of the 148 bedrooms has a radio, telephone, and tiled bath. A single rents for 2000$ ($30.60), a double for 2400$ ($36.72) daily. The bedrooms have a lighter decorative treatment than the public rooms, although the lounge, the bar, and the restaurant are quite adequate. So far I've not been able to understand the artist's meaning of the vivid, large mural in the cocktail lounge. The hotel is in the center of the city.

Albergaría de São José, 172 Rua de Alegria (tel. 38-02-61), is a modern, corner, first-class inn, with all the facilities you'll need for a pleasant stay in Porto. While the lobby, the lounge, and the regional drinking bar are furnished in a contemporary idiom, the bedrooms have antique-style furnishings that connect you with regional Portugal. The carved mahogany beds are old world in their elegance. Each room has selected music, telephones, and a tiled bath. A single costs 1250$ ($19.13) daily, a double 1700$ ($26.01) daily. If you'll accept a shower instead of a tub, doubles rent for 1500$ ($22.95) daily. There's a private hotel garage.

Grande Hotel do Porto, 197 Rua Santa Catarina (tel. 281-76), right in the heart of the town, offers comparatively moderate rates. It has been given a face lift, and contains 100 bedrooms, each with bath, central heating, and air conditioning.

Best of all are the brightly painted rooms, all modern, with many built-in tables. A single rents for $31.30 (U.S.). Depending on size and facilities, doubles are priced at $37.50. A suite costs $73. Breakfast is included.

Many Portuguese families are attracted to this hotel, drawn by the tariffs and near grandeur. Along the main-corridor lounge, with its row of marble pillars and crystal chandeliers, are small lounges. At one end is a modern bar, intimate with stained-glass windows and black leather booths. There's a fine old-world dining room with four chandeliers, a mosaic wooden floor, and ornate curtains.

Hotel do Imperio, 130 Praça da Batlha (tel. 268-61), is a recently constructed 100-room hotel, close to the railway station in the heart of the city. It's rather well designed and attractive for a railway-station hotel, with a striking interior decor. Bedrooms are well thought out, tasteful, with color-harmonized schemes. Units come with wall globe lights, bedside tables, telephones, central heating, and private tiled baths. The cost of a single is $35 (U.S.); a double, $45—including breakfast. A separate meal costs $15. Children up to 8 years are granted a 50% reduction.

Albergaría Girassol, 133 Rua Sá da Bandeira (tel. 218-91), is a modest little upper-floor inn, set over an excellent restaurant. The hotel offers 18 nicely designed and furnished rooms with private baths. Each bed has built-in headboards. Rooms at the rear are quieter. Including breakfast, a single rents for 1000$ ($15.30) daily and a double goes for 1200$ ($18.36) daily. There's a small TV lounge with soft leather chairs, all tasteful and cozy. You can have your morning meal in a little breakfast room.

READERS' LODGING SELECTIONS: "Porto-Mar, 167 Rua Brito Capelo, in Matosinhos, is a good place to stay. Matosinhos is the sardine capital of the world and only a streetcar ride away from the railway stations in Porto. We paid 1100$ ($16.83) for double with bath, which included a large room with a view of the Leixoes harbor and the ocean. Meals were copious and good, served in a huge dining room for about 300$ ($4.59) for two, including wines. The large public market is nearby and a treat to visit, with its flowers, live chickens, fish, and other items" (Mrs. Marie Bockerdorff, Ottawa, Canada). . . . "In Porto, I stayed at the **Pensão de Acúcar** 262 Rua do Almada (tel. 224-25), which was very reasonable. A bathless double, very clean, with a wash basin and venetian blinds at the windows, goes for 670$ ($10.25), including taxes and service. Larger doubles with bath range from 790$ ($12.09) to 1060$ ($16.29), the latter tariff for a suite. English is spoken by the personnel, and a simple but good continental breakfast is included in the price" (J. Barrie Jones, Paulersbury, Northamptonshire, England).

2. Where to Dine

When Prince Henry the Navigator was rounding up the cattle in the Douro Valley for his men aboard the legendary caravels, he shipped out the juicy steaks and left the tripe behind. Faced with the tripe, the denizens of Porto responded bravely and began inventing recipes for it. To this day, they carry the appellation of tripe eaters, and it has become their favorite local dish. To sample the most characteristic specialty of Porto, you can order *tripas à moda do Porto* (tripe stewed with spicy sausage and string beans). Of course, the city offers other viands, and quite good ones at that, at any of the following recommendations:

Restaurante Escondidinho, 144 Rua de Passos Manuel (tel. 210-79), is an elegant regional-style tavern, popular with the leading port wine merchants and the English. The name means hidden or masked. The entrance alone is a clue, a facade in burnt orange tile framing an arch leading to the L-shaped dining room.

Inside, it's a world of time-blackened beams and timbers, a corner baronial stone fireplace, and carved wooden shelf brackets holding a collection of antique Portuguese ceramics. The chairs are just right for a cardinal, or at least a friar, with their intricate carving and brass studs. The waiters are old world, yet proud of the prevailing informality. They feel free to speak their mind, candidly telling you the day's best dishes from the kitchen. Take their word.

The shellfish soup at 140$ ($2.14) and the charcoaled sardines for 125$ ($1.91) are always reliable. The chef's special dishes include hake in Madeira sauce, 450$ ($6.89), and a chateaubriand for two, 320$ ($4.90). A main course might be augmented by a tomato salad at 120$ ($1.84). Desserts include a kirsch omelet for 275$ ($4.21) or an orange pudding at 100$ ($1.53). Telephone for reservations. Closed Sunday.

Portucale Restaurante, 598 Rua da Alegria (tel. 278-61), perches on the rooftop of the Albergaría Miradouro. Seemingly on the highest point in town, outside the heart of the city, it offers wide views of the river, the boats, and rooftops. Two elevators zip you to the 13th floor, from which you ascend to the dining room via a spiral staircase, crossing a tiny lily and fish pond. Despite the infinity of the panoramic sweep, the restaurant is fairly intimate, with tables set with fine silver, china, and flowers. There's an appetizing pastry cart.

The hand-woven hanging is by Camarinha, the artist who designed the à la carte menu. Specialties of the house include bacalhau (dried codfish) a marinheiro, 315$ ($4.82); cabrita à serrana (kid in wine sauce), 380$ ($5.81); smoked swordfish, 280$ ($4.28); lomos do pescado, 320$ ($4.90); steak flambé, rice, and mushrooms, 390$ ($5.97); and homemade cakes, 100$ ($1.53).

Restaurante Chinês, 38 Avenida Vimara Peres (tel. 289-15), is Porto's leading Chinese restaurant. Housed in a modern building at the entrance to Dom Luís I Bridge, it is an incongruous combination of the new and the old. Setting the mood are traditional Chinese lanterns, three wide bamboo fans, and a dragon mural. In the spacious two-level dining room, soft music is played in the background, a good complement to the authentic dishes.

Appetizers include egg flower soup, 50$ (77¢); fried wanton, 100$ ($1.53); and fried almonds, 55$ (84¢). Main courses (which can be shared) include sweet-and-sour meatballs, 225$ ($3.44), and duckling with pineapple, 250$ ($3.83). The price of fried prawns varies according to the time of year. For dessert, there are many appetizing choices, such as fried bananas with honey for 55$ (84¢).

Aquário Marisqueiro, 163 Rua Rodrigues Sampaio (tel. 222-31), is one of the finest seafood restaurants in Porto—actually two, connected by a central kitchen. Its location is within sight of the City Hall, and close to either of two leading hotels: the Infante de Sagres and the Albergaría de S. João.

Marine fare reigns supreme at this "aquarium." Soup made from boiling the shells of mariscos is a good beginner for 45$ (69¢). Main fish orders include cod at 220$ ($3.37). An excellent fish dish is clams in the Spanish style, but the house specialty is an açorda (a type of bread panada) of shellfish. The prices of these two dishes vary according to the season. Sole costs 320$ ($4.90) and trout with ham, 210$ ($3.21). Closed Sunday.

Garrafão, 53 Rua António Nobre, Leça da Palmeira (tel. 995-16-60), a traditional restaurant in the suburbs, overlooks the Praia Boa Nova. Attractively situated, with a pleasant decor, it seats about 100 and serves mainly seafood. The prices of the seafood specialties vary according to the season. The Garrafão is becoming known also for its wine cellar, containing a large selection of the best Portuguese wines. À la carte specialties feature a shrimp omelet for 200$ ($3.06); shellfish soup for 80$ ($1.22); grilled sole, 280$ ($4.28); veal dishes, 280$ ($4.28); and caramel custard, 50$ (77¢). The restaurant has a pleasant dining room with windows over the beach.

Neptuno, 133 Rua Rodrigues Sampaio (tel. 279-37), as its name indicates, specializes in seafood, although all other dishes are savory. The decor is simple and modern, with white walls, and fruit on the counter. Nonfish specialties are the bife na frigideira, 265$ ($4.06); veal scallopine, 205$ ($3.14); chicken with ham, 200$ ($3.06); and tripe Portuguese style, also 200$. Try the shellfish soup for 55$ (84¢), and, more expensive, the lobsters, shrimp, and clams. Desserts include a soufflé with kirsch or rum, 110$ ($1.68), or a rum omelet, also 110$.

Taverna do Bebobos, 21–25 Cais da Ribeira (tel. 31-35-65), is perhaps the oldest (founded 1876) and smallest restaurant in Porto, directly on the riverside dock. Women sell fish on the quay, and overhead are lines of laundry waving in the wind, fluttering from wrought-iron balconies. Inside, the ground floor has a service bar with every sort of knickknack on its little tables. A narrow open staircase leads to an intimate dining room upstairs with a corner stone fireplace, a coved ceiling, an iron scale filled with sprouting onions, a five-foot-high coffee mill, farming hay forks and shovel, strings of garlic pigtails, brass and copper pans, ships' lanterns, and a flamboyantly painted pottery crèche. On the tables are hunks of dark, crusty "mother earth" bread, and when served, the portions are large enough to be shared. To begin your meal, you might order a hearty bowl of caldo verde at 35$ (54¢) or else a plate of grilled sardines, 100$ ($1.53). For a main course, we'd suggest either grilled trout with ham, 175$ ($2.68); regional codfish, 185$ ($2.83); or else pork prepared in the Alentejana style (that is, with a savory clam sauce), 200$ ($3.06). A fruit salad at 50$ (77¢) finishes the meal nicely. Because of the small number of tables, it's necessary to have your hotel call and make a reservation for you. The owner also has the antique shop next door, which provides an endless source for decorations for his restaurant.

A Brasileira, 116 Rua do Bonjardim (tel. 271-46), is an art deco coffee-house, the virtual social center of Porto, plus a first-class restaurant and a bustling snackbar. In the restaurant part of the complex you can order cream of shellfish soup at 40$ (61¢), followed by such main dishes as roast chicken at 150$ ($2.30); grilled trout, 160$ ($2.45); or veal liver, 170$ ($2.60); topped off by chocolate mousse at 50$ (77¢).

Abadia, 22 Travessa de Passos Manuel, off Rua do Atteneu Comércial do Porto (tel. 287-57), stands on a short street with a patio entrance. It has an open dining mezzanine. The cook specializes in fresh fish dishes, including such typical fare as Spanish clams, 175$ ($2.68); small fried sardines, 120$ ($1.84); and baked fish, 200$ ($3.06). The grilled red mullet at 480$ ($7.34) is especially nice, as is the paella or Valencian rice, 160$ ($2.45). Soups begin at 40$ (61¢). Large and bustling, the restaurant serves from noon to 10 p.m.

3. What to See and Do

Exploring the sights of Porto requires some probing. But your discoveries will compensate for the effort. A good beginning is:

THE CATHEDRAL DISTRICT: The Sé (cathedral), at the Terreiro de Sé, has grown and changed with the city—that is, until about the 18th century. Originally founded by a medieval queen and designed in a foreboding, basically Romanesque style, it is now a patchwork-quilt monument to changing architectural tastes. Part of the twin towers, the rose window, the naves, and the vestry are all elements of the original 13th-century structure. However, the austere Gothic cloister was added at the end of the 14th century and was later decorated with azulejos depicting events from the Song of Solomon. Opening off the cloister is the Chapel of St. Vincent, built in the closing years of the 16th century.

The main chapel was erected in the 17th century, and in 1736 the baroque architect Nicolo Nasoni of Italy added the north facade and its attractive loggia. The monumental altar is flanked by twisted columns, the nave by fading frescoes. In the small baroque Chapel of the Holy Sacrament (to the left of the main altar) is an altarpiece fashioned entirely of silver, the work so elaborate that the whole piece gives the illusion of constant movement.

Outside on the Cathedral Square is a Manueline-style pillory and a statue of Vimara Peres, the warrior of Afonso III of León, who captured ancient Portucale in 868. To the side, also on the same square, is the 18th-century **Archbishop's Palace,** sequestered for municipal offices. Noted for its granite-cased doors and windows, it also contains an exceptional stairway inside.

In back of the cathedral is one of the most charming *típico* streets of Porto: the **Rua da Dom Hugo.** Along its route, you'll pass the **Chapel of Our Lady of Truths.** It's invariably closed, but you can peek through the grillwork at the gilded rococo altar, with a statue of the Virgin at the center.

Down the same street, you'll reach the **Casa Museu de Guerra Junqueiro.** This famous Portuguese poet lived between 1850 and 1923. The house was built by the Italian architect Nicolo Nasoni (1691–1773). Each room is arranged to preserve the private art collection and memorabilia of Guerra Junqueiro.

The collection includes Georgian and Portuguese silver, Flemish chests, Italian, Oriental, Spanish, and Portuguese ceramics, and ecclesiastical wood and stone carvings. Joining the many examples of religious sculpture are an Italian Renaissance desk, metal plates said to have been made in Nürnberg, a 16th-century Brussels tapestry, as well as interesting Portuguese furniture.

Casa Museu de Guerra Junqueiro is open every day except Sunday and Monday from 10 a.m. to noon and from 2 to 6 p.m. Admission is free.

In the same district, you can cross the busy artery, the Avenida Dom Afonso Henriques, and head down the Rua Saravia de Carvalho until you reach the Largo de 1 de Dezembro and—

The **Church of Santa Clara:** Although completed in 1416, the interior was transformed by the impassioned artists of the 17th century, masters of woodwork and gilding. The facade remains squat and plain, however. The number of man-hours invested is staggering to contemplate. There is hardly a square inch that isn't covered with angels, saints, cherubs, patterned designs, and great knobbed bosses. All this dripping gilt is an architectural scramble of rococo and baroque, one of the most exceptional examples in Portugal. The clerestory windows permit the sunlight to flood in, making a golden crown of the upper regions.

If the keeper of the keys takes a liking to you, he'll take you on a behind-the-scenes tour of the precincts. In the Tribute Room, for example, you'll see a devil carved on the choir stalls. Through it all is a hodgepodge of a lot of bad, fading paintings, some not even hung—just propped casually in the corner. But it's intriguing to see what lies beyond all the glitter and glamor out front.

Sights Near the Cathedral

Passing along the water, you can look for a front row of buildings along the **Rua Nova da Alfândega.** Underneath these structures is an arcade that is a continuous row of Romanesque arches. Perhaps they faced the waterfront until the street was built at a high level like a dike.

Up from this major artery is one of the most colorful sectors of Porto. If time allows, it's good to wander through some of the back streets (often stepped), where the city's poorest people live. In other places, the area might be called a slum or ghetto, but in Porto, the district has such style—vegetable- and meat-stuffed arcaded markets, churches, museums, monuments, even such elegant buildings as the Stock Exchange and the British Factory—that it retains both punch and glamor.

A good point to begin your exploration is on the main **Praça do Infante Dom Henriques,** named after the Porto-born Henry the Navigator, who launched Portugal on its Age of Discovery. At this square, you can visit the big covered food market, where tripe is sold in great quantities.

Facing the square (entrance on the Rua da Bolsa) is the **Stock Exchange,** housed in the imposing 19th-century Palácio da Bolsa. It is known for its Moorish Hall, a much-modified pastiche resembling a room in the Alhambra at Granada. The walls, ceiling, and balcony are a gilded mass of patterns and geometrical configurations. The pastel blue column bases glow in sunlight filtered through intricately latticed octagonal skylights and floral side windows.

The **Basilica of St. Francis,** reached by steps up from the waterfront and opening onto the Rua da San Francisco, was built in the Gothic style between 1383 and 1410. But in the 17th and 18th centuries it underwent extensive rococo dressing. The vault pillars and columns are lined with gilded woodwork: cherubs, garlands of roses, cornucopia of fruit, and frenzied animals, entwined and dripping with gold. Many of the wide-ribbed Gothic arches are made of marble resembling the Italian forest-green serpentine variety. The marble almost seems to fade into an easy blending with the gray granite columns and floors.

The Romanesque rosette dominates the facade, whose square portal is flanked by double twisted columns. Above the columns, a profusely ornamented niche contains a simple white statue of the patron saint. In the rose window, 12 mullions emanate from the central circle in apostolic symbolism, ending in a swag-like stone fringe. The steps seem to spill out into the square fan-like along the base of the curved walls.

Next door you can visit the **Museum of St. Francis.** The sacristan estimates that 30,000 human skulls have been interred in the cellars. Even assuming that he may be exaggerating, this dank building was once the burial ground for rich or poor. Nowadays, it is a catacomb unique in Portugal.

A section of it looks like an antique shop. There are paintings, too, one of St. Francis of Assisi worshiping Christ on the Cross. Oddities include some of the first paper money printed in Portugal and an 18th-century ambulance

that was really a sedan chair. The Sala de Sessoes adds a note of unexpected
elegance. Built in the rich baroque style, it is now a meeting hall with a Louis
XIV table and João V chairs. Wherever you go in the room, the painted eyes
of framed bishops follow you, like Big Brother watching. The museum charges
only 5$ (8¢) for admission (but tip the guide), and it is open from 10 a.m. to
noon and from 2 to 5 p.m. daily, except Monday.

Also reached by steps up from the water is one of the city's leading
museums, sheltered on a *típico* square and rarely visited. Culture seekers are
usually beset with escudo-hungry children who live in the jumble of dwellings
nearby.

Museum of Ethnography and History of Douro Litoral, Largo S. João
Novo, celebrates the arts, handicrafts, and culture of the Douro River valley.
It's a rustic potpourri of spinning wheels, looms, and animal and fish traps
nostalgically evoking the simple lifestyle of the peasant. Roman coins and other
artifacts remind one that legions from far afield once marched in and settled
on the banks of the river.

Earthenware jugs from Vita-da-Feira, gold filigree work, a bas-relief of a
provincial cottage, and a three-faced Christ are among the exhibits, along with
primitive puppets, provincial bedrooms, ceramics, dolls in regional costume,
ship models, decorative ox yokes, weathervanes, cannon balls, spears, antique
sarcophagi, even a wine press. Any or all of the above may be viewed from 10
a.m. to noon and from 2 to 5 p.m. daily, except Monday, for a 20$ (31¢)
admission.

THE TOP MUSEUM: The **Soares dos Reis National Museum,** Rua de Dom
Manuel II (tel. 271-10) was created in 1833, by order of the king, Dom Pedro
IV. At the opening to the public in 1840, it was called Museu Portuense. One
hundred years later, it was declared a National Museum and was dedicated to
Soares dos Reis (1847-1889), the noted sculptor from Porto, and the name was
changed. *Desterrado* and *Flor Agreste* are remarkable sculptures by this artist,
but good portraits and allegorical figures can be seen in the same gallery.

In the foreign painters collection, you'll find Dutch, Flemish, Italian, and
French works, including two François Clouets portraits (1522–1572) and land-
scapes by Jean Pillement (1727–1808). Above all, the most representative and
united display is that of the Portuguese 19th-century painters, particularly from
the Porto School. Henrique Pousão (1859–1887) and Silva Porto (1850–1893)
are represented by fine naturalistic work.

Decorative arts are displayed in the museum, including ceramics, glassware, gold and silver work, furniture, and other objects.

The museum is open daily, except Monday, from 10 a.m. to 5 p.m.,
charging an admission of 15$ (23¢), except on entrance-free Saturday and
Sunday.

WHERE PORT IS KING: Across the river from Porto, in **Vila Nova de Gaia,**
are the port wine lodges. Like the sherry makers at Jerez de la Frontera, Spain,
the establishments are hospitable, inviting guests to tour their precincts.

The largest of these lodges, the **Real Vinícola,** is a prime example of the
art of wine making. It is here that the blending, aging, and selection processes
take place. Dating from 1889, the warehouses contain specially treated oaken
vats where the wine is sterilized, pasteurized, blended, and aged. The wine is
bolstered with brandies and vintage wines to maintain its character.

The vast cellars, dark, cool, and moist, are the resting place for port which ranges in age from 5 to 70 years. However, the oldest bottle in the company's museum is dated 1765. In one tunnel section alone there are two million bottles of Portuguese sparkling wines.

If you wish to learn the intricacies of production and development of port wine, from tasting to decanting, arrive and announce yourself. You'll be guided through the cask- and vat-lined cellars and tunnels and into the laboratories. If you can resist breaking away to tap a keg, there's a free sample of port, matured for 25 years, at the end of the tour. You can purchase wicker baskets packed with fine wine at the company tavern.

OTHER SIGHTS: There are many other monuments and sights worth exploring in Porto, especially the 18th-century **Torre dos Clérigos,** the landmark tower of the city, rising to a height of nearly 250 feet (it can be scaled for a fee of 25$ or 38¢). The tallest tower in Portugal, it was designed by an Italian named Nicolo Nasoni. From its summit, there's a view of the Douro River, the valley gorge, and the far reaches of the city.

PORTO AFTER DARK: The real fado is in Lisbon, but Porto does offer a club or two where you can hear these typical songs and listen to guitar music. Perhaps the best is **Arcadas Dom Vaz,** 167 Rua de Miragaia (tel. 38-07-37), right on the waterfront in a slummy part of town. Drinks begin at 400$ ($6.12).

While in Porto, you shouldn't miss having coffee in one of the old time "Brazilian" cafés. Our favorite is the **Majestic Café,** 120 Rua de Santa Catarina, one of those ornate places where burghers and poets congregated. It still oozes charm. The wood-and-mirror decor, jasper pillars, and sculpted cherubs over pilasters are eye-openers. Rows of leather-backed sofas line both sides of the oblong room, in front of which two rows of round-top tables stand. In the rear is a small garden and a counter where coffee is prepared in the old way. A coffee with milk is served in a large glass placed within a bronze holder, so you won't burn your fingers. The polite waiters are dressed in maroon jackets and wear bow ties. The wood-carved decorations are reminiscent of choir stalls in a cathedral. The café was opened in 1922 and is still going strong. You can enjoy the best port wine and also order beefsteak and light meals.

BEACHING IT: The bustling fishing village of **Matosinhos** is little more than a suburb of Porto. Separated by rocky crags, its beaches are becoming more popular with visitors who enjoy the pleasures of a seaside resort mixed with the sightseeing attractions and shopping activities of a big city nearby. Part of it sadly marred by industrial blight, Matosinhos lies but six miles north of Porto.

A much more interesting beach excursion is to the fishing village of **Espinho,** only 12 miles south of Porto, and rapidly growing into a modern beach resort. The town boasts many activities: a big gray casino with gaming tables, diverse shops, swimming pools, tennis courts, an 18-hole golf course, and wooded camping sites, plus a wide sandy beach skirted by a seaside esplanade.

Although frequented by sun-seeking families from Porto in summer, it can look like a ghost town in off-season. If you're based in Porto and venture down for a day at the beach, you can order a good and filling regional luncheon at the **Hotel Mar Azul,** Avenida 8 (it opens onto the railroad tracks). The total cost is 400$ ($6.12) for a complete meal.

4. Exploring the Coast

An underrated stretch of coastal resorts and fishing villages lies between Porto and the southern reaches of the Minho district. The Atlantic waters, however, are likely to be on the chilly side, even in July and August. The communities along this northern highway of the sun are small, ideal spots for those desiring a sequestered beach target. In some of these places, North Americans are still viewed with curiosity but welcomed warmly. Our first stopover is at:

VILA DO CONDE: Along the wharfs of the Ave River stand piles of rough hand-hewn timbers used in the building of the sardine fleet. Barefoot women repair the fish nets which hang suspended in the sun, and racks of cod dry salty and stiff. Not much has changed in Vila do Conde—that is, until recently. Now, its fortress-guarded sandy beaches, rocky reefs, and charm are being discovered.

For sights, a large squat structure sits fortress-like on a hill. It is the **Santa Clara Convent,** founded in the 14th century. In the upper rooms you can see relics and paintings garnered through the centuries by the Poor Clares. Simplicity and opulence play against each other in a combination of Gothic and Romanesque styles. The plain altar offers contrast to the gilded stalls behind the communion grilles and the ornately decorated ceilings. The church also contains two 14th-century sarcophagi: one elaborately carved tomb, depicting the founder of the monastery, his feet resting on a lion; the other, the coffin of the first Duchess of Braganza. From the grounds, you can see an 18th-century aqueduct, utilizing 999 arches to carry spring water to the precincts.

Just 17 miles from Porto, Vila do Conde is served by a modern, convenient highway.

FOOD AND LODGING: Estalagem do Brasão, Avenida Coronel Alberto Graça (tel. Vila do Condo 640-16), is a superior inn styled more like a gracious pousada. It's in the center of the village, with a lofty dining room, worth considering if only for its restaurant. The bedrooms are compact, of contemporary design with fully tiled baths. Rooms have twin beds with built-in headboards, and comfortable, stylish armchairs. The cost, including a continental breakfast, is 750$ ($11.48) daily in a single, that rate rising to 1000$ ($15.30) in a double. If two persons desire a suite, the tariff is 1400$ ($21.42). A set lunch or dinner costs 400$ ($6.12). The chef turns out three specialties on the à la carte menu—codfish Brasão at 240$ ($3.67); beef Brasão, 220$ ($3.37); and omelet Brasão, 130$ ($1.99). There's a combination bar and disco, plus a private parking lot.

PORVO DE VARZIM: In the small intimate cafés of this town, beneath ornate roofs and gables, skimpily clad tourists idyllically take their afternoon glass of port wine (some have several). Seemingly unaware of them, the *pescadores* (fishermen) of the bustling village go on with their work. Franz Villier wrote: "Here the boat-owners are kings, and morality reigns. Drunkards and debauchees may not aspire to the honour of fishing, unless it happens that the owner is one himself."

Dotting the beach are white canvas tents known as *toldo,* which are suspended on two poles. Many bathers prefer to swim in the warmer waters of the Olympic-size pool. In days of yore, a fortress dominated the coastline. Nowadays, a neoclassic-style **casino** does, drawing visitors from Porto, 19 miles away. In summer the casino offers dancing to an orchestra and, of course, gaming tables.

The **Vermar Dom Pedro Hotel** (tel. 610-41) is the latest hotel in the expanding Dom Pedro chain. Its stark white towers on the outskirts of Porvo de Varzim overlook the sand dunes and water, yet it is only a short drive to Porto.

The hotel boasts all the conveniences of a resort community, including two heated pools (one just for children), tennis courts, a health club, sauna, solarium, and a disco. The cobblestones and multilevel terraces surrounding the pools are the favorite gathering spots for sunbathers.

The restaurant, enhanced with graphics and interesting lighting effects, opens onto a view of the beaches and sea, as do the terraces of the 208 rooms. Each room is tastefully designed with practical furnishings and is equipped with air conditioning, telephone, private bath or shower, and radio. In high season, a double room rents for 4000$ ($61.20), a single for 3100$ ($47.43) daily, these tariffs including breakfast. Lunch or dinner, ordered separately, costs another 600$ ($9.18), all taxes and service included.

Grande Hotel da Povoa, Passeio Alegre (tel. 620-61), has long been the most substantial hotel along the beachfront. It faces a filled promenade and has facilities for housing the prominent Portuguese families who like to have their holiday here. The public rooms are substantial, and the dining room, with its wide arches and sea view, lends dignity to the meals. The snackbar with its stool bar is popular, and two saltwater swimming pools give the hotel a resort character. While the suites have antique furnishings, the regular bedrooms are substantial and well appointed. Some have complete baths. A single rents for 1200$ ($18.36) daily; a double for 1800$ ($27.54) daily in a bathless room. With complete bath, the charge is 1500$ ($22.95) daily in a single, 2000$ ($30.90) in a double. The hotel lies only a few minutes' walk to the casino, with its gaming tables and shows.

Low-Budget Dining

O Predilecto, 34 Avenida Mousinho de Albuquerque (tel. 648-56), is a simple restaurant on the main road to the beach (near the tourist office). It's housed in a colorful old-style building, and many of the residents from Porto stop off here when they're touring in the area. They know they'll get good regional fare at reasonable prices—baked codfish, 140$ ($2.14); stuffed rabbit, 135$ ($2.07); fish filets with rice, 140$ ($2.14); and beef dishes, 145$ ($2.22). The classic soup is, of course, caldo verde, 25$ (38¢), and chocolate mousse at 35$ (54¢) provides the finish.

Maresia, Avenida dos Banhos (tel. 61929) is another possibility if you're at the beach. It's extended right out onto the sands, with a sea-view dining room. It is both a restaurant as well as a snackbar-bar. Large and bustling in summer, it serves typically regional dishes—Spanish-style clams, 185$ ($2.83); roast chicken, 140$ ($2.14); codfish Maresia, 200$ ($3.06); and grilled pork cutlets, 140$ ($2.14). A good-tasting bowl of vegetable soup is offered for 30$ (46¢), and you can finish with a mild flan, also at 30$.

OFIR AND FAO: Once through the pine forests of **Ofir,** you gaze down on a long white sandy spit dotted with wind-swept dunes and suffused with the sharp cries of seagulls. Imagine a pure unspoiled Cape Cod. The beach is dramatic any time of the year, but exceptional during the summer months. Ofir is considered by many as the best beach resort between Porto and Viana do

Castelo. The White Horse Rocks, according to legend, were formed when fiery steeds from the royal stock of King Solomon were wrecked upon the beach.

While the hotels of Ofir offer guests every convenience in a secluded setting, the nearest shops and more local color are found one to two miles inland on an estuary of the Cávado River at Fão. Framed by mountain ridges in the background and a river valley, the village is the sleepy destination of all visitors to Ofir. Interesting are the *sargaceiros* (literally, gatherers of sargasso), who, with their stout fustian tunics, rake the offshore breakers for the seaweed used in making fertilizer. On the quays you can lunch on sardines off the smoking braziers. At the end of the day you can soothe your overdose of sunshine with a mellow glass of port wine.

The accommodations in these two towns are the best along the coast north of Porto.

Staying in Ofir

The **Hotel de Ofir,** Praia de Ofir (tel. 893-83), competes in its own way with the new resort developments on the southern Algarve. One section is quite luxurious, built motel-style right along the dunes, with a row of white tents and a pure sandy beach in full view of the second-floor bedroom balconies. There are rather well-styled public rooms for the evening's activities, but the principal focus is on the wide oceanfront terrace, where guests sunbathe and order refreshments under candy-stripe umbrellas.

A dining room opens onto the sea and is informal with comfortable armchairs, allowing guests to enjoy a near-constant parade of good meals. The nightclub, Boîte de Nuit, simulates an open patio with ceiling of heavy beams under a fake sky. Tables encircle a round dance floor, and a large stage provides an orchestra and variety shows.

It's a resort unto itself, with a vast playground terrace, two swimming pools (one for children), two tennis courts, and a flagstone terrace bordering soft green lawns. The hotel has a disco and a bowling alley as well. The hotel is divided into three sections. The older central core contains bedrooms furnished in the traditional Portuguese fashion, with reproductions of regionally styled furniture; the adjoining wings are totally modern.

The public rooms are large, well decorated, and have many areas for quiet relaxation. The bedrooms have a well-conceived sense of style, with substantial pieces of furniture placed against pleasant color backgrounds. In high season (July 1 to August 31), the full-board rate for two persons is 4500$ ($68.85), dropping to 3600$ ($55.08) in spring and fall. Full-board rate for one person is 2500$ ($38.25) in high season, 2200$ ($33.66) in spring and fall.

Estalagem Parque do Rio (tel. 895-21) is a modern first-class inn on the Cávado River in a pine-covered garden, five minutes from the main beach. It has two excellent garden swimming pools with surrounding lawns. The resort, planned for those who stay for more than one day, offers a full social life. The atmosphere is like that in a skiing lodge, including a natural stone fireplace. In the beamed dining room, a snug wood-paneled bar is set against a stone wall, and you'll find several lounges for get-togethers. Each bedroom is well conceived, having a fully tiled bath, a private balcony, a telephone, and central heating. For half board, the rate ranges from 1920$ ($29.38) in a single to 3220$ ($49.27) for two persons sharing a room.

Staying in Fão

Hotel do Pinhal (tel. 894-73) is a modern resort hotel, but somehow it captures the regional character of northern Portugal. The Hotel of the Pine Cones is set amid pine trees beside a river. The entrance is formal, but at the rear is a lawn leading to the water. Here are two swimming pools (a smaller one for children), a tennis court, and a putting green. It's just a four-minute walk to the sea and the beaches.

The public rooms are attractive, the lounge arranged with armchairs clustered to enjoy the view of the gardens through the picture windows. The restaurant captures the river view with an all-glass wall. The bedrooms are impressively furnished: some are contemporary (walls of wood paneling, lots of built-ins); others capture the character of the region with carved fourposter beds, chinz fabrics, hand-loomed rugs, ornate wrought-iron lamps and chandeliers, and old chests or desks.

There are three price levels, according to the room you select (size, balcony, outlook). Doubles are in the 1700$ ($26.01) to 2200$ ($33.76) bracket; singles, 1200$ ($18.36) to 1500$ ($22.95). Add a supplement of 750$ ($11.48) per person daily for full board. All taxes are included in the rates. Occasionally, there's dancing to music in the hotel's boîte.

5. Deep in the Environs

Before exploring the northwestern Minho, you may want to dip deeper into the Douro River Valley by driving west into the mountains for a look at the Portugal rarely seen by rushed foreign visitors. If you give yourself two targets—**Amarante,** north of the river, and **Lamego,** to the south—you'll be rewarded. Hopefully, you'll be in the Upper Douro region at the end of summer for the harvesting of the grapes.

AMARANTE: Where the lazy Tâmega flows under the **Ponte de Amarante,** completed in 1790, you can see wooden balconies extending out over the river and willow trees drooping their branches over the banks. It's a romantic setting for the town of St. Gonçalo, the protector of old maids.

On the slopes of the Marão Hills, Amarante is worth the 41-mile trek northeast from Porto. Right at the entrance to the bridge sits the former **Convent of St. Gonçalo,** with a tile-faced dome. Inside, the entire altarpiece is a cherubic romp, with silvery white-haired baby angels frolicking and cavorting all over the columns and ceiling. On each side of the altar are huge pillars festooned with bouquets and wreaths of flowers. Adjacent archways display richly gilded trompe l'oeil decorations. Four supporting columns reveal bizarre figures costumed in black, gold, and scarlet. These seemingly hermaphroditic figures exhibit the face, posture, and air of women, but are in fact masculine, as their hirsute chests will testify. The right and left platforms off the main altar continue the florid rococo ornamentation.

Another oddity amid this frantic theatrical scene is a baroque organ held by a gilded merman, the tips of his feet forming fish tails. Fellow Tritons round out the supporting cast. To the right of the altar chapel is a well of wax replicas depicting particular body infirmities. Someone even placed a replica of his sick pig. In a small chapel to the left under the altar is the enemy of every young Portuguese girl: St. Gonçalo, who sees to it that elderly spinsters or widowed women find husbands but doesn't care a bit about unattached young girls. His sculptured figure is robed, holding a staff and a book, his head resting on two **bold red** embroidered cushions with tasseled ends.

The saint's feast day in Amarante, on the first weekend in June of every year, produces a *festa* unique in Portugal. It is the custom for unmarried girls and bachelors to exchange loaves of bread shaped like phalluses. It seems as if the vestige of a pagan fertility rite has survived, or else St. Gonçalo himself is having a final chuckle.

For dining or lodgings, there's a government-owned pousada in the environs:

A Budget Pousada

Pousada de São Gonçalo, Sêrra do Marão, Amarante (tel. 461-13), is on a remote mountain pass. It's almost snowbound in winter, but a sun trap in summer. A modern version of a roadside inn, it is a retreat. The approach, between Amarante and Vila Real, is forlorn, with no signs of life. The place is called Bela Vista, near the Alto de Espinho. Pinewoods grow for miles around in every direction.

Inside, it is furnished in the regional style, more like a hilltop home than an inn. Antique console tables, high wooden chests, tiled floors, country-style armchairs, an open fireplace, and statuary add to that effect. Only 18 rooms are available—14 with bath, 4 without—so it's wise to make reservations. The rooms are furnished with a few antiques interspersed with passable reproductions. A single rents for 1500$ ($22.95), a double for 1600$ ($24.48).

Meals are hearty and filling, a complete table d'hôte luncheon or dinner going for 450$ ($6.89) to 600$ ($9.18), including homemade bread and a ceramic pitcher of wine. Hopefully, you'll be served the house specialty, a baked cod casserole (generous chunks of white fish baked in a cream sauce, under a crust of cheddar cheese), with vegetables. Kid is also savory when roasted until it's brown and crispy. Desserts are the special pride of the cook: perhaps you'll receive a creamy layer cake studded with almonds and looking just like a porcupine.

LAMEGO: This old bishopric on the wooded slopes of Mount Penude is a good example of baroque harmony. Many of its public and private buildings (even the town cinema) show this unifying style, an example of community planning rarely achieved. The main square has a public garden and adjoins a leisurely, tree-lined esplanade, where the denizens of Lamego promenade in the evenings. Behind the statue of Bishop Dom Miguel is his former palace, converted into a museum displaying sculpture and French tapestries.

Across the way is the **Cathedral of Lamego (Sé)**, originally built in the Romanesque style, then overlaid with Gothic and baroque ornamentation. The ceilings are frescoed, but in dire need of repair. Adjoining is a Renaissance cloister, with a chapel containing a large baroque altar. Ironically, two baroque picture frames, with their huge monsters, twisted scrolls, winged cherubs with bellies protruding, and fowl, obscure the canvases they frame. A second chapel contains pictorial tiles illustrating a touching scene of children bathing in a tub.

Crowning a forested sêrra, overlooking Lamego, is the well-known 18th-century mecca of **Nossa Senhora dos Remédios** (Our Lady of the Cures). Leading to it is an elegant baroque stairway, the Spanish Steps of Lamego, broken by nine fountain-centered and profusely decorated landings. The faithful scale the steps on their knees, as they do in Rome's Scala Santa (Holy Steps).

The granite balustrade is topped with various resplendent finials and statues in Roman battle dress, vases and urns, spheres and niches, plus some saccharine pictorial tiles. The fountains are interesting; one is decorated with four grotesques, each spouting water from its mouth.

READERS' RESTAURANT SELECTION: "**Restaurant Avenida,** Avenue Dr. Alfredo de Sousa (tel. 623-44), is an excellent find on the tree-lined avenue leading to Our Lady of the Cures. The northern Portuguese cuisine and the service are good, and it is moderately priced. Main dishes are 200$ ($3.06) to 350$ ($5.36). To enjoy 'Spanish Steps,' take a taxi to the chapel and walk down. It's lovely" (Mr. and Mrs. Robert M. Davenport, Huntington Beach, Calif.).

VIDAGO: An international spa, Vidago lies in remote Trás-os-Montes, the far northeastern province of Portugal. Its pure sparkling waters and good climate have made it a favorite among spa devotees.

All life centers on the **Palace Hotel** (tel. 973-56), which is set deep in a forest. On beautifully landscaped grounds, the hotel is known for its flower beds and fountains. Standing like a glistening pink birthday cake, the hotel in high season charges from 1000$ ($15.30) to 1200$ ($18.36) for two. If you request an accommodation without bath, the charge drops to 650$ ($9.95) in a single, to 1000$ ($15.30) and up in a double. If you're touring, you might want to drop in for lunch, ordering a four-courser for 500$ ($7.65), including wine. Swimming, tennis, golf, horseback riding, and badminton are among the sports offered. International races are often held on a well-known race track nearby. The hotel also shelters a nightclub.

From Porto and its environs, we now head for the last stopover in continental Portugal, the Minho district.

Chapter XVI

THE MINHO DISTRICT

1. Guimarães
2. Braga
3. Barcelos
4. Esposende
5. Viana do Castelo
6. Valença
7. Pousada-Hopping in Minho

CORN GRANARIES on granite stilts... heather-covered hills... fishing villages... poplar-shaded river valleys... terraces scaling slopes... ramparts guarding against long-dead enemies... *sargaceiros* in fustian tunics raking for seaweed... and heavily laden vines at grape harvest.

The Minho occupies the most northwestern corner of Portugal, and is almost a land unto itself. The district begins some 25 miles north of Porto, stretching to the frontier of Galicia in northwestern Spain. In fact, the Minhotons and the Galicians share many common characteristics.

Granite plateaus undulate across the countryside, broken by the green valleys of the Minho, Ave, Cávado, and Lima Rivers. Bountiful granite quarries stand agape amid the hills. From the great church facades in Braga and Guimarães to the humblest of village cottages, this material has been employed for centuries. Green pasturelands contrast sharply with forests filled with cedars and chestnuts.

The small size of the district and the proximity of one town to another makes hamlet-hopping easy. Even the biggest towns—**Viana do Castelo, Guimarães,** and **Braga**—are provincial. You can see wooden carts in the streets drawn by pairs of dappled and chocolate-brown oxen. These noble beasts have become subjects for the regional pottery and ceramics for which the Minho, and especially Viana do Castelo, are known.

Religious *festas* are excuses for bringing the hard-working people out into the streets for days of merry-making and celebrations including folk songs, dances, and, of course, displays of traditional costumes. The young girls and women often wear woolen skirts and gaily decorated aprons in floral or geometric designs. Their bodices are pinned with golden filigree and draped with heart- or cross-shaped pendants hung in many layers upon chains about their necks.

Historically, the Minho was the spawning ground of Portuguese independence. It was from here that Afonso Henriques, the first king, made his plans to capture the south from the Moors. Battlemented castles along the frontier attest to the former hostilities with Spain, and fortresses still stand above the coastal villages, ruined sentinels which once protected the river accesses to the heartland.

1. Guimarães

The cradle of Portugal, Guimarães suffers from a benign malady which the French call *embarras de richesses*. At the foot of a range of sêrras, this first capital of Portugal has successfully preserved a medieval atmosphere which shows little sign of evaporation.

Dominating the skyline is the 10th-century **Castle of Guimarães,** where Afonso Henriques, Portugal's first king, was born sometime between 1094 and 1111 (historians disagree). The castle dates from 996. High-pitched crenels top the strategically placed square towers and the looming keep, said to have been the birthplace of Afonso. The view is magnificent. With the church bells ringing in the distance, and roosters crowing early in the morning, the setting seems straight out of the Middle Ages.

Almost in the shadow of the structure is the 12th-century **St. Michael of the Castle,** a squat, rectangular Romanesque church where the liberator was baptized. Nearby is a heroic statue of the mustachioed Afonso, his head helmeted, his figure clad in a suit of armor, sword and shield in hand.

From the keep of the castle, you can see the four-winged **Palace of the Dukes of Braganza.** Although constructed in the 15th century, it has been heavily restored. Many critics have dismissed the rebuilt structure with contempt. However, if you're not a purist, you may find a guided tour interesting. Perched on the slope of a hill, the palace possesses a varied assortment of treasures, including a number of portraits such as of Catherine of Braganza, who married Charles II of England, the merrie monarch and lover of Nell Gwyn.

Copies of the large Pastrana tapestries depict scenes from the Portuguese wars in North Africa. The scabbards and helmets in the armor room, plus the antiques, Persian hangings, Indian urns, ceramics, and Chinese porcelains make the 15$ (23¢) admission seem small. Many of the rooms have beamed and coffered ceilings, plain gray stone block walls, and chocolate-brown stone floors. The chapel opens onto the throne chairs of the duke and duchess. Nearby are the double-tiered cloisters.

By far the most dramatic interior of any church in town belongs to **São Francisco,** on Largo de São Francisco. Entered through a Gothic portal, the church contains Delft-blue and white azulejos decorations on its walls. At times color tones are created which seem to bathe the whole interior in moonlight. In the transept to the right of the main altar is a dollhouse, a recreation of the living room of a church prelate. The detail is meticulous, from the burgundy-colored cardinal's chapeau resting upon a wall sconce, to the miniature dog and cat (slightly out of scale), to the grapes suspended from the ceiling. Found at the second altar on the right is a polychrome tree of life, representing 12 crowned kings and the Virgin, her hands clasped, her feet resting upon the heads of three cherubs. The palace next door, with its embellished tiled facade, may be visited by appointment only (tel. 41-22-28).

If you'd like to step into the Middle Ages for an hour or two, take a stroll down the **Rua de Santa Maria,** which has remained essentially unchanged, except nowadays you're likely to hear some blaring music, in English no less. Proud town houses, once the residence of the nobility, stand beside humble dwellings. The hand-carved balconies, aged by the years, are most often garnished with iron lanterns, not to mention laundry.

At the end you'll come upon a charming square in the heart of the old town, the **Largo da Oliveira** (Olive Tree Square). Escudo-hungry children are likely to surround you at this point. You can press on, however, to an odd chapelette in front of a church. Comprised of four ogival arches, it is said to mark the spot in the sixth century where Wamba was asked to give up the simple toil of working his fields to become the king of the Goths. Thrusting his olive stick into the tilled soil, he declared he would accept only if his stick sprouted leaves. So it did, and he did—or that was the tale told.

The church, called the **Collegiate Church of the Olive Tree**, was originally a tenth-century temple erected by Mumadona, a Galician countess. It has changed with the seasons: Romanesque giving way to Gothic, and then to more sterile neoclassicism.

In the Romanesque cloister of the church is the **Museum of Alberto Sampaio**. Besides a large silver collection and such historical curios as the crown of Our Lady of the Olive, it displays the tunic worn by João I at the battle of Aljubarrota that decided Portugal's fate. In addition, there is a myriad assortment of vestments, paintings, ceramics, faïence from Viana do Castelo, and pottery from the Beiras. A fresco illustrates a gloating Salomé, rapturous over the severed head of John the Baptist. Off the cloister you can visit a baroque chapel with two Wagnerian amazons, sans helmets, bearing torchères.

WHERE TO STAY: For years, Guimarães suffered by not having a decent hotel to lodge visitors attracted to its riches in sights. However that situation, I can joyfully report, has been relieved by the opening of **Sta. Maria d'Oliveira** (tel. 418-93), a government-run pousada. The modern pousada stands right in the historic heart of Guimarães, on a quiet and ancient square. The pousada has been converted from old manors whose original plan and features have been preserved. If you stay here, the hotel staff will be happy to start you off on a number of interesting tours.

The hotel has been handsomely furnished, and everything looks immaculate. A double room with bath rents for 2500$ ($38.25). It's most comfortable, although some readers have complained that it doesn't have the cozy feeling of many of its sister pousadas. One English visitor, Peter H. Allaway, said, "It's more like a good, impersonal hotel." Nevertheless, after the horrible accommodations I have suffered over the years in checking after Guimarães, I find Sta. Maria de Oliveira an enormous blessing.

The kitchen places emphasis on providing the local cuisine and wine (vinho verde), and does so rather well. Service is likely to improve as the staff acquires more experience. For 705$ ($11.48), I recently enjoyed a pescada filet, good cold beer, a salada with those tasty Portuguese tomatoes they grow in the north, and aromatic crusty bread from the oven, along with potatoes, too.

WHERE TO DINE: Jordão, 62 Avenida Afonso Henriques (tel. 41-14-98), is a big, first-class restaurant lying below the Jordão Theatre, a cinema. Within walking distance of the Tourist Office, the entrance is down an alleyway. Regional and international dishes are offered—grilled colin at 280$ ($4.28); steak of the house, also 280$; and escalope of veal, 270$ ($4.13). Soups begin at 35$ (54¢), and a typical dessert, a pudding, costs 40$ (61¢).

READER'S RESTAURANT SELECTION: "An excellent restaurant, *típico*, in Guimarães, or just outside, is the **Mirapenha**. A taxi ride to it cost us $1.50 (U.S.), and the proprietors drove us back to town free. Fine local food is served at a reasonable cost" (Dr. Gerald Noble, North Balwyn, Victoria, Australia).

2. Braga

Nearly everywhere you look in Braga there's a church, a palace, a garden, or a fountain. The site the town occupies has always been favored. Known to the Romans as Bracara Augusta, it also resounded to the footsteps of other conquerors—the Suevi, the Visigoths, and the Moors. For centuries it has been an archiepiscopal see and a pilgrimage site (the Visigoths are said to have renounced their heresies here).

Inside the town, interest focuses on on the Sé, the **Cathedral of Braga.** It was built in the 12th century by Count Henry of Burgundy and Dona Teresa. Following his demise, she was chased out of town because of an illicit love affair; but in death Henry and Teresa was reunited in their tombs in the Chapel of Kings.

Although built in the Middle Ages, the Sé didn't escape subsequent decorative and architectural overlays. The north triple-arched facade is austere and dominating, with a large stone-laced Roman arch flanked by two smaller Gothic ones. What appear to be the skeletons of cupolas top the facade's dual bell towers, which flank a lofty rooftop niche containing a larger-than-life statue of the Virgin and Child. Under a carved baldachin in the apse is a statue of "Our Lady of the Milk"—that is, the Virgin breast feeding the infant Jesus Christ. The statue is in the Manueline style—but somehow pious, restrained.

Once inside the structure, you'll believe you've entered one of the darkest citadels of Christendom. However, if you can see them, the interior decorations are profuse, particularly a pair of huge 18th-century organs gilded with baroque decorations. In the 1330 Capela da Gloría is the sarcophagus of Archbishop Dom Gonçalo Pereira, carved by order of the prelate himself, with an unctuous expression on his face.

For 25$ (38¢), you can visit the **Treasury of the Cathedral** and the **Museum of Sacred Art,** an upstairs repository of Braga's most precious works of art. Included are elaborately carved choir stalls from the 18th century, embroidered vestments from the 16th through the 18th centuries, a 14th-century statue of the Virgin and a Gothic chalice from the same period, plus the custódia of Dom Gaspar de Braganza. This treasury house may be visited from 8 a.m. to 12:30 p.m. and from 1:30 to 5:30 p.m. In the cloister is a pietà, reflecting human grief.

Three miles southeast of Braga is the nationally renowned **Bom Jesus do Monte.** The hilltop pilgrimage site is reached via foot, funicular, or a tree-lined roadway. A double baroque granite staircase dating from the 17th century may look exhausting; but, if it's any consolation, pilgrims often climb it on their knees.

Although less elaborate than the stairway of Remédios at Lamego, the stairs at Bom Jesus (Good Jesus) are equally as impressive. On the numerous landings are gardens, grottos, small chapels, sculptures, and allegorical stone figures set in fountains.

Designed by Carlos Amarante in 1811, the hilltop **Chapel of the Miracles** contains many reminders, even anatomical recreations, of the diseased and sick who have claimed cures. In foggy weather the mountain is enshrouded in mist, but on most days you can walk along the mosaic sidewalks and belvederes, past white and black swans, and view the provincial capital at every turn. In accommodations you have the following:

Hotel Turismo Dom Pedro, Praçeta João XXI (tel. 270-91), is the leading first-class hotel of Braga, in the city center, an 11-floor rather posh air-conditioned complex set back from a main artery. Each well-furnished bedroom has a private bath. The cost of a single is 1600$ ($24.48) daily; a double, 2050$

($31.37)–including breakfast. Evening meals cost 700$ ($10.71). On the top floor is a spacious and attractive snackbar opening onto a roof swimming pool. On the second floor is an overscale but comfortable and fine-looking lounge, with an adjoining bar and restaurant. The main lounge has soft leather sofas, large tables, and an intermixing of antiques. The hotel also has a nightclub.

Hotel João XXI, 849 Avenida João XXI (tel. 221-46), is a good stopover hotel in its bracket (second class). Just out of the heart of the city, on a tree-shaded avenue leading to Bom Jesus do Monte, it stands opposite the leading first-class hotel of Braga. The entry to this modern little six-floor hotel is a salute to the 19th century. The tiny street-floor reception room is decorated à la Louis XVI. The bedrooms are basic, in a warm modern. The social center is the living room-lounge with well-selected furnishings featuring an open fireplace for the nippy months. At the restaurant on the sixth floor you can order breakfast or an evening meal. The latter costs 500$ ($7.65) per person.

The bedrooms are furnished with semitraditional pieces, with the accent on neatness and efficiency. Each of the 28 rooms has its own private bath, the singles have double beds, and you get either a shower or tub as you require. The price, including breakfast, for a single is 950$ ($14.54), and a double costs 1700$ ($26.01).

Bom Jesus do Monte

Many visitors to Braga prefer to stay high on the hill overlooking the city at the sanctuary of Bom Jesus do Monte. If you're interested in views and don't mind mingling with a lot of pilgrims, then you might want to do the same. The views at night are among the most exciting in the north of Portugal.

Hotel do Elevador, Bom Jesus Do Monte (tel. 250-11), is not unlike a private hillside villa—furnished in a plush manner with antiques, paintings, and objets d'art—except for the 25 bedrooms which have contemporary appointments. Every bedroom has a private bath, central heating, and bedside telephone. The price for one person is 1100$ ($16.83) daily, this tariff rising to 1700$ ($26.01) in a double, including breakfast. At your table with a view, the price of a complete luncheon or dinner is around 500$ ($7.56).

Sud Americano, at Bom Jesus do Monte (tel. 225-15), on a plaza overlooking the church and valley, is like a country inn, ideal for pilgrims who want a basic budget hotel. The entry is small, the dining room has a few token antiques, and bedrooms are simplicity itself. Some are twin-bedded with private baths. In a bathless room, full board for one is 500$ ($7.56) daily; in a double, 1750$ ($11.48). With private bath a single costs 750$ ($11.48) a double 1000$ ($15.30) daily.

WHERE TO DINE: O Inácio, 4 Campo das Hortas (tel. 223-35), is an old stone-built structure with rugged walls and hand-hewn beams. In the cold-weather months, a fire burns in an open hearth. The decor is rustic, with regional pottery and oxen yokes. Your host is Francisco de Macedo, who welcomes you and will often advise about his specialties of the day. Usually these are bacalhau (codfish) à Inácio, 240$ (3.67); papas de sarrabulho (a regional stew), 270$ ($4.13); and bife na cacarola, 250$ ($3.83). Roast kid is also featured occasionally at 300$ ($4.59). Most fish dishes (and they're fresh) average around 240$ ($3.67). Soups are hearty fare, rich tasting, going for 40$ (61¢). The dessert surprise is a rum omelet soufflé at 180$ ($2.75). Mr. de Macedo has a well-stocked wine cellar, and in our opinion, serves the best cuisine in Braga.

3. Barcelos

Fourteen miles west of Braga, Barcelos is a sprawling river town, resting upon a plateau ringed by green hills. Wrought-iron street lanterns glimmer late in the evenings long after the market in the open square of **Campo da República** has closed down. Barcelos does not feature any single major attraction, only itself, taken as a whole, with its ensemble of sights and curiosities, and that is more than enough.

Market day, on Thursday, in the fountain-centered Campo da República, almost 450 yards square, is a major event. You can purchase such local handcrafted items as rugs, dyed pillows stuffed with chicken feathers, Portuguese chandeliers, crochet work, local pottery, and, of course, the Barcelos cockerels.

These hand-painted earthenware cocks are the most characteristic souvenirs of Portugal and often seem a symbol of the country. The worship of the Barcelos Rooster derives from a legend concerning a Gallego sentenced to hang, despite his protestations of innocence. In a last-hour appeal to the judge (who was having dinner at the time), the condemned man made a bold statement: If his manifestation of innocence were true, the roasted rooster resting on the magistrate's plate would get up and crow. Suddenly, a gloriously scarlet-plumed cockerel rose from the plate, crowing loud and long. The man was acquitted, of course.

Opening onto the tree-studded main square are some of the finest buildings in Barcelos. The **Igreja do Terço** from the 18th century resembles a palace more than a church, with a central niche facade topped by finials and a cross. The interior tile work around the baroque altar depicts scenes of monks at labor and a moving rendition of the Last Supper. Also fronting the campo, with its fountain, is the **Hospital da Misericórdia**, a long formal building of the 17th century, behind a spiked fence, taking up almost half a side of the square.

Of more interest, however, is the small octagonal **Temple of Senhor da Cruz**, with a cupola faced with tiles. An upper balustrade, punctuated by large stone finials and a latticed round window about the square portal, provide contrast to the austerity of the walls. The interior is more sumptuous, with crystal, marble, and gilt.

Overlooking the swirling Cávado River are the ruins of the **Palace of the Braganzas**, dating from 1786. The original palace site, as well as the town of Barcelos itself, were bestowed on Nuno Álvares by João I as a gift in gratitude for his bravery in the 1385 battle at Aljubarrota.

On the facade is a representation of the palace, recreated in splendor. You can wander through the ruins which have been turned into an archeological museum, left relatively unguarded and filled with sarcophagi, heralded shields, and an 18th-century tiled fountain. A museum of ceramics underneath the palace encapsulates the evolution of that handicraft (look for the blood-red ceramic oxen, with their lyre-shaped horns).

The shadow from the high palace chimney stretches across the old pillory in the courtyard below, with the structure even exceeding in height the bell tower of the adjoining **Igreja Matriz**. Fronting the river, this Gothic church contains a baroque altar and an interior whose sides are faced with multicolored tiles. The altar is an array of cherubs, grapes, gold leaf, and birds.

WHERE TO STAY: **Albergaría Conde de Barcelos** (tel. 820-61), is not only the one really good hotel in Barcelos, but it has a delightful pousada style with furnishings made by local artisans. Beds are intricately carved. The 30-bedroom inn, a part of a three-story complex, stands mostly on thick pillars, in the Corbusier manner, and has an inner courtyard. The hotel is just a little way from the center of town, within walking distance of the artisan sales museum. Natural wood paneling is used generously in the dining room, the main lounge, and the bar-lounge. The cost for a double is 1800$ ($27.54) daily and meals are 500$ ($7.56). The chef does both regional and international dishes.

4. Esposende

Esposende is a small beach resort in a village between Viana do Castelo and Porto, 30 miles to the south. The pines and sand dunes are swept by the Atlantic breezes, and cows graze in nearby pastures. The surrounding countryside is no longer as unspoiled as it used to be, although you'll still see an occasional ox cart in the street. The area has been extensively developed, and there's a wide new road running along the seafront. Men and women in fustian clothes and broad-brimmed hats work the vineyards in the foothills. The beach is large and fine, lining either side of the Cávado estuary. Small fishing vessels plod up the river carrying anglers to the bass upstream. Recent archeological diggings have revealed the remains of a Roman city and necropolis, but that doesn't seem to have disturbed Esposende in the least.

In accommodations there are the following:

Nélia Hotel, Avenida Valentin Ribeiro (tel. 892-44), is a handsome inn in the center of the village, which has flair and color. Perhaps influenced by the regional designs, the interior has rather a lavish style. Especially interesting are the bedrooms and wall dressing table and mirrors and hand-carved wooden beds with interwoven leather headboards. The cost of a single with private bath is 750$ ($11.48) daily in winter, 1000$ ($15.30) in summer. Doubles are 1100$ ($16.83) and 1500$ ($22.95). Evening meals are 400$ ($6.12).

The **Hotel Suave Mar,** Avenida Arantes Oliveira (tel. 894-45), is a semimodern hotel on the river, with its own swimming pool and tennis courts. It attracts budgeteers who don't want to pay for the superior first-class accommodations at neighboring Ofir and Fão.

The lodgings are pleasant and comfortable, and of its 44 bedrooms, 36 contain private baths. Full board for two persons costs either 2850$ ($43.61) or 3250$ ($49.73); whereas, one person, for a room and all meals, is charged either 1750$ ($26.78) or 2000$ ($30.60). However, of its cuisine, the food critic Raymond Postgate wrote that its "menus are a meticulous reproduction of Anglo-Saxon nurseries of the twenties—for example, vegetable soup, followed by boiled fish with boiled potatoes and a jam cake." The Suave Mar is open all year, although you may have the place to yourself off-season.

5. Viana do Castelo

Viana do Castelo sits complacently between an estuary of the Lima River and a base of rolling hills. The Princess of the Lima, as she is called, is northern Portugal's city of folklore. The setting is enhanced by an occasional ox cart with wooden wheels clacking along the stone streets. Some of the boatmen of the city, their faces weatherbeaten, can be seen near the waterfront, offering to sell visitors a slow cruise along the riverbanks.

But for the best view, scale the **Monte de Santa Luzia,** reached by a 20$ (31¢) funicular ride or, if you have a car, along a twisting road. From the Hotel de Santa Luzia at the summit, a great view unfolds, including Eiffel's bridge spanning the Lima.

Viana do Castelo is noted for its pottery and regional handicrafts (many can be purchased in the Friday market). It is even better known for its regional dress, best seen at the annual *festa* (the Friday, Saturday, and Sunday nearest to August 20) of Nossa Senhora da Agonia (Our Lady of Agony). The native women wear bright, strident colors of oranges, scarlets, and Prussian blue, with layers of golden necklaces displaying heart- and cross-shaped pendants.

The center of town is the **Praça da República,** one of the handsomest squares in Portugal. At its heart is the much-photographed **Chafariz Fountain,** constructed in the 16th century, with water spewing from the mouths of its figures. The most impressive building on the square is the **Misericórdia,** a dour, squat, three-story structure, unique in the country. The lower level is an arcade comprised of five austere Roman arches, whereas the two upper levels are ponderous Renaissance balconies. All are crowned by a rooftop crucifix. The four supporting pillars of each level are primitive caryatid-like figures between which are interspersed bright-red geraniums in flower boxes. Adjoining the Charity Hospital is a church fronting the Rua da Bandeira. Inside is a combination of pictorial tiles made in 1714, ornate baroque altars, a painted ceiling, and wood carvings.

The other building dominating the praça is the old **Town Hall,** constructed over an arcade made up of three wide and low Gothic arches (the Tourist Office occupies the headquarters upstairs). The crenel-topped facade displays a royal coat-of-arms and wrought-iron balcony windows above each arch. Originally the Paços do Concelho, it was constructed during the reign of Manuel I and completed under João III. From the small sidewalk tables and chairs, you can observe the square's activities and sample pastries such as torta de Viana.

The **Igreja Matriz,** down the Rua Cabral at Largo do Instituto Histórico do Minho, was begun by João I in 1285 and completed in 1433. Dominated by a large Gothic arched portal, the facade is flanked by two battlemented towers. The interior archway is carved with granite figures, acanthus leaves, and simplistic statuary with moonshaped faces. The inside is cold but with an excellent trompe l'oeil ceiling.

Viana do Castelo, only 44 miles north of Porto, is possible either as an overnight stopover or as the goal of a one-day trip. The beaches are large and sandy, guarded by an age-old fortress standing at the river's mouth.

Only 12 miles up the river is **Ponte de Lima,** which is exactly what one hopes a Portuguese village will be like. The drive along the north side of the river takes you through grape arbors, pastoral villages, and forests of cedar, pine, and chestnut. Red-cheeked peasants stand silhouetted against moss-green stone walls or cease their toil in the cabbage fields to watch you pass.

At Ponte de Lima, an old bridge spans the river, on the banks of which women wring out their clothes. At certain times of the year, however, this river is likely to be dry. At other times anglers try to snare trout from its waters. The numerous towers and churches reveal a secular architecture in faded elegance.

In accommodations the city is well supplied.

The **Hotel Afonso III,** 494 Avenida Afonso III (tel. 241-23), is a first-class hotel which opened in 1971. Offering eight floors of comfort, it contains 88 accommodations, each with its own bath. More than half are graced with a private balcony as well. The attractively furnished rooms rent for anywhere from 1250$ ($19.13) to 1500$ ($22.95) for one person, increasing from 1500$ ($22.95) to 2400$ ($36.72) for two, including breakfast. Lunch or dinner is an extra 600$ ($9.18).

The contemporary decor consists mainly of black and white marble. The overall tone is both simple and sophisticated. A restaurant on the seventh floor provides a panoramic view over the Lima River. Other facilities include a convention hall, a boîte, and swimming pools. Bar facilities are available.

VIANA DO CASTELO

Hotel de Santa Luzia, Monte de Santa Luzia (tel. 221-92). The first thing you do here in the morning is walk out on your terrace and drink in one of the great hotel views of Europe. The position of this hilltop establishment is awesome, with views of the harbor and ocean beyond, as well as of Viana do Castelo. With its 19th-century facade and terraced gardens, Santa Luzia appears to contain at least 100 bedrooms, although it has only 42, with six suites. The hotel is reached by a three-mile, winding, tree-lined avenue.

Not a decorator's dream, the furnishings seem more simple than would be appropriate, with an overuse of floral fabrics and paper. However, many of the rooms contain palace-high ceilings and private baths. The bedroom trappings are traditional and adequate, and the better chambers are outfitted with sitting areas and balconies. In high season, half-board rate is 2600$ ($39.78) for one person, rising to 3600$ ($55.08) for two persons.

On the grounds are a swimming pool and tennis courts, and there is a good restaurant, offering a panoramic view, as well as a cocktail bar and a nightclub.

Hotel do Parque, Parque de Galiza (tel. 241-51), is a 120-bedroom hotel at the base of the bridge crossing the Lima River on the edge of town. It has a motel-mini-resort flavor, its lounges overlooking an outdoor swimming pool with grass terrace. On its rooftop is a panoramic restaurant, serving regional and international dishes, and adjoining it is a solarium with a refreshment area. Intermixed with the main-floor lounge is an interior winter garden. The lounges have coral-colored soft armchairs. For evening entertainment there is a disco-boîte. Bedrooms are quite contemporary, with plenty of built-in furnishings, tiled baths, air conditioning, telephone, piped-in music, and balconies. One person pays a peak 1900$ ($29.07) daily, the tariff rising to 2800$ ($42.84) in a double. A meal, ordered separately, costs 700$ ($10.71).

Hotel Rali, Avenida Dom Afonso III (tel. 221-76). Set back from the waterfront, this four-story modern hotel is a pleasant choice. It faces the mountains, but also opens onto a busy thoroughfare. The bedrooms—42 in all, each with a private bath—are splashed with good strong colors, often greens and blues, with floral prints at the wall-wide windows. The furnishings seem like demonstration rooms in Copenhagen. The tariff in a single is either 800$ ($12.24) or 1030$ ($15.76), depending on the plumbing (shower or tub). For two persons, the cheapest double is 1260$ ($19.28), increasing to 1600$ ($24.48).

The lounges open one onto the other, the favored one with a raised fireplace, red lacquered armchairs, and marble coffee tables. The dining room, serving breakfast only, has paneled walls, a rear clerestory window with green plants, and dramatic drop lights of cutout white metal. Depending on the weather, guests choose between a heated indoor pool or an outside one. The bar, Prince Henrique, is an attractive rendezvous.

WHERE TO DINE: Os 3 Potes, Beco das Fornos, off the Praça da República, was an old bakery before its conversion into one of the best regional restaurants in Viana do Castelo. From the Praça da República, head down the Rua de Sacadura Cabral (the restaurant is somewhat hard to find, although worth the search). The atmosphere is rustic, and on Saturday folk dancing is offered. The food is good, too, but you should have your hotel call in advance to make a reservation. We'd suggest caldo verde at 25$ (38¢) to begin, followed by such good-tasting main dishes as codfish 3 Potes, 250$ ($3.82); lampreys, 350$ ($5.36); or else fondue bourguignonne, 260$ ($3.98). I always skip dessert, settling for the Irish coffee at 85$ ($1.30) instead. The restaurant stays open until midnight from Tuesday to Sunday; closed Monday.

Alambique, 86 Rua Manuel Espregueira (tel. 238-94). You enter this typical Portuguese restaurant through a large wine vat. Inside you'll find many of the specialties for which the cooks of northern Portugal are known, including codfish Antiga Viana, 240$ ($3.67); churrasco de porco (pork), 200$ ($3.06); cabrito (goat), 220$ ($3.37); tripes Porto style, 180$ ($2.75); and lampreys Bordelaise, 350$ ($5.36). For a beginning, you can order either sopa àlentejana at 40$ (61¢), or else sopa do mar, 60$ (92¢).

Laranjeira, 24 Rua de Manuel Espregueira (tel. 222-58), off the Praça da República, is an inexpensive restaurant serving good Portuguese food. It's on the ground floor of a simple boarding house, offering meals under 300$ ($4.59). The fish dishes are better than the meat offerings. It's closed on Saturday.

READER'S RESTAURANT SELECTIONS: "**Margarida,** Largo 5 de Outubro, is a small restaurant on the waterfront with an attractive arched frontage. If you walk through to the rear room, you can choose to sit at a blue-tiled table or in an enclosed wooden booth at the side of the room. The menu is short and rarely changes. The restaurant has an informal, family atmosphere, and only Portuguese is spoken. However, mime and a phrase book serve the purpose admirably. The croquettes Viana, sardines, and chicken with rice are excellent, and where else could you feed five hungry people a hearty two-course meal, with three soft drinks and a good vinho verde, for 700$ ($10.71) and in such attractive surroundings? . . . Another recommendation is the **Tunel** in Rua dos Manjovos, off Avenida des Combatantes. The food is good, and there is always a selection of regional specialties such as roast kid or quail, plus a number of fish dishes. It is popular with the locals and is sometimes crowded and noisy, but the cooking is well above average. The vegetable soup is the best we had in northern Portugal. Our meal, ordered for four but split among five, included beef and fish dishes and came to 1000$ ($15.30) with wine, soft drinks, and ice cream for the children. . . . If the Tunel looks very crowded, the **Bela Terra,** not far away, is also good value, with friendly, concerned service" (Valerie West, Appleton, Warrington, Cheshire, England).

NIGHTLIFE: **Solar Edite,** at Afife, six miles from Viana do Castelo (tel. 243-43), presents the typical folk dances of the north, an average evening costing around 600$ ($9.18). Spectacles are presented on Saturday at 8:30 p.m. The club is in a rustic old home, and such regional food is offered as grilled sardines. Mai bread, roast pig, caldo verde, and, of course, many green wines. Any travel agent in Viana can book you for an evening here.

6. Valença

The walled battlements of Valença, 33 miles northeast of Viana do Castelo, stand today as a reminder of ancient hostilities between Portugal and Spain. In fact, when Afonso III ruled Portugal, the forces of Castile and León besieged and destroyed much of Valença.

A narrow covered gateway across a moat takes you into the center of this walled village of cobbled streets, ancient stone houses, pots of geraniums, wrought-iron balconies, and old street lanterns. Incorporated into the 13th-century fortress, a government-owned pousada opens onto a belvedere, from which you can enjoy one of the finest views in the Minho. The old cannons are still mounted, no longer seriously, looking down on the **International Bridge** across the Minho to Spain.

On the other side of the river is the Spanish town of **Tuy,** once a blood enemy, and now a sister-town to Valença. Tuy is noted for its narrow, steep streets and walls erected on top of ancient Roman fortifications. The battlemented turrets and towers of the cathedral-fortress have stood guard on the frontier since 1170.

While in Valença, you may get hooked on the local specialty, lampreys. Order them fresh from the river, served in a spicy pepper sauce.

In accommodations, there is the following.

Pousada de São Teotónio (tel. 222-52). The Portuguese government tried to outshine its rival counterpart across the border, a Spanish parador. Although lodged among some of Portugal's most unspoiled antiquities, the pousada is contemporary in concept. It's built villa-fashion on several levels, with an entrance portico connecting the main building with an annex. Most of the lounges and bedrooms not only have a view of the river and Tuy, but also open onto a courtyard with a lawn and reflecting pool.

The public rooms are spacious, flowing one into another, containing wooden ceilings, tiled floors, and various retreat nooks. Favored is the lounge with a wide stone fireplace, a 15-foot plank coffee table, and hand-loomed rugs. Many of the bedrooms have balconies, and 14 of the 16 rooms contain private baths. Single rooms range in price from 2150$ ($32.90); doubles, 2250$ ($34.43). If you stop only for a meal (and many do), the cost ranges from 500$ ($7.65) to 650$ ($9.95) for a five-course table d'hôte luncheon or dinner. The helpings are bountiful and the dishes good, if you like regional cooking. The wooden-ceiling dining room takes full advantage of the view of the river and Spain.

7. Pousada-Hopping in Minho

Many visitors consider pousada-hopping the most rewarding way of exploring Portugal. Every government-owned inn lies in a characteristic region, as well as a special scenic spot. (The first pousada, a place to rest, was founded in the 12th century, offering pilgrims a roof, a bed, and a candle. That kindly motto today includes all the amenities of modern comfort.) Pousadas in this northern region of Portugal include the following:

Pousada de São Bento (tel. 571-90), on the Braga–Geres highway, 16 miles from Vieira do Minho at Caniçada do Minho (about 27 miles from Braga). This small pousada, in lovely countryside, has only ten double rooms, each with bath. For full board, one guest pays from 2950$ ($45.14). If you're stopping by just to sample a regional meal, the charge is 600$ ($9.18). A magnet with guests is the swimming pool.

Pousada da São Bartolomeu, Bragança, Trás-os-Montes (tel. Bragança 224-93). This government-owned inn lies just outside the town, about a half-hour drive from the Spanish frontier town of Quintanilha. Ten double rooms containing private baths are most attractively furnished. The room rate for two persons is 2100$ ($32.13) with bath. The charge for a main meal is 600$ ($9.18), if you're just passing through.

Pousada da Santa Catarina (tel. Miranda 55), at Miranda do Douro (Trás-os-Montes). About 78 miles from Bragança, this inn overlooks the great dam at Upper Douro. Enjoying a scenic spot, the pousada rents out 12 pleasantly furnished double rooms, each with private bath, all year. A party of two is charged 1600$ ($24.48), a single going for 1500$ ($22.95). A complete luncheon or dinner costs 600$ ($9.18).

Pousada de São Lourenço, Manteigas, Sêrra da Estrêla (tel. 471-50), is about 8½ miles from Manteigas, standing at a height of 4900 feet on a mountainside, with a panoramic view. Only 12 double rooms with bath are available. Singles rent for 1500$ ($22.95), doubles, 1600$ ($24.48). One main meal costs 600$ ($9.18), if you're just stopping by. The pousada lies about 56 miles from the Spanish frontier. Rustic in concept, it is surrounded by a pine-studded mountain and valley landscape. The comfort at this well-run pousada is first rate, and you're given a selection of regional dishes. It's most suitable if you're in search of a good rest, combined with tranquility and beauty. For touring, you can be directed to the fountain source of the River Mondego and can see such natural phenomena as "The Head of the Bear" and "The Head of the Old Woman."

With continental Portugal behind us, we head out into the Atlantic.

Chapter XVII

MADEIRA AND THE AZORES

1. Settling into Funchal
2. Excursions in Madeira
3. Discovering the Azores
4. Ponta Delgada
5. Exploring São Miguel
6. Terceira
7. Faial

THE ISLAND OF MADEIRA, 530 miles southwest of Portugal, is the mountain peak of a volcanic mass. Its craggy spires and seacoast precipices of umber-dark basalt end with a sheer drop into the blue water. The surrounding sea is so deep that large blubber-rich sperm whales often come near the shore.

The summit of the undersea mountain is found at Madeira's center where the **Pico Ruivo**, often snow-capped, rises to an altitude of 6105 feet above sea level. From that point project the rocky ribs and ravines of the island, running to the coast. If you stand upon the sea-swept balcony of **Cabo Girão**, one of the world's highest ocean cliffs (1933 feet above the sea), you'll understand the Eden-like quality of Madeira, Camões called it "at the end of the world."

Madeira is only 35 miles in length, about 13 in breadth at its widest point. It contains nearly 100 miles of coastline, but no beaches. In its volcanic soil, plants and flowers blaze like the Tahitian palette of Gauguin. From jacaranda and crawling masses of bougainvillea, to orchids and geraniums, whortleberry to prickly pear, poinsettias, cannas, frangipani, birds of paradise, and wisteria, the land is a botanical garden. Custard apples, avocados, mangos, and bananas grow profusely. Fragrances such as vanilla and wild fennel intermingle with sea breezes and pervade the ravines, sweeping down the rocky headlands.

Claimed by the British as a sentimental dominion, Madeira has long been popular with English people, notably Winston Churchill. The post-Victorians arrived dressed to the teeth, the women in wide-brimmed hats to protect themselves from the sun. Now that has changed: the British make their way here specifically to enjoy the sun, even though most of them visit during the rainy winter season. The climate of Madeira is mild, the mean temperature averaging about 61 degrees Fahrenheit in winter, about 70 degrees Fahrenheit in summer.

Legend has it that two English lovers discovered the island about half a century before its known date of exploration. Supposedly Robert Machim and Anna d'Arfet, fleeing England, were swept off their course by a tempest and deposited on the eastern coast. In 1419, João Gonçalves Zarco and Tristão Vaz Teixeira, captains under Henry the Navigator, discovered Madeira while exploring the African coastline, some 350 miles distant.

As it was densely covered with impenetrable virgin forests, they named it Madeira, meaning wood. Soon it was set afire to clear it for habitation. The holocaust is said to have lasted seven years until all but a small northern section was reduced to ashes.

The hillsides are so richly cultivated today one would never know there had ever been a fire. Many of the groves and vineyards, protected by buffers of sugarcane, grow on stone-wall ledges, which almost spill into the sea. The farmers plant so close to the cliff's edge that they must have at least a dash of goat's blood in them. The terraced mountain slopes are irrigated by a complex network of levadas.

About 25 miles to the northeast, **Porto Santo** is the only other inhabited island in the Madeira archipelago. *Réalités* called it "Another world, arid, desolate and waterless." Unlike Madeira, Porto Santo contains beaches, but is not yet developed for mass tourism.

GETTING THERE FROM LISBON: The quickest and most convenient way to reach Madeira from Lisbon is on a TAP flight (the trip taking one hour and 30 minutes). A one-way air passage, as of this writing, costs from $90 (U.S. dollars), but confirm that with your travel agent or by calling TAP. The plane stops at the Madeira Airport, then goes on to Porto Santo. However, if you're booking a TAP flight from, say, New York to Lisbon, you can have the side trip to Madeira included at no extra cost, providing you have a regular—that is, not an excursion—ticket.

1. Settling into Funchal

The capital of Madeira, Funchal, is the focal point of the entire island and the springboard of outlying villages. When Zarco landed in 1419, the sweet odor of fennel led him to name it after the aromatic herb, called *funcho* in Portuguese. Today, the southern coast city of hillside-shelved villas and narrow winding streets is the garden spot of the island. Its numerous estates, including the former residence of the discoverer Zarco, the Quinta das Cruzes, are among the most exotic in Europe.

THE SIGHTS: Funchal is the center of Madeira's wine industry. Grapes have grown in the region since the early 15th century when Henry the Navigator introduced vines and sugarcane to the slopes. In Funchal, the must (fresh wine) from the black and white grapes is used to make Bual, Sercial, and Malmsey. It's cultivated for its bittersweet tang (women used to scent their handkerchiefs with it). The wine growers still transport the foot-pressed must in goatskin bottles carried over the rough terrain by *borracheiros*. Naturally, it undergoes extensive pasteurization in its refinement and blending.

The **Madeira Wine Association,** 28 Avenida Arriaga (tel. 201-21), next to the Tourist Bureau, offers samples from its diverse stock. Inside this former convent, dating from 1790, are murals depicting the wine pressing (by foot) and harvesting processes which proceed according to traditions established hundreds of years ago. You can savor the slightly burnt sweetness in a setting of old barrels, wine kegs, and time-mellowed chairs and tables made from aged wine kegs. Incidentally, Napoleon passed this way on his journey into exile on St. Helena in 1815. Bottles from a vintage year were given to him, but death came before the former emperor could sample them.

Of the churches of Funchal, the most intriguing is the rustic 15th-century **Sé (cathedral)**, with its Moorish carved cedar ceiling, stone floors, Gothic arches, stained-glass windows, and baroque altars.

Just down the street from the Cruzes Museum is the baroque **Convent of Santa Clara**, Calçada de Santa Clara, with walled tiles, a painted wooden ceiling, and the tomb of Zarco, the discoverer of Madeira. The church is said to have been built by the granddaughter of Zarco the year Columbus discovered America.

The **Museu da Quinta das Cruzes**, 1 Calçada do Pico, is the ancient residence of Madeira's discoverer, João Gonçalves Zarco. The surrounding park is of botanical interest and contains an orchid collection of note. The museum houses many fine examples of English furniture and China Trade Porcelains brought to Madeira by expatriate Englishmen during the 18th century, rare Indo-Portuguese cabinets, and the unique chests, native to Madeira, fashioned from *caixas de acúcar* (sugar boxes, which date from the 17th century). Also worth noting is a superb collection of antique Portuguese silver. The museum is open daily except Sunday from 10 a.m. to noon and 2 to 6 p.m., and charges 30$ (46¢).

The aquatic, bird, and invertebrate life of the archipelago is represented at the **City Museum and Aquarium**, 31 Rua da Mouraria (tel. 297-61). Moray eels, eagle rays, scorpion fish, sea cucumbers, sea zephyrs, sharp-nosed puffers, and loggerhead turtles, as well as many of the beautifully plumed birds seen around Madeira are represented here. On weekdays, the museum is open from 9:30 a.m. to 12:30 p.m. and from 2 to 5 p.m., the aquarium from 9:30 a.m. to 10 p.m. On Sunday and holidays, both are open from noon to 4 p.m. Admission is 10$ (15¢).

The **Municipal Square** is a study in light and dark, its plaza paved with hundreds of black and white lava half moons. The whitewashed buildings surrounding it contain black stone trim and ochre-colored tile roofs. In all, it's an atmosphere of stately beauty.

Finally, you can visit the **lota** (fish auction) and many bazaars selling local handicrafts, such as wickerwork and Madeira embroidery. At the lota, seafood is auctioned off to housewives and restaurant owners. Horse mackerel, grouper, mullet, tunny (sometimes weighing hundreds of pounds), freshwater eels, even a slab of whale steak or a barracuda, will find its way to the stalls.

In the bazaars you can purchase needlepoint tapestries, Madeira wines, laces, embroidery on Swiss organdy or Irish linen, plus all sorts of local crafts such as goatskin boots or Camacha basketry of water willows. The **City Market**, at the Praça do Comércio on Saturday, is a study in color, everything from yams to papaws.

The most exciting (and most crowded) time to visit Funchal is during the **End of the Year Festival**, December 30 to January 1. Fireworks light up the Bay of Funchal, the mountains in the background forming an amphitheater. Floodlit cruise ships anchor in the harbor to the delight of passengers who revel until dawn.

THE HOTELS: In summer, when every other European resort is socking you with its highest tariffs, Madeira experiences its low season. And not because of bad weather. Rather, owing to the temperate climate, the early British

252 □ DOLLARWISE GUIDE TO MADEIRA AND THE AZORES

visitors set a pattern of mass descent in the winter, thereby crowding the hotels and inflating the tariffs. Surely when more people know of summertime Madeira and its low-season rates, the island will build more of an all-year popularity. The hotels range from one of the finest deluxe citadels in Europe to an attractive quinta for budgeteers.

One of Europe's Great Resort Hotels

Reid's Hotel, 139 Estrada Monumental (tel. 230-01). Its position is smashing, along the coastal road at the edge of Funchal, on its own 11 acres of multiterraced gardens cascading down the hillside to the rocky shores. Midway down are two saltwater swimming pools thrust out onto a cliff edge, the pair joined by a bridge and fountain. On a still lower terrace is yet another pool (reached by an elevator) built onto a ledge of rocks. You feel you're swimming in the ocean. The sentimental English who frequent the hotel in large numbers (famous guest of the past: Sir Winston Churchill) spend their days strolling along the scented walks lined with blue and pink hydrangeas, pink camellias, hedges of geraniums, gardenias, banana trees, ferns, and white yuccas.

Reid's has a tradition of quiet dignity, in its public rooms and in a wing added in 1968, all tastefully and successfully combined. The main drawing rooms are refreshingly decorated in the colors of the sea (aqua and jade) with country estate-type furnishings, utilizing either tropical prints or soft solid colors. Afternoon tea or lunch is provided in either the chinoiserie lounge or on the open terrace. There's still another place for lunch, the Garden Restaurant, built on two levels with white and blue outdoor furniture set to face the sea view. The two-level main dining room is classically dignified with Wedgwood-style paneling and ceiling, plus the inevitable and very English silver trolley holding roast beef. The Grill Room is recommended separately in the restaurant section.

The hotel is owned by the Blandy family of wine and shipping fame. On the full-pension plan, a single with an inland view goes for $89 (U.S.), increasing to $103 in a sea-view room. Inland doubles rent for $157, rising to $180 with a sea view and $199 with a sea-view balcony. These rates include three meals for two persons as well as service and taxes. Of the 168 air-conditioned rooms with radio and TV in the suites, all but 14 face the ocean, but in each case the baths are private. The spacious rooms are conservative in the finest sense, with well-chosen pieces, plenty of storage space, sitting areas, and desks. The baths are super-clean, with walls and floor of marble or tile.

Although it's hard to be lured away from Reid's garden park, there are fishing, waterskiing, and sailing trips available. The tennis courts are at your disposal.

The Upper Bracket

The **Casino Park Hotel,** Avenida do Infante (tel. 331-11), is the newest addition to the luxurious hotels of Funchal. Just a seven-minute walk from the center of town, the hotel is nestled in a subtropical garden overlooking the harbor. Designed by architect Oscar Niemeyer, the creator of Brasilia, the main building is low (only five stories) and undulating, as if poised for flight from its position on the cliff above the deep waters. The complex is made up of the hotel and conference center and a separate casino, where "indoor sports" can indulge in such pastimes as baccarat, roulette, blackjack, or French bank. The less sporting may prefer an enjoyable evening of dining and dancing at the panoramic nightclub.

Every conceivable convenience and luxury is available within the Casino Park, including shopping facilities, tennis courts, swimming pools, saunas, billiards, and a health club. Special facilities, including a shallow swimming pool, are provided for the children. You can even arrange fishing, sailing and golf excursions through the hotel. Variety in dining is also thoughtfully provided, from the luxurious and spacious dining room overlooking the port and town of Funchal or the subtly international Grill Room with its extensive wine cellar to the simpler Coffee Shop adjacent to the swimming pool for a refreshing snack after a swim.

The 400 fully air-conditioned rooms each have their own balconies offering superb views of the harbor and town. Each room also has its own private bath, telephone, and radio. The rooms are tastefully coordinated with bright, sunny colors which seem to bring the radiance of the island and the sea indoors. In addition, two comfortable lounge areas on each floor offer visitors a spot to meet and relax at the end of a busy day.

A single rents for $60 (U.S.), rising to $80 in a double. For two meals a day, add an additional $23 per person to the tariffs quoted.

Madeira Palácio, Estrada Monumental (tel. 300-01), is a luxurious hotel of 260 well-appointed rooms and 18 suites on the seaside route to Camara de Lobos, about two miles from the center of Funchal. The hotel is perched on a cliff over the sea. From the establishment, Madeira's famous high cliff, Cabo Girão, can be seen looming in the distance.

All the handsomely tended rooms are complete with private baths, telephones, radios, and balconies. The tariff depends on the location, rooms opening onto the mountain less expensive than those facing the sea. For half board, a single costs $56 (U.S.), rising to $80 in a double.

The star-shaped hotel is most contemporary, with three wings. The public salons and guests rooms are colorfully coordinated, and local woods, native construction materials, and Madeiran fabrics have been used judiciously when appropriate. During the day guests enjoy a heated swimming pool, an outdoor snackbar, tennis courts in the gardens, and a shopping arcade complete with a hairdresser and a sauna, even table tennis.

Visitors may select the hotel's restaurant with its menu of both local and international dishes, or else they may prefer the specialties of the à la carte Grillroom. Later, entertainment is provided in the nightclub with its private orchestra which plays for dancing. Occasional folk dances are staged here as well.

Madeira-Sheraton, Largo António Nobre (tel. 310-31), is a luxurious, 17-story, high-rise structure near the Casino with direct access to the sea. The 300-room hotel offers three swimming pools, a restaurant for 350 persons, plus an English pub, a specialty grill, and a nightclub for 250. The hotel has some amusing eccentricities of design—two trapezium-shaped elevators that transport clients down to their rooms from the reception area. All the accommodations, many furnished in a provincial style, are air-conditioned with private balconies, showers, radios, direct-dial telephones, and TV sets in the suites.

A single ranges from $55 (U.S.) to $70, doubles go for $75 to $90 daily. The least expensive rates are for the standard mountain view, the more expensive for deluxe rooms with a sea view. The rates quoted include service, taxes, and breakfast. For half board, add $17.50 per person daily. The hotel lies on a promontory overlooking Funchal Bay in the fashionable Vale-Verde Garden district, next to the century-old landmark, Reid's. Its oceanfront exposure to the south offers dawn to dusk sunlight on all pool terraces and seaside guestroom balconies and patios.

The Middle Bracket

Hotel Orquidea, 71 Rua dos Netos (tel. 260-91). The Orchid blooms right in Funchal. A first-class hotel, it offers 70 small, but comfortable bedrooms, each with private bath and phone. Most of the accommodations open onto their own terraces. Inside, the atmosphere is sleek modern, with polished marble surfaces and much plastic. For a room with a continental breakfast, one person in high season pays 1000$ ($15.30), that fee increasing to 1400$ ($21.42) for two, taxes included. The best feature of the hotel is its rooftop terrace, with a panoramic view of the town and port.

Santa Isabel, Avenida do Infante (tel. 231-11), was built in the early 1960s to accommodate groups who wanted completely modern lodgings in the sun. In the center of the deluxe hotel belt, it was equipped with its own rooftop terrace and swimming pool. How luxurious it is to swim, sunbathe, and lunch around the pool—without having to change one's attire.

The atmosphere is somewhat impersonal, although the bedrooms are warmly decorated, each with a triangular sun balcony. Armless soft chairs, homespun striped draperies, and combined chests of drawers with lift-up mirror dressing tables give the rooms a comfortable edge. Freshly maintained and tiled baths are included with each room. There are three grades of accommodations, extending from the more expensive ones facing the sea to the cheaper rooms opening onto a garden and a mountain view.

In high season, the half-board rate in a double is 3200$ ($48.96), dropping to 2500$ ($38.25) in a single. A public lounge with an open fireplace adjoins a bricked sun terrace.

Hotel do Carmo, off the Avenida João de Deus at 10 Travessa do Rego (tel. 290-01), provides modern accommodations right in the center of Funchal. One of the more recent hotels to sprout up in the city, it is erected in a cellular honeycomb fashion, each bedroom opening onto its own private balcony. While there is no surrounding garden, guests gather during the day for dips in the L-shaped rooftop swimming pool (good view of the harbor from here).

Created by the Fernandes family, it was designed for guests who have limited purses and want to be near the bazaars in the heart of the city's life. The bedrooms are simple, with contemporary furnishings (wall-to-wall draperies, overhead bed lights, armchairs, tiled bathrooms). For a room and breakfast, one person pays $22 (U.S.); two persons, $31. Meals are served in a spacious dining room, decorated with a green harlequin tile floor. A little lounge opens onto an inner patio.

Girassol, 256 Estrada Monumental (tel. 310-51), is a little hotel offering immaculate accommodations at reasonable tariffs. It's on the outskirts of Funchal, overlooking the Tourist Club, where guests are allowed access to the sea at a small charge. Every one of its accommodations has a sunny balcony, half overlooking the mountains, the rest viewing the sea. Each chamber also comes complete with private bath, including a shower, plus a radio and telephone. Most double rooms are, in fact, suites, consisting of bedroom, bathroom, small sitting room, and veranda. The room decor is bright and cheerful. On the half-board plan, two persons can stay here at a cost of 2300$ ($35.19) per person, including taxes and service. If double rooms are put to single use, the half-board rate begins at 3600$ ($55.08). Two swimming pools are available, one for children. Guests can also catch the sun on the 12th-floor solarium. On the street level is a bar and social lounge, even a hairdressing salon. There's a nightclub with orchestra every night except Sunday. Two other special features include an entrance courtyard with a series of octagonal reflection pools and a dining room with sea views.

The Budget Range

Miramar Hotel, Estrada Monumental (tel. 211-41), is one of the great old villas of Funchal, functioning now as a very personal hotel under the management of an American, Richard Thomas. While it appears to be much older, it was the grandiose creation of a wine and shipping merchant named Solomão Veiga França. Built in 1922, it was once considered the finest house in the city and was dubbed Solomon's Temple. Sadly, the merchant lost it during the Depression.

The style of the mansion is preserved but improved. It is built on several acres of gardens facing the harbor—hauntingly similar to a Beverly Hills estate. Its entrance is through formal gates and a central stone staircase, with balustrades covered with ivy. The front veranda is glass covered, with a climbing magenta-colored trumpet vine. Most impressive is the central two-story-high entrance hall, with a curving wooden staircase and paneled doorways. The drawing room and adjoining card salon are neoclassic, furnished in a homey fashion, more English than stylish. Log fires burn in the winter months.

Meals are served either in the coral and white dining room, which has window walls opening onto the garden and harbor view, or in summer in the garden bower under a giant camphor tree. Accommodations are offered in the main house as well as two chalets, some of which have little private gardens. The rooms are furnished with brightly painted pieces in pastel sea colors and most have wicker chairs and end tables, as well as sitting areas. Prices vary depending on whether you have the luxury of a private bath or a balcony. Single rooms with a balcony and a view of either the sea or mountains go for 1700$ ($26.01) daily on the half-board plan. The rate in a double, with a balcony and sea view (or mountain) is 2550$ ($39.02) daily for two persons, also on the half-board arrangement, all taxes included. In addition, Mr. Thomas has opened one of the largest and best discos on the island.

The Best Bargains

Quinta da Penha de França, off the Rua da Penha de França (tel. 290-87), exists because of the dash and impulsiveness of Muriel Ribeiro, who startled the substantial citizens of Funchal by turning her gracious old quinta into a guest house. Married to a successful surgeon, she took quite seriously the announcement of her son that he wanted to learn the hotel business. After a short training period in London, he now works for her at the quinta.

Their family home, chock full of antiques, paintings, and silver, is in its own garden right on a ledge almost hanging over the harbor. It's a short walk to the center of the bazaars and is opposite an ancient chapel. The four-story antiga casa is bone white with dark-green shutters, plus small-panel windows overlooking the ocean. Across the front terrace is a good-size swimming pool with white iron garden chairs arranged for lazy lounging. Set on the hillside in the midst of poinsettias, bamboo, sugarcane, and coffee plants is a wine lodge and stone washhouse now converted into guest rooms.

The furnishings of the public lounges and bedrooms are an heirloom mixture. She likes to mix people as well ("not too much of the same kind"). Twin-bedded rooms with bath go for $40 (U.S.), including breakfast.

Apart from the main house and the bungalows, the family has opened a bar. Called simply "Joe's Bar," it is decorated in a turn-of-the-century style.

Vila Lido, 17 Rua do Gorgulho (tel. 211-00), stands on the edge of a rocky cliff directly above the sea. It's surrounded by its own lawns and gardens. Owned by a German couple, the villa attracts a large patronage not only from their own country, but from the Scandinavian countries as well. The couple speak English and bring a homelike hospitality to their place. The food is excellent, and the setting is comfortable and moderately attractive. Antiques are interspersed with the more contemporary pieces, usually in floral chintz. Bright colors prevail. Tariffs for bed and breakfast range from 1100$ ($16.83) per person in some doubles to 1400$ ($21.42) per person for the best doubles, which include balconies opening onto the sea. One person, with lunch included, pays anywhere from 1450$ ($22.19) to 1700$ ($26.01) daily. The Vila Lido lies a ten-minute ride by bus from the center of Funchal.

Hotel Madeira, 21 Rua Ivens (tel. 300-71), is in the center of Funchal behind the park and in the quietest part of the town. The rooms are clean and comfortable, and there is a rooftop swimming pool with a solarium area, where the bar and snack services never give you a chance to be thirsty. It has the most extraordinary panoramic view of the town, mountains, and sea. At 2200$ ($33.66) in a double, including breakfast, this is a good buy.

READER'S BOARDING HOUSE SELECTION: "The **Pensão Santos,** 22 Estrada Monumental, has been in existence since 1936. Senhor and Senhora Santos extend a gracious hospitality to their guests that is rare to find these days. Besides the main house on Estrada Monumental, near Reid's Hotel, a lovely villa with a private garden is a short distance away by the Lido. There are 22 beds in all. The rooms range from singles without bath for 800$ ($12.24) to doubles with sitting room and private bath for 2000$ ($30.60). These prices include breakfast and a hearty evening meal. Sr. Santos speaks English and is eager to help guests in their exploration of the island" (Doris E. Widerkehr, New York, N.Y.).

MACHICO: If you don't mind living at Machico on the east coast where the Portuguese first landed, you'll find two more excellent hotels. This part of land-scarce Madeira is being rapidly developed. Already a number of tiny vacation villas are climbing the hillside. In the complex is a yacht club, plus an elegant bridge club. Machico is about 5 minutes from the airport, but a good 30-minute run along a twisting road to Funchal.

Two Hotels

Atlantis, Agua de Pena, Machico (tel. 544-01), stands gleaming white in the Madeira sun, a mammoth complex of 300 tastefully furnished rooms, which in high season (December 15 to April 30) go for $40 (U.S.) for one person, $62 for two, on the half-board plan. It's a complete resort world unto itself, featuring the only heated indoor pool in Madeira, with a sunroof in the lobby. The outdoor figure-eight pool is another highlight, especially when the weather's right. The hotel also features a game room, health club, mini-golf, and two tennis courts. Six miles away, you'll find the nine-hole golf course of Santo da Serra. Dining on international cuisine is enjoyed either in the Algarve Restaurant, done in creamy orange, or in the Madeira dining room, decorated in rose and brown. There's also a boîte for dancing. The inn's own bus makes frequent trips back and forth from Funchal.

Nearby is the **Hotel Dom Pedro da Madeira,** Machico (tel. 554-50), a modern structure that boasts sea views, private baths, and phones for every room. The sparsely furnished rooms are well kept, comfortable, and tastefully appointed. On the bed-and-breakfast plan, the single rate is 1800$ ($27.54), that tariff rising to 2600$ ($39.78) for two. Rooms with balconies and suites cost more. An extra meal is 600$ ($9.18). Good food is served in the Panoramic Restaurant. A bar, a heated saltwater swimming pool, sun terraces, a beach, even a disco, make this a nice choice.

FUNCHAL

THE RESTAURANTS: Many of the major hotels require full or half board in high season; but perhaps you'll be able to sneak away for a regional meal at one of the recommendations listed below. The list begins, however, with the pick of the hotel restaurants.

The Upper Bracket

Reid's Grill, Reid's Hotel, 139 Estrada Monumental (tel. 230-01), is generally conceded to be the island's finest restaurant. Both guests and the local gentry consider it the perfect place to celebrate a new amour or console oneself after the loss of an old love. True to English tradition, clients sometimes still dress for dinner, the women often in silk, the men sedate in black tie.

The chef combines a French, Portuguese, and English cuisine that makes for a bill of fare peculiar to Reid's. For your palatable preliminaries, you can try everything from Portuguese soup at 120$ ($1.84) to homemade terrine (potted meat in a crock) at 180$ ($2.75). The kitchen offers about a dozen specialties, worth several visits just to sample them.

Favored are the fish stew Funchal style, sea bass with fennel, and espetada, chunks of beef filet skewered on a branch of laurel tree. Americans especially are fond of the porterhouse steak for two. To top your repast, you can select from the dessert trolley. Any meal here will cost you an average of 1250$ ($19.13), and you can be sure it will be excellent.

Another elegant choice for dining, the **Grill Room** of the Casino Park Hotel, Avenida do Infante (tel. 331-11), is superb. Not only do you receive well-prepared food and immaculate service, but the view of Funchal at night is enthralling. For about $35 (U.S.), two diners can enjoy a cocktail before dinner, then perhaps the shrimp flambé, prepared right in front of you. This is one of the chef's many specialties, including not only the shrimps, but mushrooms, onions, brandy, wine, and a tomato sauce. It comes with a fresh vegetable such as peas and carrots. If you're not flambéd out, you can order for dessert a crêpe suzette flamed in brandy.

The Medium-Priced Range

Restaurante Caravela, 15-17 Avenida do Mar (tel. 284-64), is a modern restaurant right on the waterfront. You can dine on a glass-enclosed terrace with an open fireplace or else in the inner room where you sit in wicker chairs. Reached by elevator, the top-floor restaurant gives diners a view of the cruise ships arriving and departing. You can order both lunch and dinner, as well as afternoon tea with open-faced Danish smørrebröd sandwiches. What to offer daily on the menu is decided by the Caravela's Swedish owner, Otto Ullman.

The cooking is personal, with a large choice of tasty dishes. Perhaps the finest regional dish is espetada, skewered meat flavored with garlic and bay leaves, costing 425$ ($6.50) and served only on special request. Unpretentious and proud of the native Portuguese dishes, the restaurant features Caravela fish for 300$ ($4.59), but also turns out international dishes, such as chateaubriand flambé, 650$ ($9.95). A favorite dessert is a fruit salad at 70$ ($1.07). The restaurant is open seven days a week, with lunch served between noon and 3 p.m.; dinner, from 6:30 to 10 p.m.

Clube de Turismo da Madeira, 179 Estrada Monumental (tel. 203-59), is a fine place for lunch and a swim. At the edge of Funchal, it appears to be a private club, but membership isn't necessary. Approached through a lane of poinsettias, sugarcane, and bougainvillea, the club is close to the sea. It's like a small tiled villa, with a beachhouse built to adjoin a free-form swimming pool.

Meals are served in one of the intimate dining rooms or on a covered veranda where guests relax in rattan chairs. One interior salon is 19th-century formal, with crystal chandeliers and mahogany chairs. The bar, with iron lanterns, tavern chairs, and pine beams, is more rustic.

A typical meal begins with a well-prepared hearty soup, costing 30$ (46¢) to 60$ (92¢). Fish dishes include such items as grilled red mullet or a more expensive natural lobster. Meat courses include Portuguese beef or roast chicken. Regular main dishes are priced from 220$ ($3.37) to 450$ ($6.89). Even if you stop in just for a drink, you'll be welcome. A dry martini or cognac goes for 120$ ($1.84). To use the pool, you pay 60$ (92¢), the tab including a changing cabin. Lunch is served from 12:30 to 3:30 p.m.; dinner from 7 to 10 p.m. daily.

Jardim do Sol, Caniço, on the coast highway east of Funchal (tel. 931-23). This roadside inn is like a hunting lodge, with knotty-pine walls, a mezzanine, rattan chairs, and two walls of glass with a view of the sea through tall pines. The owner has installed framed murals of the local fishermen, a bamboo bar, and window boxes overflowing with orange marigolds. The proprietor caters not only to the residents of Funchal, but to the cruise ships that tie up in port.

A 780$ ($11.93) table d'hôte luncheon or dinner is offered, although the wine is extra. You'll be given a first course, usually a big bowl of good-tasting soup, followed by a fish dish such as filet of scabbard, then a meat course, a dessert, and finally fresh fruit. Lunch is from 12:30 to 2:30 p.m.; dinner from 7 to 9:30 p.m.

The Budget Range

A Seta, 80 Estrada do Livramento, Monte (tel. 203-07), is for regional cuisine supreme. The mountainside restaurant is a tavern-style place where you can order inexpensive and tasty meals. The proprietor seemingly patterns himself after Ernest Borgnine, shirt sleeves and all. The decor is rustic, with a burnt-wood trim, walls covered with pine cones, and crude natural pine tables. An inner dining room adjoins an open kitchen, with a charcoal spit and oven, ideal for those who want to watch the action.

First of all, a plate of coarse brown homemade bread still warm from the oven is put at your place. Above each table is a hook to which is attached a long skewer of charcoal-broiled meat. You slip off chunks while mopping up the juices with your crusty bread. There are three specialties: beef, chicken, and grilled dry codfish. Seasoned with olive oil, herbs, garlic, and bay leaves, these concoctions are called *espetadas.* A bowl of rich-tasting soup costs 35$ (54¢) to 55$ (84¢); a salad, 65$ (99¢); the fried potatoes, 55$ (84¢); and a skewer of beef 240$ ($3.67). The least expensive bottle of wine goes for 80$ ($1.22).

Restaurant Estrelicia, in the Hotel Madeira, 21 Rua Ivens, lies in comfortable surroundings near the City Gardens. If you'd like some light, cool fare instead of the heavy Portuguese cuisine, we'd suggest a luncheon there. It's a welcome change to have a light cold meat and salad lunch, one that's tasty, nicely served, and in a clean restaurant with several amenities, including, on occasions, orchids placed on the tables. Most platters cost only 150$ ($2.30) and are likely to feature cold roast beef (or ham) with a fresh green salad, fish and chips, or else a tuna-fish salad platter. It's under the same management as the Carochinha Restaurant.

Combatentes, 1 Rua Ivens (tel. 213-88), is a good choice for regional food, a favorite of Funchal's colony of doctors and lawyers. At the top of the Municipal Gardens, this simple Portuguese restaurant serves well-prepared dishes, including rabbit stew, roast chicken, stewed squid, and codfish. The

Portuguese eat a lot, so the portions are ample, with two vegetables and a green salad coming with the main dish if required. Desserts are likely to be simple, including caramel custard and chocolate mousse or fresh fruit, and most diners begin with a bowl of the soup of the day. A dinner for two persons is likely to cost around 550$ ($8.42). The waiters are friendly and efficient, and hours are from noon to 3 p.m. and from 7 to 10 p.m.

Pensão Restaurante Universal, 4 Rua de João Tavira (tel. 206-18), stands in the center of town, one minute from the cathedral. Although some foreigners patronize it, it is known mainly to the Portuguese. Service is slow, so plan to dine leisurely. Various steaks cost from 150$ ($2.30) to 190$ ($2.91), but you can also order pork chops at 160$ ($2.45) and a roast chicken at 150$ ($2.30). The cook specializes in filet espada at 160$ ($2.45). At lunch one of the omelets, ranging from 100$ ($1.53) to 130$ ($1.99), might interest you. Soups and desserts are also available at low prices.

Bar Restaurante A Gruta, Estrada Pontinha, has an attractive position, overlooking the harbor and lying only a ten-minute walk from the center of town. It has tables both inside and out, and serves drinks and food from 9 a.m. to 11 p.m. The layout is simple—metal tables and chairs and paper tablecloths—but the food is ample and good, and the service is friendly. The clients are both Portuguese and foreigners from all walks of life, everybody from the vice military governor of the island to the British consul. The prices are most reasonable. Two persons can dine here, enjoying an ample meal with wine and coffee, for about $8 (U.S.) apiece. Main dishes are well prepared, including hearty soups, grilled chicken, filet of swordfish, omelets (with a variety of stuffings), beefsteak (also on a spit). We prefer the gambas, those giant prawns flown in from Mozambique.

Romana, 15 Largo do Corpo Santo (tel. 289-56), lies in the old part of town. Because of the ability and good taste of its owner, João Carlos Abreu, the restaurant is most attractively decorated. For local residents it is considered expensive, but most North Americans will find it reasonably priced, particularly when considering the quality of food served. The clientele is international. Favorite dishes include chicken sauté at 300$ ($4.59) or filet espada with fried bananas, 260$ ($3.97). I'm also fond of the smoked swordfish at 320$ ($4.90). The meats are first class, and therefore you may want to order one of the steaks, priced from 400$ ($6.12) to 500$ ($7.65).

Restaurant Snack-Bar A Flor, 6 Rua da Queimada da Cima, in the center of town, about two minutes from the cathedral, is favored mostly by young people. Alcoholic drinks are served. The restaurant seats about 30 guests, and the atmosphere is pleasant, the service quite satisfactory. Prices are reasonable, the portions ample, and the quality of the food is good. Various steaks cost from 200$ ($3.06), and a well-prepared wienerschnitzel goes for 180$ ($2.76). Other main dishes include pork chops at 190$ ($2.91) or roast chicken at 180$ ($2.76). All main dishes are served with two vegetables. My latest dinner there (for two), including a bottle of good white wine, came to only 600$ ($9.18) with tip.

Gavinas, Rua do Gorgulho (tel. 269-08), won't please everybody. It's in a category by itself, the most rustic dining spot in this entire guide. Reached by driving out the Estrada Monumental to the Lido, it is a little garage-like cement cottage set among the rocks on the sea. You pass along a field of sugarcane overlooking the water, then descend the cliff via a narrow cobblestone pathway. Despite the ethnic setting (even an occasional drunk stumbling over to you), Gavinas draws a stream of well-heeled diners.

The fish is as fresh as one can imagine, practically cleaned and cooked right in front of you. No fancy sauces, no elaborate service—just hearty sea fare, cooked the way many of the Madeirans cherish it. You'll spend about 450$

($6.89) for a regular meal, including a salad, bread, plus wine or beer. Sometimes the owner-chef, Senhor Gavinas, makes a savory caldeirada (fish stew), but generally he grills or fries at his primitive stove.

READERS' RESTAURANT SELECTIONS: "The most reasonably priced restaurant in downtown Funchal is the **Casa da Carochinha,** facing the City Gardens at 2A/2B Rua de São Francisco. Owned and hosted by the congenial Roy and Maureen Maggs of Bristol, England, Casa abounds in continental charm and serves fine, homecooked meals with a European flavor. Each guest enjoys complimentary Madeira with the meal, and a flag of his or her country is placed on a spotlessly white Nottingham lace tablecloth. If you are lucky enough to join the Maggses at their dinner table, they will delight you with stories about their experiences in Madeira and elsewhere, providing the visitor with a wealth of information not available at the local Tourist Office. Dinner is served from 7 to 10 p.m. à la carte, and lunch from noon to 2 p.m. It is closed Sunday" (Connie Tonken, Hartford, Conn.). . . . "We ate frequently at the **Rotunda Restaurant** on Rua de Serpa Pinto. It's a newly opened restaurant, bar, and snackbar. The food is excellent, as is the service, and the waiters speak English. For $12 (U.S.) we had vegetable soup, pork in wine and garlic, string beans, french fries, rice, fresh baked bread, chocolate cake, and a bottle of Madeira wine" (Linda S. Neubauer, Rochelle Park, N.J.).

Tea and Pastries

Casa Minas Ceraes (The Corner Shop), Avenida do Infante, is an old-fashioned tea and pastry shop which has been around for more than 47 years. At its central serving bar, waiters make pots of tea and coffee or else pour Madeira wine. Before sitting at one of the little tables, clients pick out a pastry, paying for it separately. The waiters bring only the beverages. Against the walls are tall built-in cupboards, with glass doors in bright blue and gold. Shoeshine boys ply their trade from table to table. A pot of tea costs 40$ (61¢) for two persons. The Corner Shop opens onto a circular fountain and the busy boulevard.

READER'S TIP: "Do see **Camacha,** where the wicker factory is. You can watch employees, many of them children, making the wicker products. They are very cheap, a chair costing $15 (U.S.) and up, and well made. Near the wicker place is a restaurant, **Flor da Achada** (tel. 922-141), that is quite good. The whole restaurant is covered in wicker—the ceiling, walls, decorations, and chairs, and it also has a small store. Two of us had a meal consisting of chicken, french fries, seasoned rice, a liter of house wine, and custard for which we paid $5 apiece." (W. Michael Sharpe, Windsor, Ontario, Canada).

TOBOGGAN RIDES: Time was when the visiting Victorians (some of the men looking like Mr. Pickwick) were carried around the islands in hammocks slung on poles and supported by two husky bearers. Nowadays, the government is discouraging this form of transport, although it still exists. As one official put it: "The Communists object to it. They consider it a form of slavery." A more popular means of transport in Funchal is to hire a bullock-pulled, wheel-less sledge on the Avenida do Mar, near the pier.

By far, the most famous ride, however, is the descent by toboggan from **Monte,** about four miles from Funchal. You ascend by taxi, about a 20-minute trip. Before you begin your descent, you can visit the **Church of Nossa Senhora do Monte,** which contains the iron tomb of the last of the Hapsburgs, the Emperor Charles who died in Madeira in 1922 of pneumonia. From a belvedere nearby, you can look down on the whole of Funchal: the narrow streets, the plazas, and especially the *cais,* that long docking pier set in deep-blue mirror-like water.

The toboggan is a wide wicker basket with wooden runners. As it rushes down the slippery smooth cobblestones, it is directed and sometimes propelled by two expert, straw-hatted guides who yaw the ropes like nimble-footed seamen. You may need to fortify yourself with a glass or two of Madeira wine before taking the plunge. From Monte to Funchal the ride costs 250$ ($3.82) per person. You can also take the toboggan ride from **Terreiro da Luta** to Funchal. At Terreiro da Luta, at a height of 2875 feet, you'll enjoy another splendid view of Funchal. Here also are monuments to Zarco and Our Lady of Peace.

FOLK DANCING: The **Windsor** at Terreiro da Luta (tel. 235-88) offers a folkloric exhibition at an outside dancing ring. Dancers in native costumes perform in a circle to live musical accompaniment. The cost is 300$ ($4.59) per person, including a glass of Madeira wine. From the dining room, which seats 400 guests, there is a full view of Funchal and the port from a height of 1300 feet.

FUNCHAL AFTER DARK: The **Casino Park Complex** (tel. 331-11) is the glittering target for most visitors to the island. On its own grounds in the center of town, it is just minutes from most of the big hotels. "Indoor sports" include roulette, chemin de fer, French bank, craps, blackjack, and 120 slot machines for the "Dixie cup" crowd. Designed by the architect Oscar Niemeyer, the complex features a 400-room, five-star deluxe hotel (the Casino Park), plus a nightclub with international entertainment. At the restaurant continental and Portuguese specialties are served.

Admission to the Casino is easy for foreign tourists, who take along their passports or some other identification card. The entrance fee for two nights is 75$ ($1.15), increasing to 120$ ($1.84) for one week.

The Prince Albert, Rua da Imperatriz D. Amélia, is a Victorian pub in Madeira, complete with cut plush velvet walls, tufted banquettes, and English pub memorabilia. You're greeted with a "Good evening, sir." Next to the Savoy, the pub serves oversize mugs of beer and a cross sampling of all the accents of England. Drinks are served at the curved bar or at one of the tables under Edwardian fringed lamps. Whiskeys range from 60$ (92¢) to 150$ ($2.30); beer, from 35$ (54¢) to 100$ ($1.53).

The **Infinity** operates out of the previously recommended Miramar Hotel, Estrada Monumental (tel. 211-41). It's the largest and best disco on the island. This is where the people of Madeira meet with an international crowd. The music is the very latest hits from the U.S. and Europe. The disco opens nightly at 9 p.m. every day of the week, and drinks begin at 150$ ($2.30).

2. Excursions in Madeira

To explore and savor Madeira, the adventurous visitor with endless time will go on foot across some of the trails. Hand-hewn stones and gravel side embankments lead one (but definitely not the queasy) along precipitous ledges, down into lush ravines, across flowering meadows. These dizzying paths are found everywhere from the hillsides of the wine-rich region of Estreito de Câmara de Lobos to the wickerwork center of Camacha.

A much easier way to go, of course, is on an organized tour, although you may prefer to risk the hazardous driving on hairpin curves by renting your own automobile in Funchal, competing for space on the narrow coastal road with overloaded banana trucks.

Heading west from Funchal, you'll pass banana groves almost spilling into the sea, women doing their laundry on rocks, and homes so tiny they're almost like dollhouses. Less than six miles away lies the coastal village of **Câmara de Lobos** (Room of the Wolves), the subject of several paintings by Sir Winston Churchill. A sheltered and tranquil shell-shaped cove, it is set amid rocks and towering cliffs, with hill-climbing cottages, terraces, and date palms. In the late afternoon, naked youngsters loll and play in the cove, alongside the bobbing fishing boats in such colors as sunflower gold, kelly green, and marine blue.

The road north from the village through the vineyards leads to **Estreito de Câmara de Lobos,** the heart of the wine-growing region that produces Madeira. The men who cultivate the ribbon-like terraces can be seen laboring in the fields, wearing brown stocking caps with tasseled tops. Along the way you'll spot women sitting on mossy stone steps, doing Madeira embroidery. At times clouds move in over the mountain tops obscuring the view, then pass off toward the sea or tumble down a hillside. One visitor compared the effect to "a very expensive production of *Götterdämmerung.*"

A helpful reader, Herman Marcuse, Arlington, Va., adds this footnote: "One of the best kept secrets on Madeira is that you can make excursions on local buses at a fraction charged by the tour companies."

Scaling a hill studded with pine and eucalyptus, you'll reach **Cabo Girão,** the oceanside cliff mentioned in the introduction. Considered the second-loftiest promontory in Europe, a belvedere overlooks the sea and the saffron-colored rocks below. Close by, you can see how the land is cultivated in Madeira, one terrace seemingly no larger than a small throw rug. (Incidentally, the blondes you see in and around here aren't peroxided. Rather, the straw-colored hair was inherited from early Flemish settlers sent to the island.)

Try to return to Funchal by veering off the coastal road, past São Martinho to the belvedere at **Pico dos Barcelos.** In one of the most idyllic spots on the island, you can see the ocean, the mountains, orange and banana groves, bougainvillea in every direction, poinsettias, and the capital. Whether it's roosters crowing, babies crying in faraway huts, or goats bleating, the sound carries for miles.

By heading north from Funchal, you can visit some of the most outstanding spots in the heart of the island. Going first through Santo António, you'll eventually reach **Curral da Freiras,** a petite village huddled around an old monastery at the bottom of an extinct volcanic crater. The site, whose name means Corral of the Nuns, was originally a secluded convent which protected the good sisters from the appetites of sea-weary, woman-hungry mariners and pirates.

If you go north in a different direction, one of the goals is **Santana.** Many visitors have described it as something out of Disney's *Fantasia.* Picture an alpine setting, complete with waterfalls, cobblestone streets, green meadows sprinkled with multicolored blossoms, thatched cottages, swarms of roses, and plunging ravines. Of it, novelist Paul Bowles once wrote: "It is as if a 19th-century painter with a taste for the baroque had invented a countryside to suit his own personal fantasy. It is the sort of picture that used to adorn the grocer's calendar."

Southwest of the village is **Queimadas,** the site of a 3000-foot-high rest house. From here, many persons make the three-hour trek to the apex of **Pico Ruivo** (Purple Peak), referred to earlier as the highest point on the island, 6105 feet above sea level.

Those who stay only in Funchal miss what the island is about. If you don't care to venture into the mountains in your own automobile, then take one of the many excursions to different sections of the island. The tours reach virtually every accessible point in Madeira from Porto Moniz to Câmara de Lobos, and many of the excursions are terminated in Monte where you can finish with a toboggan ride into Funchal. Various tours leave every day except Sunday; the major jaunt to Porto Moniz runs Tuesday and Friday, and costs 500$ ($7.65). A toboggan tour departs at 2:30 p.m. on Thursday, costing 350$ ($5.36). The Santana tour is a Saturday destination, leaving at 9 a.m. and costing 750$ ($11.48), including lunch and tea. A regular Monday tour of the city of Funchal departs at 9 a.m. and finishes at 12:30 p.m., for a price of 250$ ($3.82). Madeira possesses a number of travel agencies, including Wagons-Lits Cook. If you go to any of them, you can receive detailed information about the island tours available. Not all are by motorcoach; some are by boat. You can also pick up information at the **Official Tourist Bureau**, on the jacaranda-lined Avenida Arriaga.

In the east, about 18 miles from Funchal (a short drive from the airport) is historical **Machico**, with its much-visited **Church of Senhor dos Milagres**, dating from the mid-15th century. According to legend, the church was built over the tombs of the two star-crossed English lovers, Robert Machim and Anna d'Arfet. Try to view the village from the belvedere of **Camöë Pequeno**. In the vicinity is a grotto 300 feet long, said to be the deepest in Madeira.

On the way back from Machico, you can detour inland to **Camacha**, perched in a setting of flowers and orchards. It's the island center of the wickerwork industry. You can buy here (although the stores back in Funchal are heavily supplied), or just watch chairs and other items being made by the local crafts people.

ISLAND DINING: While exploring Madeira, you may want to arrange luncheon stopovers at one of the following recommendations:

The government-owned **Pousada dos Vinhaticos**, near Sêrra de Agua (tel. 623-44), is near the top of a pass on the winding road to São Vincente. Guests can visit just for a meal or else spend the night. The pousada is built of solid stone, a tavern-style building with a brick terrace. On that terrace comfortable wicker armchairs are placed, allowing visitors to absorb the unmarred mountain views. The cooking is regional, a complete meal costing 250$ ($3.82). Most of the bedrooms are in Portuguese modern, although a few accommodations contain antiques. All have private baths, good views, and are kept immaculately. The price of a double room is 1000$ ($15.30) nightly, dropping to just 850$ ($13.01) in a single, including breakfast.

Áquàrio, Seixal (tel. 641-96), is a waterfront fish restaurant too often ignored by visitors who flock to the dining spots of Porto Moniz, where they have to fight for a seat. In less confusion, clients at Áquàrio enjoy some of the tastiest cooking on the island. Although the kitchen turns out simple fare, the cooking often outdistances the table d'hôte menus served in the deluxe hotels. Everything is prepared fresh for the diner. The tall proprietor oversees every serving by the neophyte waitresses. To begin with, one gets a heaping basket of homemade bread and a carafe of the local wine. We'd recommend the grilled fish of the day, served with three vegetables. Fish plates cost 300$ ($4.59), and the less recommended meat dishes average 350$ ($5.36). Soups are hearty, the helpings generous, and the cost is 55$ (84¢) per bowl. The decor is nautical, the walls decorated with objects rescued from the sea. On sale are handmade straw and reed baskets. Lunch only is offered, and you can arrive any time before 3:30 p.m. and be served.

A Cabana, Beira da Quinta São Jorge (tel. 572-91), is a colony of circular cottages with central roofs, arranged at the edge of a cliff on the northern coast of Madeira. True to the architecture of the region, the roofs are thatched. The furnishings are crude but attractive. Each unit has a private bath and a bed recess, along with a murphy bed. Two armchairs await one on either side of a fireplace. The cost is only 1000$ ($15.30) per person in the winter months, rising to 1400$ ($21.42) is summer. The coffee's free.

A much larger circular thatched hut with an open beamed ceiling provides good-tasting meals at about 500$ ($7.65) per person. Many of the specialties are cooked on a large open semicircular charcoal fireplace. Specialties include beef grilled on a spit, roast chicken, roast cod, panada, and bolos do caco, a typical bread.

THE "OTHER MADEIRA": There's yet another island that forms part of Madeira, although it is completely different in character. It's **Porto Santo,** only nine miles long and three miles wide with a seven-mile stretch of fine, sandy beach along the southern shore. Soft rolling hills are crowned here with a few remaining, unusual windmills. Gentle, rolling farmland gives way to sand dunes.

The town, **Vila Baleira,** where boats dock, is attractive, but very sleepy. Its mosaic sidewalks are shaded by palm trees. About the biggest event that ever happened around here was when Columbus slept on Porto Santo. His wife, Isabela Moniz, was the daughter of the first governor of Madeira who made Porto Santo their home. The house where Columbus reportedly stayed is in a tiny alley behind a small white church near the center.

The island is for escapists only (the last time I was there I'd run out of things to do after four o'clock in the afternoon).

Hotel Porto Santo (tel. 823-81) is a four-star, first-class hotel that has only two floors. It was constructed in a garden setting bordering directly on the large beach (seven kilometers) of gold-colored sand. Run by the same owners who operate the five-star Penina Golf Hotel in the Algarve, the Porto Santo offers 100 well-furnished double rooms, including four suites, each with private bath, phone, and a terrace overlooking the bay. For your room and breakfast, rates are $28 (U.S.) in a single, from $21 per person in a double room. However, as this hotel becomes more known and discovered, those fairly modest rates are subject to rapid change.

The hotel also has a large restaurant serving a bountiful lunch or dinner for about $17 per person. The main lounge has been attractively furnished, and it's mercifully air-conditioned, leading to the main terrace and garden, where there is an open bar. After the hot sun retires a bit, the tennis courts are popular. By the time you check in, the swimming pool should have opened.

The Pirata Azul sails from Funchal to Porto Santo daily, if the weather is good. The round-trip fare is 600$ ($9.18). Some hotels or quintas will pack a picnic lunch, which guests can enjoy on the beach. The boat leaves in the early morning, returning in the late afternoon, giving passengers at least four hours on the Porto Santo beach. For about the same price, you can fly over in the morning, catching a Funchal-bound plane in Porto Santo at 7:30 p.m. in the evening.

3. Discovering the Azores

The lost paradise . . . legends of enchanted princesses . . . hydrangea-bordered highways . . . lakes at the bottom of extinct volcanic craters . . . natural springs of therapeutic waters . . . windmills clacking on top of hills . . . oxen plowing the fields like a *tableau vivant* suspended in time . . . and mist and cloud-shrouded islands.

THE AZORES

Those seeking an offbeat holiday in Europe can strike out for the Azores. It is an archipelago where the winds of the ocean meet, where the cyclones call on each other. Robin Bryans called the islands a "muted mood, a pianissimo untouched by the strident dissonance of industrial Europe."

Ever since the first explorers directed their ships' prows into the Atlantic, it is likely that their crow's nests sighted the volcanic slopes of the Azores. Whether the Vikings, the Genoese, the Phoenicians, or whoever, first put into these lands remains unknown. There are those who believe that the Azores are all that remain of the lost continent of Atlantis.

The archipelago spans a distance of more than 500 miles from the southeastern tip of Santa Maria to the northwestern extremity at Corvo. The main island of **São Miguel** lies about 760 miles west of Portugal (2110 miles east of New York), making the Azores the most isolated islands in the entire Atlantic.

Completely uninhabited when discovered, the Azores were named by Diogo de Silves (a captain of Henry the Navigator) after the hook-beaked açor (compared to both a hawk and an eagle), which sailed on the air currents over the coast. The date: 1427. It wasn't long before settlements sprang up.

Eventually it was learned that the entire island group was actually composed of three distinct mini-archipelagos: the eastern section of **Santa Maria** and **São Miguel;** the central with **Terceira** (site of an Atlantic air base of the United States—scene of bullfighting in the streets), **Graciosa** (about 11 miles in length, known for its Sulfur Cave), cigar-shaped **São Jorge** (Raul Brandão's ethereal island of dust and dream). Finally the western or Horta District of **Pico** (really a cloud-capped mountain with a whaling factory); **Faial** (vulnerable to earthquakes and known for the eerie crater of the extinct volcano, Caldeira); **Flores** (Flowers) where vegetation runs riot in a setting of lakes, waterfalls, and valleys; and **Corvo** (the smallest and most westerly member—everybody knows everybody else—and a visit by a foreigner is an occasion).

The Azores are a study in color. The writer who once made the much-publicized characterization, the "Gray Azores," must have been color blind. Much of the color of the archipelago comes from the flowers that grow rampantly in its volcanic soil: azaleas, camellias, heather, agapanthus, rhododendrons. Although occasionally lashed by violent storms, the enchanted islands enjoy a mild climate, the temperature averaging around 58 degrees Fahrenheit in winter, only 75 degrees Fahrenheit in summer.

Its rugged people who daily contend with the elements of nature have emerged friendly and hospitable to strangers, even though one would have expected such isolated islanders to be insular. Coming back from a walk in the São Miguel hills, two American visitors were stopped by a boy riding a mule. Under a straw hat with a hoe slung over his shoulder, his face beamed as he bid *Bom Noite.* The word YALE was written across his sweat shirt. Learning that he spoke a bit of English, the visitors inquired about the letters. It seemed that his uncle had attended Yale. "Do you know him?" the boy asked. "He now lives in Boston."

Every man, woman, and child in the island chain seemingly has relatives living in the United States. Many settled in New Bedford, Mass. (of *Moby Dick* fame), during the whaling heyday of that port, taking jobs as sailors, fishermen, whalers, and caulkers. Many of the immigrants returned, however, after earning their fortunes across the sea.

GETTING THERE: At any TAP office or at your local travel agent, you can learn the times and frequency of flights to the Azores. For example, on your return to North America from Lisbon, you might stop off at Santa Maria airport, originally built by the U.S. in 1944 as an Allied air base. The government leased the base to the Allies in World War II, even though Portugal was officially neutral. If you hold a round-trip ticket from New York to Lisbon, you're allowed to stop free in the Azores, providing this desire is declared and arranged when you purchase your ticket. The free stopover may not be valid on special excursion tickets. From Santa Maria, you can take local SATA flights to either Terceira or São Miguel. Finally, you might prefer to make the Boston/Terceira flight, then go from there by SATA either to São Miguel or Santa Maria. Many possibilities are available for investigation and adventure.

All the red tape of the past, including such requirements as visas for Americans, has now been abandoned. You can also visit the Azores by boat; the **Empresa Insulana de Navegação** runs a regular service (consult the passenger department at 152 Rua Augusta in Lisbon).

SANTA MARIA: For many, Santa Maria is just a refueling stop, a place where passengers get out and stretch their legs. But don't judge this island by the scenery at the airport. You have to penetrate deeper to know its charm, and if you're pressed for time, we recommend that you go on to São Miguel, saving Santa Maria for another day. Those with more time can explore the sêrra-studded southernmost island in the archipelago, with its grazing ridges, scattered village houses (some thatched), and roads that are in some cases merely lanes, unpaved and lined with wildflowers.

Speeding around the island (as most visitors invariably do), you get the distinct impression that the clever farmers, like their fellow islanders in Madeira, have used the land to the maximum—and not just for produce, as flowers abound as well.

Vila do Porto, a village near the airport, is the capital, although the designation seems pretentious. It is noted for its old houses and a restored parish church of the 16th century. To the east, **Santo Espírito** contains a much-admired baroque church, the Holy Spirit. With a square bell tower to the right of its portal, it presents a severe facade that is topped by an overscale baroque scroll with finials. The simple doors are framed by an intricately carved basalt casement. In and around Santo Espírito, you'll pass some of the characteristic Azorean white-sail windmills, usually honey colored, clacking in the Atlantic winds.

On February 18, 1493, Christopher Columbus moored the *Nina* off the coast. The explorer's men attended church at **Anjos**, supposedly stripping off their pants and walking single file from the vessel to the chapel to fulfill a vow made at sea when it looked as if they would perish in a storm. The little church that stands today, Our Lady of the Angels, is a reconstruction. Anjos, about a half-hour ride from the airport, is in the northwestern sector of Santa Maria.

Picos, near the center of the island, is the highest point (about 1800 feet above sea level). From its summit, you can absorb what is considered the finest panoramic view of Santa Maria, with the sea as a backdrop.

A night on the island can be an experience to remember, as related by Robin Bryans: "... the invisible night ghouls of Santa Maria came to haunt the bay and to make the cliffs echo with their diabolical cries. The ghouls were Mediterranean shearwaters, or cagarros."

The island's accommodations are limited to the following:

The Middle Bracket

Aeroporto Hotel, Aeroporto de Santa Maria (tel. Aeroporto 117), is barely adequate as a hotel, but on this island you take what is available. In the closing months of World War II, this site was an Officers Club for the American Air Base of Santa Maria. With the opening of the airport to international jet travel, it was remade into a hotel rated second class by the government to provide stopover accommodations, bungalow-style.

The living room has fireplaces, a high beamed ceiling, and groups of furniture set for conversation and beverages. There's a bar and a spacious dining room in the Terminal Building providing a hearty and very simple Azorean cuisine.

Geared to passengers making the transition between the Old and New Worlds, the Aeroporto Hotel contains 103 rooms, 65 without private baths. Depending on the plumbing and location, a double goes from $35 (U.S.), and singles go from $21.

4. Ponta Delgada

Hopefully, you'll arrive in the capital of São Miguel in the early evening, after a 20-minute flight from Santa Maria. The zebra-striped Avenida Infante D. Henrique, encircling the waterfront, is alive with strollers taking their characteristic paseo. Traditionally, this affords a chance in Portuguese towns and villages for the parents of unmarried girls to show off their prizes to the eligible young men.

Today, of course, foreign tourists and sailors in port for the night join in the promenade. Some stop along the ledge to admire the twinkling lights from the boats in the bay. In the 1860s, a breakwater 2800 feet long was built, making possible the wide waterfront boulevard. Before that, the harbor and the lower town were completely exposed to the sea.

The next morning you can explore the southern coastal town in more detail, walking its narrow streets, looking at its new buildings, but finding the older ones more interesting. Some of the tile-roofed cottages are walled with lime, and decorated with painted earthenware tiles and black lava adornments.

Founded in the 15th century, Ponta Delgada makes a good base for exploring São Miguel, or you can go to the hotel at Furnas, about an hour's drive from the capital. It's recommended that you spend your time not in the baroque churches or the town museum (Santo André in a 16th-century convent), but rather in exploring the natural wonders of the island, which far excel any artificial attraction.

However, you should get in at least one shopping expedition. You're likely to find bargains galore. For example, you may want to browse through a basket bazaar, with not only a wide selection of baskets, but also wicker and willow chairs, handbags, even some articles made from the pith of a fig tree. A personal favorite is the **Casa Regional da Ilha Verde** (the Regional House of the Green Island), 25 Largo da Matriz. Among its best items are the Azorean embroidery and the regional pottery made of red clay from Vila França do Campo.

On the outskirts of Ponta Delgada, you can arrange to attend one of the pineapple factories, actually greenhouses, where the fruit is grown under slope-ceilinged glass which has been whitewashed. The plants are smoked several times during their growth, as this *fumo* method is said to make all of them flower at the same time.

In Ponta Delgada, you'll find the finest hotel in the Azores, as well as a few less expensive accommodations.

THE UPPER BRACKET: The **Hotel de São Pedro,** Largo Almirante Dunn (tel. 222-23). Here you can savor the ambience of past centuries, yet enjoy the comforts of the 20th. The building was the love child of the island's most colorful and legendary figure, Thomas Hickling, who came from Boston on a schooner in 1769. He and his descendants profited from a thriving business growing and exporting oranges to London and St. Petersburg (Leningrad). From their wealth, they built a family homestead, with the help of imported craftsmen, and shipped in loads of fine antiques from the continent to furnish it.

Their town house, with its Georgian colonial interior, is on the sea, with a high garden wall to provide privacy from the street. Throughout its history, it has known many vicissitudes (it was used in World War I as a headquarters for the American navy).

Nowadays, one can stay here in comparative luxury for moderate tariffs. Although there has been some modernization, such as the installation of private baths in each of the 30 chambers, the essential atmosphere has been preserved. The drawing room, the salons, and the dining room are tastefully furnished with many museum-caliber antiques. The majority of the bedrooms are equipped with traditional pieces combined with the old. The suites are furnished in the grand manner—one with a huge Napoleonic sleigh bed, another with spindle twin beds. The rates are complicated, as some of the rooms contain shower baths, others complete baths; some are deluxe, and a few are listed as suites. Singles cost $30 to $50, doubles from $40 to $60. Lunch or dinner is an extra $15.

In a noncommercial atmosphere, guests are likely to intermingle freely; and the staff is considerate. The style is set by the director, Durante M. P. Pimentel, who has won many friends and admirers in America. The drawing room is not overpoweringly stiff, but it is formal, with two bronze and crystal chandeliers, a pair of fine 18th-century fruitwood chests, velvet chairs, and a sofa set in front of an Adam-style fireplace.

The dining room, scene of many bountiful meals, backed up by a good cellar, contains mahogany chairs at tables set in either the main room or in the oak-beamed alcove, with leaded glass windows and deep paneled Georgian arches. Fresh flowers are everywhere, as important to the character of São Pedro as changing the linen sheets. The drinking lounge seems right from Old Salem, Massachusetts, with its hand-hewn beams and spoke chairs. Drinks are also served on the tiled loggia where you can sit in wicker and leather armchairs under deep arches, enjoying the view of the lawn, the water, the stone urns, and the century-old trees.

THE MEDIUM-PRICED RANGE: **Hotel do Infante,** Avenida Infante Dom Henrique (tel. 233-31), is recommended for those seeking a prominent position along the waterfront boulevard. It is a seven-story, honeycombed modern building, with most of its rooms opening onto a balcony with a view of the boat-studded harbor. The architectural and furnishing concept is contemporary, but not stylish.

On the top floor is a building-wide dining room, with three walls of glass that provide an unblocked view of the ships and the Azorean sunsets. Adequate lounges for drinking and conversation are on the street floor. The bedrooms—39 in all, each with private bath—are equipped in a modern style, pleasantly simple. A double with breakfast goes for 1800$ ($27.54), dropping to 1400$ ($21.42) in a single, also with breakfast.

Tip: Ask for fresh pineapple juice for breakfast. Grown in the glass houses nearby, it will become your comparison for all pineapple juices thereafter.

THE BUDGET RANGE: Residêncial Casa das Palmeiras, 26 Rua Diário dos Açores (tel. 22-621), is a grand old free-standing villa in the center of Ponta Delgada. Its upper floors have been transformed into comfortable suites and rooms, with many decorating touches. The stairway leading to the residence has woodwork and opera-red walls. Each private room has its own color scheme, with coordinated fabrics and furnishings. All have refrigerators stocked with drinks. Many of the chambers are decorated with antiques, although others are in a contemporary style. The better rooms have small lounge areas. Singles range from $35 (U.S.), doubles from $42. A continental breakfast is included in the rates. The villa is easy to spot, as its gables and peaked tower, even its towering palm, can be seen from many blocks away.

5. Exploring São Miguel

The largest link in the archipelago chain (290 square miles), São Miguel is called the Green Island with good reason. It offers a widely varied landscape, ranging from mountains, to volcanic lava pools, to brooks filled with trout, to cultivated checkerboard fields, to tea and pineapple plantations—everything set off effectively by the age-old customs and handmade touches, such as windmills clacking in the wind, ox-drawn carts, and medieval woolen bonnets on cowherds. Practically everything grows well in the gardens of São Miguel, especially the hydrangeas that border the roads in summer.

As interesting as Ponta Delgada is, the main reason for flying over from Santa Maria is to take one of the many excursions by rented car, inexpensive taxi, organized tour, or independently—along with the Azoreans on one of the island's buses. Nearly all visitors head east from the capital, a distance of about 28 miles, to:

FURNAS: Following in the footsteps of rheumatic Victorians who shunned the sea cocktail at Brighton to take the baths at Furnas, you'll arrive at one of the richest spas in Europe. The thermal spa season lasts from July 1 to September 30, but a visit is interesting at any time of the year. The geysers and springs make the valley steamy in the district where sulfur fumes pour forth from craters.

The *New Yorker* described the springs as a place of "bare black rock, blasted by geysers, hot oozing clay, and sulphur-scented smoke. In a grim-looking cave, water boils furiously, now and then leaping up and spilling over in a smoking stream that runs steeply downhill between lava banks." David Dodge called the waters at the baths "cold, warm, boiling, carbonated, uncarbonated, radioactive, tasty, clear, muddy and as you like it, twenty-two kinds to choose from."

The major attraction is **Hickling Park,** founded in 1770 according to an inscribed boulder, by Thomas Hickling, the American vice-consul discussed earlier in the São Pedro write-up in Ponta Delgada. Where Hickling left off, the Marquês da Praia eventually took up. However, the latter's grandson at one point was about to destroy the park; but it was rescued by Vasco Bensuade in 1937. A pavilion was built that same year at Furnas Lake, and two years later a nine-hole championship golf course was opened.

It is a botanical garden, filled with azaleas, ferns, camellias, hydrangeas, pines, japonica, and jacaranda. Plants were brought from China, Japan, South

America, Mexico, New Zealand, Asia, even the southern United States. White swans float majestically in the ponds studded with red and white lilies, and in the park is an egg-shaped swimming pool filled with muddy thermal waters. Changing cabins are nearby.

Before you go, you may want to take a trip to **Lake Furnas** for a volcano cooked luncheon. This type of cuisine can be arranged through the Hotel Terra Nostra at Furnas. The cooking is known as à la caldeira; and everything from pullet to horse mackerel is covered with paper or some other wrapping after being well spiced with aromatic herbs. It then is buried in the hot earth, the way the Haitians roast kid. Sometimes whole chickens and yams are dropped into the simmering pools. On Sunday especially, you see families coming to the lakeside setting for picnics, washing down their meals with *cheiro,* a regional wine.

For dining or accommodations, try:

A Medium-Priced Hotel

Hotel Terra Nostra (Our Land), Rûa dos Banhos, Furnas (tel. 541-04), is a living monument to art deco. The rear opens onto Hickling botanical park, with its restorative waters. A long list of European and North American visitors are drawn here, finding its setting idyllic. One of its special treats, mentioned above, are the cookouts arranged by the hotel, the food slowly done to a turn by volcanic steam. A volcano-cooked luncheon costs 500$ ($7.65) per person. But you can also dine less ruggedly at the hotel. If you're not a guest, but are visiting, say, from Ponta Delgada, you can order a 500$ ($7.65) table d'hôte luncheon or dinner.

The full-board rates are most economical. Depending on the plumbing, the tariff for two persons ranges from 2800$ ($42.84) to 3360$ ($51.41). One person can have full board at rates ranging from 1900$ ($29.07) to 2280$ ($34.88). The rooms are furnished in a 1930s style.

Of course, you have access to the thermal swimming pool, plus the tennis courts and a nearby nine-hole golf course. You can even join the British in a game of croquet.

To the west of Ponta Delgada—a distance of some 13 miles—lies the second major attraction of São Miguel:

SETE CIDADES: The Seven Cities were named after a legend; in fact, they are the subject of many myths. It is an hourglass-shaped lake, the upper one blue, the lower one emerald green. The lake, about eight or nine miles in circumference, was supposedly formed by tears shed over a broken love affair: one by a blue-eyed princess, the other by the shepherd boy she loved who was green-eyed. The appellation of Sete Cidades stems from a legend that claims that this site was actually the center of a powerful empire on the lost continent of Atlantis. You can visit a park near the blue lake, called **Jardim Pitoresco,** and enjoy the wafting aroma of the pittosporum flower. The vegetation on the slopes makes this a lush setting.

6. Terceira

Pronounced ter-say-ra and meaning third, Terceira is the third largest of the nine Azorean islands. It's about two-thirds of the way between Boston and Lisbon, making it one of the nearest parts of Europe accessible to North Americans.

SETE CIDADES/TERCEIRA

When you first land at Lages Airport, you'll think you're in the United States. Terceira is the site of an American air force base, and its personnel have their own little community near the airport. The base was originally built by the RAF in World War II.

Once you pass this, you'll have left America far behind and the real island emerges. It is rural in nature, with most of the islanders engaged in agriculture and livestock breeding. Extinct volcanoes slope down to green pasturelands crisscrossed by low stone walls. Black-shawled women duck past ox carts to enter Manueline churches of the 16th century.

Life is casual here, and for some that means Terceira is an acquired taste. In fact, it's been so quiet around here that many locals were lured to America. It's estimated that more Terceira-born persons are in California than on the island. Others settled in New England. Many were originally drawn there during the whaling days of the 19th century.

Don't come expecting to view great monuments and museums—rather, to sample the local hospitality and Terceira's own bucolic charm. Fishing and boating are excellent, by the way.

TAP offers a Boston/Terceira service, a four-hour flight to Europe. Terceira is also connected by SATA, the local Azorean airline, to the international airport at Santa Maria and to that of São Miguel, some 35 miles away.

Angra is the island's main city, about a 45-minute run from the airport. It's also the oldest settlement in the Azores, the most fascinating colonial town in the archipelago.

Considered a masterpiece of Renaissance town planning, Angra still reflects its 16th-century layout. Many mansions stand from the 17th and 18th centuries.

The finest example of military architecture on the island is the Castle of São João Baptista, where the notorious sadist, King Afonso VI, was imprisoned. At the foot of Monte Brasil, it contains a carved doorway and an arched bridge. It's one of the largest 16th-century fortresses built in the Portuguese world. Behind the castle rises the pile of São Gonçalo Convent, filled with fine ornamental tiles and some interesting carving.

In the center of town, the cathedral dates from the 16th century and is noted for its carved ceiling of cedar. The Church of São Francisco, built in the 15th century, contains the tomb of Pedro, brother of Vasco da Gama, who buried his kin there on his way back from India in 1499.

Peculiar to Terceira is the custom of rope bullfighting known as *tourada a corda*. Young bulls are brought in from the pastures and allowed to run wild in the town. A long heavy rope has been fastened to the bull's horns, and this forms the means of controlling him. Reckless young men rush into the streets to taunt these bulls with objects. This bull running takes place from May to November.

At some point you'll want to rent a taxi and explore the island, 12 by 18 miles in distance. At the eastern end lies **Praia da Vitória,** second town of Terceira, containing the largest sandy beach in the entire Azores. Whatever time of year you decide to take the excursion, the temperature's likely to be right: the average is between 50 and 70 degrees Fahrenheit all year. Terceira is still unspoiled and inviting, especially now that the following accommodations have opened their doors to new-world visitors.

LODGINGS: Albergaría Cruzeiro, Praça Dr. Sousa Júnior, Angra do Heroísmo (tel. 240-71), is the newest of the hotels built in the center of town, a most recommendable place to stay if you appreciate modern facilities. All rooms come with private bathroom, telephone, and heating. Singles cost from 1000$ ($15.30), twins from 1200$ ($18.36), breakfast and taxes included. You can also take half or full board. The hall contains wrought-iron furniture and green plants. In addition, there's a restaurant, bar, and a nearby lounge with all-white furniture.

Hotel de Angra, Praça da Restauração (tel. 240-414), is a substantial modern hotel in the heart of Angra, set back from a pie-shape little plaza, studded with trees. Although not overwhelming in any area, it does have its own dignity and style. Singles cost from $43 (U.S.), doubles from $30. Lunch or dinner goes for an extra $10.

At Cabo da Praia

Apartamentos Nove Ilhas Motel (tel. 531-35) is a holiday house for those seeking a tranquil retreat in a setting of natural beauty. A member of the staff of the hotel meets guests at Lages Airport and provides free transportation to the facilities of Nove Ilhas, about 3½ miles away.

In one of the Nine Islands apartments, clients are near the largest Azorean beach and only two miles from the historic town of Praia da Vitória. The Terceira Island Golf Course is 8½ miles away, and the city of Angra do Heroísmo is 11½ miles away.

Each apartment has two bedrooms and a full bath, with tub and shower. A combined living and dining room comes with the apartment, as does an equipped kitchenette, with cutlery, silverware, and other dishes. Linens are also provided.

On the precincts are a restaurant, a small market, plus facilities for dry cleaning and laundry. Babysitting can be arranged for parents wanting to be free to tour Terceira. One person is charged from 1470$ ($22.49); two persons, from 2000$ ($30.60); and three persons, from 2500$ ($38.25). An extra bed costs 300$ ($4.59).

7. Faial

Much less visited than any of the islands previously recommended, Faial has its own particular charm, a land of restful valleys, verdant fields, and hydrangea-hedged hillsides. It and Pico are the chief tourist islands of the Horta district. They are separated by a channel five miles wide.

The easiest way to get there is by air via São Miguel or Terceira, but Faial also can be reached by boat from Terceira. However, if you're planning to come by boat, check in advance with a travel agent or the tourist office, as service is not frequent.

Faial's chief town is the port of **Horta,** with its Church of São Francisco from the 16th century. Inside is a museum of religious art, with carving, glazed tiles, and painting. Horta is built along a bay. From its harbor (which was used as a naval base in both world wars), you can enjoy views of the neighboring islands.

Excursionists go to Caldeira, a volcanic crater covered inside with vegetation and containing a lake. Caldeira is at the top of the island, and from this vantage point the best view of Pico and the neighboring islands can be enjoyed. In 1957 a new volcano, Capelinhos, rose up from the sea and erupted in 1958. There was also renewed activity in 1973.

WHERE TO STAY: Hotel Faial, Horta (tel. 221-81), is a four-star, first-class hotel, consisting of a group of buildings like a village in a park. The situation is tranquil, as the Faial is surrounded by gardens offering views onto the sea. The hotel is the major social center for Horta. The furnishings are in an ultramodern style, with a high taste level, as reflected by the subtle autumnal colors of nutmeg, burnt orange, beige, and blood red. The rooms are well styled, often opening onto views of the bay and the inner harbor. Doubles cost from $60 (U.S.) with breakfast, and singles are charged from $53, also with breakfast. The food, served in a large room, is good and typical of the region. A complete meal costs $17 and up.

Chapter XVIII

A GRAB BAG OF CHARTS

1. Menu Translations
2. A Capsule Vocabulary
3. Currency Exchange

FRENCH IS STILL traditionally spoken by guides in provincial museums, but English is increasing in popularity, and is now taught in most schools.

Usually in Lisbon, Estoril, Cascais, Madeira, and on the major coastal resorts of the Algarve, you'll have no problem if you speak only English. However, if you venture inland—to towns of the Alentejo for example, you may find a few words in our Capsule Vocabulary helpful.

Likewise, menus tend to be bewildering, especially when a chef has named a bean and tripe dish after his favorite aunt. Nevertheless, a basic knowledge of the main dishes in the Portuguese cuisine is essential, especially if you're planning to stay at second-class hotels or local taverns where there's nobody around to translate for you.

1. Menu Translations

SOUPS (SOPAS)

caldo verde	potato and cabbage	**sopa à alentejana**	Alentejo soup
canja de galinha	chicken soup	**sopa de cebola**	onion
crème de camarão	cream of shrimp	**sopa de mariscos**	shellfish
		sopa de queijo	cheese
crème de legumes	cream of vegetable	**sopa de tomate**	tomato

EGGS (OVOS)

com presunto	with ham	**mexidos**	scrambled
cozidos	hard boiled	**omeleta**	omelet
escalfados	poached	**quentes**	soft boiled
estrelados	fried	**tortilha**	Spanish omelet

FISH (PEIXE)

ameijoas	clams	ostras	oysters
atum	tuna	peixe espada	swordfish
bacalhau	salted codfish	percebes	barnacles
cherne	turbot	pescada	hake
camarãos	shrimps	robalo	bass
eiró	eel	sardinhas	sardines
lagosta	lobster	salmonete	red mullet
linguado	sole	santola	crab
lulas	squid		

SPECIALTIES

bife na frigideira	steak with mustard sauce	porco Alentejano	pork in a sauce of tomatoes and clams
caldeirada	fishermen's stew		
cozido à portuguêsa	Portuguese stew		

MEAT (CARNE)

bife	steak	lingua	tongue
borrego	lamb	porco	pork
cabrito	kid	presunto	ham
carneiro	mutton	rim	kidney
coelho	rabbit	salchichas	sausages
costeletas	chops	vaca	beef
dobrada	tripe	vitela	veal
iscas	liver		

POULTRY (AVES)

borracho	pigeon	pato	duck
frango	chicken	perdiz	partridge
galinha	fowl	perú	turkey
ganso	goose		

VEGETABLES (LEGUMES)

aipo	celery	cenouras	carrots
alcachôfra	artichoke	congumelo	mushroom
arroz	rice	couve-flor	cauliflower
azeitonas	olives	couves	cabbage
batatas	potatoes	ervilhas	peas
berinjela	eggplant	espargos	asparagus
beterrabas	beets	espinafres	spinach
cebola	onion	favas	broad beans

feijão	bean	pepino	cucumber
nabo	turnip	tomate	tomato

SALAD (SALADA)

agrioes	watercress	salada verde	green salad
alface	lettuce	Russa	Russian
salada mista	mixed salad		

DESSERTS (SOBREMESA)

arroz doce	rice pudding	pêssego Melba	peach Melba
bolo	cake	pudim flan	egg custard
gelados diversos	mixed ice cream	pudim de pao	bread pudding
		salada de frutas	fruit salad
maça assada	baked apple	sorvetes	sherbets
pastelaria	pastry	queijo	cheese

FRUIT (FRUTAS)

abacate	avocado	melancia	watermelon
alperches	apricots	melao	melon
ameixa	plum	morangos	strawberries
ananas	pineapple	peras	pears
cerajas	cherries	pêssegos	peaches
figos	figs	roma	pomegranate
framboesa	raspberry	tâmara	date
laranjas	oranges	toronja	grapefruit
limao	lemon	uvas	grapes
macas	apples		

BEVERAGES (BEBIDAS)

água	water	leite	milk
água mineral	mineral water	sumo de fruta	fruit juice
café	coffee	sumo de laranja	orange juice
chá	tea	sumo de tomate	tomato juice
cerveja	beer	vinho branco	white wine
com gelo	with ice	vinho tinto	red wine
laranjada	orangeade		

MENU TRANSLATIONS/VOCABULARY

CONDIMENTS (CONDIMENTOS)

açúcar	sugar	mostarda		mustard
alho	garlic	compota		jam
azeite	olive oil	pimenta		pepper
caril	curry	sal		salt
manteiga	butter	vinagre		vinegar

MISCELLANEOUS

chocolate	chocolate	pão		bread
biscoito	cracker	pão torrado		toast
gelo	ice			

COOKING TERMS

assado no forno	baked	frito		fried
cozido	boiled	mal passado		rare
estufada	braised	bem passado		well done

2. A Capsule Vocabulary

		Pronounced
Hello	olá	oh-lah
How are you?	como está?	como esh-tah
Very well	muito bem	muy-toh bym
Thank you	muito obrigado	muy-toh obree-gah-do
Good-bye	adeus	adeush
Please	faça favor	fassa fah-vohr
Yes	sim	seem
No	não	naion
Excuse me	desculpe-me	dash-culpa-meh
Give me	dê-me	deh-meh
Where is?	onde fiça?	ondeh feecah
the station	a estaçao	a aish-tassaion
a hotel	um hotel	oom hotel
a restaurant	um restaurante	oom rash-tauranteh
the toilet	a casa de banho	ah cahzah de bahnhoo
To the right	à direita	aah deeraitah
To the left	à esquerda	aah ash-kerdah
Straight ahead	em frente	ym fraintah
I would like—	gostaria de	goosh-tareeah de
to eat	comer	coh-mere
a room	um quarto	oom quarr-toh
How much is it?	quanto custa	quahnto coosh-tah
The check, please	a conta se faz, favor	ah cohnta sa fahsh, fah-vohr

English	Portuguese	Pronunciation
When	quando	quandoh
Yesterday	ontem	ohntym
Today	hoje	hoyhje
Tomorrow	amanha	ahmain-hayh
Breakfast	pequeno almoç	paikainoh aahlmohssoh
Lunch	almoço	aahlmohssoh
Dinner	jantar	jain-taah

1 **um** oom
2 **dois** doysh
3 **três** traishe
4 **quatro** quaahtroh
5 **cinco** sseencoh
6 **seis** ssaish
7 **sete** ssaiteh
8 **oito** oytoh
9 **nove** nohveh
10 **dez** daish
11 **onze** onzeh
12 **dôze** doze
13 **trêze** traihzeh
14 **catorze** cahtohrzeh
15 **quinze** keenzeh
16 **dezasseis** dehzaissaish
17 **dezassete** dehrzassaihteh
18 **dezoito** dehzoytoh
19 **dezanove** dehzanohveh
20 **vinte** veenteh
30 **trinta** treehntah
40 **quarenta** quaraintah
50 **cinquenta** sseenquaintah
60 **sessenta** ssaissaihntah
70 **setenta** ssaitaintah
80 **otenta** oyhtaintah
90 **noventa** nohvaintah
100 **cem** sym

3. Currency Exchange

Escudos	Dollars	Escudos	Dollars
2	$ .03	125	$ 1.91
3	.05	150	2.30
4	.06	200	3.06
5	.08	300	4.59
10	.15	400	6.12
15	.23	500	7.65
20	.31	600	9.18
25	.38	700	10.71
30	.46	800	12.24
35	.54	900	13.77
40	.61	1000	15.30
45	.69	1500	22.95
50	.77	2000	30.60
60	.91	3000	45.90
75	1.15	4000	61.20
100	1.53	5000	76.50

Our gratitude for research aid to Mr. and Mrs. Pierre Français, and especially to Margaret Foresman for her editorial assistance.

FROMMER/PASMANTIER PUBLISHERS Date _____
1230 AVE. OF THE AMERICAS, NEW YORK, NY 10020

Friends, please send me the books checked below:

$-A-DAY-GUIDES
(In-depth guides to low-cost tourist accommodations and facilities.)

- ☐ Europe on $20 a Day $9.25
- ☐ Australia on $20 a Day $7.25
- ☐ England and Scotland on $25 a Day $7.95
- ☐ Greece on $20 a Day $7.25
- ☐ Hawaii on $25 a Day $7.25
- ☐ Ireland on $25 a Day $5.95
- ☐ Israel on $25 & $30 a Day $6.95
- ☐ Mexico and Guatemala on $15 & $20 a Day $6.95
- ☐ New Zealand on $20 & $25 a Day $6.95
- ☐ New York on $25 a Day $5.95
- ☐ Scandinavia on $25 a Day $5.95
- ☐ South America on $25 a Day $5.95
- ☐ Spain and Morocco (plus the Canary Is.) on $20 a Day .. $5.95
- ☐ Washington, D.C. on $25 a Day $7.25

DOLLARWISE GUIDES
(Guides to tourist accommodations and facilities from budget to deluxe, with emphasis on the medium-priced.)

- ☐ Egypt $6.95
- ☐ England & Scotland ... $6.95
- ☐ France $6.95
- ☐ Germany $6.25
- ☐ Italy $5.95
- ☐ Portugal $7.25

- ☐ Canada $8.25
- ☐ Caribbean (incl. Bermuda & the Bahamas) $7.95
- ☐ California & Las Vegas .. $5.95
- ☐ Florida $6.25
- ☐ New England $6.95
- ☐ Southeast & New Orleans ... $6.95

THE ARTHUR FROMMER GUIDES
(Pocket-size guides to tourist accommodations and facilities in all price ranges.)

- ☐ Amsterdam/Holland $2.95
- ☐ Athens $2.95
- ☐ Boston $2.95
- ☐ Hawaii $2.95
- ☐ Dublin/Ireland $2.95
- ☐ Las Vegas $2.95
- ☐ Lisbon/Madrid/Costa del Sol $2.95
- ☐ London $2.95
- ☐ Los Angeles $2.95

- ☐ Mexico City/Acapulco ... $2.95
- ☐ New Orleans $2.95
- ☐ New York $2.95
- ☐ Paris $2.95
- ☐ Philadelphia/Atlantic City ... $2.95
- ☐ Rome $2.95
- ☐ San Francisco $2.95
- ☐ Washington, D.C. $2.95

SPECIAL EDITIONS

- ☐ How to Beat the High Cost of Travel $2.95
- ☐ How to Live in Florida on $10,000 a Year $8.95
- ☐ Where to Stay USA (Guide to accommodations in all 50 states from $3 to $25 per night) $6.25

in U.S. include $1 post. & hdlg. for 1st book over $3; 75¢ for books under $3; 25¢ any add'l. book. Outside U.S. $2 for shipment of 1st book over $3; $1 under $3; 50¢ any add'l. book.

Enclosed is my check or money order for $ _____

NAME _____

ADDRESS _____

CITY _____ STATE _____ ZIP _____